Photography
in Focus

Fifth Edition

Photography in Focus

Jerry Burchfield
Cypress College, Cypress, California

Mark Jacobs

Ken Kokrda

Contributing Editor
Robert Johnson
Cypress College, Cypress, California

NTC *Publishing Group*
Lincolnwood, Illinois USA

Editorial Group Director: John T. Nolan

Project Editor: Sue Schumer

Cover and interior design: Ophelia M. Chambliss

Production Manager: Rosemary Dolinski

Acknowledgments

The authors and publisher gratefully acknowledge the following institutions, companies, and individuals for their generous cooperation in supplying photographs and assistance with this edition: International Museum of Photography, Department of Photography, New York; Metropolitan Museum of Art, New York; Gernsheim Collection; Humanities Research Center, University of Texas, Austin; Farm Security Administration, Library of Congress, Washington D.C.; Barbara Hitchcock, Polaroid Corp.; Vivitar Corp.; Nikon, Inc.; Canon, U.S.A.; Eastman Kodak; Globuscope; Brandess Brothers; Douglas Dodge, Minolta Corp.; Tokina Optical Corp.; and Elizabeth Forst, *Photo District News*. Acknowledgment is extended to the following individuals: Ron Miller, David Drake, Robert Johnson, Yosef Karsh, Jerry Uelsmann, W. Eugene Smith, Greg Phillips, John Charles Woods, Barbara Burchfield, Brian Burchfield, Andra Jennison, Alex Sweetman, Bill Brandt, and Norman Weisberg. A special note of thanks to our reviewers: Bill Morehouse, Huntington Beach High School, Huntington Beach, California; John Robaton, Boston University; Joseph Meehan, technical editor, *Photo District News*, New York; John Banasiak, University of South Dakota; and Bea Nettles, University of Illinois, Urbana/Champaign.

Contents

Chapter 6   Lenses   95

Chapter 7   Film and Light   115

Chapter 8   Exposure   145

Chapter 9   Shooting Accessories and Techniques   170

Chapter 10   Black and White Film Development   203

Foreword

Photography in Focus is a comprehensive book that will meet the needs of the beginning photographer and sustain advanced students. The title of the book is not only clever, but apt, if one considers the definition of focus. When something is focused it is resolved into a sharp image, or it is in a state permitting clear perception or understanding. This is a fine description of the text.

A glance at the table of contents will reveal that this is an ambitious book. It includes extensive technical information on black and white and color photography, ranging from the pinhole camera to the zone system, from pre-visualization to post-visualization. The contents are up-to-date, including descriptions of the newest developments in this rapidly changing field with sections on the impact of electronic automation and digital photography. Like a good teacher, this book tells both sides, outlining the advantages and disadvantages of different ways of working. It cautions that nothing good comes easily and tells how mastery comes through practice, experience, and a willingness to experiment.

The tone of the book is friendly and encouraging. It offers not only the *how* but the *why* of photography, with a fine discussion of what makes a good photograph and what makes photography unique. The book includes thoughts about the future of the medium as well as an acknowledgement of its history. Ethics and photographic truth are addressed. Readers will find a valuable discussion of the role of context, purpose, and communication in judging and understanding photographs. Because of its clarity and range, *Photography in Focus* will make a valuable addition to the reader's understanding of this pervasive and powerful medium.

B. Nettles

—Bea Nettles
Chair, Photography Program
University of Illinois Urbana/Champaign

Bea Nettles is renowned as a photographic artist and has taught photography to over one thousand students.

A merging of traditional photography and digital imaging from *Out of Context*, Teresa Bischak.

Chapter 1

Visual Literacy and Photography Today

The world today has been conditioned, overwhelmingly, to visualize. The picture has almost replaced the "word" as a means of communication.

—Berenice Abbott
Photographer

It seems like everyone has taken a photograph at one time or another. It's easy, with today's cameras, to take snapshots. All anyone has to do is point and shoot—everything else is automatic. Electronic technology has made it possible for people to take quality pictures without knowing the first thing about the equipment, technology, and impact of the medium.

Yet, despite the advances in technology, as well as the digital revolution, the main ingredient of all good photographs has not changed. Good photographs are made by photographers who understand photography, not by photographers who have limited themselves by just learning technique, but by the photographers who understand what makes a photograph effective. Unlike the snapshooting populace, good photographers realize that photographs have their own reality, which is separate from the reality pictured, and that the subject photographed is not as important as the ideas expressed in the picture.

Photographs capture experience, furnish evidence, and bring us the world on a piece of paper, the truth of which most people take for granted. Even though photographs are cropped, altered, retouched, and merely representative of the subject photographed, there is always a belief that something occurred or exists, which the photograph recorded. One of the inventors of photography, William Henry Fox Talbot predicted that his invention would have believability because people would presume that the photographer was present, at a specific time and place, as a witness to an event. This idea that a photograph "mirrors reality" is what gives all photographs authority and a powerful believability unshared by any other art form.

What Is Visual Literacy?

The photographic image has thoroughly infiltrated our culture. It has become our means of knowing the world and ourselves. Lens-produced images have largely replaced the written word, while giving birth to new forms of mass communication such as movies, television, mass advertising, illustrated magazines, postcards, illustrated T-shirts, and the World Wide Web.

Photography has been described as a universal language, yet most people are *visually illiterate*. On a daily basis, we are flooded with photographic images that influence what we think and how we live. Seldom is thought given to how and why those images influence us. Yet, what makes a good photographer is the ability to use the technology to make photographs that communicate. The idea of literacy is based upon the

On the Beach, P.W. Derby, 6 × 8-inch black and white print.

Figure 1-1
The presence of the photographer, although always implied, is evident in this wide-angle image. The perspective and truncated bodies draw viewers into the picture, almost as if they were part of it.

level of knowledge necessary to communicate within society, and the term literacy is generally connected with reading and writing. Early in the 20th century, a renowned artist and teacher, László Moholy-Nagy, said, "The illiterates of the future will be ignorant of the pen and the camera alike." Today, the digital revolution has come, and the computer must be added to Moholy's statement. Unfortunately, the advances in technology and the increased use of photography have not led to an increase in visual literacy.

When talking about photography, most people refer to **taking** a picture, rather than **making** a picture. Although the difference may not be obvious, it's real and it is important. When people describe a photograph, they generally talk about what it is a picture **of**, rather than what the picture is **about**. The point is, visual literacy is about *seeing* rather than *looking*. Visual literacy, then, is a developed system of thought that involves the recognition and understanding of the things around us and how they work as symbols in pictures.

To become visually literate you must study the past as well as the present. All of us are a product of our times, and our times are, in part, a product of the past. Knowledgeable photographers realize that understanding what makes a good photograph is tied to understanding the other arts as well as photography. Too many photographers look only at photographs, and often only in photo publications. Furthermore, to deny the social, political, psychological, philosophical, technological, and economic conditions that have influenced the world's cultures is like wearing blinders. Photographers who regularly make effective photographs that go beyond what we take for granted normally have a boundless curiosity and thirst for information.

To understand photography, one needs to consider *why* more than *how*. Each photograph presents its own vision and view of the world. The photograph may look natural, but the photographer's *bias*—his or her beliefs, values, knowledge, and culture—influences what is photographed and how it is photographed. Where, when, why, and by whom the photograph was made are part of its context, as are the circumstances and bias of the person viewing the photograph. In other words, context is important and must be considered if we are going to learn to **read** photographs.

Photographers often talk about learning to see as the camera sees. This is important, because it means that you are able to *previsualize* the translation of a three-dimensional reality into a two-dimensional photograph. Cameras, lenses, film, and photographic paper are all tools, each with inherent possibilities and limitations. Just like a skilled worker in any trade, a photographer must know the tools of the trade. Good photographs can be made with an inexpensive toy camera as well as with an expensive, sophisticated, state-of-the-art camera. Both can produce good photographs, provided the photographer appreciates the differences and understands the capabilities of the tools. This book will provide a technical foundation and artistic appreciation for understanding the tools and image-making possibilities available to photographers. But true understanding and the ability to use the tools effectively will only occur through trial-and-error experimentation and exploration. Knowledge, combined with awareness of both history and culture today, can lead to visual literacy—and to better photographs.

What Makes a Good Photograph?

Ultimately, good photography is about more than just taking a picture of something. It involves wise and sound decision making, often in a split second, in order not to miss a shot. It goes beyond mere surface interests associated with photography and gets to the core of what a subject or experience is really about, both for photographer and viewer. The process, almost automatic for many experienced and knowledgeable photographers, requires, for the novice, learning, thinking, analyzing, selective decision making, and gathering experience.

No two photographers will agree on all the elements that make a good photograph—although many won't hesitate to point out what they consider a bad photograph. In fact, there is no single, complete, or uniform set of rules for judging photography.

Often, however, we look to "experts" to tell us the difference between good and bad photographs. These experts may be friends of ours who have had more experience in photography. More often, however, we base our judgments of good and bad on what we see in print. Thus, pictures in newspapers, magazines, or books become important, or good, and become a basis of comparison for our own work.

Is this a fair method of comparison? Perhaps we are cheating ourselves and limiting our own individuality by constantly comparing what we do to what has already been done. On the other hand, it's easy to say, "I like this photograph—it is good." It is just as easy to say, "I don't like this photograph—it is bad." In both cases, the viewer has made a judgment about a photograph. However, this type of judgment is only useful if the viewer adds, "I don't like this photograph because. . ." or "I like this photograph because. . . ." The viewer is supporting his or her opinion by using the word *because*. Yet, before we can consider an opinion as a solid basis for judgment, we should try to understand more about the nature of photography.

In many regards, photography is similar to painting and the other picture-making arts. This is because it is, for the most past, a two-dimensional visual medium. Like other artists, photographers usually want their pictures to be seen. Thus, the photographer, like a writer or a painter, is using photography as a form of communication. *What* photographers have to communicate, *why* they want it communicated, and to *whom* they wish to communicate are just some of the questions that may help you to decide whether a photograph is good.

If a book remains unread or a photograph is unseen, then the communication is not a shared experience. Communication requires a sender, a message, and a receiver. It is presumed that the photographer has seen or created something he or she wants to share, and it is presumed that the viewer is willing to view it and thereby share that experience with the photographer.

Perhaps the more the viewer is able to share and *empathize*, or identify, the more he or she can "read" the photograph. Then, perhaps, that photograph is more successful. However, much is left up to the viewers. Are they qualified to view the photograph? Is any qualification needed? Are they basing their judgments on past experiences with the subject? What is the content of the photograph? Are the viewers sharing emotional ties with the contents? If a photograph is liked by many people,

Figure 1-2

Photographs have been described as mirrors that reflect the photographer, while providing the viewer with a window to another level of experience. This photograph by Jim Hansen captures that feeling through implication and suggestion.

Paris Turf, Jim Hansen, $9\frac{1}{2}$ × 6-inch black and white print.

does that mean it is good? Can photographers believe their work is valid even if they are the only ones who like it?

If we as photographers can define the purpose of our photographs, there will be a better chance for viewers to respond to them. If we as viewers understand more about the nature of photography, then perhaps our opinions will have more merit.

Although there is no "dictionary of values" for determining what makes a photograph good, a good photograph will have certain qualities, as you shall see. They include technical competence, aesthetics, conceptual context, and a sense of time. These qualities may, and often do, overlap.

Technical Competence

The diversity of photographic equipment, materials, techniques, and applications often overwhelms the beginner. Now, with the inclusion of digital imaging, the realm we call photography is even larger and more overwhelming. Therefore, it is important to be aware of the difference between a photograph and something that is photographic. A *photograph* is an altered camera image printed by means of light and chemicals, onto a piece of paper. In its simplest form, this is what we get from the one-hour photo service. The term *photographic*, refers to an image exhibiting some visual qualities of a photograph and having some part of it produced through a photographically related process. Such processes could range from traditional silver gelatin prints to photograms, gum printing, photo silkscreen, or digital imaging. Be aware that both the straight approach and the alternative or hybrid applications of photography are actively utilized in today's commercial and fine art arenas.

Technical competence comes with time and experience. In the professional world it is expected and taken for granted. But technical competence alone is not enough. If we accept that photography is a form of communication, then we can assume that a photograph should have something to say. An unusual or highly refined technique, like the subject of the picture, is not as important as the idea expressed in the photograph. The technical approach should be chosen to amplify what the picture is "about."

What Makes A Photo Beautiful?

Concern about what is beautiful is the subject of *aesthetics*. The aesthetic side of photography refers to such matters as design and composition, visual impact, appeal, and often a value judgment as to the picture's importance.

If technical ability is relatively easy to explain and understand, aesthetic comprehension is not. While one may argue that a print might look better on a higher contrast paper, few, if any, will argue that the picture is a waste of film and paper. Both, of course, are opinions, and opinions are always subjective, that is, personal.

Many people have tried to label certain types of photography and photographers. The results have occasionally been a flood of words with barely a trickle of meaning.

Let us assume that some broad classifications do exist. For example, a photograph of Uncle Harry probably will not have the appeal or visual impact of a photograph of some natural disaster. Uncle Harry's picture may be important to you as a member of the family, but probably not to anyone else unless Uncle Harry is famous. There is, however, a certain guarantee that the natural disaster photo will be in newspapers. But which photograph are you going to keep? Uncle Harry's, of course. Which photograph, then, is the more important one?

Uncle Harry's picture is a snapshot. The natural disaster photograph is an example of photojournalism. By far, most of the billions of pictures taken each year are snapshots. Snapshots are encouraged by all segments of the photo industry. In fact, you really can't go on vacation without a camera, for fear that you will miss some photographic mementos: records of places been, things done, events participated in, and most often, pictures of people like Uncle Harry.

Many times, snapshots are technically poor, although with today's automatic cameras, more are technically excellent. Perhaps the only difference between snapshots and the photographs that people consider art is simply a matter of intention. Snapshots show a certain directness toward the subject. In many ways, the snapshooter is free from the traditional boundaries that limit many photographers. The concern of many photographers with composition and the like is of little or no concern to most snapshooters. This is not an endorsement to go out and continue shooting unconsciously whatever appears in the viewfinder of the camera. However, many snapshots do contain at least two elements that often get lost when the education process begins: directness of approach to the subject and a freshness that can just be awe or amazement that the picture came out at all. Neither element should be forgotten.

Regardless of subject, visual impact and appeal are normally due to the formal values within the photograph. Formal values vary, but they generally consist of these elements: (1) composition, (2) proportion, (3) focus, (4) balance, (5) rhythm, and (6) texture. When you are dealing with any camera image, remember that you are "translating" a three-dimensional subject into a two-dimensional representation. Thus, every photograph, regardless of its subject, is an abstract of that subject.

You must become aware of the relationship between objects and surroundings, that is, positive and negative space. All areas of a photo—shadow or highlight, geometric or free flowing shapes—work together to create a feeling of design composition. In other words, after choosing your subject and deciding on the technical details, you have to come to grips with the visual impact that the photograph will produce. Consider its obvious visual attributes, such as shape and texture. By themselves, shape and texture may not create an interesting photograph. They can, however, create a pattern. Therefore, they become factors in the organization of a composition that will eventually determine the visual impact of a photo.

Perhaps the most important of all formal values is composition, or the satisfying arrangement of shapes and the space they occupy. However, there should be no rules concerning composition. Each photograph is made for a different purpose and by different people who see things differently. One of the most form-conscious of all photographers, Edward Weston, had this to say: "Now to consult the rules of composition before making a picture is a little like consulting the law of gravitation before going out for a walk. . . . When subject matter is forced to fit a preconceived pattern, there can be no freshness of vision. Following rules of composition can only lead to a tedious repetition of pictorial clichés."

Another formal value is rhythm, or the repetition of geometric shapes. The viewer's eye is lured into a photograph by whatever shape is being repeated. One photographer who often worked with repeated shapes is Henri Cartier-Bresson: "If a photograph is to communicate its subject in all its intensity, the relationship of form must be rigorously established. Photography implies the recognition of a rhythm in the world of real things. . . . In a photograph, composition is the result of a simultaneous coalition, the organic coordination of elements seen by the eye."

Balance and proportion result from a pleasing relationship between objects in a photograph. Balance can result from having two identical shapes in a photograph, but balance does not necessarily depend on exactly matching sizes and shapes. It may be helpful to think of a seesaw balancing objects of different sizes. Two objects of different sizes or proportions will balance if the smaller one is farther from the fulcrum or support point. The sculptures of American artist Alexander Calder offer a lesson in the subtle balance of objects of different proportions.

Focus is a factor that you can control. (There is no rule that pictures have to be sharp.) Try this experiment. Focus sharply on a subject and

Woman with Umbrella, Jerry Burchfield, 6 × 8-inch black and white print.

Figure 1-3
A woman's legs are the key visual element providing a balance of positive and negative space in this image.

Figure 1-4

Fuller used innovative printing
techniques to create this multiple
image.

Wings, Martha Fuller, 84 × 60-inch black and white print.

take a photo. Then turn the lens so that the image is slightly out of
focus and take another photo. Try again, with the image completely
out of focus. You may like one of the out-of-focus pictures better than
the one that is sharp. If your picture is visually exciting, you've achieved
part of the goal.

What Is the Purpose?

Your purpose or intent for making a photograph normally determines
the technical and aesthetic considerations. A casual snapshot routinely
involves little technical or aesthetic consideration. In contrast, profes-

sional photojournalists and portrait, advertising, fashion, publicity, and fine art photographers have a purpose that motivates and directs the form of their work. Those earning their living through commercial applications of photography do what is needed to satisfy the needs of the client, whereas fine art photographers have the freedom to determine their own direction, but often face the dilemma of compromise if they want to make something that is marketable.

Aspiring photographers generally begin by emulating others. This is fine, especially if you desire a commercial career. It provides a basis to build upon and comparisons for analyzing your own work. However, it is imperative that you increase your awareness by experiencing work that is unfamiliar. A photograph that is easily absorbed and fits conveniently within your established "comfort zone" seldom has lasting value. Growth and personal development come from going beyond what is already known. Find the bookstores that specialize in rare, uncommon, and diverse publications from around the world. Visit galleries and museums to experience original photographs as well as other art. As you broaden your foundations, you will absorb more and find that you imitate less. Sooner or later, your own personality will begin to replace borrowed ideas, and your work will be a reflection of you.

It is also necessary to show your work to others in the field. Only then can you get feedback that has a professional foundation, and only then will you be able to accept or reject the advice offered you. In photography, as with most worthwhile pursuits, you get back as much as you put into it.

A Sense of Time

Photography is forever linked to light and time.

Every time a picture is made, time is a factor. Exposure is based upon the relationship between the intensity of light and the amount of time necessary to record that intensity on photographic film or paper. Cameras are designed to allow us to vary this relationship. By opening or closing the lens aperture, or opening, we can control the intensity of the light, while variations in the shutter speed control the amount of time needed for the exposure. Both the aperture and the shutter control the visual effects that can be used to enhance or change the "look" of a picture. These technical and visual relationships are discussed throughout the book.

Mark this, however. The association of a photograph with an actual event in time makes it different from all other forms of art. Consciously or unconsciously, we acknowledge this every time we look at a photograph. Even though a picture may distort the subject, there is always a presumption that something actually occurred at the specific moment when the shutter snapped. The event may be over, but the photograph endows the event with a significance, even immortality, that it would never have attained otherwise. Any subject, frozen in time photographically, can become nostalgic.

That's how photographs made for commercial and other utilitarian purposes assume another level of importance in time. The artist, photographer, and historian Mark Johnstone suggests that the value of artworks can be validated only after the passage of time.

The Future of Photography

Photography was invented at a time when human society began to change at an accelerated rate. It became the primary means of recording that which was disappearing. Today, the rate of change is faster than ever, and photography is more prevalent than ever. Snapshots are being made at unprecedented rates, amateur enthusiasm continues to grow, educational programs flourish, career opportunities abound, and photography has been accepted into the mainstream of the fine arts world.

During the 1990s, photography has been in the midst of a transition from a chemically based medium to a digital or electronic medium. This change, while seemingly revolutionary, has been evident for many years. Computer imaging has become commonplace in photojournalism, advertising photography and the fine arts. Despite this, traditional chemical-based photography is still the primary means of visual imaging, while much of the digital imaging in the fine art and commercial realms consists of a hybrid combination of chemical and digital elements.

It is inevitable that the primary means of visual image production will become electronic, as digital cameras, electronic tools, and imaging software become more practical and economical. This does not mean that chemical-based photography will be dead. Like painting, which was presumed dead upon the invention of photography, chemical-based photography will live on. Each medium has its exclusive characteristics, so use of traditional chemical-based equipment, film, and paper for personal and aesthetic reasons will continue.

Regardless of whether you prefer traditional photography or electronic means, you will still be making photographs—and still need to learn the basic principles of photography. This book provides an introduction to electronic photography while concentrating on chemical-based photography. Its goal is to serve as a bridge between the diverse areas of photographic production today. The changes in technology offer us new opportunities as photographers, which makes this an exciting time to embark on the road to photography.

Chapter 2

The Visual Aspects of Photography

As the language or vocabulary of photography has been extended, the emphasis of meaning has shifted—shifted from what the world looks like to what we feel about the world and what we want the world to mean.

—Aaron Siskind
Photographer

Figure 2-1

Ice House, Jerry Burchfield.

Photographs record the light that is reflected from the surface of everything that is in the picture.

Surface Reflections

A photograph is a two-dimensional object formed from a mechanical and optically controlled image of light. It records delicate detail and an infinite range of continuous tones from light to dark. Color photographs provide a realistic view of the subject. Black and white photographs abstract the subject by reproducing colors as shades of gray. Because most photographs are two-dimensional, depth is an illusion that is indicated by size differences, object placements, converging lines or shapes, and modeling from shadows and atmospheric conditions caused by the quality of the light, weather, and time of day.

Whether photographs are recorded photo-chemically or digitally, they are technically a record of surface reflections. That is, they record the light that is reflected from the surface of everything that is in the picture. When we view a photograph, what we see is a two-dimensional surface reflection of the light originally reflected from a three-dimensional environment. This relationship is generally taken for granted, and the photograph is accepted as an accurate representation of reality. Unfortunately, modern technology has made it so easy to make photographs, that most photographs are surface reflections for reasons other than those just mentioned. While the automated ease, speed, and accessability of photography today offer technical advantages, they can lead to photographs whose content is a mere surface reflection. This result occurs because the makers of photographs, whether amateur or professional, seldom look beyond the surface of their subject. They want instant gratification and do not take the time necessary to adequately understand their subject. They rely, instead, on quantity-shooting rather than quality.

Remember this: Anyone can make a good photograph once in a while. The challenge facing the serious photographer is to make good photographs *consistently*. To do so, we must be willing to question our motivations for making pictures and consciously seek the essence of our subject. Considering the *who, what, where, when, why* and *how* is as important for a photographer as for a journalist. It has been said that chance rewards the prepared mind. Photographers who consistently make good photographs are not only prepared, but they are also concerned enough about their subject to give it the attention and time needed to make photographs that have purpose, meaning, and impact upon a viewer.

Slanted Truths

The content of a photograph is up to the photographer. Every photograph is biased because it is influenced by the photographer's personality, cultural background, education, technical ability, and choice of equipment. Even a *documentary* photograph is biased. The photographer decides where to stand, what to include in the picture, and how to record it optically on film. These decisions affect the content and meaning of the picture. The choice of lens alone can change the impact and meaning of an image. A telephoto lens compresses space and can imply congestion and make things look uncomfortably close together, whereas a wide-angle lens expands space and can make the same scene feel open and uncongested.

Many photographers have expressed concern about the truthfulness of the photographic image in the digital age because photographs can be altered so easily with the computer. What most people fail to realize

is that photographs have *always* been biased and that manipulation of reality begins the moment the photographer decides to take a picture. The Civil War photographs of Mathew Brady are considered accurate documents of that tragic upheaval. Yet evidence suggests that Brady and his fellow photographers moved bodies to make the photographs more dramatic. Glamour photographers have always been notorious for manipulating the subject both during the shooting and afterwards with retouching. The most important difference the computer has brought to this debate is the ease with which a far larger audience can manipulate photographs.

As photographers, we need to understand our personal biases and the technological biases within the photographic medium. This book will help you to understand the technological biases and how to use them to your advantage. For many, acknowledgment and understanding of personal biases comes through seriously questioning the what and why of their photographs. For example, I recently gave a class an assignment to photograph a particular section of a diverse urban community. Most of the students made photographs that depicted the negative aspects of that environment. They made images of abandoned buildings, street people, graffiti, and urban congestion. When I told them that they had produced a limited and biased view of the community, they became defensive and declared their view an honest and unbiased representation. To prove my point, I sent them back to rephotograph the same environment. Only this time they were instructed to photograph everything that was there. Instead of selecting a few dilapidated structures to photograph, they had to photograph every single building on that street. Subsequently, at the critique, it was universally agreed that they had been biased and overlooked many of the other aspects of that community.

Learning to See

Looking is a surface reaction, whereas *seeing* is thinking that goes beyond the obvious. Looking occurs naturally, but seeing is learned ability. Seeing means allowing our eyes and our minds to search beyond societal conditioning and our preconceptions. For photographers, seeing also means learning to understand the difference between human vision and camera vision.

Human vision consists of fragments of information that we perceive from a series of quick, scanning glances of a scene. Our eyes are unable to distinguish differences in colors, light and dark values, and depth perception simultaneously in one glance. Instead our eyes go through a series of unconscious acts, encountering element by element the various parts of a scene. This information is transmitted to our brain, which pieces it together and provides us with a selective and intelligible visual impression. This impression, although visual, is influenced by other sensory input, such as sound, smell, and temperature.

Camera vision, unlike human vision, is not selective. The camera records whatever it is aimed at. It will not emphasize points of interest or suppress distracting elements. It sees the scene as a totality and is not influenced by sensory input.

The success of a photograph is dependent upon how selective we are when taking the picture. Despite some advertising claims, a camera is merely a tool and cannot read your mind or make decisions for you. To make photographs that communicate your impressions to others, you must learn to understand how a camera sees and how a photographic print is read by a viewer.

To make an effective photograph, it helps to know where to stand— not only where you stand physically when taking a photograph, but also where you stand with respect to a purpose for the photograph. The amount of attention you give to making the picture, what you choose to include in the image, and the technical approach all depend upon your interest in the subject and your purpose for making the photograph. Often we choose what to photograph at a moment's notice, for a variety of circumstantial, social, political, cultural, and personal reasons. Regardless of the circumstance, a photographer who makes pictures without any real intent or purpose seldom makes photographs that have any lasting impact.

Composition and Visual Selection

Once we decide to make a picture, we have to consider its *composition*. The word *composition* refers to the arrangement of visual elements in a picture. We also refer to the composition of an artwork as its *design*.

Artists who draw and paint actually *compose* their work because they begin with nothing but a blank canvas or piece of paper. It is different for photographers. Photographs are made from an actual physical presence, and their composition is determined through a process of *visual selection* rather than composition.

Visual selection has several different aspects, and they affect the look, design, and content of a picture. They are as follows: (1) determining the subject, (2) camera position, (3) framing the photograph, (4) subject placement, (5) lens focal length, (6) aperture, (7) shutter speed, and (8) deciding when to make the picture.

Subject and Camera Position

Once the subject is determined, the camera position or point of view must be selected. Consider the subject in relation to the surroundings. Are they compatible? Will there be awkward visual relationships such as poles and signs coming out of people's heads? Is the lighting good from that angle? Does the subject stand out from the background or blend in with it? Should I shoot from a normal standing position or try a bird's-eye or worm's-eye view? The most common point of view is to stand and hold the camera horizontally from an eye-level position. This point of view holds especially true for 35mm cameras, which are designed to be most comfortable when used in a horizontal position. Changing the point of view can radically alter the design and feel of the photograph.

Framing

Framing the photograph by looking through the viewfinder of the camera determines the content of the picture and the compositional elements that make up the picture. Using the rectangular or square format of our viewfinder, we select from the scene the part that we feel will make the best picture. At this point, the only thing that matters is whatever is within the frame of the viewfinder. Observe the scene through the viewfinder from edge to edge. Try to notice everything within the frame and determine what should be included or excluded. Change the framing or camera position to avoid visual elements that are out of context, distracting, or awkward. You will become a better photographer faster if you learn to shoot and print *full frame* images. This helps you develop your visual awareness quicker because you learn to consider everything in the frame when you are shooting, rather than relying on cropping the image later in the darkroom.

Subject Placement and Rule of Thirds

Placement of the subject within the frame determines the emphasis and effectiveness of the picture. Most pictures have a single subject or event that is the main interest of the photographer. Snapshooters tend to

Figure 2-2

Change in the placement of the horizon line alters the emphasis in landscape photographs. Raising the horizon line emphasizes land and lowering it emphasizes sky.

center the subject, whereas more experienced photographers use various approaches to subject placement to add impact and diversity to their pictures. Many photographers use the so-called rule of thirds to determine subject placement and points of interest within a photograph. This compositional device suggests that points of interest should fall at the intersection of two sets of horizontal and vertical lines that divide an image into thirds. The resulting four points of intersection provide a geometric balance for an image. However, the rule of thirds can become a formula approach to design solutions, and many photographs that break the rule are visually exciting.

The emphasis of landscape photographs can be changed by simply moving the position of the *horizon*. With the horizon line in the center of the picture, there is an equal balance between the land mass and the sky. Raising the horizon line to the upper portion of the frame shifts the emphasis to the land mass. Positioning the horizon line in the lower portion of the picture results in an emphasis on the sky. *Tilting the horizon* can imply motion or be employed to disturb or disorient a viewer.

Another consideration for framing your subject is the direction of *actual* and *implied lines*. These lines or visual paths generally should lead a viewer into the photo or to a point of interest. Actual lines are obvious, although we normally don't consider the influence they have on our response to an image. Implied lines are more subtle but effectively influence the viewer. Converging lines take the viewer to the point of convergence. Motion implies a line of view in a specific direction and can lead the viewer to a key part of the picture. When a person is in the picture, the viewer generally responds to the eyes of the subject and follows an implied line that leads in the direction the subject is looking. Implied lines that close an area define an implied shape.

Implied Lines, Linda Lucio.

Figure 2-3

Generally it is best visually to lead the subject into the photo rather than out of it. This is done with implied lines that are due to motion or the gaze of a subject. The subject in the image on the left was placed close to the frame, and the gaze takes the viewer out of the photograph. The subject position was shifted in the image on the right so that the space between the subject and the edge of the picture provides room to lead the viewer visually into the photograph.

Focal Length

The focal length of the lens determines the distance of the photographer to the subject and the optical rendition of it. Telephoto lenses magnify things at a distance, compress space, and have limited depth of field or range of focus in front of and behind your subject. Wide-angle lenses have to be used closer to the subject, expand space, and have tremendous depth of field. A change in lens focal length can radically alter the look of any subject.

Aperture

Aperture also affects depth of field as well as the amount of light exposing the film. This important visual control allows you to have everything in focus (maximum depth of field) or to have the foreground and background out of focus (minimum depth of field). Differences in sharpness within a picture, due to depth of field, can suggest movement and draw attention to specific portions of the photograph.

Shutter Speed

Shutter speed determines the way that motion is rendered and implied. It also works in conjunction with aperture to control the amount of exposure. A fast shutter speed freezes a subject that is in motion, but often a slow shutter speed that causes the subject to blur is better for suggesting movement.

When to Shoot

Deciding *when* to take the photograph determines the final outcome of the picture. Often we have to make split-second decisions and shoot fast to capture what photographer Henri Cartier-Bresson called the decisive moment. This is the final step of visual selection. Everything must come together for this one moment. If you have prepared well, you will be rewarded with images that are easy to work with in the darkroom and interesting for others to view. Like an athlete, strive to do your personal best every time you take photographs. The more you produce, the better you will get. Eventually, you will find that you no longer have to labor over picture-making decisions. You will respond automatically, intuiting the needs as you let your creativity flow.

Color versus Black and White

Photography began as a black and white medium in the 1830s. Color photography did not become practical until almost 100 years later and was not widely used until the 1960s. Today nearly all photographs are in color. Most are family snapshots. The rest serve commercial, fine art, and serious amateur needs. Black and white has become a specialty process revered for its graphic distinction and potential for easy hands-on alteration. It also has diverse commercial applications, but it is used primarily in the fine arts and educationally, to introduce beginners to darkroom procedures.

Black and white photographs reproduce everything in shades of gray and can easily dramatize a subject because they eliminate the reality of color. They rely upon shape, pattern, texture, contrast, and light and dark value relationships to define the subject and create impact in an image.

Color photographs provide a more realistic view of the subject, so they are widely used to document and show things as they are. Unfortu-

Figure 2-4

Utilizing a large format view camera and 4 × 5-inch film, along with advanced exposure and printing controls, Vodhanel makes dramatic use of the capability for abstract realism in black and white photography.

Black Aspens, Utah, Steve Vodhanel.

nately, this ability is also a drawback of color photography. Too many people make color photographs of things in color without using color as a visual and emotional element in their photographs. Color should be thought of as a design element and used to evoke responses in a viewer. To do this one has to gain understanding or have a natural grasp of color theory and relationships. One also needs to learn about light and how types of light and times of day affect color photography.

Photographers too often feel that they have to make *accurate* or true-to-life color pictures. But this can lead to self-delusion because the human response to color is subjective. No two people see colors exactly the same, just as no two color films record color identically. What *is* important is that your photographs make *effective* use of color. Mere color accuracy often leads to boring photographs.

Neither black and white nor color is better than the other. Both have advantages and disadvantages. Most good photographers are adept with both color and black and white photography and choose the process that works better with their particular image-making needs. Just remember that each process necessitates a different way of viewing the subject. Color pictures differ from black and white and must have a different level of thought during visual selection. The same holds true for black and white. You must learn to *think color* or *think black and white* to make successful photographs.

Single, Multiple, and Sequential Images

Most of us think in terms of the single-image still photograph. However, sometimes a multiple image or sequence of photographic images allows us to present more levels of information. If you are just making a picture *of something*, it will not matter. But if you want to present an idea or tell a story *about something*, multiple or sequential images may be worth considering.

Whenever we look at a group of pictures, whether in a magazine or an exhibit, our response to a particular image is always influenced by the picture that preceded it and the one that follows. Magazine editors and exhibition curators use this way of responding to involve and lead the viewer. Photographers also need to consider this factor whenever they present their work, whether a slide show, exhibition, book, magazine, portfolio, or family album.

Multiple images and sequential photographic images have been common since the beginning of photography. Multiple exposures can be made with the camera as well as in the darkroom. Some of the camera techniques will be discussed in Chapter Nineteen and the darkroom techniques in Chapter Sixteen. Digital imaging has made possible new levels of multiple image manipulation, and these techniques will be discussed in Chapter Seventeen. Photography offers many possibilities and methods for presenting ideas. Just because paper comes precut in certain sizes does not mean that we have to crop our images to fit that size. Nor does it mean that we have to make rectangular images. In today's world, photography has no boundaries.

Previsualization, Postvisualization

Most people just take pictures, seldom giving thought as to how the photograph will look. But a good photograph has to stand on its own, separate from the subject and the picture-taking. Experienced photographers have learned to *previsualize*, or see the subject as it will appear in the final photographic print. Previsualizing enables them to make better pictures because they are thinking about the final result. Too often, though, at the moment of shooting, we are so preoccupied with the subject that we don't consider how the final print will look.

To previsualize you have to become very familiar with photographic techniques and materials. A photograph is a representation of your subject. The equipment and materials you use to make the photograph translate the subject in many different ways. Photographer Ansel Adams, for example, developed a refined technique known as the zone system, discussed in Chapter 19, to control the contrast and values in photographs. This technique has enabled many photographers to control and previsualize in any picture-taking situation. Regardless of the type of photography or the process you use, learning to previsualize is an important step towards consistent and rewarding results.

Postvisualization is used by photographers who intuitively shoot many diverse images for use as a stockpile of raw material. Subsequently they combine and manipulate the images either in the darkroom or with the computer. The creative act for them is not in the shooting but in recreating or reinterpreting their images. Some use images found in magazines or other sources to combine with their own camera images.

Most photographers combine pre- and postvisualization in their work. Control, both creative and technical, is easiest to maintain when the photographer does everything. However, few people process their own color prints and fewer yet do their own color film. They rely on custom photo labs, just like most commercial photographers who find it impractical or too time-consuming to do their own lab work. Digital photography is also usually printed by someone other than the photographer. This situation makes it more important than ever for photographers to be able to previsualize and understand how their work will translate into a final print.

Traditionally, fine art photographs were considered suspect or were regarded with less respect if printed by someone other than the photographer because printing is such an important and subjective part of image making. This attitude is changing and will likely evolve as we become more dependent on electronic technology. Ultimately, it is the result that counts, regardless of how the print was made or who made it.

Symbolism and Metaphor

In the visual arts, including photography, symbols are visual elements that suggest or represent something else through association, relationship, or resemblance. Photographers use symbols, which can be objects, shapes, or designs, to influence the viewer. The response to symbolism depends upon the cultural background and education of the viewer. Humanlike forms and sexual symbols seem to be universally understood.

Floating Rock, Pebble Beach, CA, Neal Chapman.

Figure 2-5

Chapman uses the concept of equivalence in this photograph of a rock "floating" in water. Despite the subject recognition factor, the rock looms off the surface of the photograph and seems to have a living presence.

But many symbols have meaning only to a specific culture and may have a limited or different meaning to others.

Photography has been called a universal language, but the interpretation or level of meaning in a photograph will vary among people because of their different cultural backgrounds. Consequently, photographers who use symbols in their photographs must be aware of their audience.

A metaphor is the use of one thing to mean another. For instance, when we say someone is *drowning in money*, it doesn't mean the person is literally drowning, it means she has a lot of money. Photographically, metaphors are used to imply one thing but show something else.

The term *equivalence*, like *metaphor*, refers to photographs that evoke feelings that go beyond those associated with the subject of the picture. Early in the 20th century, Alfred Stieglitz made a series of black and white cloud photographs to suggest feelings of transcendence. He sought to produce pictures that would not limit the response of the viewer to direct associations with the subject of the picture. Stieglitz chose clouds because he thought they provided a neutral subject that opened the door to emotional response. In 1988, after 20 years of making landscape photographs, Richard Misrach raised his camera above the horizon and began taking pictures of the cloudless sky. Despite the fact that most people expect more tangible subjects in a photograph, Misrach realized that he had been ignoring the sky and that it provided a purity of color and feeling that went beyond subject matter.

"Finding Your Own Parking Lot"

Early in his career, one of the authors of this edition, had an opportunity to show his photographs to a renowned photographer. At that time he had been working on several different projects, each distinct from the other. One involved the exploration of form and color in photograms. Another consisted of black and white images emulating long established traditions of street and social landscape photography. After careful examination, the photographer suggested, "Find your own parking lot."

Although disappointed and perplexed, in time Burchfield realized the words rang true. Photography is a diverse medium with a short, but involved history. To enjoy making photographs is easy and does not require excessive effort, extensive equipment, or much technical knowledge. To go beyond that, however, whether in the fine arts or some commercial application of the medium, it is critical to "find your own parking lot."

The only way to find yourself is to become involved. Make and look at many pictures. Try producing a series of images that deal with a particular subject or idea. That will help develop your skills and ability to visualize your ideas faster than if you rely on the results of random shooting. Have a motivation or purpose behind your work. When shooting, do not limit your intuitive response by *overthinking* the picture. But afterwards, critically evaluate your results so that you can improve your intuitive responses when shooting.

Show your work to others in the field and enter juried exhibitions and competitions. Learn to accept, yet question rejection and criticism. Be it good or bad, criticism provides you with another perspective to evaluate your work. Most photographers find it hard to be objective about their own work and need outside feedback for growth.

With the advent of digital imaging, photography is rapidly expanding with many opportunities for both amateurs and professionals. Photography alone in the visual arts has a direct connection with real experience. That association has raised snapshots and commercial images to status as historical documents and some as fine art. In this way, many advertising, fashion, and journalistic images have gained importance beyond their original intent. At the same time, ideas and techniques developed by fine art photography are infiltrating everyday approaches to photographic imaging. You can strive to make a contribution too.

Chapter 3

Photograms

Light is the shape and play of my thought, my reason for being a photographer.

—Barbara Morgan
Photographer

The word *photography* comes from two Greek words that mean "light drawing." Light is the physical phenomenon that makes photography possible, from the initial exposure of a picture to the final development and printing of the film.

Cameras and film have always been the essential tools of photography, but not all photography is based on them. Digital imaging is still dependent upon cameras to record the image, but it can be done electronically without film. Another method for making photographic images, the photogram, is made with neither camera nor film. Photograms are cameraless images resulting from the interaction of light with objects placed on light-sensitive materials, such as photographic print paper. Put simply, making a photogram is similar to getting a suntan—skin exposed to the sun's rays darkens, while "unexposed" skin remains the same. The amount of exposure time and the intensity of the light affect the degree of darkening of both a suntan and a photogram.

Some of the first photographic experiments resulted in photograms. The calotypes, or *photogenic drawings*, made in the early 19th century by William Henry Fox Talbot, were photograms. In the 1920s artists such as Christian Schad, Man Ray, and László Moholy-Nagy started experimenting with photograms as a means of deviating from straightforward realism and into the strange and dreamlike exploration of surrealism and the abstract use of light and space. Like many photographic pioneers, each gave his own name to the process: Schad referred to his as Schadographs, and Man Ray called his Rayographs. Moholy-Nagy, however, simply referred to his as light drawings, or photograms.

The techniques for making photograms are basically simple, but results can be highly sophisticated. Many artists today find the photogram to be a versatile and stimulating way to make pictures. Most

Figure 3-1

Talbot, the inventor of the negative/positive photographic process, initially made photograms by laying plants on top of drawing paper, which he had sensitized by coating it with a chemical emulsion that turned dark upon exposure to light. This image was one of the first photograms ever made.

Photogenic drawing, 1839, William Henry Fox Talbot.

photographers use traditional black and white or color print materials for photograms, but some work directly on film or other types of light-sensitive materials.

Making photograms provides an excellent understanding of how light and the photographic process work. It also requires us to begin composing images much as a painter does. Unlike camera work, where we select from an existing environment what we wish to include in the picture, to make an effective photogram we have to compose a picture on a blank sheet of paper. Moholy-Nagy considered it the purest form of photography because it was based on the direct interaction of light, objects, and light-sensitive materials.

Printed-out Photograms

A printed-out photogram does not require a darkroom or any special equipment. It uses light, time, black and white photographic paper, and whatever objects you decide to use. Photographic paper has an *emulsion*, or coating, on one side that is made with silver halide particles that turn dark with exposure to light. When objects are placed on top of the emulsion side of the paper and subsequently exposed to light, a shadow image is formed, with the covered portions of the paper staying light.

To make a printed-out photogram, start with a sheet of 8×10-inch *resin-coated* (RC) paper because it is large enough to allow for flexibility in composing your photogram. Many brands are available, and most will work well with this process. To begin, try to avoid *fiber-based* papers. RC papers are quicker and easier to use.

To begin, remove one sheet of photographic paper from the package while in the dark or under safelight conditions of a darkroom. Be sure to put the unused photo paper back into the package and seal it so that no light can fog (partially expose) the paper. Once the unused paper is safe, determine the emulsion side of the piece of paper you removed from the package. This can normally be done by feeling the surfaces of the paper. The emulsion side usually feels smoother and has a slight shine that should be apparent under safelight illumination. Next, lay the paper down, emulsion side up, and place the objects that you planned to use on top of the paper. Think of the objects as *light modulators*. Flat opaque objects will create a silhouette, but rounded ones will allow light to "bleed" around the object and result in shades of gray with an illusion of depth. Objects that aren't completely opaque will allow light to go through them, depending upon the degree of opacity. Making use of any translucence will allow you to record the inner textures and forms of the object. Using a magazine page, for example, enables you to get a blend of images from both sides of the page.

In making a photogram, think in terms of composing a picture, rather than just laying objects on the paper to see what happens. Make cutouts and create scenes or stories. In all cases, the character of the result will depend upon the amount of light and time that you give to the project. The same object can result in quite different images, based on differences in the amount of exposure. Be prepared to experiment.

After the objects are arranged on the paper, expose the photo paper to daylight, regular room lights, or better still, light from an intense source such as a spotlight or a lamp directed at the paper. You can

Figure 3-2

This large multipanel photogram, or light painting, was made by lighting a baby, two women, a skeleton, and a toy figure with a penlit flashlight covered with colored gels. Ilfochrome print paper was used because it is a positive-to-positive material, which results in a positive image and makes it easier to determine the color relationships.

The Last Supper, Jerry Burchfield.

observe the paper getting slowly darker in the uncovered areas. The amount of exposure time will vary depending upon the objects and the intensity of the light source. Through trial and error experimentation, you will be able to determine when the exposure is giving you the result you desire. Different types of black and white photographic paper produce an array of colors from blues to rust when exposed to light over a period of time. Try different brands to see what results you can obtain.

Once you have an image that pleases you, you face a problem that plagued early photographers. Your printed-out photogram is not a permanent image and will continue to darken if exposed to light after the objects have been removed. To make your photogram permanent, it has to be *fixed* in a chemical called *hypo* or *fixer*, which will be discussed next in the next section. Note, however, that when a printed-out photogram is fixed, it changes color and gets a little lighter.

Developed-out Photograms

Developed-out photograms are made in a manner similar to that of printed-out photograms, except that a chemical process is used to shorten exposure times and ensure a permanent black and white image. Because the photographic chemicals enhance the light sensitivity of the photographic paper, it is necessary to make developed-out photograms in a darkroom equipped with safelights.

To make a developed-out photogram, you begin as you did with printed-out photograms, but do not remove your paper from the package until you are ready to make an exposure. Safelights are safe for only limited amounts of time. Also, remember to reclose your paper package so that the remaining sheets are light safe.

To expose the paper you can use room light, a flashlight, or whatever else might be available. Just remember that you will need very little light to have an effect when the paper is chemically processed. To find out how much, you will have to do some experimental tests. Start with 1 or 2 seconds.

After making the exposure, remove the objects from the paper. At this point, you will notice that nothing seems to have happened to the paper. It is still white, seemingly unaffected by the shorter exposure. However, an invisible image has been recorded on the sensitized paper. This is called a *latent image* and can only be seen after being chemically processed. Photons of light react with silver halide crystals and produce an invisible (latent) image.

A

B

Figure 3-3

Three-dimensional plastic toy cowboys were used to make this basic silhouette photogram. When the exposure was increased from 3 seconds to 60 seconds, the light bled around the objects, giving form and dimension to the photogram. (B) Changing the angle of the light source distorted the toy figures. The photograms in A and B were exposed with light from the enlarger, but was exposed (C) with a penlight flashlight.

C

The Chemical Steps

The chemical for making the invisible latent image visible is the *developer*. A developer chemically changes the latent image on the emulsion to a visible image composed of metallic silver. The greater the exposure, the denser the silver. Different brands of developers have their own particular characteristics. However, since we are using photographic paper for these photograms, be sure to acquire a developer made for photographic paper, not for film.

The length of time that the photo paper remains in the developer is determined by the type of paper, the type of developer, and the temperature of the developer. A chart is usually provided with the package of paper or the developer. If none is available, refer to the chart at the end of this chapter.

The second chemical, the *stop bath*, halts the action of the developer. It usually consists of a mild solution of acetic acid. The stop bath also helps preserve the useful life of the next chemical, the *fixer*.

The fixer (or hypo) removes the unexposed silver from the paper. After the paper is treated in the fixer, it is no longer sensitive to light, and thus the print can be viewed in normal room light.

Although not a photographic chemical, running water must be used to remove any excess fixer. If this is not done, the print stains after a few weeks, and eventually the image bleaches itself because of certain ingredients in the fixer.

To begin the chemical process, set up four processing trays. If the darkroom you are working in has a large counter or sink, position the trays in a line and work from left to right with the developer first, followed by the stop bath, fixer, and finally water.

When working with photo chemicals, make sure that you work in a well-ventilated room. Also, always try to keep one hand dry, or use tongs to keep your hands out of the chemicals.

After you have made the exposure and are ready to process it, immerse the paper in the developer and gently rock the tray to agitate the print. The agitation helps ensure even chemical development. With RC papers, the developing time with most developers is one minute. For information on the chemical times for fiber-based prints, refer to the chart at the end of this chapter. Be sure to time the development and keep it consistent. If your print is too dark, you need to expose it to less light, not reduce the developing time. Reducing developing time will only lead to uneven, mottled results that lack normal image contrast. If your print is too light, you need to expose it longer. Increasing the development time will have little effect. Be sure to work under safelight conditions.

During the last 10 seconds of the developing time, lift the print out of the tray and let the excess developer drain off. Then immerse the print into the second chemical, the stop bath. Gently agitate it in the stop bath for 30 seconds. During the last 10 seconds, remove the print and drain off the excess stop bath before immersing it in the fixer. With RC prints, the fixing time, with agitation, is normally 2 minutes. Extended times in the fixer can cause an adverse bleaching of the print and should be avoided. Once the print has been adequately fixed, you can turn on the room lights to view your results better.

The next step is to wash out all residual chemicals with running water. This can be done by using a tray with running water from a

Figure 3-4

The cardboard cores from two toilet paper rolls provide the eyes of this "face" photogram made with toilet paper and colored light, printed orginally in color on Agfacolor print paper.

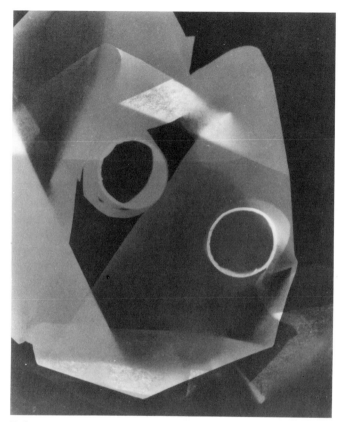

Toilet Paper Cubism, Jerry Burchfield.

faucet in either a sink or bathtub. RC papers need to be washed for 2 to 5 minutes, fiber-based papers for at least 30 minutes.

Once washed, prints need to dry. The simplest method with RC prints is to hang them by a corner with a clothes pin or push pin and let them drip dry. Another method is to squeegee or to gently wipe off the excess water with a sponge or towel before laying the prints on paper towels to dry. Fiberglass window screens are often used to dry the prints on because they can be positioned to allow air to reach both sides of the print. Hair dryers can also be used to speed up the process. Always be sure to squeegee off the excess water to avoid water spots on the dry print unless you are using the drip dry method. Fiber-based papers take much longer to dry and have a tendency to curl. A simple way to dry them is to squeegee the washed prints and place them face down on a clean window screen. This method takes several hours to dry fiber prints. A blotter book can be purchased and also used to dry squeegeed prints. This method will take several days for drying.

Negative-Positive Relationships

Both the printed-out and developed-out methods of making photograms produce *reverse*, or *negative* images. In other words, they reverse the normal tonal scale, substituting white for black. These negative image photograms can be used as *paper negatives* to produce positive images. This is done by *contact printing* them onto another piece of photographic paper.

Figure 3-5

A record-winning black sea bass was placed on black and white mural paper and exposed to light, creating this "documentary" photogram. A mop was used to apply the developer, which caused the watery look in the background.

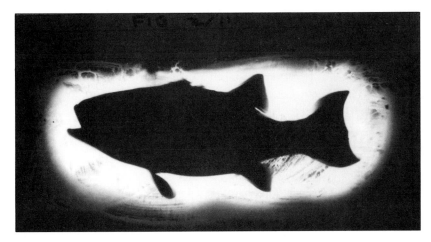

Figure 3-6

The original negative image photogram of *Ted's Dad's Big Fish* was copied onto 4 × 5-inch black and white film, and a smaller print of the image was made. This was then used as a paper negative and placed on top of an unexposed piece of enlarging paper held in place with a piece of glass and exposed to light. The result was a positive or reversed image of the photogram.

Ted's Dad's Big Fish, Jerry Burchfield, 40 × 96-inch black and white mural paper.

There are two methods for contact printing of paper negatives, the *wet process* and the *dry process*. The wet process can be done immediately after washing a newly made print. In safelight conditions, take out an unexposed piece of photo paper and put it in a tray of clean water. Then take the wet photogram and the wet piece of unexposed paper and place them in contact with each other, emulsion to emulsion. Then take this *sandwich* and lay it on a smooth, flat surface, with the negative image on the top. Starting at the center, take a rubber squeegee and remove the excess water and air from between the two prints. Then expose them to light for several seconds. The light will go through the back of the negative photogram and expose the photo paper that is in contact with it. If given the right amount of exposure, the result will be a reverse, or positive, image of the original negative photogram image. To determine the right exposure, experimental tests will be necessary. A controllable light source with a timer works best. Most photographers use their enlargers for contact prints as well as enlargements.

For making photograms with the dry process, a piece of glass is used to hold a dry print in contact with and on top of a piece of dry and unexposed enlarging paper. The remaining process is the same as with the wet process.

Creative Options

Photograms offer endless possibilities for creative image making without a camera. The techniques discussed in this chapter are merely a starting point. Experiment with different shapes and sizes of objects as well as different types and sizes of photo paper. Also try varying your light source. With the light directly overhead, it will create a specific shape from your objects. However, if the light is used at an angle to the surface of the paper, the light will cast long shadows and make little objects look gigantic. Variations in the amount of exposure will also give different results with the same object, often producing graduated gray tones that give a sense of form and depth to the picture.

Don't be afraid to experiment with a variety of different types of objects. You can create silhouette shapes with almost anything. Many objects, even an inch-thick steak, will allow light to go through if you give enough exposure. When an object is in direct contact with the paper, a well-defined hard edge will result in the photogram. If parts of it are elevated and not in direct contact, then the edges and textures of the object will be diffused and soft.

Another thing to try is drawing with light and chemicals. A penlight flashlight or fiber optics can be used for light drawing or accenting specific areas of a photogram. You can also apply the developer selectively with your fingers, a brush, or a sponge, or by just splattering it onto the photo paper to get some unusual effects.

Vaseline or other petroleum jelly can be used for making hand- and footprints. Lightly apply the jelly onto your hand and carefully place it in contact with a piece of unexposed photo paper. Lift your hand off and a jelly impression of your hand will be left on the photo paper. Then expose the paper to light and develop it with the jelly still in place. The jelly will mask the print and keep the developer from affecting the part of the paper where you placed your hand. A white handprint will result, showing the textures and patterns of your hand. Once the print is developed, put it into the stop bath and then the fixer. With the safelights on, take the print out of the fixer, rinse with water, and use a paper towel to wipe off the jelly. Then refix and wash the print to make the handprint permanent. To make dark handprints, put your hand into the developer and then place your wet hand in contact with a piece of unexposed photo paper. Expose it to light and let the hand area develop. When it is dark enough, put it into the stop bath and follow through with the remaining chemical steps.

These are just a few of the possibilities for making photograms. You can make photograms from plants in your garden, by contact printing

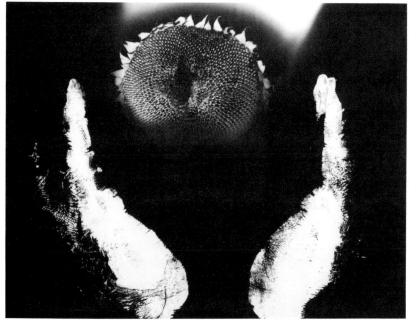

Vaseline, Palms & Sunflower, P. W. Derby, 8 × 10-inch black and white print.

Figure 3-7

Derby made this photogram by coating the sides of his hands lightly with petroleum jelly and then putting them in contact with the surface of the printing paper. The sunflower image was printed separately and dodged (covered to block additional exposure), while the rest of the paper was exposed to light. The petroleum jelly impeded development and, thus the hand images stayed white. However, the petroleum jelly must be removed during the fixer bath for the white areas to be permanent.

through magazine pages, by making cutout shapes, or by placing photo paper in contact with a TV screen. As you become more experienced and learn how to make enlargements of your camera images, you may want to combine camera images and photograms, or make color photograms. The possibilities are endless.

The chemical steps described earlier provide a working knowledge only. They are not intended as a complete description of the chemical process.

Chemical Time Chart

Step	Time	Additional information
1. Developer	1 to 3 minutes for fiber-based papers; 45 seconds to 2 minutes for RC papers	Agitate constantly; safelight conditions only
2. Stop bath	30 seconds for fiber-based papers and RC papers	Agitate constantly; safelight conditions only
3. Fixer	5 to 10 minutes for fiber-based papers; 2 to 4 minutes for RC papers	Agitate constantly; safelight conditions for first half of time
4. Wash	30 minutes to 1 hour for fiber-based papers; 4 to 6 minutes for RC papers	Empty tray of all water once every 5 minutes

* Chart provides guidelines only. Solutions should be between 65 and 75°F (18.5 and 24°C). The primary recommendation for processing is 68°F (20°C). When possible, refer to manufacturer's instructions.

Color Gallery A

List of Plates

Plate 1.1

This color image presents a negative photogram image of a magazine article celebrating the 150th anniversary of the invention of photography. It was meant to suggest that visual literacy is learned and that photography is not universally understood.

Context, Jerry Burchfield, 14 × 11-inch Ektacolor photogram in a glass box.

Plate 1.2

The word *photography* means "light drawing" and this image was made by "painting" the scene with a flashlight covered with colored gels. Hesketh uses the primary colors of light—red, blue and green—and paints with each separately, creating the color combinations he wants during a half-hour time exposure.

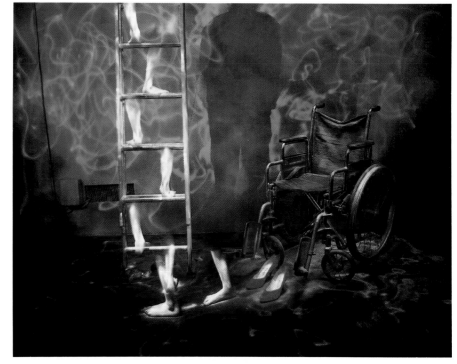

Ascension, John Hesketh, 16 × 20-inch Cibachrome print.

Illusive Landscapes #4, Arches National Park, Robert Johnson, 16 × 20-inch Ektacolor print.

Plate 1.3

Our sense of reality and the truth of photographic representation are questioned in this photograph. Through the use of rephotographic techniques, Johnson combines black and white with color in a spatial relationship.

Goody's Coffee Shop, Jerry Burchfield, 11 × 14-inch Cibachrome print.

Plate 1.4

Many "serious" photographers appreciate and are often inspired by the innocent vision that generates snapshots.

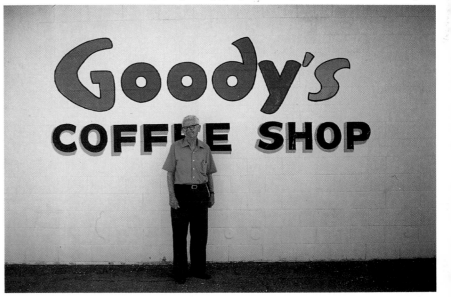

Plate 1.5

This photograph is about relationships between painting and photography. The paintings and chairs were shot with 35mm color slide film, which was subsequently "hand painted" with a black felt pen.

Considering Painting, Jerry Burchfield, hand painted 35mm color slide film.

Plate 2.1

Light and time are essential ingredients in any photograph. A long, hand-held exposure and flash were used to create this radiating image from the photographer's *Night Walking* series. The intent of the photograph went beyond rendition of subject to exploration of the impact of light and color as energy.

Untitled #1651, Jerry Burchfield, Cibachrome print.

Plate 2.2

For his *Gridlock* series, Clayton Spada combines the human element with the scientific. Spada lights his subjects and projects scientific information onto them. Once the film is developed, the images are digitally scanned and then encapsulated onto a grid of more scientific data via computer imaging. The images are then outputted onto a 4 x 5-inch transparency film and printed onto Ilfochrome photographic paper.

Gridlocked II, Clayton Spada, Ilfochrome print.

Plate 2.3

Camera vision is not selective. This photograph was shot from a car driven through downtown Los Angeles. It is a record of what the camera saw and does not emphasize points of interest or suppress distracting elements.

Drive By, Jerry Burchfield, Ilfochrome print.

Plate 2.4

The unusual positioning of the giraffes emphasized the interplay of the shapes and patterns in this photograph.

Giraffes, Clayton Spada, Ilfochrome print.

Plate 2.5

The *point of view* or *camera position* can radically alter the impact of a photograph. A different perspective from the normal standing position, such as a bird's-eye or worm's-eye view, is always worth considering. By shifting the camera position to a lower viewpoint, the photographer gave the glove an almost lifelike feeling.

Point of View

Rule of Thirds

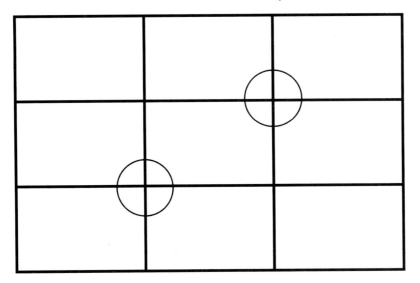

Plate 2.6

A commonly used compositional device, the *rule of thirds* is used to determine subject placement and points of interest. According to the rule, points of interest should fall at the four intersections of two horizontal and two vertical lines that divide the image into thirds. Following the rule slavishly may result in predictable and uninteresting images.

Convergence to Center

Plate 2.7

Most snapshooters tend to center their subject, often resulting in a static and boring composition. The converging lines add impact and emphasis to the centered subject in this photograph.

Untitled, Jim Hansen.

Plate 2.8

Hansen uses line, shape, and contrast in value and color to make this fountain pen image visually exciting.

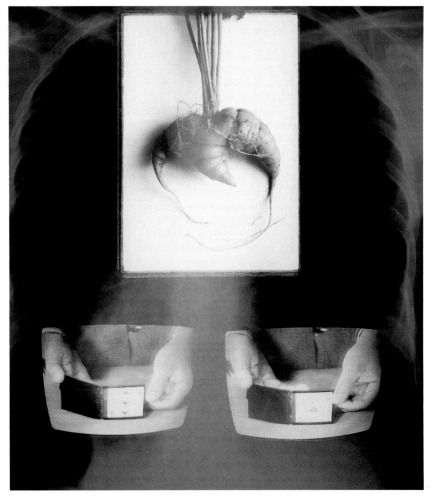

Plate 2.9
Multiple images were combined in the darkroom to suggest ambiguous relationships about life, death, and the passage of time.

Card Trick, Jerry Burchfield, Cibachrome print.

Plate 2.10
Symbolism can be a powerful communication tool for photographers, but many symbols are not universally understood. Interpretations vary from culture to culture. The cross symbol in this photograph, usually associated with Christianity, evokes many different responses throughout the world.

Untitled #1602, Jerry Burchfield, Cibachrome print.

Plate 3.1

This color photogram, from the *Totem Series*, is made from a group of books laid on top of long, thin strings of unexposed Ilfochrome paper. Penlight flashlights covered with different color gels are used to "paint" with light the spaces around the books. Print sizes vary from 5 to 8 feet high and 16 inches wide.

Totem #1, Personal Referents, Jerry Burchfield, light painting on Ilfochrome, 60 × 13-inches.

Plate 3.2

In the same way that the first photographs were made, objects were placed on black and white enlarging paper and then exposed to sunlight until the uncovered portions turned dark. The paper was then fixed, washed, and dried. Note the color possible with "printed-out" paper.

Printed-out Photogram

Plate 3.3

Here the same objects were used, but for a shorter exposure, because the image-making was accelerated by using a developer. Early photographers discovered that a short exposure produced an invisible, or latent, image, that would appear when bathed in the appropriate chemicals. Chemical development also enabled them to control contrast and achieve richer and more detailed prints.

Developed-out Photogram

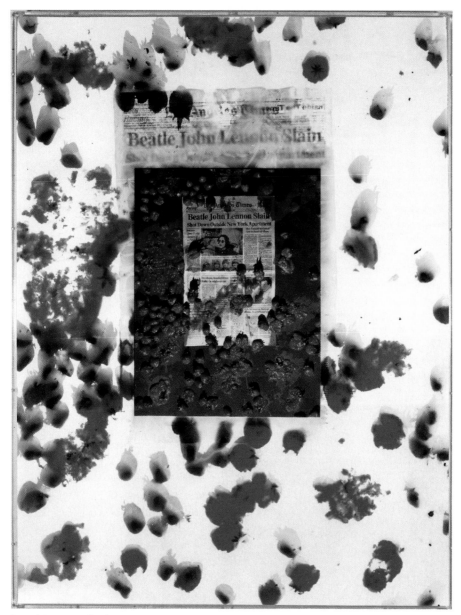

Second Degree, Still Life #43, Jerry Burchfield, 38 × 28-inch photogram.

Plate 3-4

This image, made in response to the death of John Lennon, combines a photogram and a camera image of the photogram as it was produced. In the dark, a newspaper and smashed strawberries were placed on the surface of 30 × 40-inch Ilfochrome paper with a camera overhead. The photogram and camera image were exposed simultaneously with a flash. After processing, the camera image was double-printed into the unexposed center of the paper.

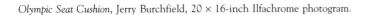

Plate 3.5

An inflatable plastic seat cushion from the 1984 Olympics was used to make this "documentary" photogram on Ilfochrome. If enough exposure is given, light will go through an object and record its inner form.

Olympic Seat Cushion, Jerry Burchfield, 20 × 16-inch Ilfachrome photogram.

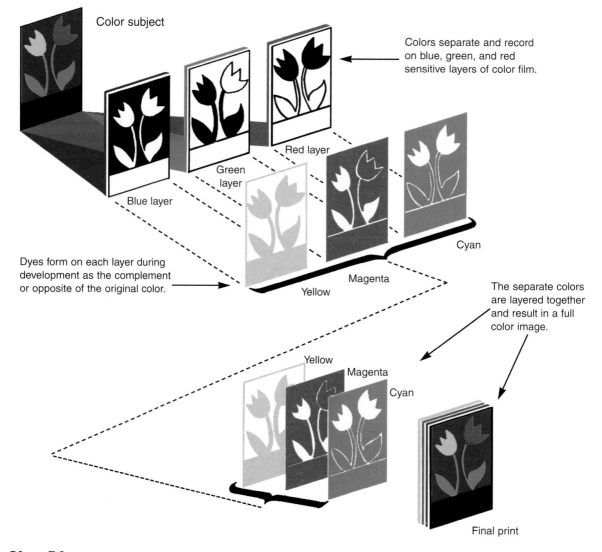

Color subject

Colors separate and record on blue, green, and red sensitive layers of color film.

Red layer

Green layer

Blue layer

Cyan

Dyes form on each layer during development as the complement or opposite of the original color.

Yellow

Magenta

The separate colors are layered together and result in a full color image.

Yellow

Magenta

Cyan

Final print

Plate 7.1
How Color Film Works.

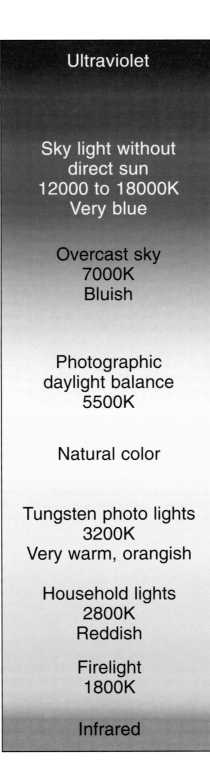

Ultraviolet

Sky light without
direct sun
12000 to 18000K
Very blue

Overcast sky
7000K
Bluish

Photographic
daylight balance
5500K

Natural color

Tungsten photo lights
3200K
Very warm, orangish

Household lights
2800K
Reddish

Firelight
1800K

Infrared

Plate 7.2

The warmer or redder the light—
candle, for example—the lower the
kelvin temperature; the cooler or
bluer the light—a cloudless summer
sky, for example—the higher the
kelvin temperature.

Chapter 4

The Pinhole Camera

In an era of point-and-shoot cameras, with lenses focused by computer-chip electronics, the notion of using a handmade camera with a pinhole instead of a lens appears to be at least curiously anachronistic if not perversely eccentric.

—John Upton
Photographic historian

Figure 4-1

Cannon used a homemade pinhole camera to make a 4 × 5-inch black and white negative of this scene. Subsequently, he made a Van Dyke emulsion, which is an old photographic process, and painted the emulsion onto Arches watercolor paper. The pinhole camera negative was then contact printed, and this image resulted.

Two Trees and a Rock, Glenn Cannon, hand-coated Van Dyke emulsion on Arches paper.

The camera has undergone a tremendous evolution since the invention of photography in the early 1800s. The diversity of types and models of cameras is astounding. Yet as cameras become more sophisticated, they remain basically the same. The pinhole camera, primitive by today's standards, provides an inexpensive and simple tool for learning about the basis of photography.

A camera is often compared to a human eye. Both a camera and an eye are enclosed chambers with an opening that allows light to enter the chamber from the front and then pass through a lens. Both have a light-sensitive area behind the lens.

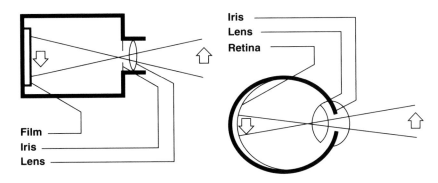

The lens in both the camera and the eye serves the same function. It gathers rays of light reflected from objects in the scene being viewed and then transmits them, in an expanding cone, back to the light-sensitive area behind the lens. In the eye, this light-sensitive area is called the retina; in a camera, it is the film.

In both the eye and the camera, a device in the lens controls the amount of light transmitted. In the eye, this device is a muscle called the iris. In the camera, the device is called the iris diaphragm. Both the eye and the camera work best when there is a moderate amount of light—too little light, and the details cannot be seen; too much, and the light is blinding, again obscuring details.

Both the camera and the eye must be focused, or the image will be blurred. In the eye, the lens, which is controlled automatically by the brain, focuses the light rays on the retina. The brain also translates the image on the retina into something meaningful. In the camera, the lens focuses the image onto the film plane.

The one very important difference between your eye and a camera is that the camera has no intelligence of its own—no brain to control it. Camera manufacturers try to make cameras easier to use by installing electrical circuitry that will make instantaneous calculations of the picture-taking situation, and by providing digital readouts much like a calculator's. Yet no camera, no matter how new or expensive it is, can see for you. The camera is a tool: It serves the photographer, but it is not the master. The photographer has to recognize what makes a good photograph and when to release the shutter.

The Origins of the Camera

As far back as 400 B.C., people have investigated the phenomena of image formation through a small aperture or opening. The earliest forerunner of the camera—the camera obscura—did not initially use a

lens. The term *camera obscura* is Latin for "dark chamber," and at first the camera obscura was simply a dark room with a small hole in one of the walls. People inside the dark room could see fuzzy, upside-down images of things outside on the interior wall opposite the aperture.

The image within the camera obscura was formed by unfocused light rays coming through the aperture. The sharpness of the image depended on the size of the aperture and the distance between the aperture and the opposite wall. A large aperture with a long distance to the opposite wall produced a blurred image, but a small aperture would create a sharper, but fainter, image because it reduced the amount of light hitting the wall. Consequently, such lensless devices had to compromise between sharpness and brightness. The image reflected on the wall

Figure 4-2

In this pinhole image of the Cologne Cathedral in Germany, a long exposure was necessary to expose the 4 × 5-inch color transparency film. This lapse of time caused the leaves of the windblown trees to blur on the image, resulting in an effect similar to the look and "feel" of many early landscape photographs.

Cologne Cathedral, from the *Holy Images* series, Glenn Cannon, a 4 × 5-inch transparency made in a pinhole camera and printed on Ilfochrome.

would be upside down because of the way light refracts through a small opening.

According to many historians, the camera obscura began to be equipped with lenses in about the 16th century, making possible the development of portable models with sharper, brighter images. Artists used the improved camera obscura to learn three-dimensional perspective drawing and to trace images directly from nature. The next advance in the use of the camera obscura was the invention in the early 1800s of the chemical means of recording images direct from nature—the process that we call *photography*. Today, one simple type of camera still does not have a lens: It uses the basic principle of the camera obscura—light entering a dark chamber through an aperture and producing an image. We call it the *pinhole camera*.

How to Make a Pinhole Camera

The first thing you need to make a pinhole camera is a box that can be made light-tight so that no stray rays of light will enter and fog the film or photographic paper. Boxes that can be used for this purpose include shoe boxes, oatmeal boxes, or any similar box that has a tight-fitting lid and will hold a 4 × 5-inch sheet of photographic paper or film.

Next, you need to make the pinhole, which will serve as the lens on the camera. Take a smooth piece of aluminum foil about an inch square. Lay it on a flat, hard surface such as metal or glass and press only the point of a needle straight down through the foil. The hole should be perfectly round and free from ridges, and the foil should not be pushed out where the pinhole was made. The hole itself will be hard to measure, but it should be too small for the entire pin to fit through.

After you have selected the box, paint the inside with black paint that has a flat (not shiny) finish. If the inside is not painted, it will reflect or bounce the light passing through the pinhole in all directions and fog your paper. Next, make a hole in the center of one side of the box and tape the aluminum foil with the pinhole securely over the larger hole, using an opaque tape such as black electrical tape or masking tape. Make sure that the pinhole is in the center, and then take another piece of opaque tape and cover the pinhole. This piece of tape will act as the shutter of your camera.

Loading the pinhole camera with photo paper must be done in a darkroom, using a safelight. Use a fresh sheet of photo paper, like that used in making the photograms, and center it on the side opposite the

Figure 4.C

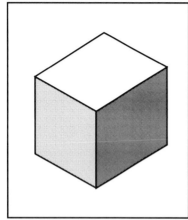

Find a light-tight box

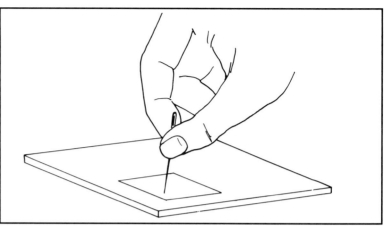

Carefully puncture the aluminum foil

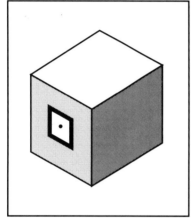

Tape aluminum foil over square hole

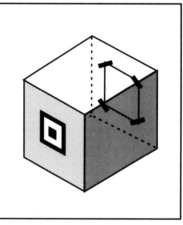

Tape pinhole closed and position photo paper

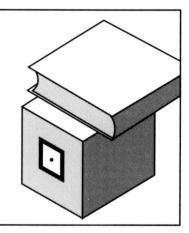

Secure box with heavy object; remove tape and expose

pinhole. Make sure that the emulsion side is facing the hole. After this is done, tape the four corners down so that the paper won't move around inside the box. (See the accompanying illustration.) Replace the lid on the box and you are ready to take a picture.

Taking a Pinhole Picture

In photography, the term *exposure* can mean two things: (1) the actual taking of the picture and (2) the time that light is allowed to enter the light-tight camera. For instance: Elaine *exposed* thirteen pictures today,

each one having an *exposure* of 2 minutes. Luckily for her, it was a bright day—otherwise her *exposure* would have been 8 minutes each and she couldn't have *exposed* as many pictures.

To take a picture (or *expose* a picture) with a pinhole camera, place it on a firm support such as a table, a window sill, a rock, or a chair. Tape or weight it so that it won't move accidentally. This is important because any movement during the exposure will cause your picture to be blurry or out of focus. After your camera has been securely fastened to the support, remove the tape that is covering the pinhole. Expose the picture for two minutes if it's sunny outside, for about eight minutes if it's cloudy bright. You must then develop your picture in the darkroom as you did the developed-out photogram. The resulting image will, of course, be a negative. Making a positive is done in the same manner as with a photogram. If your negative is too light, or underexposed, then increase your exposure time. If your negative is too dark, or overexposed, shorten the exposure time. Just remember that the brighter it is outside, the shorter your exposure time should be; the darker it is, the longer your exposure time will be.

You may want to make three or four pinhole cameras so that you'll be sure of getting the correct exposure. With camera 1, make an exposure of 2 minutes; with camera 2, a 4-minute exposure; with camera 3, a 6-minute exposure. This procedure is called *bracketing* the exposure.

Movement (or lack of it) is the main consideration in choosing subjects for pinhole camera exposures. Most people can't sit still for a 2-to-8-minute exposure; they move and cause a blurry image. It is best to shoot unmoving subjects such as landscapes or buildings.

There are actually four variables that affect the exposure time: (1) the sensitivity of the paper or film to light; (2) the size of the pinhole; (3) the pinhole-to-paper distance; and (4) the lighting conditions.

All photographic papers and films are sensitive to light. However, some kinds of film and paper are more sensitive than others. In general, film is more sensitive to light than paper is. Therefore, you may want

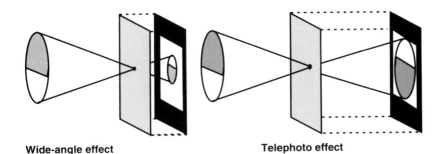

Wide-angle effect   **Telephoto effect**

to use film instead of paper in your pinhole camera, especially if you intend to photograph something other than a still life. Sheet film is available in both black and white and color in 4 × 5 inch and larger sizes. A pinhole camera, designed around a 126 film cartridge, is explained later in this chapter.

The size of the pinhole also affects the necessary exposure time. A small hole, of course, will allow less light to pass through it. Then, why not just make a bigger pinhole? The reason is that many more rays of light will pass through the larger hole, and because there is no way to guide them, they will record themselves over a much larger and less well-defined spot on the paper or film. What about using a more sensitive film and a smaller hole to get a sharper picture? This would work if it were not for the effect of diffraction. *Diffraction* refers to the scattering of light rays as they pass close to any edge. As the hole is made smaller, the proportion of scattered rays of light to unscattered rays increases, thus also producing a less defined image. In short, a pinhole camera cannot ever produce as clear or sharp a picture as a camera with a lens.

The shorter the distance from a pinhole to the paper (or film), the shorter the exposure time can be. Conversely, the longer the pinhole-to-paper distance, the longer the exposure necessary.

Distance can also be used to create an optical effect you may want to use in your picture taking. A camera in which the pinhole-to-paper distance is substantially less than the diagonal measurement of the paper will produce a small image that includes a wider field of view. For example, the diagonal measurement of a 4 × 5-inch sheet of paper is about 6 ½ inches. If you put such a sheet of paper 2 inches from your pinhole, you'll get a "wide-angle" effect. That is, more area will be shown in your picture because the subject and its surroundings will be reduced in size.

Conversely, if the pinhole distance to the paper is much greater than the diagonal measurement, the image will be magnified to look much greater in size than it really is. This is called a "telephoto" effect. If the pinhole-to-paper distance is about the same as the diagonal measurement, the effect will be "normal"—that is, about what your eye would see within the same space from the same distance as the camera.

The last factor that determines exposure is the amount of light. The more light, the shorter the exposure time. The less light, the longer the exposure time. Bracketing the exposure by making several pinhole cameras and photographing the same scene under the same lighting conditions with different exposures will help you in getting a properly exposed picture.

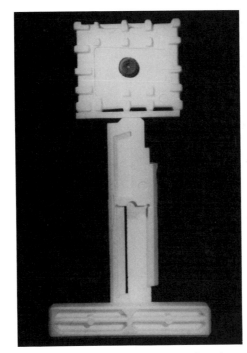

Styrofoam Camera, Peggy Ann Jones, styrofoam, brass, 50 × 25 × 10 inches.

Figure 4-3

For years, Jones has made pinhole cameras that are intentionally designed to utilize the unusual characteristics of the materials and objects from which she makes them. The cameras for her *Black Hole Photography* series are made from styrofoam packing materials for protecting electronic equipment. Jones intentionally uses the light leaks from the styrofoam to get an "astro photography" look in her images.

Experimental Pinhole Cameras

Pinhole cameras can be made in many sizes and shapes. For instance, a 20 × 30-inch cardboard drum can be used to make a 16 × 20-inch pinhole photograph. The requirements needed are a tight-fitting lid for the container and large sheets of photographic paper. However, since photographic paper that large is costly, it is advisable to practice with smaller-size images first. It will be necessary to increase the exposure time with a large image. A 10-minute exposure time is a reasonable starting point.

Multiple-Image Pinhole Cameras

Another interesting area that can be explored is the use of the multiple-image pinhole camera. A multiple-image camera will allow you to record more than one image on the same sheet of photographic paper. It is

Figure 4-4

Another image from the *Black Hole Photography* series, this looks like a picture of a flying saucer in space. In actuality, Jones made this picture of a kitchen colander in her studio, using her styrofoam pinhole camera.

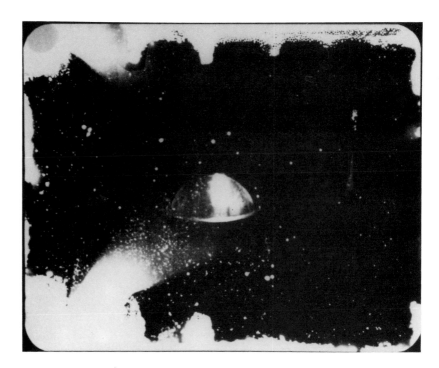

Kitchen Colander, Peggy Ann Jones, black and white print from styrofoam camera.

much like a double exposure except that the different images do not have to overlap.

In constructing a multiple-image camera, the major item needed is a long tube that again has a tight-fitted end cap. The tube should measure approximately between 20 to 30 inches long with a 3-to-4-inch diameter. Mailing tubes, such as the type sold in many stationery stores and art supply stores, fit the requirements and will generally cost between $1.50 and $3.00. The major difference between constructing this type of camera versus the other pinhole cameras is the number of pinholes.

After securing a tube, paint the inside black as before. Next, measure out 2- or 3-inch intervals in a row on the front of the tube. It is at these 2- or 3-inch spaces that the pinholes will be placed. For example, if your tube is 20 inches long, you will need to make 10 pinholes if you use 2-inch intervals. When making the individual pinholes, be careful to make each pinhole the same size. After making the pinholes at the predetermined intervals, cover them with an opaque tape.

The camera is now functional, and all that remains to be done is to load it with the photographic paper. The paper should be cut so that

Candy Camera, Peggy Ann Jones, pinhole camera made from candy packaging.

Figure 4-5

The 33-aperture "candy camera" and the print *Self-Portrait with O-Jizo-Sama* came about in the following manner. Jones explains, "The candy was a holiday present, and when we'd eaten all of it, the box was so beautiful, I said 'It's a camera!' To make it lighttight, I painted it over and over, then poked a hole in each candy cup with a pushpin. After inserting a piece of unexposed b/w photo paper behind, and opening the box's flap, I struck a worshipful pose with a little Jizo statuette that I'd brought back from Japan, closing the flap again after about a minute." She then made a positive print (Figure 4.6) from the paper negative produced in the candy camera.

Figure 4-6

Self-Portrait with O-Jizo-Sama, Peggy Ann Jones.

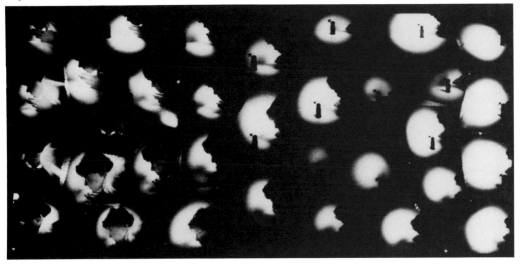

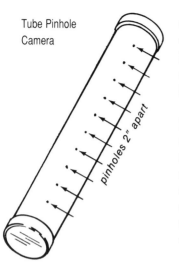

Tube Pinhole Camera

pinholes 2" apart

the length equals the length of the tube. Thus, it is recommended that you use a tube no longer than 20 inches because photographic paper larger than that is hard to come by. The height of the paper should be cut to half of the inner diameter of the tube. For example, if your tube is 20 × 4 inches, your paper should measure 20 × 2 inches.

The exposure will be a little shorter than with the single-hole camera because the pinhole-to-paper distance will decrease. It will be possible, though, to control each pinhole separately if you desire to give some areas of the picture a different exposure. It will also be possible to record an image in sequence by exposing through one pinhole at a time instead of having them all open at the same time. Also, by repositioning the camera, and if each pinhole is controlled separately, it will be possible to record entirely different images next to each other. There are endless variations with which to experiment.

Cartridge Film Pinhole Cameras

As explained earlier, film is generally more sensitive to light than photographic paper is. Thus, exposure time can be reduced to a few seconds when you are using film. This is especially important if your images were fuzzy because of camera movement during the long exposure of the photographic paper, or because you want to photograph something that won't remain still for more than a few seconds. A cartridge of film will also allow you to take twelve pictures without having to unload the camera after each exposure. The following materials will be necessary to make this type of pinhole camera: A cartridge of Kodak Verichrome Pan film, size 126, (Instamatic size), a piece of thin black cardboard cut to 1¼ × 5 ¾ inches, a piece of thick black cardboard cut to 1½ × 2 ¾ inches with ½-inch opening cut in the center, a one-inch square of aluminum foil for the pinhole itself, an opaque piece of paper cut into a one-inch square, two rubber bands, and some black masking tape (or cloth tape).

To assemble the camera, first measure and mark the large black cardboard into four equal sections. Each section will measure 1 and 7/16-inches wide. Next, using a knife or single-edged razor blade, cut through the top layer of the cardboard along each of the lines you made. *Do not cut through the cardboard!* You just want to score the top layer. Next, fold the cardboard into a box and tape the edges together with the black tape. Now, make the pinhole in the foil and attach it over the opening in the smaller piece of cardboard. Once your pinhole is secure, put the small piece of opaque paper over the pinhole and tape

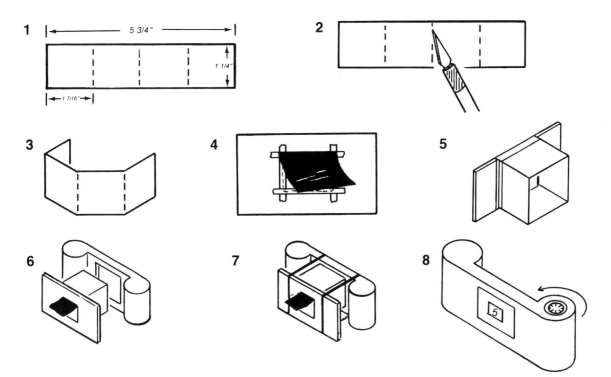

it along the top edge. Use a smaller piece of tape on the bottom edge to hold the flap down after the exposure has been made. You can now tape the cardboard with the pinhole to the box. Be sure to use an opaque tape (electrical), making sure all the edges are taped together so that no light can get into the box. Install the camera box into the grooved recess of the square opening of the film cartridge. Make sure that the box fits snugly so that no light enters the camera box. Once this is done, use two rubber bands, one on each side of the pinhole, to secure the camera box to the film cartridge. To advance the film for each picture, insert the edge of a coin into the round opening on the top of the cartridge and turn it counter-clockwise. The yellow paper, which is visible from the outside of the cartridge, will begin to move. The yellow paper has numbers printed on it. Turn the coin slowly until the third and fourth numbers in each series show in the window on the outside of the cartridge. The film will then be in the correct position to take the picture.

The exposure time for this type of pinhole camera will be considerably faster than it was for the photographic paper. Again, in order to get a sharp and clear image, it is essential that the camera remain very still when you are making the exposure. Since this camera is very small,

Making a Cartridge Film Pinhole Camera

you might try taping it down to a firm support, such as a chair or table. It is, of course advisable to experiment on the amount of time to give the film the necessary exposure. As a guide, you might try a 2-to-4-second exposure if it is a bright sunny day, or an 8-to-16-second exposure if it is cloudy bright.

Basic Cameras

Pinhole camera enthusiasts often find that the making of the camera is as involved as the picture making because the visual character of the pinhole image is dependent upon the shape and size of the camera from which it was made. Unfortunately, pinhole photographs lack the clarity and quality of images made from even the most inexpensive cameras. The primary reason is the one feature that separates pinhole cameras from all others—the lack of a lens.

Lenses, like cameras, vary in quality, but they all serve the purpose of focusing the light that passes through them onto a film plane. Lenses in many inexpensive cameras are made of plastic. Better quality lenses are generally made of glass, which can be polished to a finer degree than plastic and produces a sharper image. Because a pinhole camera lacks a lens, the image it produces may have the illusion of sharpness. In actuality, though, no single point within a pinhole image is completely sharp.

Stenopaic Pinhole Camera, Peggy Ann Jones.

Figure 4-7

Peggy Ann Jones calls this basic camera her Stenopaic camera. One of the first pinhole cameras she made, it measures 6 × 6 × 6 inches and is constructed of cardboard and tape with a piece of brass that has the pinhole in it.

Figure 4-8
Chocolate Camera Obscura,
Peggy Ann Jones, camera made
from chocolate candy
packaging.

Fish Photo, Peggy Ann Jones, 2 × 2 3/4-inch print made
from a paper negative form the Chocolate Camera Obscura.

Figure 4-9

As Jones explains in her book
Chocolate Camera Obscura,
this camera exploits the light
leaks that came through the
folds of the triangular box. The
"chocolate camera" was
originally packaging for
Japanese white chocolate
candies called *netsuke,* which
have the same shapes as the
traditional ivory carvings by the
same name. The fish is one of
the candies that served as
subject matter for a series of
photos made with this camera.

Most cameras with lenses share certain basic features. They include: (1) a light-tight box to keep out all stray light and to serve as a frame to hold other parts; (2) a lens to focus the image, which also has an adjustable aperture, or opening, to control the amount of light that reaches the film; (3) a shutter to control the length of time the film is exposed to the light; (4) a trigger to release the shutter; (5) a device to advance film in roll film cameras; and (6) a viewfinder to look through and frame the picture.

The frame, or body, of many cameras today is made of plastic, although metal is also used. The frame is designed so that other parts, such as the lens, can be attached to it without destroying its lighttight body.

Much like the diameter of the pinhole, the lens aperture, or opening, controls the amount of light that reaches the film. In inexpensive cameras, the aperture size remains the same and does not vary even if lighting conditions change. This situation is similar to that of a pinhole. However, more sophisticated (and expensive) cameras have diaphragms that can change in size. This diaphragm works much like the iris in your eye, which adjusts the size of your pupil to let in more or less light, depending on the lighting conditions.

While the lens aperture (opening) controls the amount of light that reaches the film, the shutter of a camera controls the amount of *time* that light is permitted into the dark chamber. Some inexpensive cameras have shutters that do not vary in speed. Thus, if there is not enough light available, the resulting negative may be underexposed. In many newer cameras, the shutter is controlled electronically so that the speeds vary from very fast (1/2000th of a second) to very slow (four or more seconds). The shutter release in most cameras is simply a button that releases the shutter so that the light can enter the camera.

A film advance lever or a motor drive (in many newer cameras) moves film through the camera, making it possible to take many pictures on a roll or film.

A viewfinder is built into most cameras so that the photographer can see what the picture will include. This feature allows the photographer to frame and compose the photograph. In some cameras, for example, the single-lens reflex (SLR), the photographer looks though the picture-taking lens directly.

Chapter 5

Cameras and Basic Camera Functions

We are passive onlookers in a world that moves perpetually. Our only moment of creation is that 125th of a second when the shutter clicks.

—Henri Cartier-Bresson
Photographer

Figure 5-1

This full frame 35mm photograph presents a natural view of the subject while alluding to the passage of time and aging. The black border was made by printing with a filed out negative carrier, which allows the clear edges of the film to expose the black border.

Mrs. Pillard, Mark Chamberlain, black and white print.

In the previous chapter, you learned that cameras are basically the same. Yet there are many different types of cameras with a wide range of controls and options. The reason for this diversity is that cameras are designed for different needs. The average person, mainly concerned with getting good family snapshots, has very different needs from the advanced amateur or professional photographer.

Other than the pinhole cameras, all cameras have the same basic parts: (1) a light-tight body or box; (2) a lens with an aperture, or opening, to control the amount of light that reaches the film; (3) a shutter to control the length of time the film is exposed to light; (4) a trigger or button to release the shutter; (5) a winding mechanism to recock the shutter and advance the film; and (6) a viewfinder to look through while framing and focusing the pictures. Additional controls vary from camera to camera, but they are designed to allow the photographer the type of technical control that will be necessary for different picture situations. The type of camera to purchase depends upon your needs and expectations. An automatic *point-and-shoot* camera is great for snapshots, but it will not allow the type of picture control needed by a photographer who seeks more control. On the other hand, a new multifunction, fully electronic 35mm SLR is beyond the needs of most snapshooters. This chapter will provide information on various types of cameras and their applications, camera care, and what to consider when buying a camera.

Types of Cameras

Point-and-Shoot Cameras

For casual snapshots of family and friends, compact point-and-shoot cameras are ideal. They are inexpensive, nonadjustable, automatic cameras that more serious photographers often call "no brainers" because they give no options except to point and shoot. Even the disposable

Figure 5-2
Compact 35mm camera

cameras can produce a result that is normally satisfactory, provided the shooting conditions are normal.

Compact 35mm point-and-shoot cameras allow you to shoot under a variety of conditions and have become very popular. They are totally automatic in that, once you put the film into the camera, the camera sets the film speed, advances it to the first frame, focuses the picture, calculates the exposure, provides flash if needed, advances the film to the next frame, and rewinds the film when the role is done. Some even talk to you. A zoom lens, available on the higher priced models, lets you select the image magnification, while the camera does the rest. But if you are serious about photography, you will want an adjustable camera that gives you more picture-making versatility.

Rangefinder Cameras

Most point-and-shoot cameras are rangefinder cameras, that is, the viewfinder is separate from the shooting lens. There are also adjustable-control 35mm rangefinder cameras that provide shooting flexibility and excellent picture quality. These cameras are popular with photojournalists and photographers who want a light, quiet, and inconspicuous camera that is quick and easy to use. The rangefinder is a separate viewfinder that approximates the image formed by the lens. Because it is a separate viewing system, you do not see exactly what the taking lens sees and cannot visualize *depth of field*, the distance in front of and behind the point of focus that appears sharp. The problem caused by the separate viewing system is called parallax, and it is due to the

Figure 5-3
Rangerfinder camera

Farmyard and Dog, St. Donatus, Iowa, Mark Chamberlain, black and white print.

Figure 5-4

Using a manual 35mm camera with a wide-angle lens, Chamberlain had to react fast to capture this moment. At the time of the shooting, he was unaware of the hand on the right side of the picture. Subsequently he felt that it was a subtle, yet integral, part of the picture.

difference between the viewfinder image and the image seen by the shooting lens. For distance shots, parallax is not a problem; unfortunately, it becomes a problem as you get closer to your subject, and it could mean that you miss part of the picture you want because what you see is not what you get. Some rangefinder cameras correct for parallax or have indicator marks in the viewfinder so that you can adjust the position of the camera to avoid the problem when you are shooting a close-up.

Single-Lens Reflex Cameras

Beyond the snapshot level, the 35mm *single-lens reflex camera,* or SLR, is the most popular. With an SLR, you view through the *taking lens,* which means that what you see is what you get. SLRs also offer more options than most other types of cameras and have the greatest variety of interchangeable lenses and easy-to-use through-the-lens exposure metering. The SLR's through-the-lens viewing is a definite advantage for close-up photography or any other work where you need to see exactly what you are getting in the picture.

Most of the newer SLRs provide a number of automatic features including autoexposure, autofocus, autoflash, autofilm winding, and

Figure 5-5

Figure 5-5

35mm manual SLR (single-lens reflex) camera

automatic setting of the film speed or ISO. The better models provide the option of both automatic and manual features. Cameras that have full *program* (completely automatic), *aperture priority*, *shutter priority*, and completely *manual* controls are the best choice for the serious photographer because they allow options to fit any picture-taking need. Many also come with built-in flash, but it is important that they have a manual override and provide a *sync* cord connection for a supplemental flash.

A 35mm SLR can satisfy a diverse range of professional and nonprofessional needs. *Medium format SLR cameras*, however, use 120 film that results in negatives that are 2¼ inches wide; these cameras vary in format from square to rectangular, and the bigger format film provides a sharper and finer grain result than that of a 35mm. The medium format cameras retain most of the versatility of 35mm SLRs yet are

Figure 5-6

35mm automatic SLR (single-lens reflex) camera

Swans, Edouard de Merlier, black and white print.

Figure 5-7
De Merlier shot this image with a 2 ¼-inch SLR camera and printed it in a glass carrier so that the clear edges of the film would print and create a black border. A four-bladed adjustable easel was used to provide the clear, sharp edges of the print.

only slightly more cumbersome. One big difference is price. Medium format SLR cameras, which are used mainly by fashion and advertising photographers, are much more expensive than 35mm SLRs.

Twin-Lens Reflex Cameras

Twin-lens reflex cameras (TLRs) also use medium format 120 film, but they have two lenses: one for viewing and one for exposing the film. Much less expensive then medium-format SLRs, TLRs have the disadvantage of parallax problems with shots closer than 5 feet from the subject. This is due to the separate taking and viewing lenses. Interchangeable lenses are only available on a few models, but supplemental attachments such as tele-extenders and close-up accessories are generally available. TLRs are used mainly by portrait and wedding photographers.

Figure 5-8

Cokas used a toy Diana camera to make this diptych about time and culture. The Diana camera and other toy cameras are used by many art photographers because of their flaws, limitations, and the characteristic look that results.

Garden of Eden, Jim Cokas, original in color.

TLRs were very popular cameras in the fifties and sixties, but improvements in SLRs have reduced their popularity.

View Cameras

Generally called *large-format cameras*, view cameras are totally manual and give the photographer more control over the image than does any other type of camera. View cameras consist of a *front standard*, which holds the lens; an accordion-like *bellows* for focusing; a back standard, which has a ground glass for viewing and for positioning the film holder; and a support *rail* that holds it all together. The most important feature is the camera's adjustability. Unlike most other cameras, which have a rigid lens and film plane, the view camera has *swings* and *tilts* that enable the photographer to correct or create distortion by moving the lens and film planes (front and back standards).

Exposures are made on separate sheets of film that vary in size from 4 × 5 inches to 8 × 10 inches and larger, depending upon the size of the camera. This gives the photographer individual control of each shot in the processing as well as the shooting. The large film size ensures maximum sharpness and minimum grain. The biggest drawback to a view camera is its size. View cameras are heavy, awkward to handle,

Figure 5-9
View camera

need to be used with a tripod, and are slow to operate. They are used mainly for architectural and studio work (especially product photography), and any other use where control and superior picture quality are needed.

Specialty Cameras

Many different types of specialty cameras are available to fulfill a variety of needs.

Instant cameras produced by Polaroid have long been popular. These vary from the snapshot variety to those designed for professional use. Polaroid also makes instant films for use in regular 35mm cameras, as well as special backs so that their film can be used with view cameras and many medium format cameras. Polaroid even has several cameras that will produce 20 × 24-inch instant color prints.

Underwater cameras vary from the throw-away variety to sophisticated professional models. Many underwater cameras use 35mm film and can be used in wet conditions out of water, as well as underwater. Special flash attachments are available for underwater illumination and provide more natural color.

Figure 5-10

Polaroid instant camera

Untitled, Danette Whitcomb,
Polacolor print.

Figure 5-11

Most people are familiar with Polaroid cameras and the "pop-out" prints that develop as they watch. This unique photo resulted when Whitcomb moved the emulsion around with a blunt object while it was still fluid.

Panoramic cameras are available in a variety of film formats, including throw-away models. Most rotate the lens from one side to the other as the picture is being exposed, whereas some rotate completely and give a 360-degree view.

Stereo cameras use two side-by-side lenses to take two exposures of the same scene simultaneously. When printed side-by-side and viewed through a stereo viewer, the offset images give a three-dimensional illusion. Stereo images, called stereographs, were very popular in the 19th century but are mainly a novelty now.

3-D cameras are rare, but several models are available. Most have four side-by-side lenses that expose four images simultaneously. The film is then sent to a lab designated by the camera manufacturer. At the lab, the four slightly different images are printed on lenticular paper that gives a 3-D illusion, just like 3-D postcards.

Electronic cameras are on the forefront of the technological revolution. Most photographers still rely on chemical-based film cameras, but with the fast pace of technical innovation it is expected that electronic cameras will play a bigger role in the future. This means that photogra-

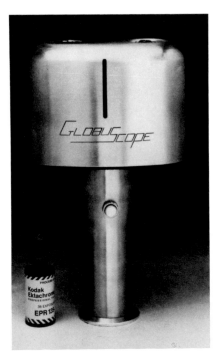

Figure 5-12
Panoramic camera

Figure 5-13
Digital camera

phers will no longer need to use traditional film. Everything will be done electronically, enabling the photographer to edit, select, manipulate, and send pictures anywhere in the world via modem while still in the field. To date, electronic cameras have enough disadvantages to make traditional cameras and film the main means used to generate images for normal photographs and digital imaging purposes.

Buying a Camera

Buying a camera is a lot like buying a car. There are many models available, with a variety of options, sizes, variations in price, conflicting advertising claims, and plenty of sales people who sometimes lead you to hasty decisions. Before buying a camera, first consider the *use factor*. Do you want a camera for more than snapshots? If so, what type of pictures do you plan to make? Do you have professional aspirations? If so, what type of professional photography interests you?

Cameras are designed for specific amateur and professional needs. To buy a camera without considering your current and future needs is wasteful. For the snapshot photographer, a fully automatic compact 35mm point-and-shoot camera with an autozoom would be the best

Figure 5-14

A complete camera system

bet. Advanced amateurs will want more control and options, such as interchangeable lenses. They should consider a 35mm SLR that offers auto and manual focus, interchangeable lenses, a supplementary flash, and exposure options that include full manual, full automatic, aperture priority, and shutter priority. Many professionals use 35mm SLRs, but they may also have other needs, based on the type of photography they produce. Portrait photographers generally use medium format cameras, and advertising photographers use a variety of cameras, including large-format view cameras.

The second thing to consider when buying a camera is how much you want to spend. Cameras vary tremendously in cost, and the price of a camera does not always determine the quality. Generally, the more expensive the camera, the more versatility and features it offers. Unfortunately, this flexibility isn't always a blessing. Many newer cameras have become complex electronic toys that often make camera use more complicated and confusing than it needs to be. An important thing to remember is that a camera is a *tool*, and too many features are often more limiting than helpful. If you are serious about photography, you will need to learn how a camera functions manually to fully understand its automatic options.

Generally, any brand name camera will perform well given proper care and use. Before shopping consider your needs, the various types of cameras, negative formats, viewing systems, versatility, size, weight, metering system, accessories, handling, service availability, and, of course, price. Then shop around to compare equipment and prices before buying. It may be worth extra expense to get extra service from a dealer who takes the time to explain the differences in equipment and will help you if you have problems later.

Used Equipment

Many photographers cannot afford a new camera, so they turn to used equipment. By shopping carefully, they can probably find a fairly recent model in good condition at a reasonable price. Although some photographers think they must have all the latest features, this expectation is needless. Although when buying a used camera you may end up with someone else's troubles, most photo dealers are reliable and will let you return a used camera if it is not working right. Usually a camera is sold either because its owner didn't understand how to use it or because it was old and didn't have the latest features.

When buying a used camera, look it over for signs of misuse. Dents or rust in the body or around the lens rim indicate that the camera was dropped or banged. Though it may still be usable, it probably is not worth the risk to buy it. Look at the rear and front sides of a lens to see whether the lens is free from scratches. Make sure the aperture ring on the lens turns and stops at each *f*-stop setting. The focusing ring, like the aperture ring, should turn smoothly, not too tight or too close. If the lens is interchangeable, remove it from the body to check the wear and tear on the lens mount. Next, check the shutter speeds. With older cameras, the slower speeds tend to stay open or stick. Shutter overhauls are very expensive. If the camera has a built-in meter, check it against a handheld meter, using an 18 percent gray card. If possible, try the equipment first by shooting a roll of film. Use a 36-exposure

Figure 5-15
A Fuji panoramic camera was used to make this photo.

The Mitten, Monument Valley, Tom Lamb, panoramic photo, original in color.

roll of film to check for overlapping negative frames on the processed roll. Check the developed negatives for even sharpness edge to edge.

In any case, get a warranty in writing. Most camera shops will provide a short-term, written warranty (30 to 90 days being the norm). A private party may or may not be willing to do the same.

Camera Care

The camera you are using is a fine, precision instrument. It was made with care and contains a great many moving parts, which must work in harmony. Care of your camera is primarily common sense. The following are some basic tips for keeping your camera in good condition.

Storage. When the camera is not in use, it should be protected from dust, preferably in a case. Avoid storing the camera in excessively hot, cold, or damp places. Normal room temperature is best. Always attach a body cap when the camera body is to be stored separately from the lens. Never leave the shutter or self-timer cocked if the camera is to be stored overnight or longer. Remove any batteries if the camera is not to be used for several weeks. Batteries can leak, causing corrosion. Be sure to check your batteries periodically. An electronic camera uses a lot of energy. When the batteries go out, the camera doesn't function. Manual cameras continue to function mechanically without batteries, but they lose their exposure metering system. Most newer cameras have a battery check built in, but you can also get them checked at camera stores.

Camera Body. Brush the inside of the camera periodically, using a soft brush. This is especially important after you have used the camera on a beach or under conditions where dust or sand can infiltrate into the mechanism. If you have an SLR, keep the mirror free from fingerprints and dust.

Use. Keep the camera away from water. Avoid excessive moisture. If the camera is to be used near water, guard it against splashes, especially from salt water. If some lever or moving part does not operate with the usual pressure, do not force it. A stopped level is usually caused by an oversight in the sequence of operation. The shutter will not trip, for example, unless it is cocked, or unless the film is advanced in an automatic-cocking camera. No amount of pressure on the shutter release will active the shutter. When all steps of operations have been checked, and the mechanism still does not operate with normal pressure, it's time to see a camera repairperson.

Repairs. Camera repairs are expensive. If a repair is in order, obtain a written estimate of the cost from a reliable repair shop before approving any work. Be prepared for some shops to charge for estimates. Be sure that any work done is covered by a written warranty. New cameras are covered with a warranty that is issued by the maker, usually for a period of 1 year after purchase. If this is the case, return the camera to the store where you bought it.

Basic Camera Functions

A camera is a tool that enables an individual to document places and events or to record personal interpretations of reality. When used creatively, the camera can be a means to a new level of seeing, understanding, and experiencing the world. When used intelligently, the camera can be a vehicle for the communication of feelings and ideas.

All cameras are basically similar. Each is a light-tight box with film at one end and a hole or a lens at the other to admit light. A camera enables you to focus and record the light that is reflected from the surface of your subject. All cameras, no matter how expensive, work in this manner. Today, you can choose from many types of cameras and hundreds of models. Most newer cameras offer a variety of electronic and automatic functions. Regardless of the type of camera you use, if you are serious

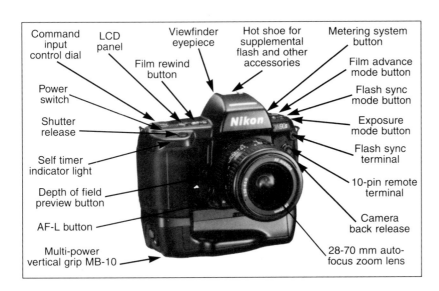

Command input control dial
LCD panel
Viewfinder eyepiece
Hot shoe for supplemental flash and other accessories
Metering system button
Film rewind button
Film advance mode button
Power switch
Flash sync mode button
Shutter release
Exposure mode button
Self timer indicator light
Flash sync terminal
Depth of field preview button
10-pin remote terminal
AF-L button
Camera back release
Multi-power vertical grip MB-10
28-70 mm auto-focus zoom lens

Figure 5-16

The features of a 35mm SLR camera

about photography, you need to learn the basic camera functions. These will vary somewhat from model to model, but the basic functions apply whether you are using an automatic camera or a manual one. In this chapter the emphasis is on the basic functions and use of the 35mm SLR. However, the principles discussed apply to all types of cameras.

Loading and Unloading 35mm Film

First, buy a film that suits your needs. For prints, a negative film in either color or black and white is best. If you want slides (transparencies), choose a reversal film. Reversal films produce positive images and are most commonly available in color, although some black and white reversal films exist. Detailed information on films is provided in Chapter 7, "Film and Light."

Before opening the back of your camera to load your film, check and make sure that the camera is empty. It is frustrating to open the camera and discover that film is still in it, particularly since it will be exposed to light and therefore ruined. To open the back of most 35mm cameras, lift the rewind knob located on the top left side of the camera. Other cameras will have a release lever that you push to open the camera. Once the camera is opened, insert the cassette under the rewind knob so that the extended part of the cassette points down.

Manual Film Loading

When the cassette is in place, push the rewind knob down so that it locks the film cassette into position. Pull the *film leader*, or tapered end, to the right side of the camera and insert the end of the film into the take-up spool slot. Then advance the film forward, using the shutter release and film advance lever until the sprocket holes on both the top and bottom of the film have caught on the film-advance teeth (gears). Next, close the back of the camera and advance the film forward three times to go beyond the exposed film leader to unexposed film. The frame counter on your camera should correspond to this by registering on frame number 1 at this point. To make sure that the camera is loaded correctly, watch the rewind lever as you advance the film. If it moves, then the camera is loaded properly. However, if the rewind lever doesn't move when you advance the film, the film was not loaded properly and you need to reopen the camera and reload the film. Once the film is correctly loaded, the next step with manual cameras is to set the film

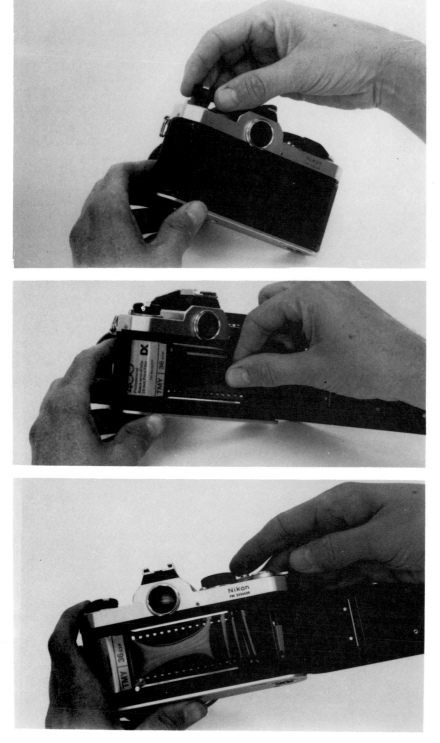

Figure 5-17
To load film in a manual camera, first lift the rewind knob.

Figure 5-18
Next, pull the film leader.

Figure 5-19
After advancing the film forward, as shown, close the camera.

speed (ISO) to program the exposure meter for the light sensitivity of the film you are using. This will be covered in Chapter 7.

When you have shot the last frame, the film advance will no longer move. At that point, you need to push in the *rewind release button*, normally located on the bottom of the camera. This reverses the mechanism so that you can use the *rewind knob*, located on the top left of the camera body, to rewind the film back into the cassette. Once the film is rewound, you can open the camera back and remove the exposed film.

To load film in a manual camera, first open the back of the camera by pulling up the rewind lever, or other release device. Second, place the film cassette in the open space on the left side of the camera; push the rewind lever down to lock the cassette in place; and pull the film leader to the right side of the camera. Finally, push the film leader into the slot located on the right side of the camera. Once the film leader is in place, advance the film until the top and bottom spocket holes "catch" onto the top and bottom film advance sprockets. Close the camera, gently wind the rewind lever to take up the slack, and advance the film three times until the number *1* appears on the film counter. When advancing the film, watch the rewind lever; it should be moving if the film is located properly. (See Figures 5.17–5.19).

Automatic Loading

To load film into an autoloading camera, open the camera back and put the film cassette, extended part down, into the space provided on the left side of the camera. With some automatic cameras, the cassette loads on the right, but most load on the left. (see Figure 5.20) Once

Figure 5-20

Loading an autoloading camera.

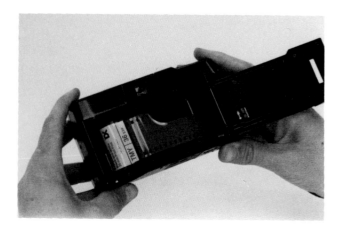

the cassette is in position, pull the film leader to the opposite side of the camera. (Normally there is an indicator mark on the inside of the camera.) Close the back of the camera, and the film will automatically load itself, advance to the first frame, and set the film speed (ISO).

If the number *1* does not appear, it means that you didn't get the film leader into the right position. You need to open the back and reposition the film leader. When you have shot the last frame, the camera automatically rewinds the film back into the cassette. You can then remove the film for processing.

Focusing Methods

Your eyes are constantly focusing and refocusing as they look at a subject. If your eyes focus improperly and you wear glasses, then you know how blurry things look without them. This should give you a good idea of how a camera will record subject matter if it is not focused properly.

There are at least six basic systems of focusing found in different types of cameras: (1) fixed-focus, (2) "zone-focus", (3) rangefinder; (4) twin-lens reflex ground glass, (5) single-lens reflex, and (6) automatic focus.

In a *fixed-focus camera*, there is no device on the lens to control focus. These cameras are set at the factory to be in acceptable focus at a distance of around 10 feet. Usually, as long as the subject isn't closer than 5 feet, the image will look sharp. Pictures taken with these types of cameras at too close a range are unrecognizable blurs.

If the lens on a camera can be moved to compensate for changes in distance, but has no device to indicate the actual focusing, then the photographer must estimate the distance. The second method ranges from pure guesswork ("That looks like about 6 feet, so I'll set the scale there") to a *zone-focus* scale on the camera. The scale for zone focus usually shows three or four drawings. If your subject is between 3 and 5 feet away, the scale will show a picture of head and shoulders, which corresponds to that approximate distance. For subjects between, say, 6 and 15 feet away, you would set the scale to the focusing picture of the group scene. Anything beyond 15 feet is "infinity," and thus the focusing scale would be set on a mountain scene. Cameras with finer scales may have settings for close-ups (about 4 feet), for medium shots (up to about 8 feet), for groups in a background (to about 17 feet), and for distance of infinity. Both zone-focusing and fixed-focusing cameras supply only relative sharpness. However, even just estimating distance will produce a sharper image than having a camera with no means of focusing, assuming you accurately estimate the distance.

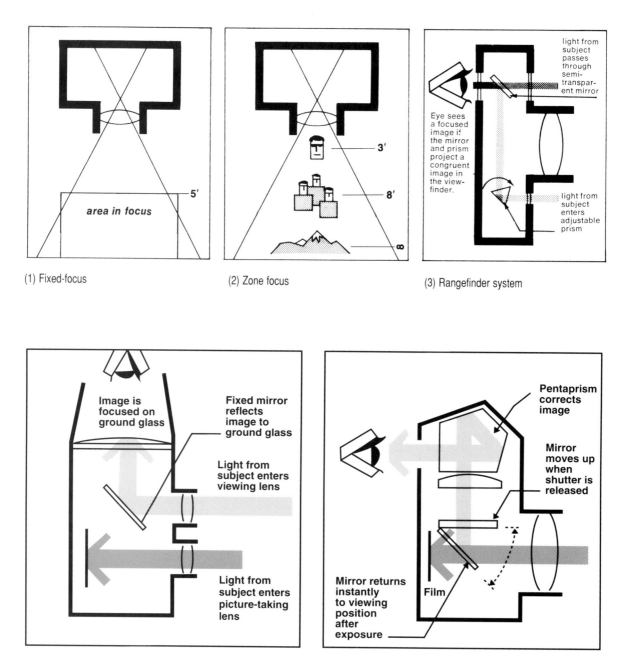

(1) Fixed-focus

(2) Zone focus

(3) Rangefinder system

(4) Twin-lens reflex (TLR)

(5) Single-lens reflex (SLR)

A *rangefinder* is an optomechanical device that produces two images in the viewfinder of the camera. One image is usually tinted a light color (yellow or red) for better visibility. To bring the camera into focus, rotate the lens until the two images coincide with each other. A double image indicates an out-of-focus subject; a single image indicates an in-focus subject. A small rectangular area in the center of the viewfinder is used to bring a subject into focus.

The *twin-lens reflex* method of focusing is used in some larger roll-film cameras. These cameras have two lenses, one for focusing and the other for exposing the film. The lenses are attached to the camera so that they move simultaneously. A mirror installed at a 45° angle behind the upper lens, which reflects the image onto a ground glass, where the photographer can see it. A hood over the ground glass keeps out strong light and makes the image easier to see. Sometimes a magnifying glass is built into the hood for more critical focusing. In this type of focusing, the camera is held about waist level (the other ways of focusing are usually done at eye level) and the photographer looks down into the hood.

One of the most popular cameras today is the *single-lens reflex* (SLR). This kind of camera allows the photographer to view and focus a subject through the actual picture-taking lens. The photographer sees the same image that the film records. Hence, the name single-lens reflex refers to the single lens that forms the image that you view and the image that the film records, as shown in the illustration. The word *reflex* refers to the image formed by reflection and, indeed, the single-lens reflex camera is a derivative of the twin-lens reflex, since both use a mirror to reflect the image-forming light. In a single-lens reflex camera the mirror is placed behind the picture-taking lens at a 45° angle. The light that forms the image comes through the lens and is reflected upward by the mirror to a viewing screen or ground glass. Then it passes through a prism that turns the image right side up and right side around and delivers that image to the eye. The type of ground glass used determines the manner of focusing. Although there are many modifications in the various types of ground glass used, they generally fall into two categories: *split-image and microprism*.

A *split-image* screen is one in which the subject is divided into halves. The idea is to focus the lens so that the top half does not overlap the bottom half of the screen. In using this type of screen, it is helpful to find a straight line to focus on.

The other type of screen found in many single-lens reflex cameras is the microprism. A *microprism* screen consists of many small dots that cause the image to appear shimmering where it is out of focus. As the lens is focused, the pattern phases out until the dots are no longer visible. The image is then in correct focus.

Practice focusing your camera until you focus naturally. Try to develop

Focus screens

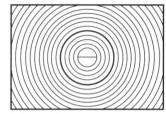

(1) Matte fresnel screen with split-image rangefinder

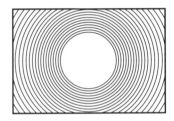

(2) Matte fresnel screen with clear ground glass

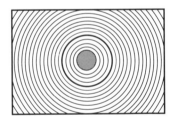

(3) Matte fresnel with microprism

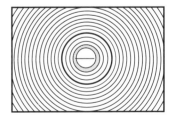

(4) Matte fresnel with microprism and split image

the ability to focus with no more than two motions—one on either side of correct focus—so that you don't waste time and possibly miss the best moment to take the picture.

Automatic Focusing Cameras

Automatic focusing is a recent technological development in cameras. Essentially, there are three types of automatic focusing systems in use at present. *Sonar autofocusing* is used with Polaroid instant cameras; *infrared autofocusing* is used with most 35mm point-and-shoot cameras— the compact 35mm; and *phase-detection* or *phase-contrast*, sensors are used in most single-lens reflex cameras.

With a *sonar-focus* camera, as you press the shutter release button, the sonar device releases sound waves. These sound frequencies, traveling at the speed of sound (1,100 feet per second), are beyond our own range of hearing. The fraction of a second that it takes for the sound to reach the subject and bounce back is fed into a very small electronic computer inside the camera. The computer in turn will use this time measurement to calculate the distance between the sonar device and the subject. It will then signal a motor in the camera to turn the lens so that that image is in focus.

The *infrared system* is employed on most compact 35mm point-and-shoot cameras. Like the sonar autofocusing system, the infrared systems measures the distance, but by sending out an invisible infrared signal rather than a noise signal. Instead of measuring elapsed time—light being faster than sound—infrared systems work like rangefinders; they judge the angle of the light's return. This is the reason for having two translucent windows, or a single long panel, on the front of infrared focusing cameras. Behind the windows lies an infrared emitter and a receptor.

Infrared systems can be made more accurate by increasing the distance between the emitter and the receptor. Because of size considerations, however, most manufacturers limit their systems to a few autofocusing zones, in effect producing automatic zone-focusing cameras. The number of zones has, of late, been increasing, from three or four on early models to more than twenty on later ones. The more zones, the more accurate the focus.

A camera that has infrared focusing is equipped with a viewfinder that has an area in the center to show what part of the scene the camera will focus on. This focus area in the viewfinder is usually indicated by a small rectangle or oval. To focus, aim the camera so that the main subject (for example, a person) is centered in the viewfinder focus area. The camera will then focus automatically as you press down the shutter release. Be sure to keep your fingers from covering the emitter and receptor windows on the front of the camera so that the focus is not affected.

One problem with the *center-oriented* infrared focusing systems is that you have to have your main subject in the center of the picture. If you have two people in the picture standing next to each other, the camera will focus on what is in the center. In this case it would probably be the background, which would result in your main subjects being out of focus. To alleviate this problem, many infrared focusing cameras provide a *focus lock* so that you can select what it is you want to focus on. To use the focus lock, you view through the viewfinder and place your main subject in the center of the frame. You would then press the shutter release partway down to *lock the focus.* Then recompose your picture while keeping the shutter release partially depressed. When you have it the way you want it, press the shutter release all the way down to make an exposure. Another caution with infrared autofocus cameras is that they can't focus through windows or on mirrors. They get confused and you have to use the focus lock.

Unlike the majority of point-and-shoot cameras, the type of autofocusing found in SLR cameras has no zones because the camera is capable of moving the lens through an infinite series of adjustments. Therefore, the *phase contrast-sensor,* or *phase-detection* system, is more precise than infrared systems. By comparing the contrast, or the optical separation of adjacent lines within the viewfinder frame, the microcircuitry built into the camera knows when the correct focus has been obtained.

The major limitations of SLR phase-detection systems involve their lack of ability to function in low-light situations and their selectivity in reading either horizontal or vertical lines. Thus, certain subjects will fool the system if their features do not match the computer's memory chip. For example, if the camera is designed to read vertical lines, the system may not recognize a particular subject if the lines are all horizontal. Nevertheless, phase-detection systems are highly accurate and technological improvements are making nearly all manual focus 35mm SLR cameras obsolete.

Most autofocus SLRs are capable of *single-shot* and *continuous* operation autofocus. Single-shot, as the name suggests, adjusts the focus automatically for each shot. With the continuous mode, the camera will follow moving subjects, continuously adjusting the focus as long as you partially depress the shutter release. This is helpful when sequence shooting at several frames per second in motor operation.

Exposure Controls

As you learned by using the pinhole camera, exposure is based on the quantity of light that reaches the film. A correct exposure is the amount of light needed to produce an easily printable image upon the film. *Overexposure* makes negatives too dark and results when too much light has been allowed to reach the film. *Underexposure* makes negatives too light and occurs when too little light reaches the film.

The two devices on the camera that control the amount of light that strikes the film are the *shutter* and the *aperture*, or lens opening. The aperture can be adjusted to make it larger or smaller, like the iris of our eyes. The shutter and the aperture work together to control exposure in conjunction with the light sensitivity (film speed or ISO) of the film. When one variable is changed, it affects the relationship with the others and changes the exposure.

The Shutter

The shutter serves two functions. Its primary function is to control the amount of light that reaches the film by controlling the length of time the shutter remains open. Its second and more creative function is to control the way that moving objects are depicted in the picture. A fast shutter speed severely limits the amount of light that reaches the film, while freezing motion—from a race horse at full gallop to a drop of

Figure 5-21

A slow shutter speed was used to heighten the sense of audience involvement. Heads that moved during the exposure came out blurred.

Military Appreciation Day: Yuma, Arizona. Jim Stone, black and white photo.

sweat falling off your brow. A slow shutter speed allows more light to hit the film and causes moving objects to blur. When the shutter speed is changed to get different motion effects, it is necessary to adjust the aperture to compensate for changes in the amount of light that will reach the film.

There are two main types of shutters. The 35mm SLRs have what is called a *focal-plane* shutter, which is built into the camera itself. Most other cameras have *leaf* shutters that are located between the lens elements of each individual lens. Interchangeable lenses are much less expensive for focal-plane shutter cameras because the shutter mechanism is not built into each lens.

Focal-Plane Shutters

Focal-plane shutters are located directly in front of the film and consist of two overlapping curtains that form an adjustable slit or opening that generally moves horizontally across the film plane. (Only the Copal Square shutter moves vertically across the film plane.) Because focal-plan shutters expose one end of the film before the other, objects moving rapidly parallel to the shutter are sometimes distorted, and this problem limits the shutter speeds that can be used with flash. With many 35mm cameras, especially older ones, the maximum shutter speed with flash is 1/60th of a second, whereas some newer models allow flash sync shutter speeds of 1/400th of a second. The reason for the problem is that at faster speeds, the focal-plane "slit" does not completely uncover the film at any one time. Consequently, if you shoot flash with a focal-plane shutter at any speed faster than the *flash-sync* speed (the highest speed for flash recommended for that camera), you will only expose part of the picture. Fortunately, there is no problem using shutter speeds slower than the flash-sync speed; just avoid using faster ones.

Leaf Shutters

A leaf, or between-the-lens, shutter is built into the lens itself and consists of a number of small overlapping metal blades. They function much like the iris of our eyes in that they open and close all at once in a circular pattern. Leaf shutters are quieter than focal-plane shutters and can be used with flash at any shutter speed. Because they have to open, stop, and then reverse direction to close, leaf shutters seldom go beyond 1/500th of a second, whereas focal-plane shutters can go as fast as 1/10,000th of a second.

Shutters, Shutter Speed, and Exposure

In the pinhole camera, using photo paper, the exposure could vary between 2 and 8 minutes, so a difference of 30 seconds would not change the image much. However, photographic film is much more sensitive to light than photographic paper. Because of this difference, the time needed to correctly expose a negative is more critical, more precise, and usually shorter. Thus, shutter speed, the time during which the shutter is open, is usually measured in fractions of a second, rather than in minutes. The shutter speeds ordinarily found on today's cameras are expressed as 1000, 500, 250, 125, 60, 30, 15, 8, 4, 2, 1 and B. Each number represents a fraction of a second. For example, a shutter speed indication of 4 means 1/4 of a second; a shutter speed of 250 means 1/250 of a second. A shutter speed of 1/30 seconds allows twice the amount of light to reach the film as does 1/60. The speed of 1/60 permits about twice as much light to enter as 1/125. Similarly, by selecting 1/125 over 1/250, you allow twice the light to reach the film. Conversely, using the speed 1/500 instead of 1/250 means that only half as much light will reach the film. The setting of 1/500 is twice as fast as 1/250, and therefore only allows half as much time for light to enter. In other words, using a faster shutter speed lets in only half the light that the next slower speed does; and conversely, the slower shutter speed permits twice as much light to enter as the next fastest speed.

The setting B is an exception; it is a variable speed. When the dial controlling the shutter speed is set at the B (for "bulb") position, the shutter remains open for as long, as the shutter-release button is depressed. This position is used only for long exposures (called *time exposures*) such as are used when photographing the stars. Shutter speed selection is mostly determined by the amount of light illuminating a scene. Low light levels require long, or "slow," shutter speeds, such as 1/30, 1/15, 1/8, and 1/4. Short, or "fast," shutter speeds—1/125, 1/250, 1/500—are normally needed when bright light illuminates a scene.

On many cameras, the device for setting the shutter speed, the shutter speed dial, is located on the camera's top, usually next to the shutter release button. On many newer cameras, however, the shutter-speed dial has been completely eliminated and replaced with a liquid crystal display (LCD) window on top of the camera, which digitally expresses and changes the shutter speed by pressing the appropriate buttons. With other newer cameras, the shutter speed display is located in the camera's viewfinder.

In older cameras, the shutter is controlled by a dial that activates various gears and springs. Called mechanical shutters, these must be set

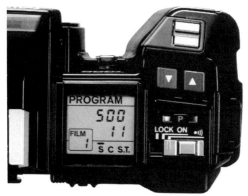

Liquid crystal display window

at the speeds designated on the dial. Electronic shutters, found in many newer cameras, are controlled by circuits powered by tiny batteries. The major advantage of the electronic shutter is that it provides a stepless shutter-speed range. One manufacturer's model has a stepless shutter-speed range from 1/4000 to 30 seconds so that any shutter speed in between is possible. However, the disadvantage of the electronic shutter is that, unlike the mechanical shutter, it will not function if the battery needed to power the shutter is exhausted.

Shutter Speed and Motion

The shutter speed determines how movement is rendered in a photograph. Although a sharp stop-action or frozen-motion image is usually desirable, there may be occasions when a less sharp blurred image is appropriate. In many cases, a slightly blurred image suggests speed better than a frozen image. Understanding the relationship between the shutter speed and motion allows the photographer to exercise this creative option.

The selection of a shutter speed is influenced by the speed at which the subject is moving, the angle of the moving subject to the camera, and the distance between the camera and the subject.

Stopping Action

Faster-moving subjects require faster shutter speeds to "freeze" the action. For example, the relatively slow action of a person walking may

Figure 5-22

A fast shutter speed was used to "freeze" the action of these marching soldiers.

Russian Soldiers, Changing of the Guard, *Glenn Cannon, black and white photo.*

Shutter Speed Guidelines for Stopping Action*

Approximate Speed of Subject: Miles per hour	Description or Type of Action	Example	Distance from Camera (in Feet)	Direction of Action from Camera Position ↔	↕
5	Slow Action	People Walking	10	1/500	1/125
			25	1/150	1/60
			50	1/125	1/30
10	Moderate Action	Swimmers, Parades	10	1/1000	1/250
			25	1/500	1/125
			50	1/250	1/60
25	Fast Action	Bicyclists, Runners	10	1/2000**	1/500
			25	1/1000	1/250
			50	1/500	1/125
50	Very Fast Action	Race Cars, Tennis Players	25	1/2000**	1/500
			50	1/1000	1/250
			100	1/500	1/125

* With normal focal-length lenses.
** Many cameras do not have this shutter speed. Use the fastest shutter speed available on your camera.

be frozen by a shutter speed of 1/125. The very fast motion of a race car will appear blurred at that same shutter speed. A shutter speed of 1/500 or 1/1000 is necessary to freeze the action of a race car.

The angle at which the subject is moving in relation to the camera must also be considered. If a fast-moving subject is moving at right angles to the camera, use the fastest shutter speed possible to stop the action. If, however, the subject is moving directly toward or away from the camera, the need for a fast shutter speed is greatly reduced. Thus, a faster shutter speed is needed to freeze the motion of the subject traveling across the viewfinder than a subject traveling toward or away from the camera.

The distance between the camera and a moving subject will also influence the selection of a shutter speed. The farther away a moving subject is from the camera, the slower the shutter speed needed to freeze its motion. For example, a shutter speed of 1/1000 might be needed to freeze the action of a race car at 50 feet away; a shutter speed of 1/250 would freeze the action of the same race car, traveling at the same speed, if it were photographed from a distance of 200 feet.

The chart on the preceding page offers guidelines in the selection of a shutter speed. The best guidelines, however, are those that you develop yourself by experimentation.

Blurring Action

A moving subject that is slightly blurred provides a graphic means to visually accentuate the feeling of motion in a photograph. Often, a stopped-action picture of a moving subject makes it appear as if it is not moving, though a slight blur caused by the use of a slower shutter speed can heighten the sense of movement.

Unintentional long or slow blurred images are usually the result of camera movement during exposures. To minimize unwanted blurring, the camera should be held as steady as possible during the exposure. This means keeping your arms against your body—not suspended in midair—while you hold your breath pressing the camera against your face as you depress the shutter release. Although people differ in their ability to hold the camera steady, the rule of thumb is that at shutter speeds of 1/60th or slower you need to take extra care. If possible, use a tripod and cable release to ensure a steady picture. If not, rest the camera on any firm support you can find—a wall, a chair, the hood of a car, a table, or a tree.

There are several types of blurred motion effects that are worth trying. The simplest effect is the type of "total image blur" that occurs when

Figure 5-23

A slow shutter speed and camera movement caused the blur and double image in this photograph.

Camera Movement, Glenn Cannon, black and white photo.

you use a slow shutter speed and move the camera while shooting the picture. Blurred patterns will result based on the direction and amount of your camera movement. City lights at night can produce interesting patterns and streaks when you set the shutter on "B" and leave it open for several seconds as you move the camera.

To heighten the sense of motion in a picture, it generally works best when you have a moving subject that is blurred while the rest of the picture is static and sharply rendered. To get this effect, use a slow shutter speed and hold the camera steady when you take the picture so

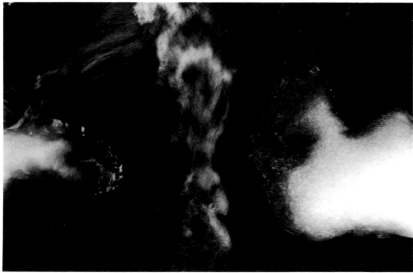

Blurred Water, Jerry Burchfield.

Figure 5-24

The water is slightly blurred in this black and white photograph adding to the feeling of motion. A shutter speed of 1/15th of a second was used.

that the only thing blurred will be the moving subject. The shutter speed that you should use depends upon how fast your subject is moving. A fast moving subject can be blurred using shutter speeds as fast as 1/125 or 1/60th of a second, whereas it may be necessary to use a shutter speed as slow as 1/4th of a second with a slower moving subject. Experimentation and practice are necessary to determine what shutter speeds to use.

Panning

Moving the camera during the exposure in the same direction as the subject's movement is another way to show motion in a photograph. Called *panning*, this technique allows you to make sharp pictures of moving subjects while creating streaked patterns (horizontally blurred) in the background that correspond to the direction of the camera movement. A slow shutter speed is necessary, but it will vary depending upon the speed of your moving subject.

Panning works best when the subject is moving perpendicular to the camera. Predetermine the path of the moving subject and focus for the distance it will be when you plan to release the shutter. Then center the subject in the viewfinder and move the camera *with* the moving subject so that it stays centered in your viewfinder. When the subject reaches your predetermined exposure point, release the shutter while

Panning the camera

Figure 5-25

Panning minimizes background distractions and heightens the feeling of motion in this photograph.

Panning, Steve Cvar, black and white photo.

continuing to move the camera with the subject still centered in the viewfinder. Since you are moving the camera at the same relative speed as the moving subject, it will appear sharp while the background will be streaked. This technique is used a lot in sports photography to accentuate motion and to hide visually conflicting backgrounds. When you first try it, experiment by shooting the same subject with different shutter speeds so that you can get a feeling for the technique.

The Aperture

The aperture is an adjustable opening made by a diaphragm inside the lens. This diaphragm is very similar to the iris that controls the size of the pupil of your eye. You can see the pupil get smaller or larger as more or less light strikes it. Try the following experiment: Look into a mirror in dim light. You will see that your pupil is rather large in order to let in as much light as possible. Then, turn on a bright light, and

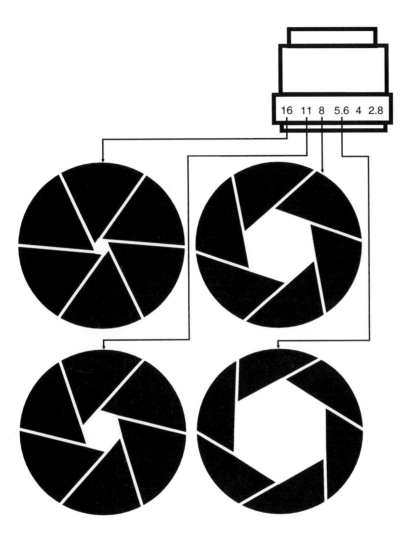

The apertures in this illustration are exaggerated in order to emphasize the increase in diameter as the *f*-stop number is decreased.

you will see the pupil suddenly getting smaller as the iris automatically adjusts the opening to the brighter light. Some cameras with an automatic exposure system adjust the opening in the diaphragm automatically when the amount of light changes. On a manual or adjustable camera, the aperture must be set by the photographer. This setting is often made with the aperture control ring, or "*f*-stop ring," which is usually located around the lens housing of the camera.

The aperture, like the shutter, has two main functions: It controls the amount of light that passes through the lens and it determines the amount or range of sharpness on either side of the subject on which the camera is focused. This second function is referred to as *depth of field*.

Aperture, *f*-stop, and Exposure

The different aperture sizes are referred to as *f*-numbers or just *f*-stops. There are usually seven to nine *f*-stop positions on an adjustable camera lens, each designating an opening of a different size. Some common *f*-stop numbers are 22, 16, 11, 8, 5.6, 4, 2.8, 2, and 1.4. The large *f*-numbers produce small lens openings, and the small *f*-numbers produce large lens openings. This may be confusing at first, but remember that each *f*-number is really a fraction: since 1/8 is smaller than 1/4, an *f*-stop of 8 is smaller than an *f*-stop of 4. The numbers used to designate the *f*-stops and the corresponding lens openings may not seem to fall into any regular order because the *f*-numbers express the ratio between the diameter of the lens and the focal length of the lens, discussed in more detail in Chapter 6. What is more important to understand, though, is that *f*/1.4 lets in twice as much light as *f*/2. Similarly, *f*/2.8 allows twice as much light to pass through the lens as *f*/4, and *f*/5.6 allows twice as much light as *f*/8. Conversely, *f*/16 allows only *half* as much light to enter the lens as *f*/11, and *f*/11 permits only half as much light as *f*/8. In other words, opening the lens by one *f*-stop permits twice as much light to pass through the lens. By opening the lens two stops, four times the amount of light will reach the film. Closing the lens down a stop allows only half as much light to reach the film. This is the same correlation that exists between the shutter speeds. It is also important to understand that on a lens of any focal length, the same *f*-stop delivers proportionately equal amounts of light to the film.

Lenses are designated, and generally priced, according to the maximum *f*-number to which they open. For example, a lens that opens to *f*/1.4 is called a "one-four lens." Lenses that open wider than *f*/2 are called fast lenses. Slow lenses are generally those with a maximum aperture of *f*/4. However, rating lenses by this system tends to be quite subjective because other important factors are not taken into account.

On some lenses, the designated maximum aperture is a half-stop number. For example, *f*/1.8 allows more light to pass through than *f*/2 but not twice as much light, as *f*/1.4 would permit. Similarly, *f*/3.5 is a half-stop between *f*/2.8 and *f*/4; it allows more light to pass through than *f*/4 but not twice as much.

Aperture and Depth of Field

The selection of aperture is a major factor affecting depth of field. Depth of field is the zone of apparent sharpness that extends ahead of and

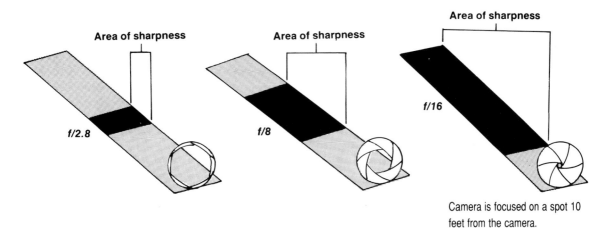

Camera is focused on a spot 10 feet from the camera.

behind the subject on which the camera has been focused. Depth of field is determined by lens aperture, distance to the subject, and the focal length of the lens.

Lens Aperture

The smaller the aperture, the greater the depth of field.

Depth of field refers to the area of apparent sharpness in front of and behind the point of camera focus. A wide aperture, such as $f/2.8$, yields minimal depth of field. Each time the lens is closed down (stopped down) to a smaller aperture, such as $f/4$, the depth of field is increased. With a small aperture such, as $f/16$, the depth of field is much greater.

Distance to Subject

The farther the camera-to-subject distance, the greater the depth of field.

The depth of field will change as you increase or decrease the distance you are from your subject. With an aperture of $f/11$, a picture taken 5 feet from the subject will have a lot less depth of field than a picture made at $f/11$ and 20 feet from the subject. Even with the same aperture, the difference in distance will cause a dramatic change in the depth of field. For example, with a 50mm lens at $f/11$ and 5 feet from the subject, the depth of field, or range of focus, would be from 4 1/4 feet to 6 3/4 feet or 2 1/2 feet of subject area in focus. With the same lens at $f/11$ and focused on a subject 20 feet away, the depth of field would be from 11 feet to infinity, which is a much greater depth of field.

Figure 5-26

Photographers can use depth of field as a creative tool. In this and the following shot, the palm tree trunk on the right was focused upon. The image with the most focus has what is called *maximum depth of field* and was made by using the smallest *f*-stop and a slow shutter speed to get the right exposure.

Figure 5-27

This image still has the palm tree trunk in focus, but because of the use of the biggest aperture, it has *minimum depth of focus*. Everything in front of and behind the palm tree is out of focus. To maintain a proper exposure, a faster shutter speed was needed. Neither the focus nor the camera position was changed in either exposure, just the aperture and shutter speed combination.

Focal Length

The shorter the focal length of the lens, the greater the depth of field.

Focal length can be defined as the distance between the optical center of the lens, when focused at infinity, and the focal point, where the image is in focus in the camera. The film in the camera is positioned at the focal point, also known as the focal plane.

You will recall that you could create wide-angle and telephoto effects with the pinhole camera by varying the pinhole-to-paper distance. When that distance was shorter than the diagonal measurement of the paper, the result was a wide-angle effect. Wide-angle lenses are made for most cameras. They have a short focal-length lens because the distance between the lens and the film is shorter than the film's diagonal measurement. Conversely, when the distance between the lens and the film is longer than the film's diagonal measurement, the result is a telephoto effect. The telephoto, then, is a long focal-length lens.

Depth of field is greatest with a short focal-length lens (wide-angle). In other words, the shorter the focal length, the greater the depth of field. A longer lens, such as a telephoto, will have much less depth of field.

To summarize, three factors determine depth of field: (1) aperture or lens opening; (2) subject-to-camera distance; and (3) focal length. The smaller the aperture, the greater the depth of field. The greater the distance between the lens and the subject, the greater the depth of field. Finally, the shorter the focal length, the greater the depth of field.

Film Speed

The speed of a film indicates its relative sensitivity to light. Speeds are expressed in terms of ISO (formerly ASA) numbers. These numbers appear on the film carton and on the cassette, cartridge, or backing paper. The higher the speed, or ISO number, the more light-sensitive or "faster" the film; the lower the speed, the less light-sensitive or "slower" the film. A fast film requires less light for proper exposure than a slow film. For example, a film of ISO 400 is more sensitive to light than a film of ISO 200. ISO 400 requires less light than ISO 200 or shorter exposure to produce a properly exposed negative.

The ISO film speeds are classified into four groups: low speed (ISO 25–32), medium speed (ISO 64 to 200), high speed (ISO 400 to 640), and very high speed (ISO 800 and up).

There is a correlation between these numbers. Suppose we start with a base of ISO 100. ISO 200 would be twice as fast as ISO 100. ISO

Three factors determine depth of field.

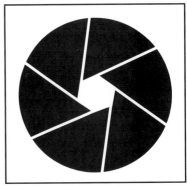

(1) *f*-stop

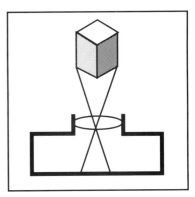

(2) Subject-to-camera distance

(3) Focal length of lens

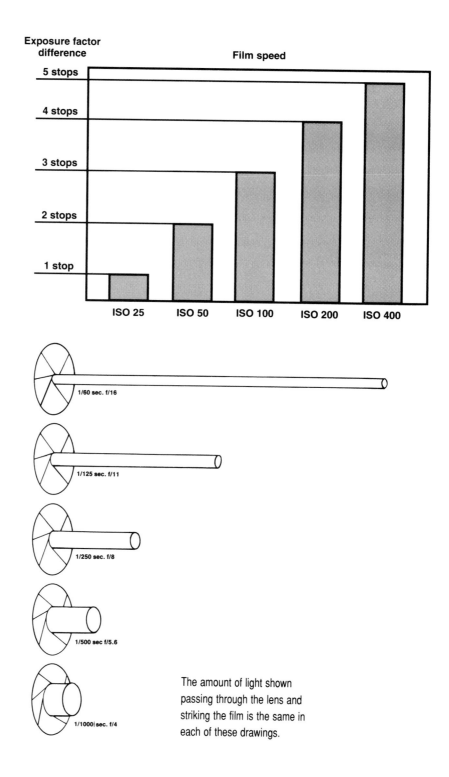

The amount of light shown passing through the lens and striking the film is the same in each of these drawings.

400 would be twice as fast as 200 and four times as fast as ISO 100. This is precisely the same correlation that exists between shutter speeds and f-stops. Therefore, another way of expressing how much more sensitive one film is than another would be in terms of how many more stops are gained. For example, ISO 400 is one stop faster than ISO 200.

Film speeds are determined according to International Standards and American National Standards and are designated ISO speeds. These speed values replace ASA speeds. ISO speed numbers are numerically the same as the ASA speed numbers they replace. For example, a film that had an ASA number of 400 would now have an ISO number of 400. Some film manufacturers outside the United States express film sensitivity in ISO° (formerly DIN) logarithmic numbers. An ISO/ASA/DIN film-speed conversion chart is provided in Chapter 8.

Since most of the photographic equipment now sold in the United States uses ISO speeds, this speed system will be used throughout this book. (Chapter 7 will provide more technical information concerning black and white and color films.)

Aperture, Shutter Speed, and Film Speed

The combination of aperture and shutter speed determines how much light actually reaches the film. Thus, *the selection of an aperture and a shutter speed will always work together to determine exposure*, and exposure is always expressed in terms of both aperture and shutter speed.

As previously explained, each designated f-number or shutter speed doubles or halves the amount of light allowed to pass through the lens and reach the film by the next designated f-number or shutter speed.

Therefore, *the same quality of light allowed to reach the film can be produced by a variety of aperture and shutter speed combinations*. Apertures and shutter speeds have a reciprocal relationship. If the aperture is wide open, a faster shutter speed is required to make an equivalent exposure. Conversely, if the shutter speed is slowed down, a smaller aperture is required. The following aperture and shutter speed combinations, as shown in the bottom illustration on page 92, allow the same amount of light, and thus will produce the same exposure:

$$
\begin{array}{ll}
1/1000 & \text{at } f/4 \\
1/500 & \text{at } f/5.6 \\
1/250 & \text{at } f/8 \\
1/125 & \text{at } f/11 \\
1/60 & \text{at } f/16 \\
1/30 & \text{at } f/22
\end{array}
$$

Then why choose one aperture and shutter speed combination over another? Although equivalent exposure combinations produce the same exposure, each combination produces a visually different picture. Your choice depends upon what effect you, the photographer, want to commu nicate to the viewer. *When depth of field is more important than movement, choose an exposure combination that gives more consideration to apertures than to shutter speeds. When stopping the motion of a subject is more important than depth of field, choose an exposure combination that gives more consider- ation to faster shutter speeds. Remember, the shutter speed and aperture always work together. Change one, and the other must change.*

Film speed is the third factor affecting exposure. Fast films are more sensitive to light than slow films. Therefore, a subject photographed with an exposure of *f*/8 at 1/500 with ISO 400 film will need an exposure combination that produces two stops more light if ISO 100 film were used instead. Equivalent exposure combinations include *f*/4 at 1/500, *f*/5.6 at 1/250, *f*/8 at 1/125.

Chapter 6

Lenses

Let the eyes work from the inside out.

—Edward Weston
Photographer

Figure 6-1

Taggert used a wide-angle lens with a small aperture to produce maximum depth of field.

View from the Paramount Hotel, Judith Taggert, black and white photo.

The purpose of a camera lens is to gather light and direct it to the film. The pinhole camera, which had no lens, produced images that were not sharp and had little tonal contrast. A lens provides a definite plane of focus, giving a sharp, focused image, and increases the tonal contrast. A photographer need not know everything about lens design or construction in order to take a good photograph. However, the more you know about how lenses work, the better your chances are of taking good photographs.

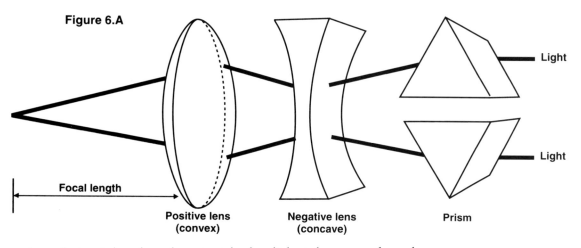

Figure 6.A

Focal length

Positive lens
(convex)

Negative lens
(concave)

Prism

Light

Light

Lens design is based on the principle that light is bent, or refracted, as it passes from air to glass or glass to air, as it does in a prism. In the case of a double prism, a second ray of light begins at the same point. It enters the lower prism and is eventually bent back upward so that both rays meet at a common point. Lenses are made in different shapes and sizes, but they can be classified as negative or positive, based on how they disperse light rays. In a negative lens, the light rays diverge, or spread out, as they pass through the lens. In a positive lens, the light rays converge at a common point. More sophisticated lenses contain not one piece of glass but many. In these lenses, each piece of glass is called an element. The various shapes and combinations of elements (called groupings) determine the quality and use of a particular lens.

Terminology

Understanding lenses requires knowing some of the technical terms used in describing them.

Focal point. All rays of light approach a lens from a point of infinity. These rays of light are parallel as they travel through air until they enter a lens. After they are bent by the lens, they converge at a common point, the *focal point.* More specifically, the focal point is the point where the light rays converge when the lens is focused at infinity. Basically, a thin lens causes light rays to converge at a farther point than a thick lens. The film in the camera is placed at the focal point of the lens. This area of the camera is called the *focal plane.*

All lenses, regardless of focal length, transmit the same amount of light to the film when focused at infinity and set at the same f-stop.

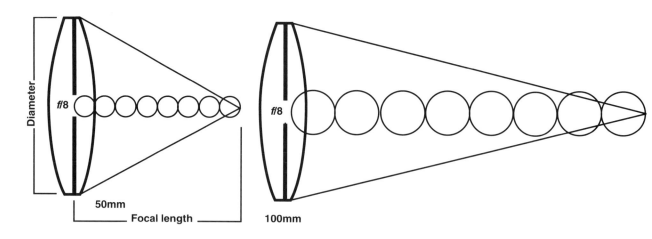

Lenses set at the same *f*-stop

This uniform transmission of light is the result of the constant ratio that can be maintained by dividing the focal length by the *f*-stop diameter. The setting of *f*/8 for both lenses (50mm and 100mm), as shown in the accompanying illustration, was determined by dividing their respective focal lengths by the *f*-stop diameter.

Focal length. Lenses are normally referred to by focal length. For a 35mm single lens reflex (SLR) camera, a 50 mm lens is a normal focal length, whereas a 200mm lens is a long focal length, or telephoto, lens. A 21mm lens would be a short focal length, or wide-angle, lens. The focal length of a lens determines the size, or magnification, of the image on the film, that is, the area of the subject included in the picture. The focal length of a lens is the optical distance from the lens, when focused at infinity, to the focal point. In Chapter 4, you learned about pinhole-to-film distance in the pinhole camera. Had there been a lens on the pinhole, this distance could have been called the focal length.

The focal length of a lens never changes, even if the lens is removed from the camera, or if it is focused at a closer point than infinity. It is the result of the fundamental design of the lens.

F-number. Because of the variety of lenses available, a formula is used to describe the ability of a lens to gather light: $F - N = FL/D$. $F - N$ represents the *f*-number, the maximum light-gathering ability of a lens. D represents the diameter of the lens. FL represents the focal length of the lens as shown in the lens illustration. The *f*-number, as you already know, is a fraction. It represents how many times the full effective diameter of the lens can be divided by the focal length. For example, if *f*/8 is the widest opening on a lens, then the widest diameter of that lens is 1/8 the focal length. Because an *f*-number is based on the relationship of focal length to diameter, *f*/8 on a lens with a 12-inch focal length allows just as much light to reach the film as *f*/8 on a 6-

Minolta lenses

Figure 6-2

A diverse array of lenses is available for most 35mm SLR cameras. These lenses include from left to right: AF Zoom 75-300mm, *f*/4.5–5.6; AF APO Tele 300mm, *f*/4; AF Soft Focus 100mm, *f*/2.8; and MD Zoom 35-70mm, *f*/3.5–4.8.

inch focal length lens, although the actual size of the opening will be different.

Lens speed. Lens speed refers to the maximum ability of a lens to admit light. It has nothing to do with shutter speed. The widest aperture of any lens is the opening at which the lens's speed is based, because it is the aperture that admits the most light. Some lenses have wider maximum apertures than others and are referred to as "faster" lenses.

The Vatican, Jerry Burchfield.

Figure 6-3

While on a tour of the Vatican, the author made this photograph in the Sistine Chapel. To ensure the longevity of the paintings, flash is not allowed in the Sistine Chapel and the light level is very low. To capture the ambience of the chapel, a 35mm *f*/2.8 medium wide-angle lens was used with an ISO 400 film which was push-processed one *f*-stop.

These are advantageous because they are easier to use in dim light or can enable the use of faster shutter speeds.

Depth of field. Depth of field, which was discussed in relation to the aperture in Chapter 5, is also affected by different focal length lenses. This range of focus, which extends before and behind the point of focus, has three main factors that affect it: (1) lens aperture, (2) focal length, and (3) focus or subject distance.

The smaller the lens aperture, the greater the depth of field. The larger the lens opening, the less the depth of field. Depth of field is influenced not only by aperture size but also by the distance from camera to subject. The simple rule is, the closer you are to the subject, the fuzzier everything else will be, and the less your depth of field.

Another factor that affects depth of field is the focal length of the lens. A short focal length lens (wide-angle) has great depth of field at a given *f*-stop. The normal focal length lens has a longer focal length than the wide-angle, so depth of field is not as great. The telephoto lens, which has an even longer focal length, has very little depth of field. To summarize: the shorter the focal length, the greater the depth of field. The longer the focal length, the less depth of field.

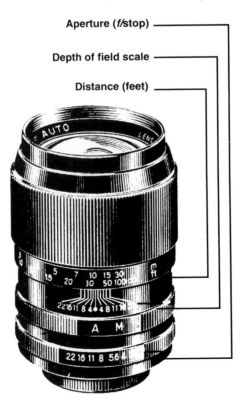

Aperture (*f*/stop)

Depth of field scale

Distance (feet)

Depth of field scales. The way in which depth of field is indicated on a camera depends on how the camera is focused. If the camera cannot be focused, its depth of field is fixed. Usually, such cameras have great depth of field, giving acceptable sharpness between 6 feet and infinity.

Zoom, or variable focus, lenses often do not have depth of field scales either, because the changes in focal length cause the depth of field to change and are hard to indicate accurately. Most fixed focal length lenses have depth-of-field scales. On most SLRs the depth-of-field scale is on the lens barrel, as shown in the illustration of a lens barrel on page 000.

To help you understand how to use a depth-of-field scale, first focus your lens at 10 feet, using the center line and the distance scale on the lens barrel as a guide. Below the footage indicator is the depth-of-field scale. It has a double series of numbers corresponding to the *f*-stop or aperture numbers for your lens. These numbers begin at the center of the lens barrel and repeat themselves as they go out in either direction. Since the widest opening (the lens speed aperture), is the beginning point, it is not listed on the depth-of-field scale.

To find the depth of field at a given *f*-stop, *f*/16 for example, read the distance scale at the points opposite the number 16 on either side of the center line of your lens. You will find that the depth of field, or focus range, for a subject 10 feet away may be as close as 6 feet and extend as far as 15 feet. Now change the aperture to *f*/4, while keeping the distance focused at 10 feet. Locate the 4 on the left side of the center line and you will find that the depth of field starts at around 9 feet—while to the right of the center line the 4 indicates a depth of field of around 12 feet. At *f*/16 the depth of field, or range of focus, is about 9 feet total, but at the wider *f*/4 the depth of field is reduced to about a 3-foot range. These distance relationships will vary with different lenses and cameras, but the principles remain the same. Depth of field is greater with small apertures and less when the aperture is opened up. The farther you are from the subject, the more depth of field. The closer you are, the less depth of field you have. Also, lenses of shorter focal length have more depth of field than lenses of longer focal length.

The depth-of-field scale provides a means for you to know the depth of field, based on the subject distance, aperture, and lens focal length combination. This is important because you are not able to physically see the amount of depth of field you are getting with most commonly used cameras. The lenses on most SLRs are designed to make viewing and focusing easier by remaining at the widest aperture until the picture is exposed. Then the lens automatically stops down to whatever aperture setting you might have. This means that what you see is not always what you get. Even though you are viewing through the taking lens,

Figure 6-4

F-stop and depth of field
variations

A. *f*/2.8 at 1/500th of a second with 50mm lens

B. *f*/11 at 1/30th of a second with 50mm lens

C. *f*/11 with 50mm lens, subject distance
    5 feet

D. *f*/11 with 50mm lens, subject distance
    20 feet

you will always see your subject and set up your shot with the aperture wide open and minimal depth of field. However, some cameras provide a depth-of-field preview, which enables you to view your shot through the actual *f*-stop you will be using. Because it is a smaller *f*-stop, the scene will be darker, but you will be able to see what will be in focus and what will not.

Some lenses, like those for large format view cameras, have no depth of field scale and no automatic features to keep them open at the widest aperture for easier focusing. These lenses get darker as the lens is stopped down to a smaller aperture. To use these lenses takes more time. Focusing is done first with the lens wide open. Then the lens is slowly stopped down, making it possible to observe the extension of the depth of field as the image gets darker and harder to see.

The depth of field varies tremendously in images A and B in Figure 6.4, both of which were shot with a 50mm lens from the same distance without changing the focus. The only thing that was changed was the f-stop (aperture) and shutter speed. The setting $f/2.8$ is a large aperture and provides minimum depth of field, making it easy to throw the foreground and background out of focus. Because a large aperture lets more light hit the film, a faster shutter speed is needed to maintain a proper exposure. The setting $f/11$ is a smaller aperture providing more depth of field and letting less light into the camera, necessitating the use of a slower shutter speed. Distance also affects depth of field. Regardless which lens or f-stop you use, depth of field will decrease the closer you get to your subject.

Interchangeable Lenses

New cameras come equipped with a "normal" lens. Normal lenses provide a view that is similar to what people would see at that distance with their eyes. Frequently, you either need to make the subject larger or have a wider view in the picture. This is no problem as long as you are able to move the camera position closer or farther away. But when you can't, being able to change to a different focal length lens can be a real advantage.

Many kinds of interchangeable lenses are available for most SLRs, varying from extreme telephotos to super–wide-angle fisheye lenses. Each different focal length changes the magnification and the angle of view of the image, but not the perspective. The distance of the camera to the subject is what affects perspective. Because the visual effect varies with changes in distance and lenses, it is best to experiment until you can visualize how each of your lenses will affect a picture.

Interchangeable lenses are designed to be changed quickly so that you won't miss a picture opportunity. Lenses can be switched whenever you need to change the focal length. Changing the lens will not fog your film, even in bright sunlight.

Autofocus and Manual Focus Lenses

The autofocus lens, which was first introduced in the 1970s, has become standard for 35mm cameras. Speed and simplicity, along with continued improvements in technology, have made autofocus lenses practical for the amateur and the professional. Early autofocus lenses for SLRs allowed manual focusing but made it difficult. Because of the need of serious photographers for occasional manual control, lens manufacturers have begun making models that combine convenient manual focusing with autofocusing.

Autofocus (AF) lenses are operated by a small motor, located either in the body of the camera or in the lens itself. Those lenses in which the motor is built-in are bigger and heavier than those operated by a motor in the camera. Several manufacturers make lenses with built-in motors. The line of one manufacturer includes 31 different AF lenses, ranging from 16mm to 600mm.

AF lenses operated by a motor in the camera are also made by several manufacturers, but usually they can only be used with the camera for which they were designed. For these cameras, manufacturers also make adapters so that the cameras may use regular lenses. The disadvantage of the adapters is that they significantly cut down on the light passing through the lens, often by as much as 75 percent. AF adapters are not a wise choice unless you are using fast film or are working in bright light. (Also see the discussion of autofocusing in Chapter 5.)

Zone Focus

Zone focusing—presetting the depth of field—is useful when you are photographing active, fast moving subjects or events such as a hockey game, people dancing, a carnival, or a race. Whether the camera is equipped with autofocus or manual-focus lenses, it can be difficult to focus and refocus constantly. Zone focusing ensures sharp focus for a distance range where the subject is most likely to be. Then, as long as the subject remains within that distance range, pictures can be made without refocusing. The depth-of-field scale or visual depth preview can be checked to determine the zone of focus. To increase the zone of focus, go to a small f-stop for more depth of field and to a slower shutter speed to compensate for the loss of light. If this isn't sufficient, switch to a shorter focal length lens to get more depth of field. With a 50mm normal SLR lens focused for a distance of 10 feet at f/16, the in-focus zone would be 6 1/2 feet to about 25 feet, whereas with a 35mm medium wide-angle lens set for the same f/stop and distance, the in-focus zone would be 4 feet to infinity.

Though zone focusing is used with all formats, it is most commonly used with the easy-to-handle 35mm cameras. Some automatic cameras have systems that can be activated for zone focusing and controlling depth of field.

Untitled from The Streets of L.A. series, Tamie Niinuma.

Normal Focal Length Lenses

When viewing from the same distance, a normal lens and the human eye see objects with the same size relationship. Normal lens size varies with different film sizes. A normal lens for a 35mm camera is a 50mm lens, but the normal lens for a medium format camera is an 80mm. A 50mm lens on a medium format camera is a wide-angle lens. A normal focal length lens is determined by the diagonal measurement of the film. For instance, the diagonal measurement of 35mm film is 43mm, while the lens size is 50mm. This is because the image produced by all lenses is a circular image that gets soft around the edges. To ensure edge to edge image sharpness and a rectangular or square format, the size of the lens is normally bigger than the actual measurement of the film.

New cameras come equipped with a normal lens. The speed of normal lenses is generally *f*2 or below and is faster than most other lenses. They

Figure 6-5

Tamie Niinuma primarily photographs people on the streets of Los Angeles. She believes that it is important to take the time to communicate with the people she photographs, but she relies on zone focusing with a normal 50mm lens so that she can be assured of catching the right moment with everything in focus.

are also capable of closer focusing than any lens other than a macro, which is designed for close-ups. These features make the normal lens very practical.

Telephoto Lenses

Sometimes your subject is too far away to be very big in the picture, or perhaps you don't want the subject to know you are taking a picture. Such occasions call for a telephoto lens. A telephoto lens, like a telescope, magnifies the subject so that it appears closer than it really is. Telephoto lenses are lenses with a long focal length. In other words, the focal length is longer than the diagonal measurement of the film. The longer the focal length, the larger the image on the film. As with normal lenses, a telephoto lens is relative to a particular film size. Because there are many telephoto lenses available for different format cameras, we will discuss only those used on 35mm cameras, whose format has the most variety in lens selection.

Telephoto lenses for 35mm cameras are generally divided into three types—short, medium, or long. Short telephoto lenses range between 85mm and 105mm. Though small, they increase the image size recorded on the film. Many photographers use a short telephoto lens both for shooting subjects at a distance and for portrait work. The telephoto has two advantages for portrait work: (1) The camera can be placed farther from the subject's face and, therefore at a more comfortable distance,

Untitled, Clayton Spada.

Figure 6-6

A 200mm telephoto lens was used to compress the space and create a stronger sense of pattern in this picture.

thus allowing a more relaxed, natural pose; and (2) a telephoto distorts facial features less than a normal lens used at minimum focus.

Medium focal length telephoto lenses are in the 135mm to 200mm range. These middle-range lenses are probably the most popular telephotos. The 135mm lens can be used for portraits, sports events, and landscapes. They are also quite widely used for candid photographs of people. While a 100mm lens will double the image size on the negative, a 200mm lenses will magnify the image four times.

Lenses longer than 200mm are usually classified as long telephoto. These are used when the distance between photographer and subject is great—at a football game or ski run, for instance. They are also quite useful for photographing animals in their natural habitats. A 400mm lens will magnify the subject by 8. That is, if the subject were 80 feet away, it would appear to be only 10 feet away in the film image. One problem, however, is that perspective may be distorted.

Perspective is the relationship between objects in terms of position and distance, as seen from a certain viewpoint. A long focal length lens, which is generally used at a great distance from the subject and has a field of view narrower than that of a normal lens, appears to compress or shorten the distance between objects. Because of this, long focal length lenses are seldom used for portraiture. However, they are useful tools in many picture-taking situations.

When using a telephoto lens, remember that the longer the focal length, the less the depth of field. Telephoto lenses are usually heavier than other lenses, and they generally are rather slow. Very few telephotos are faster than $f/4$. Because of the weight and the loss of depth of field, a fast shutter speed should be used. A tripod will provide good support for the camera with a long, heavy telephoto lens, especially if the focal length exceeds 200mm.

Wide-angle Lenses

Wide-angle, or short focal length lenses, are the opposite of the telephotos and are shown in Figure 6.2. They allow the photographer to record more of the total area of the scene without moving the camera back. For example, if you had to be 20 feet away to photograph an object while using a normal lens, using a wide-angle lens might allow you to shoot the same area from only 10 feet away.

The term *wide-angle* refers to the angle of acceptance, the area seen by the lens. How wide this angle is depends on the focal length. Wide-angle lenses have short-focal lengths. They are shorter than the diagonal measurement of the film. The shorter the focal length, the wider the

Figure 6-7

Limited by a narrow street and parked cars, Edouard de Merlier took this photograph of a burned-out building during the 1992 riots in Los Angeles with the only lens that would allow him to get the whole scene in the picture, a 17mm extreme wide-angle lens which severely distorts anything close to the camera.

Torn Apart, Edouard de Merlier.

angle of acceptance, also called the angle of view. For example, a 50mm normal lens for a 35mm camera has an angle of acceptance of 46°. A 500mm telephoto for a 35mm camera has an angle of acceptance of only 5°. Clearly, the 500mm lens has a much narrower angle of acceptance, or angle of view. A 28mm wide-angle lenses for a 35mm camera, however, has an angle of acceptance of 76°. A much wider area is covered. The focal lengths 20mm, 28mm, and 35mm are wide-angle lenses for 35mm film. The 50mm and 55mm are normal focal length lenses. In the telephotos, 85mm and 105mm are considered short, whereas 135mm and 200mm are medium telephotos. Beyond 200mm are the long focal length lenses. Starting with the 20mm wide-angle lens, notice (in the

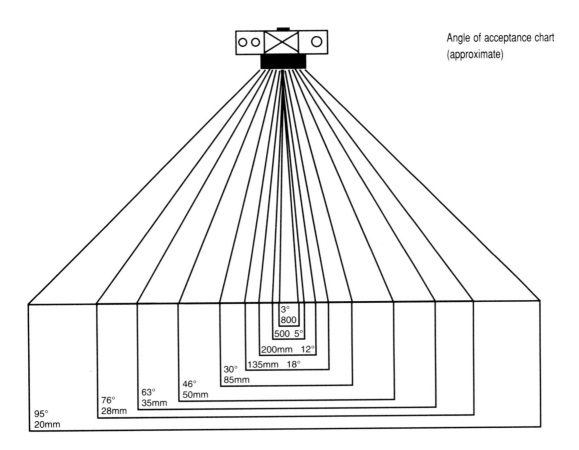

Angle of acceptance chart
(approximate)

illustration above) how the angle of acceptance gets narrower. The next diagram (page 110) illustrates the difference in area covered by a wide-angle, a telephoto, and a normal lens for a 35mm camera.

As shown by Figure 6.9, a wide-angle lens also appears to distort perspective, but differently from a telephoto lens. Rather than compress space or shorten the distance, it appears to extend space or make it longer. In reality, the apparent differences in perspective between various lenses are a result of the differences in area covered by each. Thus, because a wide-angle lens covers more area, objects close to the camera appear unusually large.

Zoom Lenses

The most popular lens today is the zoom lens—a variable focal length lens. By internal shift of the elements, zooms can vary their focal length.

How subject distance affects depth of field
Same focal length, same aperture

4 ft

◄——10 ft——►

◄————————25 ft————————►   INFINITY

How focal length affects depth of field
Same aperture, same subject distance

Long focal length—telephoto lens

Medium focal length—normal lens

Short focal length—wide-angle lens

INFINITY

Shading indicates area in
acceptably sharp focus.

Figure 6-8

To take a head shot with a normal
or wide-angle lens, you have to
get very close to the subject to fill
the frame. As in image A, this
results in an abnormal distortion
of the face. However, the same
type of shot (B) made with a
medium telephoto lens results in a
more natural and pleasing
"compression" of facial features
and allows the photographer to
take the picture from a more
comfortable distance.

A.

B.

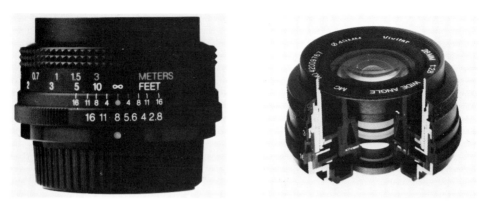

28mm lens   **Cut-away version of 28mm lens**

Figure 6-9
Closeup of lens

The degree to which zoom lenses vary their focal length is expressed as their range. Ranges generally fall into these categories:

1. Wide-angle (21 to 35mm, 24 to 35mm)
2. Wide-angle to normal (24 to 45mm, 28 to 50mm, 28 to 55mm)
3. Wide angle to telephoto (28 to 80mm, 28 to 135 mm, 35 to 70mm, 35 to 135mm)
4. Normal to telephoto (55 to 220mm, 40 to 300mm, 50 to 135mm, 50 to 200mm)
5. Short telephoto to telephoto (70 to 150mm, 70 to 210mm, 75 to 300mm, 80 to 200mm)

Figure 6-10
Auto-focus zoom lenses (Minolta)

6. Telephoto to telephoto (100 to 200mm, 100 to 300 mm, 100 to 600mm, 200 to 500mm)

Because of their flexibility and convenience, zoom lenses dominate the marketplace. They allow the photographer to stand in one position and vary the angle of view of the subject without the need to change lenses. In addition, many zooms are capable of focusing at very close distances. This type of zoom is referred to as a macro lens and appears in Figure 6.10. Two notes of caution concerning zoom lenses: Their quality varies widely among the brands available, and while they will allow for greater flexibility, use of them does not ensure successful pictures.

Specialty Lenses

There are a wide array of specialty lenses produced for 35mm and medium format cameras. These include the *fisheye, perspective control*, and *macro*.

The *fisheye* is an extreme wide-angle lens that has total depth of field and never needs focusing. It usually produces a circular image on the film, and some fisheyes are even capable of photographing objects slightly behind the lens because they have a 220-degree field of view.

PC, or *perspective control*, lenses are adjustable lenses that can be raised or lowered in relation to the film plane of the camera to correct or create distortion. When a camera is tilted upward, as in shooting a picture of a tall building, the sides of the building converge towards the top. In other words, the building may look more like a pyramid than a rectangular structure. A PC lens, however, can be used to correct this distortion, making it practical for 35mm architectural photography.

Macro lenses are designed for close-up photography, but then can also be used like a normal lens. They are generally available in 50mm or 100mm focal lengths. They provide excellent image quality and are easier to use than other close-up devices such as extension tubes, bellows, and close-up filters. Macro lenses also function with through-the-lens metering systems.

Tele-extenders

A supplementary lens is one that is attached either in front of or behind the existing lens. One type of supplementary device, the tele-extender, can increase the effective focal length of the lens attached to it by two or three times. The tele-extender is placed on the camera body, and

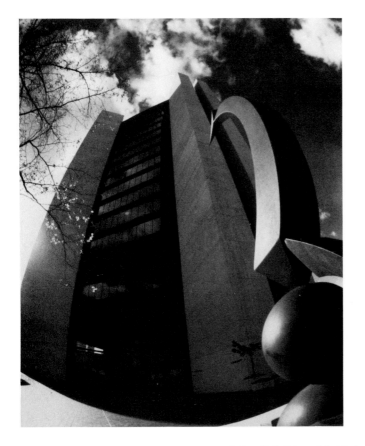

Figure 6-11

The extreme distortion in this photograph by Edouard de Merlier was achieved by using a fisheye lens.

Long Beach City Hall, Edouard de Merlier.

Tennis Ball, Kevin Starr.

Figure 6-12

A macro lens was used to take this extreme close-up shot of a tennis ball.

then the lens is attached to it. A 2X extender (converter) will double the focal length of the lens. For instance, a normal 50mm lens attached to a 2X converter will make it a 100mm telephoto. A 3X converter will triple the power. A 50mm attached to a 3X converter will make it a 150mm lens. The tele-extender is useful because it gives the photographer a telephoto lens inexpensively. However, it absorbs considerable light. A 2X converter will require opening the lens two more stops. A 3X converter requires three more f-stop openings. A tele-converter also will reduce the sharpness of the lens being used with it.

Care of Lenses

Most good lenses are made of glass and are susceptible to scratching. A scratch on a lens may reduce its sharpness. Protective lens caps are made for both the front and back of a lens. If the lens is off the camera and not in use, it should be protected with a rear lens cap as well as one on the front.

Lenses must also be free from dirt, dust, or fingerprints, since these will all cut down the sharpness. Cleaning a lens requires care because the glass is so easily scratched. A camel's hair brush is used to clean any dust or lint from the surface of the lens and lens tissue is used to wipe away dirt. Use the lens tissue with a circular motion; scrubbing with the tissue may scratch the lens. Be sure to use only tissue designed for camera lenses. Tissue for cleaning eyeglasses contain a cleaner that is harmful to the lens coating.

For fingerprints, use a commercial lens cleaner. These are solvents that dissolve away the fingerprints without too much rubbing with the lens tissue.

Many photographers like to keep either a UV (ultraviolet) or 1a (skylight) filter on the camera lens to protected it at all times from scratches and dust.

Chapter 7

Film and Light

I have seized the light, I have arrested its flight.

—Louis-Jacques-Mandé Daguerre
Inventor of the daguerreotype

Figure 7-1

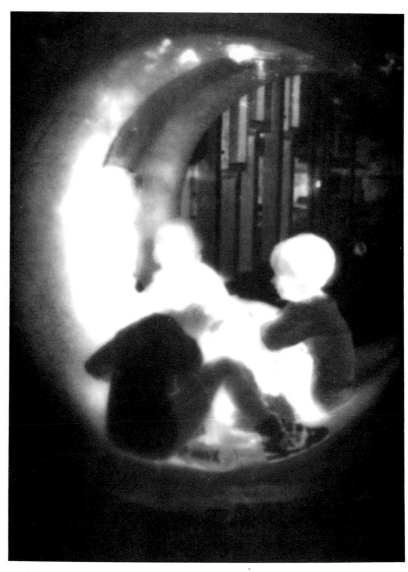

Untitled, Michael Zahler.

Light makes photography possible. Light is a wavelike energy that extends far beyond the narrow band of the visible spectrum, from radio waves to cosmic rays. Photographic film and paper are light sensitive and undergo a chemical change upon exposure to light. If the light is focused with a camera or enlarger lens, an image is formed. The effectiveness of that image depends upon the photographer's perception, control, and handling of light.

Too much or too little light results in a poorly exposed and inadequate photograph. The way a subject appears to us, and to the film, is directly influenced by the quality of the light that is illuminating it. When a light condition changes a scene, the photographer needs to be aware of that change, not only because it may affect the exposure, but also because it affects the look of the picture. Light is never stable. It is always changing from minute to minute.

Film Characteristics

Many varieties of photographic films are available today to satisfy the needs of diverse picture-taking situations. Despite their differences, modern films all have a light-sensitive silver-halide gelatin emulsion, which is coated onto sheets or strips of polyester or acetate. Upon exposure to light, a latent or invisible image is formed on the film. When developed, the exposed silver-halide crystals are changed to particles of metallic silver, which form the visible image in black and white film. Color films and chromogenic black and white films, like Ilford XP2 400, differ in that color dyes are also formed during development. Later in the processing, the silver is bleached out leaving only color dyes to form the image.

Light-sensitive silver-halides respond mainly to blue and ultraviolet wavelengths. This factor plagued early landscape photographers. In their pictures the sky was always overexposed to white, because their film was overly sensitive to the blue end of the spectrum. Today, dyes are incorporated into the film to increase the range of color sensitivity. Most modern black and white films are *panchromatic (pan)*, meaning they are designed to be sensitive to the same color range as the human eye. *Color films* have three layers of emulsion, each sensitive to only a third of the color spectrum. The effect of light on these layers is the same as in black and white photography. A latent image is recorded in the silver-halide of each layer; then, when the color film is developed, the dyes are formed and the silver is bleached out.

There are also other types of *special purpose* films designed to be sensitive to specific parts of the spectrum. *Orthochromatic* (ortho) black

and white films, like high-contrast litho films, are sensitive to blue and green, but not red. *Infrared* films, in both color and black and white, are sensitive to infrared wavelengths, which are invisible to the human eye.

The silver particles that form a photographic image are called *grain*. The grain overlaps randomly and varies in size with different films. *Fast films* are very sensitive to light and have large silver-halide particles that produce an obviously coarse grain in an enlargement. *Slow films* are less sensitive to light and have smaller silver-halide particles that form fine-grain images, which are sharper and have more subtle detail. Most modern films use a flat, waferlike grain structure, rather than the previous clumped, uneven particles. These flattened grains provide a larger and more even surface for the light to strike, while consisting of less mass overall, for sharper, crisper prints.

Some photographers like "grainy" pictures and use very fast films to make the grain more evident. To maximize grain, start with a fast film, such as Kodak's T-Max 3200, and consider push processing. Most photographers prefer minimal grain and use a medium or slow fine grain film. The size of the film format affects the amount of grain evident in an enlargement. The grain in an 8x10-inch print made from a 35mm negative will be much more apparent than the grain in an 8x10 print made from a 4x5-inch negative. The 35mm negative is greatly enlarged compared to the 4 times necessary for a 4x5 negative to make an 8x10 print, and the difference in grain is obvious. Consequently, many photographers, who are concerned about maximizing sharpness and detail, turn to larger-format cameras.

To minimize grain without switching to a larger format camera, be careful to avoid overexposure, overdevelopment, and big enlargements. Also, be sure to use a slow speed film and to investigate different types of film developers. Some developers are designed for use with fine-grain films, whereas other developers produce a harsher grain with the same film. Also, the method of film development can affect the grain structure. Refer to Chapter 10, on film development, for more-detailed information.

In addition to color sensitivity and grain, film has five other main characteristics: (1) speed, which is referred to as ISO, (2) contrast, (3) latitude, (4) reciprocity, and (5) resolving power.

Film Speed

The light sensitivity of film, called its speed, is indicated by an International Standards Organization number, ISO number for short. That film speed number is measured by a numeric scale. The higher the speed or

Figure 7-2

Two interwoven trees stand out boldly as symbols of life in this dramatically illuminated photograph. It was shot with a view camera on 4x5-inch film to maintain the delicate detail of the trees and to maximize control of the rich contrast provided by the lighting.

Trees, Silverado Canyon, California, David F. Drake.

ISO number of the film, the more sensitive it is to light. The lower the ISO number, the less sensitive the film is to light. An ISO 100 film is twice as fast as an ISO 50 film, or ISO 50 is half as fast (twice as slow) as ISO 100. The following, is a portion of the ISO film speed number sequence: 20, 25, 32, 40, 50, 64, 80, 100, 125, 160, 200, 250, 320, 400. Going up the scale, note that every third number is doubled. This means that the ISO film speed sequence changes in one-third stop intervals. For instance, an ISO 125 film is 1 1/3 stops faster than an ISO 50 film and 1 2/3 stops slower than an ISO 400 film. Slow speed films have ISO numbers lower than ISO 64, medium speed films go up to ISO 200, and high speed films are anything over ISO 200.

The ISO rating system was started in 1974. Prior to that, there were the ASA, or American Standards Association, and the German DIN, or Deutsche Industrie Norm, the main European rating system. The two were combined to create one uniform rating system, the ISO. Because the ASA system was numeric and the DIN was logarithmic they are now rated together, but separately. For example: Ilford FP4 black and white film has an ISO of 125/22. The first number is the old ASA number and the second number is the old DIN number. Film speeds are normally printed on the film box and cassette. Often, they are included in the name of the film, such as Kodak T-Max 100.

Contrast

Films vary, whether black and white or color, in their ability to record a range of tones or values. This range of values, from light to dark, is referred to as the film's *contrast*. The majority of films are designed to reproduce a natural looking tonal or value range and are referred to as medium or normal contrast films. *High contrast* films have a limited range of tone. Some films, such as litho films, are designed to reproduce only black and white. They have no gray tones and are used mostly for graphic effects and copying line drawings. Generally, slow speed fine-grain films have more contrast than medium and high speed films.

Solitary, Michael Zahler.

Figure 7-3

The graphic impact was increased in this image by maximizing the grain through the use of a high speed film.

Contrast can also be affected by the amount of camera exposure and film development. To get *normal contrast*, start with a medium speed film, expose it properly and develop it normally.

To *reduce contrast*, overexpose film, underdevelop it, or do both. To *increase contrast*, underexpose film and overdevelop it. For high contrast, with no gray tones, use a litho sheet film or one of several high contrast roll films available. The *zone system* is a method of controlling contrast by using variations in the exposure and development of film. Contrast control and the zone system will be explained in more detail in Chapter 19.

Latitude

The amount of deviation from the correct film exposure that still produces quality pictures is called *latitude*. You always obtain the best quality with any film when the exposure is correct. Over- and underexposures lead to compromises in print quality, the acceptance of which is up to the individual photographer.

Figure 7-4
Film latitude

Underexposed negative and resulting print.

Normal exposed negative and resulting print.

Overexposed negative and resulting print.

The type of film used, the subject brightness, and the needs of the photographer determine the amount of acceptable latitude. Negative films in both black and white and color have more latitude than the positive image transparency (slide) films. Most color negative films are very forgiving and that is why they are used so much for amateur snapshots. An overexposure of two to three *f*-stops and an underexposure of one to two *f*-stops can still produce a print acceptable for the average consumer, but not for the more serious photographer. Black and white negative films also have a lot of latitude; their processing times can be altered more than color films to compensate for exposure problems and contrast, as discussed later in this chapter. Transparency films offer the least latitude. The exposure needs to be as accurate as possible or there will be a definite compromise in quality.

Reciprocity

Reciprocity refers to the relationships between time and *f*-stops that enable you to use different exposure combinations and still get the right exposure. It means that the same film density can be achieved through either a change in the exposure time or the intensity of the light exposing the film, provided one is adjusted to compensate for the other. For instance, an exposure of *f*/11 at 1/125th of a second will give the same film density as an exposure of *f*/5.6 at 1/500th of a second. Thus, an increase of two stops of light intensity (*f*/11 opened to *f*/5.6) is balanced by an increase of two stops in the shutter speed, which reduces the light reaching the film by two stops (1/125 adjusted to 1/500).

Reciprocity failure refers to the inability of film to respond properly to either extremely long or extremely short exposures. All films are designed to function under certain exposure conditions. Most films offer accurate exposure, provided the exposures are faster than 1/10th of a second and slower than 1/1000th of a second. When you make an exposure that goes beyond either of these extremes, the film's sensitivity diminishes and its assigned speed number is no longer accurate. To compensate for reciprocity failure, the film's exposure must generally be increased for both long and short exposures. The amount of reciprocity failure varies with each type of film. Reciprocity failure causes color films to lose color sensitivity as well as exposure sensitivity. Because of this problem, there are special color films designed to be shot with long exposures. For general shooting, reciprocity failure is seldom a problem. However, it is wise to check the information sheet packed with your film to determine the reciprocity corrections needed for that particular film.

Resolving Power

The ability of a film to record fine detail is referred to as *resolving power*. Resolving power is measured with the use of a parallel-line test chart. The chart is first photographed at a great reduction in size. The lines of the test chart are separated by spaces of the same width. The negative is then examined under a microscope at a certain predetermined magnification, and the number of lines per millimeter that can be seen as separate lines are then counted. Lines closer together than this number (in other words, more lines per millimeter) are indistinct from each other on the film and appear as a mass of gray.

The resolving power of the film is altered by incorrect exposure. This is one reason to have properly exposed negatives. Because resolving power is measured by the eye, it is subject to some variation, depending on the person making the measurement. By looking at the data sheet packed with the film, you can usually determine what the resolving power of that film is. The following table can serve as a guide.

Film has other characteristics: definition and sharpness. Briefly, the term *definition* in photography refers to the overall appearance of detail. *Sharpness* is a factor in determining definition and describes the appearance of edge sharpness between details.

The factors that affect definition are sharpness, resolving power, and grain. As a general rule, resolving power and sharpness increase as graininess decreases. To ensure maximum definition when taking the picture, you should remember the following points: (1) Expose correctly because overexposure increases graininess. (2) Hold your camera steady, or use a tripod to reduce camera movement. (3) Focus carefully. (4) Use a high-quality lens that is free of fingerprints and dirt. To ensure maximum definition when printing a photograph, remember these

Resolving Power Reference

Resolving Power	Lines per mm
Ultra High	630 or above
Extremely High	250 to 500
Very High	160 to 200
High	100 to 125
Medium	63 to 80
Low	50 or below

Figure 7-5

The contrast between the soft horizontal movement of the water with the delicate detail of the vertical forms of the trees was heightened by the use of a fine grain film, a proper exposure, and control of the film developing process. A poorly-exposed negative combined with a lack of controlled processing generally leads to grainy images and a loss of detail.

Birch Trees, Robert Johnson.

points: (1) Use a high quality enlarger lens, free of fingerprints or dust. (2) Make sure that the enlarger doesn't vibrate when you make the exposure. (3) Choose a smooth surface enlarging paper. (4) Print on a paper that will not cause either excessively high or low contrast.

Sharpness is the visual impression of good edge contrast between details. Several factors affect sharpness: thickness of the emulsion, thickness of the film base, type of emulsion, and type of antihalation backing on the film. Sharpness measurements are made by the manufacturer of the film, although the sharpness of some films can be increased when developed in diluted developers. This is one reason why many photographers favor using D-76 diluted 1:1.

The science of sensitometry is related to the study of film characteristics and exposure. If you are interested in this field, there are many technical reference books on this subject.

Films: Black and White

There are many different film manufacturers and their products are constantly being improved and changed. Following is a list of popular black and white films, currently available, manufactured by Kodak, Ilford, Agfa, Fuji, and Polaroid. "X" indicates film format availability.

Brand Name of Film	ISO	35mm	120	4x5
Kodak				
Technical Pan	25	X	X	X
Ektapan 4162	100			X
T-MAX 100	100	X	X	X
Plus-X Pan	125	X		
Plus-X Pan Pro	125		X	X
Verichrome Pan	125		X	
Tri-X Pan Pro	320		X	X
Tri-X Pan	400	X	X	
T-MAX 400	400	X	X	X
Recording 2475	1000	X		
T-MAX 3200	3200	X		
High Speed Infrared	50/125	X		X
Ektagraphic HC Slide	12	X		
Kodalith Ortho 4154	12			X
Ilford				
Pan F Plus	50	X	X	
Delta 100	100	X	X	X
FP4 Plus	125	X	X	X
Delta 400 Pro	400	X		
HP5 Plus	400	X	X	X
XP2* 400	400	X	X	
Agfa				
Agfapan APX25 Pro	25	X	X	X
Agfapan APX100 Pro	100	X	X	X
Agfapan APX400 Pro	400	X	X	X
Scala 200**	200	X	X	
Fuji				
Neopan 1600	1600	X		
Polaroid Instant Films				
55 Pos./Negative***	50			X
54/Polapan Pro 100	100			X
Polapan CT 35mm	125	X		
51 High Contrast	320			X
Polapan 400	400			X
Type 52	400			X
Polagraph HC 35mm	400	X		

* Chromogenic black and white film, processed with C-41 color-negative film-processing chemicals.

** Black and white positive image transparency film that needs special processing available through retail outlets selling the film.

*** Produces both an instant 4x5 black and white positive image print and a 4x5 negative for making enlargements.

Films: Color

Color films are generally grouped into three categories: negative films, reversal positive films, and instant color films. Negative films are often referred to as *print films* because they are the most popular, most forgiving, and least expensive for making color prints. They are used primarily for snapshots, weddings, and portraits. They produce a negative image, in which the tones and colors are the opposite of those in the original scene. Color negative films also have an overall orange color cast called a *color mask*, which helps control contrast and color fidelity. Most color negative films have a relatively wide exposure latitude, particularly for overexposure, and are very forgiving when shot under the wrong type of lighting. Color negative films are designated by the name of the manufacturer plus the word *color*, as in Kodacolor, Fujicolor, and Agfacolor.

Reversal or positive films are called *transparencies*, *slides*, or *chromes*. The word *chrome* is used in conjunction with the manufacturer's name to designate individual reversal films, as in Kodachrome, Fujichrome, and Agfachrome. Reversal films react to light in the same manner as all other films in that a negative image is created. The difference occurs during the development of the film, when it is either physically (with light, as with Kodachrome) or chemically (as with most other reversal film), reversed from a negative image to a positive image. Unlike color negative films, reversal films have no orange mask and produce an accurate color image of the scene that was photographed.

Exposure is critical with reversal films. Overexposure causes the image to be too light and underexposure makes it too dark. Reversal films are used by professionals and serious amateurs for lithographic reproduction, slide presentations, and prints. Because the film is primarily designed for reproduction and projection, it is not as forgiving as negative films and more demanding when it comes to printing. Consequently it is generally only the more serious amateurs and fine-art, magazine, stock, and advertising photographers who shoot reversal films.

Polaroid instant color films consist of three types. Polachrome 35mm color slide film is available in 12- and 36-exposure rolls and comes with a chemical pod used to develop the film in a special Polaroid processor. This easy-to-use and inexpensive processor produces a developed roll of color slides, which can then be mounted for projection or printing, in two minutes. The cost of the film is reasonable considering that it includes the cost of processing. Polaroid produces the "*pop-out*" develop-as-you-watch color print film, which originated with the SX 70 camera and several varieties of "*peel apart*" color print films for their cameras and for special backs designed for 35mm SLRs, medium format cameras, and 4x5 cameras.

RGB and How Color Films Work

The light that makes up the visible spectrum as a whole is called *white light*. A specific color, such as red, is visible when other portions of the spectrum are missing. White light consists of equal parts of three colors: *red*, *green*, and *blue* (*RGB*). These are called the *primary colors* or *additive colors*. They are the basic colors of light and, when added together in equal parts, they make white. The primary colors of light are different from the primary colors of pigments (paint), which are red, blue, and yellow. This is because pigments have no color of their own; that is, they absorb and reflect the colors of light. (See Color Gallery A, Plate 7.1.)

Color film and print papers have three distinct color-sensitive layers, one for each of the three primary colors of light. Whatever the colors of your subject, they are recorded as separate red, green, and blue values on color film. When the film is developed, pigment-based dyes are formed through a dye-coupler chemical interaction. Each of the three color-sensitive layers has absorbed a primary color of light, and the dyes that result reflect the other two colors of light. For instance, the red-sensitive layer absorbs all of the red light in the scene that was photographed. The subsequent dye that is formed reflects the remaining two primary colors of light, green and blue, which together form the color called cyan. The green layer absorbs green and reflects red and blue, which makes the color magenta. The blue layer absorbs blue and reflects red and green, which makes yellow. Cyan, magenta, and yellow are called the complementary or subtractive colors of light. When mixed together in even amounts, they appear black. When we look at color photographs, what we are seeing is cyan, magenta, and yellow dyes layered on top of one another to produce a full color image.

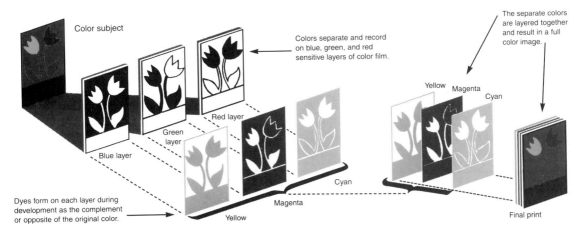

Color subject

Colors separate and record on blue, green, and red sensitive layers of color film.

The separate colors are layered together and result in a full color image.

Red layer

Green layer

Blue layer

Yellow   Magenta   Cyan

Cyan

Magenta

Dyes form on each layer during development as the complement or opposite of the original color.

Yellow

Final print

Color Balance

The color of light varies with different light sources, weather conditions, and times of the day. Color films are balanced for *daylight* (midday sun and electronic flash) and *tungsten* light (incandescent light bulbs). Color temperature is the name given to the mixture of wavelengths that make up the light from a particular light source or condition. Daylight is much bluer than light from an ordinary incandescent light bulb. Daylight-balanced film produces natural looking colors when shot with daylight illumination and electronic flash. When daylight film is exposed with ordinary household light bulbs, the warm color of these tungsten (incandescent) light bulbs makes the color have an artificial reddish orange cast. See Color Gallery A, Plate 7.2.

Tungsten balanced films have extra blue built into the film to compensate for the warm color temperature of tungsten-light sources. These films are designed to produce natural color when used with lights that have a color temperature of 3200 K (kelvin), as indicated on the kelvin color temperature chart which follows. They will give acceptable results when used with any type of tungsten-light source. Because of the extra blue in tungsten films, an overall blue cast will occur when these films are shot in daylight or with electronic flash. Color negative films balanced for tungsten are designated as *Type L* and tungsten reversal films are designated as *T* or *Tungsten* films.

Fluorescent lights give a greenish cast regardless of what type of color film you use, because their color temperature does not match either daylight or tungsten. The color temperature also varies depending upon the type and age of the fluorescent tube. It is best to try to correct this problem at the time of shooting by using filtration on the camera to counteract the green cast. Try a 30 cc magenta filter or a FL (fluorescent) filter and adjust the exposure for the filter factor.

Color negative films are the most forgiving when shot with the wrong type of light. Reversal films record the color of the light as it is and can only be minimally corrected in the printing without looking awkward. Black and white film can be shot with any color temperature.

Color Temperature

The quality of light varies with the time of year, the time of day, the weather, and several other factors. Outdoors in the early morning, for example, the light is much warmer—has more red and orange in it—than

---

The warmer or redder the light—a candle, for example—the lower the kelvin temperature; the cooler or bluer the light—a cloudless summer sky, for example—the higher the kelvin temperature.

Ultraviolet

Sky light without
direct sun
12000 to 18000K
Very blue

Overcast sky
7000K
Bluish

Photographic
daylight balance
5500K

Natural color

Tungsten photo lights
3200K
Very warm, orangish

Household lights
2800K
Reddish

Firelight
1800K

Infrared

Practical sources of illumination and their approximate color temperatures

Source	Color Temperature (°K)
Skylight (without direct sun)	12000 to 18000*
Overcast sky	7000
Photographic daylight—midday	5500**
Flash (electronic, bulbs, cubes)	5500
White-flame carbon arc	5000
3400 K photolamp	3400***
3200 K tungsten lamp	3200
Sunrise, sunset	3100
200-watt general service	2980
100-watt general service	2900
75-watt general service	2820
40-watt general service	2820
Candle, firelight	1800

* blue cast; ** normal daylight balance; ***warm, yellow to red balance.

a little later in the day. At noon, particularly during summer months, the contrast between colors is high and the shadows dark. At night and indoors, the quality of light also varies, depending on the source—streetlights, photographic lamps, ordinary light bulbs, candles.

The quality of light is measured in degrees kelvin, a unit of temperature. Light with a lot of red in it—a candle for example—has a low kelvin number. Light with a lot of blue in it—a cloudless summer sky—has a high kelvin number. The warmer the color, the lower the kelvin temperature. The cooler the color, the higher the kelvin number.

Color Negative Film

Following is a list of popular color-negative film products currently available, listed according to manufacturer and format. "X" indicates film format availability.

Brand Name of Film	ISO	Cart.	135	120	4x5
Kodak					
Ektar 25	25		X	X	
Royal Gold 25	25		X		
Royal Gold 100	100		X		
Royal Gold 400	400		X		
Royal Gold 1000	1000		X		
Gold Plus 100	100		X		
Gold Super 200	200		X		
Gold Ultra 400	400		X		
Vericolor III	160		X	X	X
Vericolor 400	400		X	X	
Vericolor HC	100		X	X	
PRN-Pro 100	100			X	X
Pro 400	400		X	X	
Vericolor II, Type L (tungsten film)*	100			X	X
Pro 400 (PPF)	400		X	X	
Pro 400 MC	400				
Ektapress Plus 100	100		X		
Ektapress 200					
Ektapress Plus 400	400		X		
Ektapress Plus 1600	1600		X		
Fuji					
Fujicolor 160	160		X	X	X
Fujicolor 160, Type L*	160			X	X
Fujicolor NPS 160	160		X	X	X
Fujicolor NPL 160, Type L*	160		X	X	X
Fujicolor 400	400		X	X	X
Fujicolor HG 400	400		X	X	X
Fujicolor Reala	100		X	X	
Fujicolor Super G 100	100		X	X	
Fujicolor Super G 200	200		X		
Fujicolor Super G 400	400		X	X	
Fujicolor Super G 800	800		X		
Fujicolor Super HG	1600		X		

Brand Name of Film	ISO	Cart.	135	120	4x5
Agfa					
Agfacolor Portrait 160	160		X	X	
Agfacolor Optima 100	100		X		
Agfacolor Ultra 50	50		X	X	
Agfacolor HDC 100	100		X		
Agfacolor HDC 200	200	X	X		
Agfacolor Optima 200	200		X	X	
Agfacolor HDC 400	400		X		
Agfacolor XRS 400	400		X	X	X
Agfacolor XRS 1000	1000		X	X	
3M					
Scotch ATG 100	100		X		
Scotch ATG 200	200	X	X		
Scotch ATG 400	400		X		
Konica					
Impresa 50	50		X	X	
VX 100	100		X		
SR-G 160	160		X	X	
VX 200	200		X		
VX 400	400		X		
SR-G 3200	3200		X	X	
Polaroid					
High Definition 100	100		X		
High Definition 200	200		X		
One Film	200		X		
High Definition 400	400		X		

* Type L films are balanced for exposures of ± 5 seconds and tungsten light sources.

Color Reversal Films

Following is a list of popular color reversal films, currently available, manufactured by Kodak, Fuji, Agfa, 3M, and Polaroid.

Brand Name of Film	ISO	Cart.	135	120	4x5
Kodak					
Kodachrome 25	25		X		
Kodachrome 40 Type A					
(tungsten film)	40		X		
Ektachrome Underwater	50		X		
Elite II 50	50		X		
Infrared	50		X		
Ektachrome 64	64		X	X	X
Ektachrome 64 T (tungsten)	64		X	X	X
Ektachrome 64X	64		X	X	
Kodachrome 64	64		X		
Ektachrome 100	100		X	X	X
Ektachrome 100 Plus	100		X	X	X
Ektachrome 100X	100		X	X	X
Elite II 100	100		X		
Ektachrome E 100	100		X	X	
Ektachrome E100S	100		X	X	
Ektachrome E100 5W					
Ektachrome 160T (tungsten)	160		X	X	
Ektachrome 200	200		X	X	X
Elite II 200	200		X		
Kodachrome 200	200		X		
Ektachrome 320T (tungsten)	320		X		
Ektachrome 400X	400		X	X	
Elite II 400	400		X		
Ektachrome P1600	1600		X		
SE Duplicating Film	12		X		
Fuji					
Velvia	50		X	X	X
Fujichrome 64T	64		X	X	X
Fujichrome 100 D	100		X	X	X
Provia 100	100		X	X	X
Sensia 100	100		X		
Sensia 200	200		X		

Brand Name of Film	ISO	Cart.	135	120	4x5
Provia 400	400		X	X	
Sensia 400	400		X		
Provia 1600	1600		X		
Agfa					
Agfachrome RSx 50	50		X	X	X
Agfachrome CTx 100	100		X		
Agfachrome RSx 100	100		X	X	X
Agfachrome RSx	200		X	X	
Agfachrome CTx 200	200		X		
Agfachrome RSx 1000	1000		X	X	
3M					
ScotchChrome 100	100		X		
ScotchChrome 400	400		X		
ScotchChrome 640 T (tungsten)	640		X		
Polaroid					
PolaChrome (needs Polaroid instant processor—comes with chemicals)	40		X		
Presentation Chrome	100		X		

Specialty Films

Most films are designed to produce photographs that appear realistic. However, there are a number of specialty films that reach other visual realms that are far from normal reality. Several of the more distinctive ones are discussed here. Most of these films can be found at better equipped camera stores, but some will have to be special ordered.

High Contrast Films

A common technique that photographers use to increase the graphic impact of their images is to alter the contrast. Normal black and white

Figure 7-6

A. Normal continuous tone print made from a 35mm black and white negative.

B. High contrast print, made by enlarging a black and white negative onto 4×5-inch high contrast litho film.

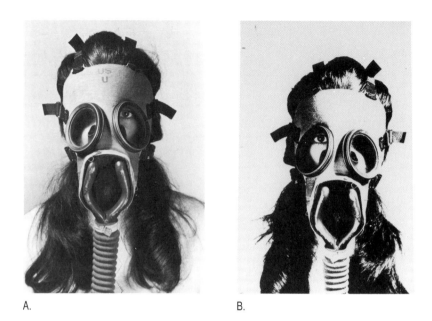

A.   B.

films are continuous tone and panchromatic, meaning that they produce a wide range of tones and are sensitive to all colors of light. There are a variety of black and white high contrast films available that achieve contrast ranges beyond the capabilities of normal films and papers.

Many high contrast films, such as most *litho* films, are not sensitive to all colors of light. They are *orthochromatic*, which means that they are sensitive to blue and green, but not red. When used with litho developers, the high contrast films have no gray tones, just pure black and white. This quality simplifies photographs by emphasizing the other graphic quality and reducing realism.

High contrast films can be shot directly in the camera, or regular continuous-tone negatives can be contact printed or enlarged onto them. High contrast films are used extensively in the graphic arts and lithographic printing industry. They are also used with many alternative non-silver photographic processes such as Van Dyke, cyanotype, and photo silkscreen. Litho films, such as Kodalith, are made by most film manufacturers but are generally available only in sheet film sizes. In 35mm, Kodak makes Contrast Process Pan Film 4155, which is a negative film, and Ektagraphic HC Slide film for high contrast positive images. Polaroid makes a 35mm high contrast instant slide film called Polagraph HC 35mm. High contrast films all need special processing, most of which you can do yourself.

Infrared Black and White Film

Images with dark dark skies, luminous glowing trees, and other surreal touches are giveaways of landscape photographers who use black and white infrared film. Infrared light waves are invisible to the human eye. They are longer than the wavelength of visible red light and are in the thermal, or heat-producing range next to red light. Because it records by heat temperatures, infrared film can be used to photograph in the dark.

Infrared light sources include the sun, tungsten lights, flash bulbs, and electronic flash. Infrared radiation is absorbed differently from visible light. Living vegetation, such as grass and leaves, reflect infrared light and appear very bright and white in infrared photographs. Clouds

Palm Trees & Garden, Southern California, Bill Agee.

Figure 7-7

Infrared film was used to create the dramatic contrast and unusual tonality of this image.

also reflect large amounts of infrared light and appear brighter than in regular photographs. In contrast, blue skies have no infrared light and appear unusually dark or black in a print.

Infrared film must be refrigerated because heat will cause fogging. Before use, let the film warm to room temperature before opening any of the packaging. This warming keeps condensation from forming inside the cassette and prevents water spots on the film. The film is extremely sensitive and must be loaded and unloaded from the camera in complete darkness. Because infrared wavelengths are different from visible wavelengths, most cameras have a red indexing mark on the lens barrel to show the adjustment needed for infrared light. To use, focus manually, and then move the lens forward slightly as indicated by the infrared indexing mark. A No. 25 red filter is recommended for shooting to enhance the infrared effect by absorbing blue light.

There is no ISO for infrared films because exposure meters do not provide accurate readings for infrared light. Experience is the best teacher. A suggested ISO, based on experience, would be 400 or 500, using a red filter and a through-the-lens exposure meter. Kodak recommends the following exposures as a starting point with High Speed Infrared black and white film when used with a No. 25 red filter in sunlight: distant scenes—1/125th sec. at $f/11$; nearby scenes—1/30th sec. at $f/11$. Because it is a negative film, overexposure is better than underexposure. To ensure that you get a usable exposure, overexpose and underexpose two f-stops, using half-stop increments. Additional advice on bracketing is offered in Chapter 8. Once shot, follow the processing instructions or have the film commercially processed by a competent custom lab.

Infrared Color Film

There is only one type of infrared color film. It is Ektachrome Infrared Film, a 35mm reversal (slide) film made by Kodak. Infrared color slide film was originally developed for the military to detect camouflage. It produces unusual colorations that creative photographers use to evoke fantasy. Like black and white infrared film, Ektachrome infrared film has no ISO. Kodak recommends the use of a No. 12 filter and suggests a trial exposure of 1/125th sec at $f/16$ in sunlight or an ISO of 400 with a through-the-lens meter. Unlike the black and white infrared, color infrared can be focused normally.

When a filter is not used, you will generally get a purplish hue; a yellow filter brings out blues; an orange filter makes neutrals and browns green, while green plants turn red; a green filter gives everything a blue cast; and a red filter makes green reddish and other colors yellow. Naturally, these results will vary with differing equipment and shooting conditions. Experimentation will be necessary. Once shot, Ektachrome Infrared film needs to be sent out for special processing in E-4 chemistry and will take several weeks to get back.

Polaroid Instant 35mm Films

Most people are familiar with the instant color print films made by Polaroid, but Polaroid also makes excellent black and white and color 35mm instant reversal films for projection and printing. These include *Polapan*, a black and white slide film; *Polachrome*, a color slide film; *Polagraph HC*, a high contrast black and white slide film; and *PolaBlue*, a film used primarily to produce title slides with white lettering and a blue background from normal text.

All of these films are available in rolls of 12 and 36 exposure and come with a throw-away chemical packet. They are processed in a Polaroid 35mm AutoProcessor, which normally takes about two minutes to process a whole roll of film. The processor rewinds the film back into the cassette at the end of the processing sequence. The film should be mounted as soon as possible because it is very delicate after processing and can be easily scratched. Polaroid makes an excellent and easy-to-

Polaroid film processors.

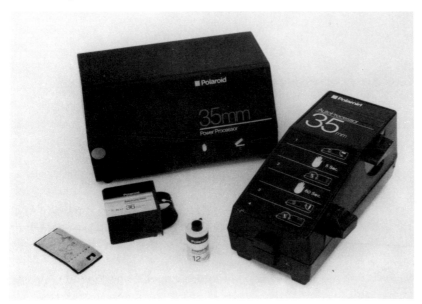

Figure 7-8

Polaroid makes several types of instant 35mm black and white and color slide films. The chemistry comes with the film in a special packet as shown.

Figure 7-9

Polagraph HC 35mm black and white instant slide film was used to produce a grainy, high contrast effect for this photograph.

Untitled, Michael Weschler.

use slide mounter designed to mount the individual slides as they are pulled out of the cassette.

These Polaroid films serve well when you need quick results. Polapan has an ISO of 400 and produces very rich, fine grain, black and white slides. The color slides from Polachrome, which has an ISO of 40 (although ISO 25 normally gives better results), have their own distinctive look and are grainy compared to normal color slide film. Polagraph HC has an ISO of 400 and gives excellent high contrast images. All four should be experimented with to ensure that you get the most out of them before using them for something important.

Chromogenic Black and White Films

Chromogenic black and white films were designed to be processed at a one-hour photo lab in the same C-41 chemistry used for color print film, thus making it easier for the average person to get black and white

Radio Telescope, David F. Drake.

Figure 7-10

This photograph, and photography as a medium, exemplify the technological progress of modern times and its dependence upon the source of our existence—light from the sun.

photographs. Unlike standard black and white film, chromogenic films employ chemical dyes rather than silver compounds to form the negative image. Chromogenic film emulsion contains both silver-halide crystals (like regular black and white films) and dye couplers (as in color negative film). During processing, the C-41 developer becomes exhausted from working on the exposed silver halides, which, in turn, activate the dye couplers. Next, these activated couplers produce a dye density, creating layers on the film according to the amount of silver halides that have been exposed and processed. After the dye layers are created, the remaining silver is bleached out. Thus, unlike a standard black and white negative, the chromogenic negative is silverless.

Photographers who like chromogenic films claim these films produce finer grain and sharper negatives with wider tonal ranges than conventional films. One interesting quality of chromogenic films is the ability to change the ISO rating from exposure to exposure. For example, the first exposure can be shot at ISO 400, the second at ISO 100, and the third at ISO 800. While all the negatives remain printable, the slower speeds tend to produce the best negatives.

The C-41 process used for black and white and color chromogenic films is designed for machine processing and is hard to maintain and control adequately with hand processing. Fortunately, the cost of *processing only* is nominal, and most photographers have their chromogenic films processed either at a one-hour or a professional lab. Currently, Ilford XP 2 is the only chromogenic black and white film that is readily available.

The New APS Film Format

In early 1996, a consortium of major film and camera manufacturers (Eastman-Kodak, Fuji, Minolta, Nikon, and Canon—to name a few) introduced a new film format called advanced photo systems or APS. Developed primarily for the large "point and shoot" consumer market, it is ultimately hoped that APS will appeal to professional photographers as well as amateurs as a replacement for the popular 35mm format.

APS film uses a conventional light-sensitive emulsion to capture an image, but the film base is entirely covered with a transparent magnetic material. The magnetic coating has no adverse effect on the image, but enables the film to carry extensive data, such as exposure information that is read by computerized/digital processing equipment for better print control. A photographer will be able to write electronically on the film additional text data for each frame, choose from three different formats (standard, wide-angle, and panoramic) for each shot, and replace a partially shot roll and begin to reuse it at the point left off. Another option is the ability to display the photographs on television sets or transfer images into a personal computer and make prints electronically.

Marketed in the United States as Smartfilm by Fuji and as Advantix by Kodak, APS will be available initially as a color negative film only. Success of this phase will determine future film options. APS film is slightly smaller than 35mm film, but is has only two sprocket holes per frame on only one side of the film, allowing for a slightly larger image area. The film comes in a cartridge that automatically loads and rewinds itself. Once processed, the film cartridge becomes the storage container and is encoded with lab processing data for future printing needs. Because the negatives are confined to the cartridge, unavailable for viewing, processed film will be returned with an "index print" containing thumb-nail images of each shot for reference and ordering purposes.

The success of this new format depends upon its popularity with the consumer market and the eventual carryover of digital imaging applications. Traditional 35mm photography will maintain its impor-tance, at least for the foreseeable future, and may even outlive the APS format. However, ultimately, APS or derivative products of that nature will force change and have a long term impact on photography.

Bulk-loading Film

Bulk-loading your own film has two main advantages: It is less expensive than buying prepackaged film, and it allows a choice of different exposure lengths. For example, you can load a 5-, 10-, or 25-exposure length into a cassette, depending on your need.

In order to bulk load film, you will need a daylight bulk-film loader, reusable film cassettes, scissors, masking tape, and bulk film.

Bulk film is made in different lengths. Common lengths are 271/2, 50-, and 100-foot rolls. One hundred feet of film is equal to about 18 rolls of 36 exposure film. The longer the bulk-film length, the greater the savings realized.

A bulk-film loader is a light-tight container that allows the bulk-film to be loaded and spooled into empty, reusable film cassettes in normal room light. Different models offer slightly different features.

The reusable film cassette looks like any other type of film cassette. However, the ends of the reusable cassette either screw on or snap on, while the ends of packaged film cassettes peel apart to open.

Cleanliness is necessary when using bulk film. A single piece of dirt or sand on the felt side of the cassette can scratch an entire roll of film as it is being loaded onto the film spool. A fleeting light leak will fog an entire roll. To compound matters, the problem will not be known until the film has been developed.

To prevent these problems, be sure that the inside of the loader is clean before inserting a roll of bulk film into the chamber of the loader. Compressed cans of air can blow the dust from the felt on both the loader and the empty film cassette. Also, empty cassettes should not be used, because it is inevitable that they will pick up some dust.

The steps for bulk loading vary somewhat from brand to brand, so read the manufacturer's instructions. Here are some general guidelines to follow:

1. Unwrap the package of bulk film in total darkness, and drop the film into the chamber designed for it in the bulk loader.
2. Pull the end of the roll through the light trap in the loader so that the film sticks out to the compartment where the film cassette fits.
3. Close the top of the loader (usually the top will screw on). Room light can be turned on after closure.
4. Take apart the cassette, and tape the end of the bulk film to the film spool with masking tape.

Figure 7-11
35mm daylight bulk-film loaders.

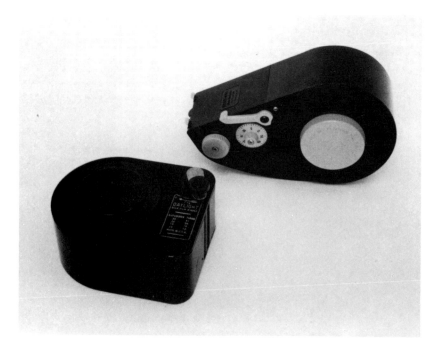

5. Reassemble the cassette. Make sure the ends of the cassette fit tightly on the cassette shelf.
6. Be sure the cassette fits properly in its compartment. Close the compartment door.
7. Put the knob on the loader in place.
8. Turn the knob slowly. The spool inside the loader will begin to rotate. The number of times the knob is rotated determines the length of the roll. On most loaders, one turn indicates one exposure. Some loaders have frame counters.
9. Once the film length has been loaded, remove the cassette from the loader. Cut the exposed end of the film into a curved shape to form a film leader. Remember, the beginning and end of each roll was exposed to light. Therefore, waste a couple of shots at the beginning of each roll and don't shoot the last two frames.

Storage and Care of Film

Photographic films are highly perishable products and can be damaged easily. Some of the characteristics of film, such as speed, contrast, and fog level, change gradually after manufacture. Adverse storage conditions accelerate these changes.

For best results, handle and store unprocessed film with adequate protection against heat, moisture, and harmful gases before and after exposure. Unprocessed films must be protected from X-rays and radioactive substances.

Protection from Humidity. Film is usually supplied in special packaging that protects it from high humidity. Do not open a package of film until you are ready to use it. Otherwise, the protection originally provided is no longer effective.

Protection from Heat. Special packaging around film is not heat-proof. Do not leave films near heat registers, steam pipes, radiators, or any other sources of heat. When you are traveling in a car, do not leave your film in a closed car parked in the sun on a warm, sunny day. The temperature can quickly reach 140°F or more.

The coolest area in a car for protecting your film from sun heat is in the passenger compartment with the air conditioner on or the windows open, especially when the car is moving. The best location is on the floor in the shade. Never keep film in the glove compartment or on the rear window shelf or in areas of direct sunlight inside the car.

Protection from X rays. X-ray equipment can fog unprocessed film when the radiation level is high or the film receives several low-level doses. The effect of exposure to X rays is cumulative. Film that has been processed is not affected.

If you travel by commercial airlines, your luggage may be subjected to X rays each time you board an aircraft. Also, all carry-on luggage is X-rayed.

To avoid X rays, hand-carry your film and ask that the film be visually checked rather than X-rayed. Also, a special lead bag is made to protect film from this type of exposure.

Expiration Date. You should expose and process film before the expiration date printed on the package. Films kept beyond this date without special treatment may be unsatisfactory because of changes in speed, contrast, fog level, and color.

Long-term Storage. For storage over long periods of time, try to maintain the following storage temperatures:

Storage Period	2 Months	6 Months	12 Months
Temperature	75°F	60°F	50°F

Refrigerating is the best way to ensure cool temperatures and extend the life of your film. Freezing will keep the film stable indefinitely. When refrigerating and freezing film, it is best to keep the film sealed in the original packaging and to put the film in a sealable plastic bag to keep it from getting wet. Before using, take the film out of the refrigerator or freezer and allow enough time for it to come up to room temperature while still fully packaged. If you unwrap it prematurely, condensation may form on the inside of the film package and cause spots on the film. Give refrigerated film as least 20 minutes and frozen film an hour or more to defrost before you use it.

Chapter 8

Exposure

An excellent conception can be quite obscured by faulty technical execution, or clarified by faultless technique.

—Edward Weston
Photographer

Figure 8-1

Technical control is a means, not an end. A slow shutter speed (shutter priority) blurs a moving subject and suggests moving water in this photograph. Control of detail from highlights to shadows by selectively metering and exposure avoided extremes.

Garropata Canyon, Robert Johnson.

In Chapter 5 you learned that there are two controls on the camera that determine the amount of light that reaches the film and how long it is exposed—aperture and shutter speed. The correct combination of these two controls, when adjusted to the film speed, or ISO, will result in properly exposed film. Shutter speed and the lens aperture, correlated to ISO, always work in tandem to determine exposure.

Proper exposure is the most important step toward achieving a good print. Over- and underexposed negatives and positives will print, but not without a compromise in quality. To secure a properly exposed negative or positive, photographers use exposure meters. An exposure meter, or light meter, measures light and expresses that measurement in terms of shutter speed and aperture. An exposure meter can be built into the camera, or it may be a separate, hand-held device.

For effective camera use, you not only need to know how to get a proper exposure, but also how to use the visual effects determined by the aperture and shutter speed. The size of the aperture opening affects the depth of field, which is an optical, yet creative, visual effect. Shutter speed affects how motion is depicted in a photograph. Aperture and shutter speed work together to control exposure. If you adjust one without adjusting the other, the exposure will change. If you adjust one to allow more exposure and adjust the other for less exposure, then the exposure will remain the same, provided you adjusted each the same amount. For instance, an exposure of $f/11$ at 1/125 sec. will give the same exposure as $f/8$ at 1/250 sec., but the motion-stopping capacity will vary and the depth of field will differ.

Once you understand how to effectively *control* and *use* these affects, your photography will improve tremendously. Exposure, depth of field, and shutter-speed motion affects are the creative and technical basis of all camera work.

Film Speed Selection with Older Exposure Meters

To use an older exposure meter, you need to program it manually to correspond to the speed of the film you are using. In the United States and other parts of the world, film speed is currently expressed in ISO

Walk-by, P. W. Derby.

Figure 8-2

The extreme value range from dark to light, forced the photographer to use a compromise exposure to hold the mid-range values, while overexposing the brighter areas and underexposing the darker parts of the image. Slow exposure caused the moving figure to blur.

Typical handheld exposure meter; ASA and ISO ratings are the same.

numbers. However, older meters will usually express film speed in either ASA numbers or DIN numbers. *Both ASA and ISO speeds are numerically the same, and you use them in the same manner.*

DIN speeds, used on meters made outside the United States, are logarithmic numbers. They have been replaced by ISO numbers marked by a degree symbol (°). Film manufacturers provide both ISO and ISO° film speeds on the outside of film cartons or with instruction sheets packed inside. A carton may be marked ISO 100/ 21°. The 100 is the ASA equivalent and 21° is the DIN equivalent. You use ISO speeds in the same way as the speeds they replace. For example, if the speed of a film is 100 ISO, you would set 100 on the ASA dial of your meter.

If the meter you are using is marked with a different scale of film speed numbers, you can convert these numbers to ISO speeds. See the conversion chart that follows for obtaining equivalent ISO logarithmic or DIN speeds.

Most photographic equipment now sold in the United States uses ISO numbers. These are the numbers that will be used throughout this book.

The following table is for converting ISO (ASA) speeds to ISO (DIN) speeds.

ISO (ASA)/ISO (DIN) Film Speeds

ISO (ASA)	ISO (DIN)	ISO (ASA)	ISO (DIN)
6	9°	160	23°
8	10°	200	24°
10	11°	250	25°
12	12°	320	26°
16	13°	400	27°
20	14°	500	28°
25	15°	640	29°
32	16°	800	30°
40	17°	1000	31°
50	18°	1250	32°
64	19°	1600	33°
80	20°	2000	34°
100	21°	2500	35°
125	22°	3200	36°

DX Coding

Nearly all brands of 35mm film available today have DX coding. As shown in the accompanying illustration, this code looks like a checker-board on the outside of the film cassette. It acts like a miniature electronic circuit board and enables newer 35mm cameras with DX coding sensing ability to perform certain functions automatically. These cameras sense the speed of film and set the camera's exposure meter accordingly. They make it unnecessary to manually program the exposure meter to the film speed. Other functions available on such cameras include the sensing of the number of exposures on a roll of film (film length), which may, in turn, indicate to the photographer when to rewind, or even to cause the camera to rewind automatically when the last exposure has been made. DX coding may also automatically adjust the exposure system in the camera for over-and-underexposure tolerances of the film being used. Under certain lighting conditions, the camera might even discourage a photographer from taking a picture if color slide film is in the camera; under the same conditions, the exposure system in the camera would "know" that black and white film has greater exposure latitude and thus allow the picture to be taken.

On some cameras, a window has been built into the camera back. This window aligns with a line of print on the 35mm film cassette,

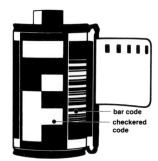

bar code
checkered code

allowing the photographer to look through the window to determine whether the camera is loaded and, if it is, to determine film type, speed, and exposure length.

DX encoded film can be used in cameras that are not equipped with DX sensing ability. You would simply adjust manually the film speed dial on the camera or on the handheld exposure meter, such as the one shown on page 148.

Reflected-Light Exposure Meters

A reflected-light exposure meter measures the brightness of light reflected from the subject. The information provided by a reflected-light exposure meter is influenced by both the amount of illumination emitted from the light source falling onto the subject and the reflective qualities of the subject itself. One of the main advantages of a reflected-light exposure meter is that it allows the photographer to take the meter reading from the camera position for most situations.

Exposure meters built into cameras and many hand-held meters are reflected-light meters. The information on reflected-light exposure meters provided in this book applies to both kinds. Some hand-held exposure meters, called *incident-light* exposure meters, are designed to read the brightness of the light illuminating the subject; they are discussed later in this chapter.

Once the reflected-light exposure meter measures the light, usually with the aid of a battery-operated light-sensitive cell called a photocell, it indicates the appropriate aperture and shutter speed combination. Some meters (usually, but not always hand-held meters) indicate a variety of aperture and shutter speed combinations. Each combination that the meter indicates yields the same exposure to the negative. For example, if a reading indicates an exposure of f/8 at 1/60, any equivalent combination, such as f/5.6 at 1/125 or f/4 at 1/250 will produce the same exposure on the negative.

Camera Meters

Most cameras manufactured today have built-in exposure meters. In newer 35mm single-lens reflex (SLR) cameras, the built-in exposure meter measures the intensity of the light that passes through the picture-taking lens and is therefore called *through-the-lens* (TTL) metering. In many non-SLR cameras, the exposure meter is mounted on the front of the lens. Since the meters built into the cameras are reflected-light

Reflected light
Measuring from
the camera
toward the subject

Incident light
Measuring from
the subject
toward the camera

The Loading Zone, Jerry Burchfield.

Figure 8-3

A reflected-light, through-the-lens meter was used to determine the exposure for this shot. If metered as the camera would normally "see" the image, the meter would have averaged the light and dark values of the scene, resulting in a middle-of-the-road exposure that would have underexposed the interior without completely saving the exterior. For this photograph, the interior was metered and the exterior *intentionally* overexposed.

exposure meters, you would normally aim the meter from the camera position in order to take a reading.

Built-in meters can be classified according to the type of exposure systems they employ. In this book four classifications are used: manual, semiautomatic, automatic, and program/multimode.

Manual Metering

With a manual-metering camera, both the aperture and the shutter speed must be chosen and set manually with the aid of a separate exposure meter. In some older 35mm cameras, an exposure meter may have been built onto the body of the camera but not integrated into the workings of the camera. In other older cameras, usually manufactured in the 1940s and 1950s, exposure meters were designed to clip onto the camera body. Most medium and large format cameras lack built-in exposure meters, so hand-held meters have to be used.

A match needle system; semiautomatic metering.

Needle is not centered.

Needle is centered.

Semiautomatic Metering

Semiautomatic-metering cameras feature exposure meters that are integrated or coupled internally with the camera. The most common systems used in semiautomatic-metering systems are matching needles, electronic diodes, and digital readouts.

In a match-needle system, the viewfinder shows two needles on one edge of the frame. One needle moves up and down depending on the intensity of the light reaching it while the other needle moves up and down as either the ƒ-stop or shutter-speed selections are made. The needles match with the correct combination.

A variation of this system involves a single needle that moves as ƒ-stops and shutter speeds are set. As shown in the illustration on page 151, the proper exposure results when the needle is centered between a stationary marking inside the viewfinder.

Newer cameras have electronic diodes instead of needles. One system has three diodes placed vertically on the right side of the viewfinder. The center diode lights up when the correct exposure combination is selected. The top diode indicates underexposure while the bottom diode indicates overexposure. A variation of this system has three diodes placed horizontally on the bottom of the viewfinder. When the correct combination is made, the center diode shows green. The diodes on either end light up red to indicate over- or underexposure.

Digital readouts in the viewfinder are found on many newer cameras. Usually, the readout displays a blinking ƒ-stop and shutter speed until the correct combination has been reached.

With rare exception, nearly all 35mm SLRs that feature semiautomatic-metering systems employ TTL exposure meters. However, production of semiautomatic-metered cameras has nearly ceased.

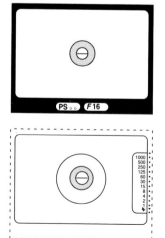

Automatic Metering

With some automatic-metered cameras, the photographer selects the lens opening, and the meter automatically selects the correct shutter speed. This system is called *aperture priority* (AP). With *shutter-priority* cameras (SP or TV), the photographer chooses the shutter speed, and the meter automatically selects the proper aperture.

AP is useful when depth of field is important. For example, you may want to use a small aperture (ƒ/16) to give great depth of field or a wide aperture to blur the background. When using an AP metering system, be sure to monitor the shutter speed selected by the camera. Sometimes the meter will select a shutter speed too slow to stop subject movement.

An SP metering system is useful when a fast shutter speed is required in order to stop or freeze action or to produce blurred motion effects when using a slow shutter speed.

When using an AP or SP metering system, check indicators on your camera to make sure you are working within the limitations of your camera. The aperture opens and closes only so far. The shutter speed goes only so fast. Even long exposures, which aren't limited physically by the camera, can blur from camera movement if you are hand-holding the camera.

When shooting with SP to stop motion, set your shutter speed for the fastest speed possible. Then focus on your subject and check the aperture and exposure meter to make sure that you can use that shutter speed and still be within the *f*-stop range that you have available to you. For instance, at a motion-stopping shutter speed of 1/1000 sec., what aperture did the camera select for you? The camera selects an aperture based on retaining as much depth of field as possible with that shutter speed and lighting situation. If you are shooting in the sunlight

Untitled, Mark Metcalf.

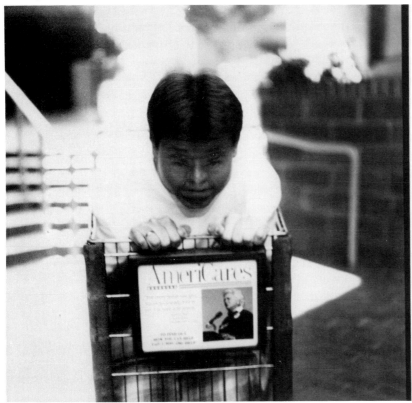

Figure 8-4

Aperture priority selection for the fastest or biggest aperture opening ensures minimum depth of field. A low light situation forced use of a slow shutter speed. The double image of the eyes was a "lucky" accident caused by subject movement during the long exposure.

with ISO 100 film, the aperture might be *f*/4. If you shoot in the shade, you may need an *f*-stop of *f*/1.8, which is fine as long as you have a fast lens that opens to *f*/1.8. But if your lens opens only to *f*/2.8, then you can't use a shutter speed of 1/1000 without underexposing the film by one full *f*-stop. To get the right exposure, you will have to go to a slower shutter speed. In this case use 1/500 sec.

AP works in the same manner. You set the camera for aperture priority and select an aperture that gives the depth of field that you need. The camera will automatically select a shutter speed that is as fast as possible to avoid slow-exposure camera-shake problems. If you want to throw the background of a medium to close-up subject completely out of focus, you will need a wide open aperture for minimum depth of field. Set your aperture for the widest aperture possible and then check to make sure that the shutter speed and exposure selected by the camera are workable. If you use a 100 ISO film in bright sunlight at an aperture of *f*/1.8, you will have to have a very fast shutter speed to keep from overexposing the film. Most cameras have shutter speeds that go only as high as 1/1000 sec. If a speed faster than that is needed, you will have to compromise on depth of field and go to a smaller aperture.

Some cameras indicate these problem situations by flashing lights or symbols, but others leave it up to you to check before shooting. Manual cameras function the same way, except that you have to adjust everything yourself, using the exposure meter as a guide.

Program/Multimode Metering

Cameras that feature program and multimode metering systems differ from aperture and shutter priority cameras in that they offer various options of exposure automation. These options, or modes, often include both AP and SP metering systems. Other modes may include an action and a telephoto program, a depth or wide-angle program, and a metered-manual program. This list does not begin to exhaust the variations found on electronic cameras, so check your camera instruction book for specifics.

Standard program mode. With cameras that feature standard or normal program mode, the meter selects both the shutter speed and lens aperture, emphasizing neither. Using this mode, the camera will choose a shutter speed that will stop moderate action and an aperture that will give reasonable depth of field. This is the only mode found on some basic automatic cameras such as the compact 35mm cameras. Most SLR cameras that offer a standard program also feature alternative modes, such as AP or SP metering systems.

Action or telephoto program mode. With action or telephoto program mode, the camera will select the fastest shutter speed that the existing light allows. This mode is designed to stop moving subjects. Depth of field is a secondary consideration. With some cameras, attaching a telephoto lens automatically shifts the camera into this mode. With other cameras, the photographer selects the mode.

Depth or wide-angle program mode. This model is designed to emphasize smaller aperture settings over faster shutter speeds in order to maximize depth of field. With some cameras, this program mode is automatically activated when a wide-angle lens is used with the camera. With other cameras, you set the program.

Metered-manual mode. This mode allows the photographer to override the various program modes in a camera. When this mode has been selected, the camera essentially reverts back to operating much like any semiautomatic-metered camera because both the shutter speed and aperture are operated manually with the aid of the built-in exposure meter.

The extremely sophisticated exposure systems now available on many cameras, especially 35mm SLRs, represent a technological breakthrough made possible by electronics and the computer chip. Yet, they have their down side. The more modes available (some cameras currently offer 15 alternatives), the more complicated your decision and the more time it takes to get used to your camera.

In-Camera Exposure Meter Coverage

It is important to remember that different cameras with through-the-lens (TTL) metering systems read reflected light from different areas of the picture. A reading from an unimportant area may cause over- or underexposure, especially if the subject is darker or lighter than other areas of the picture. To accurately determine exposure for a subject, the meter should read light reflected from that subject.

Basically, there are three kinds of TTL metering systems: the averaging meter, the spot meter, and the center-weighted meter.

The main difference between the averaging meter and the spot meter is the angle of light each reads. Most averaging meters read a large angle of light, usually 30° to 50°, whereas spot meters read a much narrower angle of 1° to 10°.

The center-weighted meter is a combination of the spot and averaging meters. These meters read light through the lens and assume that the

averaging meter

center-weighted averaging meter

spot meter

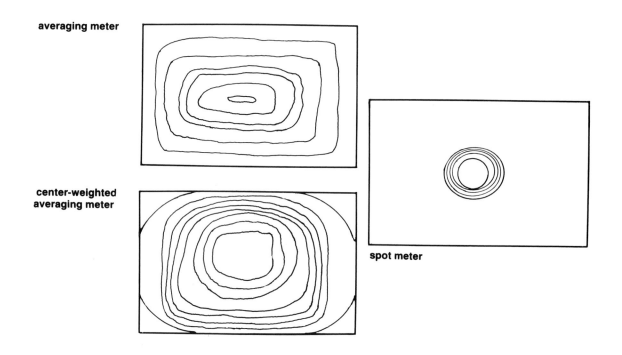

subject in the center of the viewfinder is more important for exposure than other areas. Thus, the light in the center of the frame is weighed more heavily than surrounding areas.

Note that the terms *average* and *spot* are somewhat misleading. Both meter types average light because they record all the values, light and dark, in a subject, and they average them together for an exposure. The difference is that a spot meter simply averages the values off a smaller area of the subject than does an averaging meter. With a spot meter, it is especially important to know the tonal area that is most important in the photograph.

Two variations of the in-camera spot meter are the selective-spot and multiple-spot metering systems. Although most in-camera spot meters read no more than 2.7 percent of the total area in the viewfinder, the selective-spot meter measures about 13 percent of the area. With multiple-spot metering, you can accumulate several spot readings from different areas of the scene, and the meter will then average them out.

Photographers should guard against getting carried away with new technologies. Good pictures can be made with any camera, even a plastic toy camera, as long as you understand the camera's capabilities and limitations. The variety of TTL metering systems available for 35mm cameras is endless and always changing. For example, one manufacturer recently introduced a metering system with a programmed memory

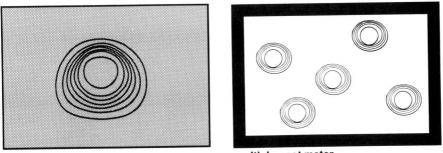

selected-spot meter   **multiple-spot meter**

capable of comparing four thousand light variations with the one seen in the viewfinder at the time of exposure. When buying a new 35mm camera, make sure that it has TTL metering and the four basic metering options—full manual, full program, aperture priority, and shutter priority.

Hand-Held Reflected-Light Meters

Hand-held meters work independently of the camera. Some older cameras have exposure meters attached to the camera body that work like hand-held meters. These exposure meters do not read the light through the lens, nor are they coupled to the camera in any way.

To use a hand-held meter, first set the film ISO speed and then point the meter at the subject. The meter reads light reflecting from the subject and translates that reading into one or more exposure combinations. Like TTL meters, some hand-held meters have a needle to indicate exposure, but others use a digital readout or liquid crystal display (LCD). A typical hand-held meter operates in the following manner:

After the meter is pointed at a subject, the needle on the meter moves to indicate how much light reflects from the subject. The greater the intensity of the light reflecting back, the farther the needle swings. The needle then points to a scale, known as a light-intensity scale. This light-intensity scale is usually rated numerically. These number ratings vary, depending on the brand of the meter. Usually, the low numbers represent dim light, whereas the high numbers represent bright light. After the numerical value of light has been determined on the light-intensity scale, it is matched up to a dial. A marker on the dial can then be matched up to the light value, and the various f-stops and shutter speeds can be implemented.

Some hand-held meters do not use light value numbers. Instead, the needle points directly to a possible exposure combination.

Figure 8-5

A reflected-light meter reads the light reflected from the subject, whether it is a hand-held meter or a meter built into the camera.

Hand-held reflected light-meter reading

Figure 8-6

A. A typical dial of a needle-type reflected light exposure meter.
B. A digital readout of a liquid crystal display (LCD) reflected-light meter.

A.

B.

Digital and LCD hand-held meters have no needle. Instead, they provide a direct readout of a shutter speed and *f*-stop combination.

The debate over hand-held meters versus TTL meters has been raging for years. Photographers who prefer hand-held meters argue that they provide more accurate exposure information, such as a wider range of exposure choice in dim light. Although technology has improved the low-light measuring ability of TTL meters, the better hand-held meters will outperform even the most sophisticated TTL meters in low-light situations. Also, a hand-held meter can be brought up close to the subject for precise reading. In addition, hand-held spot meters read a far narrower angle of light than TTL meters. Finally, if a hand-held meter should break, you still have use of the camera; but with many of the newer, electronic cameras you lose camera function when the meter does not operate.

Considering Exposure

The key to understanding how exposure meters work is to know that they read for a middle gray. That is, meters average whatever light they read, whether from a light, dark, or gray subject. The average represents the gray halfway between black and white.

This reading usually works well enough because most subjects have equal amounts of light and dark areas. However, meters are fooled when the subject is primarily light *or* dark. Meters do not discriminate between important subject matter and unimportant areas. They are calibrated

Untitled, P. W. Derby.

Figure 8-7

Selective metering of highlight values enabled the photographer to make the drive-in theater stand out against a dark sky. A normal meter reading would have resulted in the meter's reacting to the overall scene and produced a much less dramatic shot.

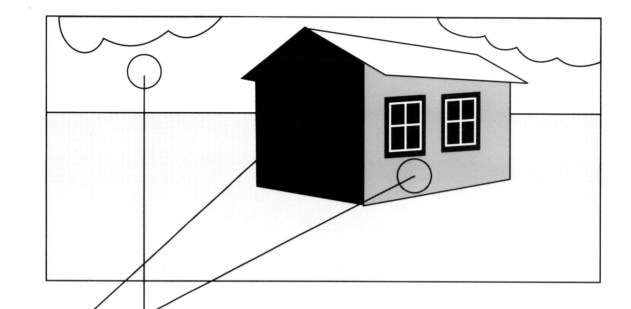

only to average the light. For this reason, the photographer must do the choosing.

When you see an object, you are really seeing the light that is reflecting off that object. The more light that falls directly on the object, the brighter that object seems. All objects reflect a certain amount of light. However, a light-colored object reflects more light than a dark-colored object. Stated another way, a dark-colored object absorbs more light than does a light-colored one. For instance, suppose you are taking a reading of an outdoor scene that contains a house, ground, and sky. Part of this house has sunlight directly on it while part of it is in shade. If the meter is pointed only at the shaded part of the house, the meter may give a reading of f/4 at 1/125.

If, instead, the meter is pointed at the sky (the lightest area of the scene), it will read on the high end of the light scale and indicate more light reflecting back. This is because light areas reflect more light. Therefore, the meter reading would indicate an exposure combination geared to compensate for the intensity of light by allowing less light to reach the film. In this case, the meter may indicate an exposure of f/16 at 1/125 as being correct.

A meter reading made off the sunlit side of the building would provide a reading of f/11 at 1/125. This setting would reflect less light than the sky but more light than the shaded areas of the building.

In effect, we now have three entirely different readings for the same subject, depending on where the meter was pointed. Readings from the darkest and lightest areas would each produce incorrect exposures because meters read for a middle gray where they are directed. Most subjects provide enough dark and light areas to simulate gray. However, when light meter readings are made from either extremely light or extremely dark areas, devoid of any middle gray, the resulting exposure is incorrect.

The Gray Scale

Photographic metering systems are based on the principle of the gray card. This card, which can be purchased at photography stores, is neutral gray with no color cast and reflects 18 percent of the light cast on it. It represents the middle gray value on which exposure meters base their measurements. Many professional photographers meter from a gray card rather than the subject. That way there is no confusion or need for interpretation of the meter reading. But most photographers find this inconvenient and meter off the subject with either a TTL or hand-held meter.

Since all exposure meters, whether in-camera, hand-held, reflected, or incident, read everything as a middle gray, it is often necessary to make adjustments from what the meter indicates. A normal scene that has a mixture of values from light to dark works well with a normal meter reading, but problems occur when you expose for a specific value. For instance, if you were to make separate pictures of a black dog, a white dog, and a gray dog, metering each individually, the meter would indicate an exposure that would make all three into gray dogs when printed normally. Naturally, the images could have contrast adjustments and be lightened or darkened when printed. But to get the best result, it is often necessary to use an exposure that is different from what the meter indicates.

You can choose how light or dark a subject should be by adjusting the aperture or shutter for a different exposure than the meter suggests. This adjustment enables you to make your subject look more natural or to change the feeling of the picture by making it lighter or darker than normal. If you give more exposure than the meter indicates, the image will be lighter than middle gray. If you give less exposure, the image will be darker than middle gray.

Such exposure would not pose a problem with the gray dog because the meter reads everything in terms of gray. To make the white dog look more natural, however, you would need to give more exposure than normal. To make the black dog appear more natural, you would need to give less exposure than normal.

Figure 8-8

This back-lit shot of mounds of snow was intentionally underexposed to emphasize the back-lighting.

Untitled, Jerry Burchfield.

The photographic *tonal* or *gray scale* goes from pure white to pure black with middle gray in the center. The values on this scale are often referred to as zones. The zone system is a system for controlling value ranges by adjusting film exposure and development. Each zone is one *f*-stop apart from the next one on the scale. Therefore, to make the white dog look more natural, you would take a meter reading directly from the white fur and then open your aperture two *f*-stops or slow your shutter speed by two times. The control you choose to adjust depends upon the depth of field and motion needs of that particular photo. The result will be an exposure that will render the dog more naturally by placing the light values higher on the "zone scale." The Zone System is covered in detail in Chapter 19.

Overriding Automatic and Fully Programmed Exposure Meters

To expose for certain scenes correctly—snow and sand, for example—you may need to override the exposure systems of your camera. Cameras that have a *metered manual mode* allow you to do this easily. But with some cameras, the automatic mode will not allow you to manually adjust either the aperture or the shutter speed. Some of these cameras, however, do have a *memory lock* or *exposure lock*. Therefore, if you have a problem with back lighting, for instance, you can take a close-up reading, press the lock button to freeze the correct setting, and then move back and shoot.

If the camera you are using doesn't have this feature, it may have a shutter release that will hold the meter reading as long as the release is held partway down. If this is the case, use the release in the same manner as a lock button. Just remember not to let up on the shutter release.

Another feature on some automatic cameras is an *exposure compensation dial*. This dial can be used to change exposures set by the meter by as much as two stops in half- or third-stop increments. Instead of a dial, other cameras have an exposure compensation button or a back-light button that can increase exposure by as much as two stops. This button is usually used in photographing back-lighted subjects. If your camera lacks these controls, you can compensate by using the film speed dial to increase or decrease exposure. If, for example, you are photographing a dark subject against a bright background (someone on a beach), divide the speed of the film you are using by two, and set your film speed dial on that number. If you were using a film with a speed of 400 ISO, you would set the dial at 200. This would increase the light on the film 100 percent by opening the lens or decreasing the shutter speed one stop.

Sometimes you may be photographing a light subject against a dark background. If this is the case, then multiply the speed of the film by two and set the meter accordingly. For example, suppose you were photographing a person wearing a very light-colored outfit standing in front of foliage. A normal meter reading would "see" mostly the dark area and thus indicate an exposure that would be too much for the

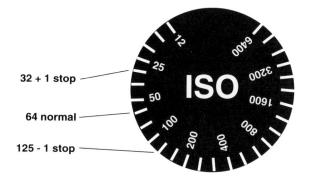

32 + 1 stop

64 normal

125 - 1 stop

ISO dial. For a film speed of ISO 64, you can set the dial on 125 to obtain 1 stop less exposure or 32 for 1 stop more exposure.

subject. The result would be that the subject is overexposed. If you were using a film speed of 100, you would multiply that number by two and use 200 instead. The result would cut the exposure time in half. In either case, remember to reset your film speed dial to the normal setting when you finish photographing the problem scene.

Some cameras are designed to read DX encoded film and do not have a film speed dial or any other mechanism to alter exposure. Despite that, it may be possible to increase the exposure time by switching on the flash unit usually built into this kind of camera. Even though you may be taking photographs in daylight, activating the flash unit automatically decreases the shutter speed, thereby exposing more light to the film.

Exposure Hints

Most of the time a general light meter reading of an entire subject produces an accurate exposure. However, before accepting that reading as the ultimate truth, examine the subject carefully. Try to think or visualize what that subject will look like in black and white. Do the dark, middle, and light areas balance? If this is the case, use the exposure combination indicated by the reading without any correction. If this is not the case, try one of the following:

1. For a predominantly light or white subject, more light will be necessary—generally the equivalent of one *f*-stop or more than the meter indicates. You can either open the aperture or slow the shutter speed to obtain the added light. For example, if the meter indicates an exposure of *f*/8 at 1/250, use *f*/5.6 at 1/250 or *f*/8 at 1/125 instead.
2. For a predominantly dark subject, do the opposite—close the aperture or make the shutter speed faster. If the meter reading is *f*/5.6 at 1/125, use *f*/8 at 1/125 or *f*/5.6 at 1/250 instead.
3. Use a gray card. An 18 percent gray card is useful to determine a correct exposure. An 18 percent gray card has a medium gray surface that reflects 18 percent of the light that reaches it. Thus, gray cards reflect an average amount of light falling onto the subject rather than the light reflected off the subject.

    To use a gray card, simply place it in front of the subject and aim it toward the camera position. Take the reading off the card only. Be careful not to cast your own shadow upon the card. Use the exposure indicated by the meter without additional compensation.

Figure 8-9
Gray card reflected-light metering.

4. Expose off the skin. Skin can be measured in the absence of a gray card. One method involves taking the meter reading directly off the palm of the hand, which is positioned directly in front of the subject. Another method entails taking the reading directly off the subject's face. Again, be careful not to cast a shadow over the hand or face when taking the reading.

   Needless to say, skin tones do vary, and thus exposure adjustments may be necessary. For average Caucasian skin, add one stop more to the exposure indicated by the reading. Dark skin will probably need no exposure compensation, although

Figure 8-10
Metering a skin value off the photographer's hand.

extremely dark skin may require one-half to one f-stop less exposure than the meter suggests.

5. Average the shadows and highlights. Since meters read for middle gray, the correct exposure will fall somewhere between the readings for dark and light areas of the subject. To obtain this exposure, first read a dark area, then a light area of the same subject. For example, if the reading for the dark area is *f*/5.6 at 1/125 and that for the light area is *f*/11 at 1/125, then the average reading would be *f*/8 at 1/125.

6. Exposure bracketing. To bracket an exposure, first determine the exposure, using an exposure meter. Take a picture at that setting. Next take another picture at one stop less exposure and a third picture at one stop more exposure. For example, if the recommended *f*-stop and shutter speed combination is *f*/8 at 1/60, take a picture at that setting, but also take one at *f*/5.6 at 1/60, and another at *f*/11 at 1/60. For more subtle exposure variations, some photographers bracket using half-stop increments on the aperture scale. Many of the newer electronic cameras have built-in bracketing systems that can be activated to function automatically. However, bracketing is not always practical, for example, when you are shooting candid or moving subjects. Also, bracketing becomes expensive because you use a lot more film. Therefore, learn to expose well and bracket only when it is really necessary.

Problem Exposures

In a back-lighted scene, the background reflects more light than the subject. The light behind the subject may also shine directly into the exposure meter. Both factors cause the exposure meter to read too high, resulting in underexposure of the subject. The pictorial effect is a silhouetted subject.

One solution to this problem is to take a close-up meter reading of the subject while you shade the meter with your hand. If that is not possible, then add the equivalent of one or two *f*-stops to the meter reading (depending on how dark the subject is). For example, if the subject is a person lit by the sun from behind and the meter recommends *f*/22 at 1/125, use *f*/11 at 1/125, instead. If the sun is especially bright, use *f*/8 at 1/125.

Another problem area is photographing a scene that includes a large proportion of sky. Since the sky is usually brighter than other parts of the scene, the exposure meter may indicate too little exposure. As a result, any subject that is darker than the sky will be underexposed. This effect is more common with overcast skies than with blue skies.

Figure 8-11

A. The cat was back lit and a normal metering was done from the camera position. Because of back lighting, flare resulted; the meter underexposed the shot by reacting to the bright back light.

B. By a subtle shift in camera position, the photographer was able to position the sunlight directly behind the cat's head to eliminate the flare. The exposure was then taken specifically for the cat so that the bright background did not influence the meter reading, and a much better picture resulted.

In this case, take your exposure with the meter pointed downward slightly to avoid undue influence from the sky.

Scenes that have large areas of snow, white sand, or concrete present certain problems. If you expose according to an overall meter reading, chances are your negative will be underexposed. The light areas would come out gray. To avoid this problem, add one stop more to the exposure indicated by the meter.

Incident-Light Exposure Meters

Until now, we have been discussing meter readings based on reflected light. A reflected-light exposure meter reads and measures the light that is reflected from the subject. There is a second type of light meter called an incident-light exposure meter. An incident-light exposure meter

Figure 8-12

Incident-light exposure metering.

measures the light illuminating the scene. In other words, it is measuring the light falling on the subject from one direction rather than the light being reflected by the subject. An incident-light reading requires the use of a hand-held meter. The meter must be equipped with an incident-light dome or diffuser. This diffuser extends the angle of acceptance or coverage of the light meter. In a reflected-light meter, coverage is normally somewhere between 30° and 50°. In an incident-light meter the angle of acceptance is generally 180°. This allows the light meter to measure the light coming toward the subject from the direction of the camera.

Taking an Incident-Light Exposure Reading

To take an incident-light exposure reading, you must position your meter in the same light illuminating the subject and point the meter toward the camera.

An exposure that is determined by an incident-light reading assumes that the scene to be photographed has average reflectance. Because an incident-light exposure meter measures the light source, rather than the reflectance, dark or light areas in the scene will not influence the reading. Be sure then that a very dark or very light area is not important in your photograph. If, however, a very dark or very light area is important, then it is necessary to modify the exposure. For instance, if a bright area is important, use a lens opening one stop smaller than the meter indicates. An example of that situation would be a snow scene. Suppose an incident-light reading indicated that 1/125 at *f*/11 was correct. By using *f*/16 instead of *f*/11, the detail and texture of the snow would still be seen in the photograph. If a dark area were important, just the opposite would be true. You would use a lens opening one stop larger than your meter indicated.

It is possible to average an incident-light reading of the area receiving the most light and the area receiving the least light. It is done in the same manner that you average a reflected-light reading. Do not, however, use an incident-light reading of a subject that emits light from a lamp or a neon sign.

More Considerations about Hand-Held Metering

Today, so many cameras have built-in, through-the-lens metering systems that it seems as if hand-held meters are obsolete. Yet, hand-held meters are a necessity for the serious photographer. Built-in meters are convenient and easy to use, but they lack sensitivity and limit your ability for making exact multiple-exposure readings. As you become more experienced, you will want more-exacting and reliable results. Relying on bracketing and the film's exposure latitude is fine when you are a beginner, but not when your results become more important. Also, most medium- and large-format cameras, such as 4x5-inch view cameras, do not have metering systems, and hand-held meters are therefore a necessity.

Most of the more recent hand-held meters are electronic, have digital readouts, and do multiple functions. The most important functions to consider are reflected and incident capabilities, low-light sensitivity, flash metering capacity, and accessories such as spot-metering attachments. But older meters are also worth considering too. One advantage of most older meters and some newer meters is that they display a whole range of usable aperture and shutter-speed combinations, while digital meters and in-camera meters normally only indicate one combination.

Chapter 9

Shooting Accessories and Techniques

The simpler I work ... the easier it is to get good pictures.

—Paul Caponigro
Photographer

MOCA, Edouard de Merlier.

Figure 9-1
Whenever the camera is pointed in the direction of a bright light source, lens flare is a possibility. Lens shades help alleviate the unpredictable hexagonal shapes that result. Sometimes, however, as in this image, lens flare adds visual impact.

The more you know about photography, the more you need to know. Every day a new process, product, or technique is introduced that may make obsolete an existing process or piece of equipment. Techniques that may have taken hours of painstaking patience to use a few years ago may now be accomplished within a few minutes.

In recent years the biggest changes have been with the electronic automation of cameras and the rapidly changing world of digital imaging equipment. Most shooting accessories, such as tripods, lens shades, and filters, remain relatively unchanged. Shooting accessories are available at most photography stores and many discount stores. They vary widely in price and quality. Before buying, consider your current and possible future needs. Many products, although attractively priced, may be limited in application. If possible, buy only black shooting accessories because silver or other colors will show up in pictures of reflective surfaces, whereas black does not reflect.

Camera Accessories

Camera accessories consist of equipment that aids the photographer in special shooting circumstances. A cable release and tripod for maintaining camera stability during long exposures are two widely used accessories.

Cable Releases

Cable releases provide a flexible cable for releasing the shutter when using long exposures. They are available in lengths from 10 inches to 25 feet long. They are used to minimize the chance of camera movement when you are depressing the shutter and enable you to shoot from a position away from the camera. Most cable releases are manually activated by depressing a plunger at the end of the cable, and they screw into the top of the shutter release. However, some of the electronic cameras use remote electronic releases that cost more but that don't have to be attached to the camera.

Figure 9-2

Camera with a cable release mounted on a tripod.

Tripods and Monopods

Tripods are necessary for controlled picture making with as long exposures, for studio and staged photography, and with large format cameras such as 4 × 5-inch view cameras. Tripods need to be lightweight, yet sturdy enough to provide a rock-steady support for your camera under various conditions. For large format cameras, a heavy duty tripod is a necessity, especially for shooting outdoors. Tiny, almost pocket sized tripods are also available for those who need to travel light.

The most important feature of a tripod is ease of use. The legs must extend and retract easily. The head of the tripod needs to provide movement in all directions yet be simple and easy to adjust. Many tripods have a quick release camera attachment screwed onto the bottom of the camera that snaps into the tripod head. Some tripods have reversible center columns. This feature allows for mounting the camera near ground level. Other tripods have "side-arms" that can be attached onto the top or bottom of the center column for low-level camera positioning that won't be obstructed by the tripod legs.

Monopods are one-legged camera supports that are quicker and easier to use than a tripod, but they don't provide the same amount of stability as a tripod because a monopod has to be held in place or leaned against something. Sports photographers use monopods to support cameras when they are using long telephoto lenses or to raise the camera up high above a crowd.

Figure 9-3
Reversible tripod.

Copy Stands

A copy stand is used to support the camera for making copy photographs of pictures or other two-dimensional objects that are too small to be hung on a wall and shot with the camera on a tripod. A copy stand is like an enlarger without a head. It consists of a vertical pole, an adjustable arm that can move up or down the pole, and a camera-holding plate or head. When mounted on a copy stand, the camera can be used with any lens or other type of close-up attachment because the copy stand provides the necessary support. The two-dimensional object that is to be copied is placed on the baseboard of the copy stand with the camera facing down towards the object. A cable release should be used to avoid camera vibration.

Copy stands are generally illuminated by two 3200K photoflood light bulbs or two strobe lights with 10-inch or 12-inch reflectors mounted on each side of the copy stand or on light stands placed next to each side of the baseboard. The lights need to be of equal intensity and at

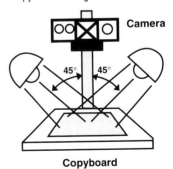

Copy stand with lights.

Camera

45° 45°

Copyboard

a 45° angle to the baseboard. This arrangement will provide uniform lighting, with no light reflecting back into the camera lens. Use an incident meter reading or a gray card for reflected meter readings. If you are shooting an object that needs to be held flat by a piece of glass, a glossy photo, or some other reflective subject, it will be necessary to cover the vertical pole with a black cloth and hide everything above the object behind a piece of black mat board. The easiest way to do this is to cut a hole in the black mat board that is the diameter of the outer element of your lens. Attach the mat board to the camera so that the lens sticks through the hole with everything else "masked" by the black board. Since the front of the lens is dark, nothing will reflect and interfere with the final picture. Use black masking or electrical tape to hold the mat board in place.

Remote and Specialty Devices

Each year camera manufacturers come out with new features and devices to expand our pictorial horizons and make photography easier. These innovations generally increase costs and often make things more confusing. But electronic photography is here, and it offers options that go beyond DX Coding, autoload, autofocus, autoexposure, and dedicated flash, an automatic flash designed with a particular camera.

Remote cable releases are becoming more common. They cost more but enable the photographer to shoot the picture without having to be tethered to the camera. Most newer 35mm SLR cameras have a built-in flash and several options for supplemental flash attachment. Hot shoes, located on the top of the camera pentaprism, are the most common option, but the better cameras provide a flash sync cord connection and wireless remote flash, some with full TTL control and high flash sync speed.

For many years, *interchangeable viewfinders,* such as prism, waist-level, and sport finders have been available for professional cameras. These options are seldom available on consumer cameras, but most of the better brands offer interchangeable viewfinder elements for people with special eyeglass needs.

Motor drives or winders once were an accessory item for most cameras. Now, however, many newer cameras can be purchased with a built-in winder that will allow rapid shooting of two to four frames per second.

Data backs are also quite common and enable the photographer to record the date the picture was shot. Minolta offers "Creative Expansion Cards," which can be purchased for its Maxxum cameras. These "computer chips" provide additional functions beyond the normal camera

Figure 9-4
Minolta Maxxum *9xi* with Creative Expansion Cards.

functions, such as programming depth of field, bracketing, and sports photography needs.

Polaroid backs are another useful shooting accessory for the serious amateur or professional photographer. They provide a quick and easy means to determine exposure, depth of field, cropping, and lighting at the time of the shooting. This capability is especially important for the professional photographer who has to make sure that everything is right, since reshoots are normally out of the question. Polaroid backs are available for large format sheet film cameras and many 2 ¼-inch cameras and can be adapted to some 35mm cameras.

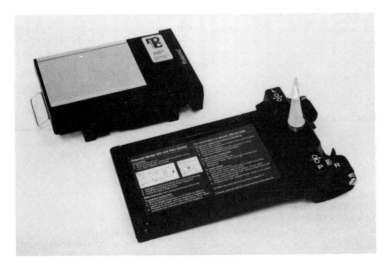

Figure 9-5
Polaroid backs for 4 x 5-inch and 2 ¼-inch cameras.

Figure 9-6

Polaroid 4 x 5-inch positive/ negative film Type 55 was used to make this image. The edges of the film were printed and serve as a framing device for the photograph. The black border was also printed in by the photographer to further frame the image and to provide a space for the title.

Driveway: Teacup, Texas, Jim Stone.

Lens Accessories

A lens shade is the most common lens accessory. They shade the lens from stray light that might cause the kind of lens flare shown in Figure 9.1. Lens shades are built-in features in many telephoto and zoom lenses, but they must be purchased separately for most other lenses. Lens shades are not normally used with wide-angle lenses because the angle of view is so wide that the lens shade vignettes or cuts into the corners of the picture. Rubber lens shades that can be retracted and made smaller work well because they can be adapted to fit both normal and medium wide-angle lenses. Most other lens shades are metal. Some have an adjustable bellows that serves as a combination lens shade, vignetter, and filter holder.

Supplementary Lenses and Close-up Photography

Supplemental lenses are attached either in front of or behind an existing lens. They are an inexpensive means to get a variety of visual effects.

Figure 9-7
Lens shades.

There are wide-angle and fisheye supplemental lenses. Tele-extenders are another supplemental device. They increase the magnification or effective focal length of an existing lens by two or three times.

The easiest way to do close-up photography is with a macro lens. Macro lenses are specially designed to deliver optimum resolution (sharpness) and contrast for subjects that are focused at close distances. Most standard lenses are designed to deliver their optimum performance at infinity focus; therefore, their quality, in terms of resolution and contrast, falls off at closer distances. A practical rule is that when the lens-to-subject distance equals the lens-to-film distance, the magnification is life-size (1:1). As this distance to the subject is reduced, the magnification increases beyond life-size.

Macro lenses are made in various focal lengths to meet different requirements. Focal lengths may include 20mm, 38mm, 50mm, 80mm, and 100mm. Generally, the 20mm, 38mm, and 80mm lenses are used in conjunction with a bellows unit. A 20mm lens mounted on a bellows will normally provide optimum resolution at 5X–12X magnification. A 38mm lens used in conjunction with bellows will allow a magnification range of 2X–6X, whereas the 80mm is designed to offer optimum resolution at a 1:1 magnification. The 20mm, 38mm, and 80mm are generally designed to be used with photographing flat field copies (similar to copy slides made from books).

The two most common macro focal lengths, however, are the 50mm and 100mm. A 50mm macro can be used in place of a normal 50mm, since both have the same angle of view (47°). The major difference is that most 50mm macro lenses can focus down to approximately 9 inches, which provides a magnification of ½ life-size. In addition, if an extension tube is placed between the lens and camera body, a 1:1 image can be obtained. Also, the 50mm macro lens can be used in reverse position with an adapter, which in combination with extension tubes, would allow for a magnification of up to 4X.

Many photographers prefer the use of a 100mm macro lens. The 100mm is an ideal focal length for general portraiture. In addition, this lens allows twice the working distance of the 50mm macro. This extra distance helps prevent perspective exaggeration with close-ups of three-dimensional objects and provides a greater distance between the subject and the lens. This capability allows for more working space between the lens and the subject so that lighting is more flexible. The 100mm macro lens is used on bellows or tubes in the same manner as the 50mm.

Definition of Close-up Terms

The relationship between the size of the image on the film and the size of the subject being photographed is usually expressed as a ratio, such as 1:1 or 1:10. The first number refers to the image size and the second is the subject size. This is the image ratio or reproduction ratio. When it is expressed as a multiplier, such as 1/10X or 1X, it is often called magnification. For example, a one-tenth life-size image is expressed as 1/10X, or 1:10. A life-size reproduction on the negative of a subject is expressed as 1X or 1:1, whereas a twice life-size image on the negative is 2X or 2:1. In many of the data sheets packed with lenses, bellows, or tubes, magnification is given in decimal units, such as 0.10 (1/10X) or 1/0 = (1X).

The following terms are used interchangeably, and all indicate close-up photography: microphotography, photomicrography, and close focus. However, in reality, there is a distinction among these terms. Refer to Chapter 13 for a color example of photomicrography.

Macrophotography describes the recording of a life-size (1:1) reproduction on the negative of a subject, reaching its effective limit at magnifications at 10. life-size. *Microphotography* is defined as an image larger than 10. magnification but not taken through a microscope. *Photomicrography* is any magnified image taken with the use of a microscope. Finally, any image of at least 10. life-size, but not larger than life-size on the negative, is defined as *close focus*. These terms all apply to the negative image, not enlarged, in ratio to the size of the subject.

For most types of close-up work, it is preferable to use a single-lens reflex camera with through-the-lens (TTL) metering and interchange-

Close-Up, Ron Leighton.

Figure 9-8

A small thistlelike bud, barely one-half inch in height, was photographed with a macro lens. Depth of field is very critical with macrophotography because the closer one gets to the subject, the less depth of field. In this instance the photographer chose to have "limited" depth of field and used a wide aperture.

able lenses. Because you are looking directly through the lens, focusing is considerably easier. The TTL metering simplifies exposure calculations, and many of the close-up attachments require that the lens be removed from the body of the camera.

An easy and inexpensive way to do close-up photography is with supplementary close-up or plus lenses. These supplementary lenses are positive magnifying glasses of various powers that are attached to the

Figure 9-9
Close-up lenses.

front of the picture-taking lens. They enlarge an image in two ways. They allow the picture-taking lens to focus closer to the object than it normally could, and they add their own power to that of the taking lens.

The power of a supplementary lens is expressed in diopters, a term usually reserved for optometrists. The diopter describes both the focal length and the magnifying power of the lens. Thus, the +1 diopter lens will focus on an object one meter (3.25 ft.) away. The +2 diopter focuses at half that distance (approximately 19.5 inches). The +3 diopter will magnify three times as much, and so on.

Supplementary lenses of varying diopters can be combined to provide a greater magnification, as long as the strongest lens is attached to the picture-taking lens first. Thus, a +2 diopter lens can be added to a +4 to create a +6. However, the image quality tends to suffer when lenses are combined because extra lens flare is created from the two glass surfaces.

Once a supplementary lens is attached to the front of the picture-taking lens and set at infinity, the next maximum focusing distance will be that of the focal length of the supplementary lens. This is true regardless of what focal length camera lens is being used. For example, a 50mm lens set at infinity focus, with a +2 diopter, will always focus at an object 19.5 inches away. If a 135mm lens was used instead, and again the focus was set at infinity, with a +2 diopter, it, too, could focus on an object 19.5 inches away. However, the ultimate image size will depend on the focal length of the lens being used. This is because the degree of magnification is determined not only by the diopter of the supplementary lens, but also by the magnifying power of the picture-taking lens. Thus, a +2 diopter on a 135mm lens will give a greater magnification than a +2 attached to a 50mm lens, if both lenses are set at the focus distance.

Another variable in the magnifying power of supplementary lenses is dependent on the distance set on the focusing scale of the lens. When a lens is focused closer than infinity, it will allow that lens to focus closer, increasing the degree of magnification.

Supplementary lenses are quite popular because they do not require any type of exposure compensation, are inexpensive, and can be used with many types of cameras (although the SLR is recommended). The major disadvantage of supplementary lenses is a loss of resolution and, therefore, sharpness. Also, since most people seem to use supplementary lenses on normal focal length lenses, which normally do not focus closer than three feet, true macrophotography is not possible unless the negative is enlarged.

The following chart gives important information about supplementary lenses:

Close-Up Data for 35mm Cameras

Close-up Lens and Focus Setting (in feet)		Lens-to-Subject Distance (in inches)	Approximate Field Size (in inches): 50mm Lens on a 35mm Camera	Approximate Field Size (in inches): Magnification Range
+1	Inf	39	18 × 26¾	1:20
	15	32¼	14¾ × 22	1:20
	6	25½	11¾ × 17¼	1:20
	3½	20⅜	9⅜ × 13¾	1:20
+2	Inf	19½	9 × 13½	1:10
	15	17¾	8⅛ × 12	1:10
	6	15½	7⅛ × 10½	1:10
	3½	13⅜	6⅛ × 9⅛	1:10
+3	Inf	13⅛	6 × 8⅞	1:6.6
	15	12¼	5⅝ × 8⅜	1:6.6
	6	11⅛	5⅛ × 7½	1:6.6
	3½	10	4⅝ × 6¾	1:6.6
+3 plus +1	Inf	9⅞	4½ × 6⅝	1:5
	15	9⅜	4¼ × 6⅜	1:5
	6	8⅝	4 × 5⅞	1:5
	3½	8	3⅝ × 5⅜	1:5
+3 plus +2	Inf	7⅞	3⅝ × 5⅜	1:4
	15	7½	3½ × 5⅛	1:4
	6	7⅛	3¼ × 4⅞	1:4
	3½	6⅝	3 × 4½	1:4
+3 plus +3	Inf	6⅝	3 × 4½	1:2.9
	15	6⅜	2⅞ × 4¼	1:2.9
	6	6	2¾ × 4⅛	1:2.9
	3½	5⅝	2⅝ × 3⅞	1:2.9

Bellows and Extension Tubes

Another method that can be employed to achieve close-up photography involves the use of extension tubes and bellows. Either accessory is mounted between the body of the camera and the lens. In effect, they extend the lens closer to the subject while moving the lens farther from the film plane. This shift will magnify the subject because the lens is focused on a smaller portion of the subject but will project the image of that portion onto the same area of the film. Therefore, the closer the lens is focused to the subject, the larger the image size on the film.

Versatility is the major difference between bellows and extension tubes. Extension tubes are rigid metal tubes, which are generally sold in sets of three. Each succeeding tube is longer than the one preceding it. Some common lengths of tubes are 12mm for the shortest, 20mm for the middle length, and 36mm for the longest. Thus, seven different combinations of extension lengths can be achieved, 12mm, 20mm, 32mm, 36mm, 48mm, 56mm, and 68mm. A 12mm extension used with a 50mm lens focused at infinity will allow the subject-to-lens distance measure 10.1 inches, resulting in a ratio of image size to subject size of 0.24. If a 50mm lens is used with the 68mm extension instead, the subject-to-lens distance would only be 3.4 inches, resulting in a greater magnification ratio of 1:36.

Bellows, on the other hand, are made of a flexible material (usually leather), and provide a continuous focus over their extendible range. Bellows are mounted on a rail. In some cases, twin rails are used for support. Thus, while tubes are set at predetermined steps, depending on the length of each tube and how many are used in combination,

Figure 9-10

Camera with bellows attachment.

Figure 9-11
Clockwise starting in the front and center: close-up lens, extension tubes, bellows slide duplicator, and close-up bellows.

Close-up equipment.

bellows are flexible over an entire range and, depending on the length of the bellows, offer greater magnification. The rail on the bellows unit almost always has a magnification and a millimeter scale engraved on it. This allows for easier computation of the exposure factor increase. Other variables for bellows units may include a copy attachment for duplicating slides or making negatives from color slides, and lens reversal rings, which allow the lens to be used in the reversed position for greater magnification.

Exposure Considerations

Nothing comes easily in photography. For every rule, there are at least ten exceptions, and so it is true with close-up photography; exposure must be compensated.

The *f*-stop on the lens is a precise indication of the diameter-focal length relationship when focused at infinity. As the lens is focused to closer distances and the lens-to-film distance increases, the light diverges over a wider field. The effect is that less light is received on the film at any given point. However, this effect is not important up to image ratios of 1:8. When the image ratio is closer than this, an exposure-factor increase is necessary. An exposure-factor is like a filter factor—a certain amount of light has to be increased.

Close-Up Data for 50mm Lenses*								Exposure Dat
Lens Combinations			Total Tube Extension	Subject-to-Lens Distance		Subject-to-Film Distance		Ratio of Image Size to Subject Size	Exposure Increase Factor**	Open this mi f-stops
				mm	inches	mm	inches			
			0	—	—	—	—	—	1.0	0
	12		12mm	258	10.1	320	12.6	0.24	1.5	½
		20	20mm	175	6.9	245	9.6	0.40	1.9	1
12		20	32mm	175	5.03	210	8.3	0.64	2.7	1½
		36	36mm	119	4.7	205	8.1	0.72	3.0	1½
12		36	48mm	102	4.01	200	8	0.96	3.8	2
	20	36	56mm	95	3.7	201	7.9	1.12	4.5	2
12	20	36	68mm	87	3.4	205	8.1	1.36	5.6	2½

* This chart is designed as a guide only. Exact data will vary slightly, depending on the lens-camera combination used. F best results keep your lens focused at infinity.
** This column shows the factor by which the camera shutter speed must be multiplied if you wish to leave the lens f-stop set as indicated by your meter or exposure chart.
*** This column shows the number of f-stops to open your lens if you wish to leave the camera shutter speed set as indicated by your meter or exposure chart.

In general, if you are using an SLR camera with TTL metering, your meter will take into account the loss of light due to the lens-to-film distance. This would be true for automatic bellows or automatic extension tubes. An automatic bellows unit or automatic extension tubes usually provide a link-up with the light meter in the camera and allow for automatic diaphragm control.

With almost all bellows units, a magnification scale is engraved on the rail supporting the bellows. Extension tubes usually come with a chart that supplies the magnification ratio based upon the lens being used with the various combinations of tubes. The chart above lists the combinations of tubes using lengths of 12mm, 20mm, and 36mm with a 50mm lens.

If you are using a bellows unit with an engraved image ratio, the chart at the right will provide the necessary exposure factor increase.

It is possible to estimate image ratios by comparing the size of the subject with the size of the image on either the long or short side of the picture frame (negative size). For example, the format of a 35mm negative is 24mm × 36mm (1 × 1 ½), so the short side is one inch. If a one-inch portion of your subject fills approximately one-third of the size, the ratio is 1:3. If a one-inch subject fills half the short side of the

Exposure Factor Table for Image Magnification

Image Ratio[1]	Exposure Factor[2]	f-stop Adjustment	Image Ratio	Exposure Factor	f-stop Adjustment
0.1	1.21	¼	4.8	33.64	5
0.2	1.44	½	5.0	36.00	5¼
0.3	1.69	¾	5.2	38.44	5¼
0.4	1.96	1	5.4	40.96	5¼
0.5	2.25	1¼	5.5	42.25	5½
0.6	2.56	1¼	5.6	43.56	5½
0.7	2.89	1½	5.8	46.24	5½
0.8	3.24	1¾	6.0	49.00	5½
0.9	3.61	1¾	6.2	51.84	5¾
1.0	4.00	2	6.4	54.76	5¾
1.2	4.84	2¼	6.5	56.25	5¾
1.4	5.76	2½	6.6	57.76	5¾
1.5	6.25	2¾	6.8	60.84	6
1.6	6.76	2¾	7.0	64.00	6
1.8	7.84	3	7.2	67.24	6
2.0	9.00	3¼	7.4	70.56	6¼
2.2	10.24	3¼	7.5	72.25	6¼
2.4	11.56	3½	7.6	73.96	6¼
2.5	12.25	3½	7.8	77.44	6¼
2.6	12.96	3¾	8.0	81.00	6¼
2.8	14.44	3¾	8.2	84.64	6½
3.0	16.00	4	8.4	88.36	6½
3.2	17.64	4¼	8.5	90.25	6½
3.4	19.36	4¼	8.6	92.16	6½
3.5	20.25	4¼	8.8	96.04	6½
3.6	21.16	4½	9.0	100.00	6¾
3.8	23.04	4½	9.2	104.04	6¾
4.0	25.00	4¾	9.4	108.16	6¾
4.2	27.04	4¾	9.5	110.25	6¾
4.4	29.16	4¾	9.6	112.36	6¾
4.5	30.25	5	9.8	116.64	6¾
4.6	31.36	5	10.0	121.00	7

Notes: 1. Image ratios are variously expressed as 0.9X, 9/10, and 9:10, all being equivalent.

1/10X is expressed as 0.1. It may also be expressed as 1:10. Similarly 0.5 equals 1/2X equals 1:2; 1X equals 1:1; 2.6X equals 2.6:1; etc.

2. Shutter speed compensations may be made by multiplying the nominal shutter speed by the shutter factor.

frame, the ratio is 1:2. In other words, if a half-inch high portion of the subject fills this side (high side) the ratio is 2:1 or 2X. The exposure factor can then roughly be calculated as below:

Image Ratio	Exposure Factor
1:8 to 1:4	1.5X (½ f-stop)
1:3 to 1:2	2X (1 f-stop)
2:3 to 3:4	3X (1½ f-stop)
1:1	4X (2 f-stops)

As mentioned in earlier chapters, depth of field generally advances ⅓ while it recedes ⅔ from the plane of focus. This, however, does not apply for photographs taken at high magnifications. In extreme magnifications, depth of field extends equally in front of, and behind, the plane of focus. The other problem with depth of field is its virtual nonexistence at high magnification. For example, at a 1:1 image ratio with an aperture of f/11 the depth of field is about 4/100 inch (1mm). Thus, as long as the image size remains the same, depth of field will be the same, regardless of the type of lens being used. Using a small f-stop to compensate for shallow depth of field will produce only very small changes.

Another problem often encountered is lighting the subject. All lighting arrangements for extreme close-up photography must be designed to produce an intensity of light in an extremely small area. This is so the exposure times are kept as short as possible, and that the image projected on the focusing screen of the camera is as bright as possible. Because the subjects are small, lights can be brought in quite close to the subject. However, because the lens-to-subject distance is also close, the lens protrusion may interfere with the placement of the light. This is why many photographers prefer the use of a short telephoto (such as a 100mm), since the subject-to-lens distance is increased while maintaining the same magnification ratio.

Two problems may occur if the lights are throwing off too much heat; the photographer will be uncomfortable, and there may be possible harm to the subject under the lights. For example, if you are photographing a small insect, using two 500 watt photo-reflector bulbs, you may find your subject a burnt mass of dead animal life. One way to avoid this is to use an electronic flash or a ring-light. Another possibility is to use one or two small light sources, such as a high-intensity desk lamp.

Filters and Light

Although panchromatic black and white films are sensitive to every color in the spectrum, they are more sensitive to certain colors. Because of this, filters are used to lighten or darken objects of a particular color.

A filter is usually a colored piece of glass placed in front of the lens. Usually, it screws into the diameter of the lens. Like any filter, it absorbs what is not wanted and passes or transmits what is. Understanding filters requires some knowledge of the behavior of light. Light is radiant energy that travels in waves. In visible light, the longest wave is red, the middle length, green, and the shortest, violet. With those wavelength groups are the various hues of red, orange, yellow, green, and blue. If there are no waves, then there is no light. When all the waves travel together, the result is white light.

Figure 9-12

The interaction between the earth and sky was heightened by the use of a red filter on the camera. The red filter darkens blues and greens, while making reds lighter. The shadows are darker because they have more blue light than sunlit areas.

Rock Forms, Pt. Lobos, Robert Johnson.

In a way, any object we see as having color is acting like a filter, because it is absorbing part of the white light. The color we see is part of the light that is reflected back to us. For example, a red apple seems to be red because it absorbs blue and green light and reflects red light. Yellow paper looks yellow because it absorbs blue light and reflects both green and red. The table that follows lists certain types of color as they appear in white light and color of lights that are absorbed.

Color Seen in White Light	Colors of Light Absorbed
red	blue-green
green	red and blue
blue	red and green
yellow (red plus green)	blue
magenta (red-blue)	green
cyan (blue-green)	red
black	red, green, blue
white	none
gray	equal portions of red, green, blue

Understanding filters is easy once you understand the principle that they always *subtract* some of the light from a scene. Remember that you are dealing with negative-positive relationships. When a filter absorbs a color, the area of that color will appear to be lighter in the negative. However, when the negative is printed, that area will appear darker.

Figure 9-13

No filter used.   Red filter used.   Green filter used.

Filters for Black and White Film

Filters used for black and white pictures can be classified into three groups: (1) correction filters, (2) contrast filters, and (3) haze filters. Although panchromatic film is sensitive to all the colors of the spectrum, it is not sensitive to all of them equally. For instance, blue sky generally prints out very light in tone. To compensate, use a *correction filter*, which changes the tonal response of the film so that all colors are photographed at about the same as the eye originally saw. The most popular correction filter is a medium yellow (No. 8). A photograph, taken with a yellow filter, reproduces the clouds as they were seen in their relative brightness values. They appear "bolder" because the blue sky appears darker. The yellow filter absorbed some blue light, thereby making blue appear darker in the print.

A *contrast filter* can either increase or decrease (lighten or darken) the contrast between colors. To make an object appear lighter than it is, use a filter that is the same color as the object. To make an object appear darker than it really is, use a filter that will absorb the color of the object. For example, compare the three black and white photographs of a red flower against green leaves in Figure 9.13. In the first photograph, no filter was used. Both the red and the green appear about the same tone of gray. In the second photograph, a red filter was used. A red filter transmits red light and absorbs green. Therefore, the red flower appears light while the color green, which was absorbed by the red filter, appears dark in the print.

In the third photograph, a green filter was used. Green absorbs red light, thereby making the red flower appear darker than the green leaves. Keep in mind that a filter transmits its own color, making that color lighter. To make a color darker, use a filter that will absorb that color. Refer to the chart to help you select an appropriate filter.

Contrast filters are also used to darken the sky. The medium yellow (No. 8) filter is used to reproduce the sky as your eye would see it if you saw things in black and white instead of color. The deep yellow (No. 15) filter will make the sky seem even darker than it normally appears. For even more dramatic effects, a medium red (No. 25) filter can be used. A deep red filter (No. 29) will make the sky almost black.

When you photograph distant landscapes or take pictures from high altitudes, the pictures tend to lose a certain amount of detail. This is caused by the bluish atmospheric haze of very small particles of dust and water vapor. The haze scatters ultraviolet light to which film is very sensitive although the eye cannot see it. To reduce atmospheric haze when photographing, you can use *haze* or *UV filters* to filter out some of the ultraviolet light. The amount of haze also is decreased with

Figure 9-14   With polarizing filter.   Without polarizing filter.

the following filters: No. 8 (medium yellow), No. 15 (deep yellow), No. 25 (medium red), and No. 29 (deep red).

One filter that can be used to eliminate both haze and reflections or glare is the *polarizing filter*. As light is reflected from nonmetallic surfaces, it is polarized. That is, the light vibrates in only one direction. The light from the sky is polarized because it is reflected from nonmetallic particles in the atmosphere. The polarized filter removes glare by stopping the path of the polarized light. The angle of the light source is important when a polarizing filter is used. To get the maximum effect from such a filter, the angle at which you view the reflecting light must be equal to the angle at which the light strikes the reflecting surface. For instance, if the sun were at approximately a 60° angle from a scene, you would get maximum effect with the polarizing filter if you took the picture at a 60° angle.

Most polarizing filters are double-threaded. One thread screws into the camera, while the other one lets you rotate the filter. If the camera you are using is not a single-lens reflex or view camera, place the filter to your eye and rotate it until the desired effect is obtained. Note that a marking on the filter, usually a white dot, is used to indicate the position of the rotation. After the desired effect is produced, place the filter on the camera, making sure that the marking is in the same position. If you have a single-lens reflex camera, you can see the effect by looking through the viewfinder as you rotate the screen.

The polarizing filter is useful when photographing water, glass, or most other shiny surfaces. The reflections are eliminated, allowing more detail to be seen. Polarizing filters are also used with color films. They not only reduce or eliminate reflections, but they also make colors richer and more saturated.

In recent years, the designation system used to identify filters was changed from a letter code (such as K2 for medium yellow, A for red), to a numerical code. Below is a conversion chart showing both designations.

Filter Designations for Black and White Films

Current Designations	Old Designations
No. 6	K1
No. 8	K2
No. 11	X1
No. 15	G
No. 25	A
No. 47	C5
No. 58	B

Filter Types for Black and White Film

Filter Type	Color or Description	f-stop Increase		Applications
		Daylight	Tungsten	
No. 8 (K2)	Yellow	1	2/3	Renders an accurate tonal reproduction of daylight scenes as the eye sees them. Natural rendition of contrast between sky and clouds, flowers and foliage.
No. 11 (X1)	Light Green	2	2	In portraiture, renders an exact tonal reproduction of skin as the eye sees it. Increases contrast between blue sky and clouds; lightens foliage, darkens flowers and earth.
No. 15 (G)	Deep Yellow	1-2/3	1	Emphasizes contrast between blue sky and clouds, increases brilliance of sunsets. Special applications in architectural photography.
No. 25 (A)	Red	3	2-1/3	Darkens blue sky to create spectacular contrast with clouds, simulates moonlight scenes in daytime with slight underexposure, increases contrast between foliage and flowers. Special applications in document copying and with infrared film.

A. Yellow filter used.   B. Red filter used.

Figure 9-15   Filter Factors

Because filters absorb some light, you must increase the exposure to compensate. The number by which you multiply the exposure is called the filter factor. If a filter has a factor of 2, you must either double your exposure time by decreasing your shutter speed by one speed or open the lens one stop. For example, a yellow filter has a factor of 2. If the proper reading without the filter were 1/250 at f/8, then with the filter it would be either 1/125 at f/8 or 1/250 at f/5.6. Generally, it is best to change the f-number rather than the shutter speed, unless depth of field is a concern. If two filters are used together, the filter factors are added together. For example, the filter factor of a yellow (No. 8) is 2. The filter factor of a polarizer is 3. If both are used together, your factor will be 5. You should then multiply your exposure time by 5 or increase your lens opening by 2-⅓ stops.

Filter factors depend on the type of light and the film being used. The deep yellow (No. 15) filter has a daylight factor of 2.5 with Kodak Plus-X film. However, when you use artificial light (tungsten), like that from photofloods, the factor is 1.5. The reason for this is that sunlight contains more ultraviolet and blue light than photofloods. Therefore, outdoors in sunlight the deep yellow filter absorbs a greater portion of the light, and additional exposure is needed to compensate for this loss.

If your camera has a TTL metering system, you generally do not have to figure filter factors. Most meters of this type read the light after it has already passed through the filter; the exposure reading is therefore based on the reduced amount of light.

However, with some filters, usually the polarizer, the built-in meter may require some correction in the film speed. Therefore, if in doubt, check with your instruction book or write the manufacturer.

Figure 9-16

A red filter makes the blue sky darker and more dramatic.

The following chart is a conversion table that lists the equivalent *f*-stop corrections for filter factors.

Filter Factor	*f*-stop	Filter Factor	*f*-stop
1.2	+1/3	5	+2-1/3
1.5	+2/3	6	+2-2/3
2	+1	8	+3
2.5	+1-1/3	10	+3-1/3
3	+1-2/3	12	+3-2/3
4	+2	16	+4

Filters for Color Film

The quality and color of natural light varies throughout the day and the year. Color film, unlike black and white film, reacts to these changes in light and has to be balanced to result in photographs that look natural. Most color films are balanced for daylight and electronic flash. Daylight-balanced films give a natural looking rendition of the subject when shot with flash or under normal daylight conditions. In the early morning or late afternoon, the color of the light is warmer, and so is the cast to the film, which normally looks appropriate because of the time of day. Overcast, stormy days and shots taken in shade tend to be bluer because the light is less warm when there is no direct sunlight. These results seem to be natural atmospheric effects and often can be used to our creative advantage. However, to make a picture that has "accurate" color, it is often necessary to use filters when shooting to make the color of light more accurate. Some color correction can be done when making color prints, but it is always best to try and get the right result when shooting the picture.

Artificial lights, other than electronic flash, pose other problems. Tungsten or incandescent lights, which include photofloods, quartz lights, many street lights, and ordinary household light bulbs, look natural to our eyes but are very warm in color and cause daylight color films to produce images that have an overall yellow-orange cast. To correct the color, a filter can be used—in this case an 80A conversion filter, or you can use tungsten balanced film, which has extra blue built into it to counteract the warm color cast of the tungsten light. Since most of us do not ordinarily have tungsten film available, filtering is the easier and more immediate solution. Fluorescent lights and mercury vapor lights also cause color problems because they emit light that results in a green cast, regardless of which type of color film is used. A 30 magenta filter or a special fluorescent filter is needed to provide a natural-looking result.

The color of light is measured in Kelvin degrees or temperature, the system that was introduced in Chapter 7. Because of the great range in the color of both natural and artificial light, it is not possible to achieve a critically accurate color rendition without the use of filters. For a first step, it is always wise to select the kind of film that most nearly matches the light source you expect to encounter. Next, it is important to have access to the appropriate color correction filters. These filters can also be used to alter or artificially enhance a color cast to make color photographs that are more distinctive. Accurate color can be important,

Figure 9-17
Medium format 2¼ camera with bellows type filter holder and lens shade.

but ultimately what is most important is whether the color is effective in generating the right feeling and response to the subject. Accurate color does not always do that.

There are three types of color filters for balancing the Kelvin temperature of the light with the kind of film being used. These are *conversion filters, light-balancing filters,* and *color-compensating filters.* All three are available in different sizes in gelatin squares or as plastic or glass filters. The gelatin squares can be held in front of the lens, taped to the lens or placed in a filter holder that attaches to the front of the lens. Plastic or glass filters can either be used in a filter holder or be of a type that screws onto the front of your lens. When purchasing a filter holder system or a screw-on type filter, be sure to get a size that is large enough to work on your largest diameter lens. Step-down rings can be purchased to adapt the filters for smaller diameter lenses, but you cannot use a small diameter filter on a larger lens without getting vignetting. The following chart shows which filters to use to produce major changes in Kelvin temperatures. Notice that in all cases, you will have to increase exposure. Filters, after all, cut down on the amount of light striking the film. When color balance is critical, check the values given in this chart with test exposures.

To Convert	Use Filter Number	Filter Color	Exposure Increase in Stops
3200 K to Daylight 5500 K	80A	Blue	2
3400 K to Daylight 5500 K	80B	Blue	1⅔
3800 K to Daylight 5500 K*	80C	Blue	1
4200 K to Daylight 5500 K**	80D	Blue	⅓
Daylight 5500 K to 3800 K	85C	Amber	⅓
Dayligth 5500 K to 3400 K	85	Amber	⅔
Daylight 5500 K to 3200 K	85B	Amber	⅔

* Clear flashbulbs, such as M2, 5, and 25.   ** Clear flashbulbs, such as AG-1, M3 and M5.

Light-Balancing Filters

To produce moderate shifts in color temperature, you can use light-balancing filters. Suppose, for example, you were shooting Type A film and using 3200K photographic lights. To raise the temperature 200K and absorb some red light, you could use an 82A filter.

In the chart that follows, notice that there are times when more than one filter can be used. Again, when color balance is critical, check the values in this chart with test exposures. To accurately determine

To Obtain 3200 K From:	To Obtain 3400 K From:	Use Filter Number	Filter Color	Exposure Increase in Stops
2490 K	2610 K	82C + 82C		1⅓
2570 K	2700 K	82C + 82B		1⅓
2650 K	2780 K	82C + 82A		1
2720 K	2870 K	82C + 82	Bluish	1
2800 K	2950 K	82C		⅔
2900 K	3060 K	82B		⅔
3000 K	3180 K	82A		⅓
3100 K	3290 K	82		⅛
3200 K	3400 K	No Filter Necessary	—	—
3300 K	3510 K	81		⅓
3400 K	3630 K	81A		⅓
3500 K	3740 K	81B	Yellowish	⅓
3600 K	3850 K	81C		⅓
3700 K	3970 K	81D		⅔
3850 K	4140 K	81EF		⅔

the color temperature, color temperature meters are available. This feature is often included with many of the better electronic hand-held exposure meters.

Color-Compensating Filters

For small changes in color balance or for special effects, color-compensating filters are used. They differ from light-balancing filters in that they absorb only one of the colors of the spectrum, allowing the other two to pass through. If, for example, you were shooting in the early morning sunlight with Daylight film, your images might be too red. To absorb some of this warm light, you might use a color-compensating filter—say, a CC10B. Then you should have accurate color rendition. (The letters CC stand for color compensating; 10 stands for a density of 0.10 to red light; and B for blue, the color of the filter.)

The following chart shows the CC filters available and the colors they absorb:

Yellow (Absorbs Blue)	Exposure Increase in Stops*	Magenta (Absorbs Green)	Exposure Increase in Stops*	Cyan (Absorbs Red)	Exposure Increase in Stops*
CC025Y	—	CC025M	—	CC025C	—
CC05Y	—	CC05M	$\frac{1}{3}$	CC05C	$\frac{1}{3}$
CC075Y	—	CC075M	$\frac{1}{3}$	CC075C	$\frac{1}{3}$
CC10Y	—	CC10M	$\frac{1}{3}$	CC10C	$\frac{1}{3}$
CC20Y	$\frac{1}{3}$	CC20M	$\frac{1}{3}$	CC20C	$\frac{1}{3}$
CC30Y	$\frac{1}{3}$	CC30M	$\frac{2}{3}$	CC30C	$\frac{2}{3}$
CC40Y	$\frac{1}{3}$	CC40M	$\frac{2}{3}$	CC40C	$\frac{2}{3}$
CC50Y	$\frac{1}{3}$	CC50M	$\frac{2}{3}$	CC50C	1

Red (Absorbs Blue and Green)	Exposure Increase in Stops*	Green (Absorbs Blue and Red)	Exposure Increase in Stops*	Blue (Absorbs Red and Green)	Exposure Increase in Stops*
CC025R	—	CC025G	—	CC025B	—
CC05R	$\frac{1}{3}$	CC05G	$\frac{1}{3}$	CC05B	$\frac{1}{3}$
CC075R	$\frac{1}{3}$	CC075G	$\frac{1}{3}$	CC075B	$\frac{1}{3}$
CC10R	$\frac{1}{3}$	CC10G	$\frac{1}{3}$	CC10B	$\frac{1}{3}$
CC20R	$\frac{1}{3}$	CC20G	$\frac{1}{3}$	CC20B	$\frac{2}{3}$
CC30R	$\frac{2}{3}$	CC30G	$\frac{2}{3}$	CC30B	$\frac{2}{3}$
CC40R	$\frac{2}{3}$	CC40G	$\frac{2}{3}$	CC40B	1
CC50R	1	CC50G	1	CC50B	$1\frac{1}{3}$

More information on color film's reaction to light and the nature of color correction is provided in Chapter 18.

Specialty Filters

There are many types of specialty filters available. Some are gimmicky, but others provide important creative alternatives for photographers.

Neutral Density Filters

Neutral density filters are used to reduce the amount of light that enters the camera. Because they are neutral in color, they only affect exposure and not color. They come in densities that will reduce light by 1, 2, or 3 *f*-stops. The most common use is to reduce the amount of light reaching the film so that a longer exposure can be used for panning or blurred motion effects or for attaining minimum depth of field in a bright sunlit situation. Too often, a combination of film speed and bright light makes it impossible to stop the lens down enough to use really long exposures, or to go to a fast enough shutter speed to get minimum depth of field with a wide open aperture. That is when a neutral density filter is useful.

Diffusion Filters

There are many different types of diffusion filters, some of which are extremely expensive. They are used most often in portraiture to soften features, blemishes, and wrinkles. Some have a frosted appearance, but others are made from a net-type mesh. Hair spray applied lightly onto a piece of glass can be an inexpensive alternative.

Diffusion filters come in different degrees, from subtle to very obvious. They can also be stacked together to provide even more diffusion. Better diffusion filters affect mainly the highlights without diffusing the overall definition of the image. Subtle diffusion is used in most professional portraiture, whether the subject is male or female. Extensive diffusion causes the highlights and white areas of the picture to have a glowing aura-like effect.

Center spot diffusion filters soften the outer portions of the picture while maintaining an unmodified central image. There are also *graduated* diffusion filters that will diffuse half of the picture with a graduated transition to the nondiffused portion of the image.

Star, Prism, Diffraction, and Multiple Image Filters

Star filters give maximum effect when a very bright light or specular highlight is in contrast with dark surroundings. Depending upon the filter and the desired effect, you can get stars with between two and sixteen rays. An inexpensive alternative is to use a small aperture and shoot with a piece of window screen held in front of the lens. This will result in a four-ray star. If you use two pieces of window screen with the meshes offset, you will get an eight-ray star.

Prism filters abstract a subject by creating a separation of yellow, red, and blue colors around the fringes of the subject. Generally contrasty subjects produce the most dramatic effects.

Diffraction filters have millions of prismatic grooves that decompose the light like a prism, but without abstracting the overall image. Bright light sources will have prismatic color affects radiating from them with the shape determined by the filter.

Multiple Image filters break the image up into five to seven images that repeat within the picture frame. These can be used in combination with other filters for very unusual effects.

Color Effects

There are a wide array of filters designed to give special color effects. *Graduated* and *center spot* filters are also made with colors added to give an altered color to part of the picture. Another option to consider is referred to as "Color Back Filters" by some manufacturers. These involve using flash and two color filters that are opposites on the color wheel. The colors, such as yellow and blue, are referred to as complimentary colors. When using the color back approach, you get a natural color, flash-lit foreground, and an artificially colored background.

For example, a yellow filter over the camera lens will cause the whole image to go yellow. However, if you place a complimentary blue filter over a flash head and light a person or object in the foreground of the picture with the blue filtered flash, the blue light from the flash will neutralize the yellow color from the part of the picture illuminated by the flash. The rest of the picture will have a yellow cast.

Vignetting

Vignetting is done in the camera as well as in the darkroom. It is an easy means of getting rid of a distracting background, but it is used

Figure 9-18

Vignetting equipment.

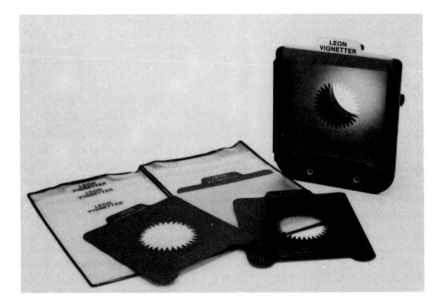

most often for traditional portraiture. It involves masking or blocking a portion of the picture during exposure, to produce a white or black area that softly fades into the subject. Vignetting filters have sawtooth edges that provide a subtle blending into the image. To ensure a soft transition to the subject, the filter needs to be in a filter holder that places it away from direct contact with the lens. An opaque black vignetter will produce a black vignette of the image, and a transparent diffused vignetter will produce a white vignette. The most common approach is to do a circular vignette, but many portrait photographers vignette only the lower part of the picture to hide hands and legs and provide a subtle transition to the main part of the picture.

Mask Effects

Filter holder systems provide other opportunities for creating distinctive images. Double masks, which allow you to blend two photographs into one, can be made or bought to fit your filter holder. This technique will allow you to create images that are similar to the morphing effects done with digital imaging and in the movies. To achieve such results, you will need a camera that will allow you to do multiple exposures. Most 35mm SLRs do not allow for this option. However, some allow you to cock the shutter without advancing the film, by depressing the rewind film release button before cocking the shutter. If that does not

Figure 9-19

A. A vignetter was used on the camera to darken the lower portion of this image.

Vignetting examples, Richard Grannis.

B. This image was vignetted to lighten the lower portion of this image.

work, load the film into the camera and mark it at the edge of the cassette before you close the back of the camera. Then shoot the whole role, keeping track of your multiple exposure needs for each frame. Once shot, rewind the film, leaving the leader out so that you can reload it. When you reload it, make sure that the mark you made lines up exactly as before. Then reclose the camera and reexpose each frame for the double masking effect.

A simple *double mask* technique is to have two half-frame masks, one that blocks the top half of the picture and one that blocks the bottom half. They need to be placed in a filter holder that will position the masks an inch or more from the lens. The distance from the lens, along with a wide-open to medium aperture will cause the edge of the mask to blur and gradually fade into the other side. The size of the aperture will vary, depending upon the focal length of the lens and the distance the mask is from the lens. Some experimentation will be necessary. To get a "twins" effect, have the camera on a tripod, and have a person stand on the left side of the scene. Shoot the first exposure with the mask that blocks the right side of the picture. Then have the subject move to the right side of the scene and use the mask that blocks the left side of the picture. If done right, the background will blend together seamlessly and you will have the same person appear on either side of the picture.

A *center spot* double mask can also be used to put a different image into the center of the picture. For the outer image, have a mask in place that consists of an opaque circle in the center of a clear filter. After making that exposure, switch masks, and put a mask in place that is clear in the center and blocks the outer previously exposed area. Make your second exposure for the center of the picture. The two will blend together.

Masks can also be used to isolate your subject with a black frame around them. The shape is up to you. All you have to do is cut it out of an opaque material so that it fits into the filter holder. The edges of the shape will be soft with a wide aperture and sharper with a small aperture.

Half frame double masks.

Center spot double masks.

Chapter 10

Black and White Film Development

Work of sight is done. Now do heart work on the pictures within you.

—Rainer Maria Rilke
Poet

Figure 10-1

Untitled, Michael Weschler.

After you have taken a picture, curiosity alone should make you want to see it, even if you suspect it is overexposed, underexposed, or out of focus. Developing the film is the halfway point between taking the picture and making a print. It makes visible and permanent the latent image that is recorded on the emulsion of the film. Film development is a chemical process involving a series of steps. It is the least creative and most critical part of the photographic process. If the camera exposure was correct and the film development procedure is followed carefully, you will produce a good quality negative, which is necessary to make a good quality photographic print. However, if the film developing procedure is handled incorrectly or carelessly, the quality of your photographs may be severely compromised, or they may even be unprintable.

The equipment and procedures used for film development are similar with both black and white and color films. This chapter will cover equipment, basic processing procedures, and several advanced techniques for processing black and white negatives and transparencies. In addition, the care and handling of processed film will be discussed.

Most professional labs process film, regardless of the type, in machines. When maintained properly, machines provide the upmost in consistency, but they are not practical for the small volume needs of the individual photographer. Fortunately, the film processing procedure is relatively easy and can be done in a kitchen or bathroom.

There are two methods for hand processing photographic films: one uses open trays of chemicals, and the other uses a light-safe tank. The tray method is generally used for sheet film and must be done in total darkness. The tank method is more efficient for roll films and can be done in the light once the film has been loaded onto a developing reel and placed into the developing tank.

Roll Film Processing Equipment

The Developing Tank

The basic developing tank consists of the tank itself, the lid (which makes it lighttight), and the reels (which holds and separates the film). Tanks are made of either plastic or stainless steel. Plastic tanks are less expensive and easier to use, but less durable. Stainless steel tanks have reels that are more difficult to load, but they are more durable, use less chemicals, are easier to clean, and enable better agitation procedures

Figure 10-2

Roll film developing tanks and reels.

for more even development of the film. Most serious amateurs and professional photographers prefer the stainless steel tanks. The easiest tank to use is one made by Kinderman. It is stainless steel but has a rubber lid. Among the variety of stainless steel reels on the market, the easiest 35mm reel to use is the Pro Model by Tundra. It has two pins that stick up on the inside of the reel for the sprocket holes of the film to catch on when you start to load the film onto the reel. Should you opt for a plastic tank, be sure to get one that allows for a complete inversion of the tank without chemical leakage.

Thermometer

Because the temperature of the chemicals is critical and must be checked often, a good thermometer is very important. Good thermometers have a range from 30° to 120°F and measure chemicals accurately within one degree. Do not trust thermometers that come preshipped with some plastic tanks—they have been known to be off by as much as six degrees. A thin-stemmed metal dial-type thermometer is the easiest to read. A glass thermometer designed specifically for photographic use should also be fine. Try to use the same thermometer each time to ensure consistency because thermometers can vary in their readings.

Graduates and Mixing Implements

You will need plastic or glass graduates for measuring and mixing chemicals, plastic stirring rods, funnels, and possibly a plastic bucket for mixing larger quantities of chemicals. You may also want to have a pair of plastic gloves in order to avoid direct contact with the chemicals. Many of these items can be purchased at a grocery store or camera store. Make sure that you have at least one 32-to-64-ounce graduate and an 8-to-12-ounce graduate for measuring smaller quantities.

Storage Containers

Photographic chemicals are sensitive to air and light, so storage containers should be dark and kept filled to capacity. Dark brown glass or plastic storage bottles provide the best protection. Be sure to use the right size container. For example, do not use a one-gallon container to hold a quart of solution because the excess air causes oxidation and shortens the life of the chemical. Also, all containers should be clean and free of chemical contamination before use. Always use the same type of chemical in the same bottle. Do not intermix chemicals and bottles or you will get contamination. For quantities over one gallon, professionals use plastic or stainless steel tanks with floating lids, which minimize oxidation.

Timer

Since the chemical steps must be timed, select a timer that measures both seconds and minutes. A luminous dial is also helpful for tray processing or other darkroom applications. However, a clock or watch with a second hand is adequate for roll film processing in light-safe tanks.

Accessories

You will also need a bottle opener, scissors, squeegee, film clips or clothespins, sponge, towel and film storage sleeves. The bottle opener is used to open 35mm film cassettes in the dark. The scissors are also used in the dark, to cut the leader off the film prior to loading it onto the reel. A squeegee, photo sponge, film wipe tissue, or a clean chamois is used to wipe the excess liquid off the film prior to drying. Film clips or clothes pins are used to hang the film from the top and placed on the bottom to keep the roll from curling while drying. Naturally the sponge and towel come in handy for cleanup and help keep at least one hand dry. Once dry, the film is cut into strips and put into clear plastic film sleeves for protection and preservation.

The Tank Development Method

Developing tanks come in a variety of sizes. Stainless steel tanks can be purchased to hold one roll of 35mm film or as many as twelve rolls. Since film processing is a methodical and time-consuming procedure, most photographers prefer to develop more than one roll of film at a time. The most practical size to purchase initially is a 16-ounce tank that holds two 35mm reels or one reel of 120 film. Plastic tanks have adjustable reels that can hold any size film from 35mm to 120. Consequently, a 16-ounce plastic tank can do only one roll of 35mm film at a time, while a stainless steel tank will process two 35mm reels in the same amount of chemistry.

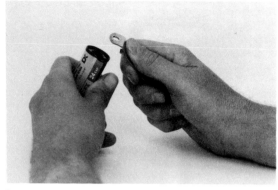

A.

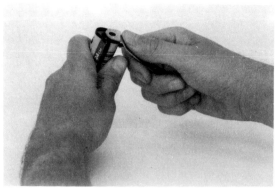

B.

Figure 10-3

Prepare to open the film cassette.
In total darkness, use the round
end of a bottle opener to pry off the
top of the flat end of the film
cassette. Then, while still in the
dark, use a pair of scissors to cut off
the film leader. The next step is
to load the film onto the developing reel.

C.

120 roll film

Tape
Film
Opaque paper

Preparing the Film for Loading on the Reel

The next steps must be carried out in total darkness. Make sure that the reel and tank are clean and dry before attempting to load the film into it. Otherwise, you may get contamination, streaking, or water spots on the film. To load 35mm film, first remove the film from it's cassette container using a bottle opener to pry off the flange on the flat end of the cassette. Be careful not to cut yourself on the metal edges of the cassette. Once the flange is removed from the flat end of the cassette, push up on the plastic end that sticks out of the bottom of the cassette. This makes it easy to grab the film and pull it out of the cassette without unraveling it. Once the film is out of the cassette, keep the film on the spool and use scissors to cut off the tapered leader (beginning) of the film.

With roll films (sizes 828, 127, 620, 120), you need only break the seal to load it. The film curls as it is separated from the paper backing, and it should be handled only by the edges to prevent fingerprints on

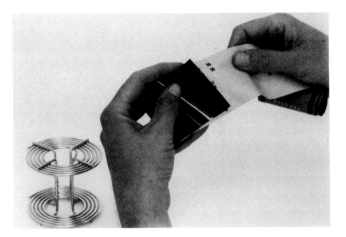

Figure 10-4

Separating 120 film from the paper backing.

The paper backing on 120 film needs to be removed before you can load the film onto a reel. The backing paper is attached with tape. In the dark, separate the backing paper from the film, removing it and the tape.

the emulsion. The film is attached to the paper with tape, which must be removed before the film is loaded into the reel. Otherwise it will prevent proper loading.

If 126 film is used, remove the film by gripping the cartridge with both hands and twisting it until it breaks in half. The film is in the larger of the two chambers. After the chamber is open, separate the film from the paper backing in the same manner as roll film.

Loading Stainless Steel Reels

Loading stainless steel reels is slightly more difficult to get used to than loading plastic reels. Before trying to load exposed film, get a scrap roll of film and practice loading the reel in the daylight as well as in the dark. Once you are comfortable with your ability to load the scrap roll onto the reel, load your exposed film. Just remember, every time you hear a crackling or crinkling sound, you are putting a crimp in the film that will show up in a print as a crescent moon shape. Also, if the film is not loaded evenly, it will touch and not develop in the spots that are in contact. Consequently, it is important to learn how to load the film properly to avoid losing your shots.

The Procedure

Begin by holding the reel in your left hand and make sure the outside end of the spiraling metal points toward your right hand. In your right hand, hold the rolled up film so that the end is pointing towards the

Figure 10-5

The procedure for loading 35mm is as follows: In the dark, hold the reel so that the outer end of the metal spiral is pointing towards the end of the film. This ensures that the film will be loaded in the direction that goes "with" the spirals of the reel.

A.

The film is the same thickness as the reel and must be curled slightly during loading. Curl the film with your thumb and forefinger and insert the end of the film into the center of the reel. With clip-type reels, insert the end of the film under the clip. With reels that have prongs on either side to catch onto the sprocket holes, insert the end of the film into the open "slot" above the metal bar with the prongs. Once the film is inserted, pull down on the film, and it will catch onto the sprocket holes.

B.

Once the film is attached to the center of the reel, hold your thumb and forefinger adjacent to the edges of the reel so that the tips touch the outer edge of the reel. This control ensures that you will maintain even pressure on the edges of the film and get a uniform curl to the film as you load it onto the reel. If you allow your hand to move away from the reel, maintaining a uniform and evenly balanced curl becomes harder, and the film will be more likely to "buckle" during loading. Next, gently turn the reel with your left hand while letting the "curled" film glide through your right thumb and forefinger until the whole roll is loaded onto the reel.

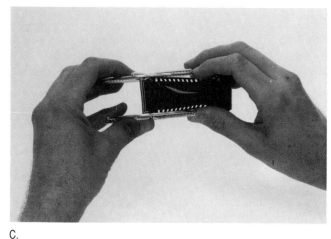

C.

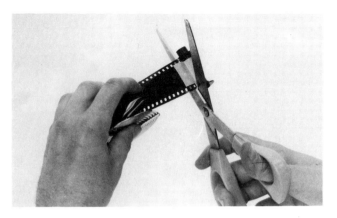

After the film is loaded onto the reel, either tear the tape or use scissors to cut the end of the film and free it from the film cassette's center spool.

D.

Finally, place the loaded reel into the film developing tank. If it is a double tank, either do two rolls at once, or place an empty reel on top as a spacer. Put the lid on, and you can turn on the lights for the chemical part of the processing.

E.

reel in your left hand. (Do the opposite if you're a "lefty.") If the outside end of the metal spiral and the end of the film are pointing towards each other, then the film will be loaded on properly.

Note that the film has the same width as the reel. Once loaded, the film rests in between the spirals so that it doesn't touch itself. To get it loaded properly, the film has to be curled to fit in between the spirals. Hold the rolled-up film in the palm of your right hand with the end curled between your thumb and forefinger. Then insert the curled end of the film into the center of the reel. The Tundra Pro Model has two pins on each side of the center of the reel, which correspond to the position of the sprocket holes of the 35mm film. When the curled end of the film is pushed into the center of the reel, just above the two pins, and then pulled down, the sprocket holes will catch on the pins and hold the film in place. Then position your right hand so that your

thumb and forefinger, which are curling the film, are resting against the outer edges of the reel. This will enable you to keep the curl constant as you turn the reel with your left hand to wind the film onto the reel. As you wind the film onto the reel, let it glide through your right thumb and forefinger. If you hold it too tightly, the film may "jump" a spiral and go on unevenly. Work on a flat surface for extra stability.

Other brands of stainless steel reels have clips in the center of the reel to hold the leading end of the film in place. Generally these are harder to use than the Tundra Pro Model with the pins. But this design is the same type that you have to use with 120 film and other types of roll film, which lack sprocket holes. To use the clip design, insert the curled film in the

Figure 10-6

Loading 120 film onto reels.

Reels for 120 film are larger than 35mm reels and normally have a clip to hold the film in place. In total darkness, unroll the film and separate the paper from the film by tearing the tape from the film. Insert the end of the film into the clip at the center of the reel. Keep your right thumb and forefinger touching the edges of the reel to curl the film consistently as you turn the reel with your left hand. Once the film is loaded onto the reel, tuck the end of the film into place on the reel, place the reel into the developing tank, and put the lighttight lid on the tank. Then you can turn on the lights to do the chemical steps.

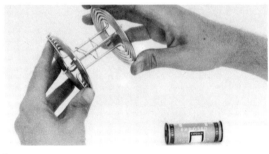

A.

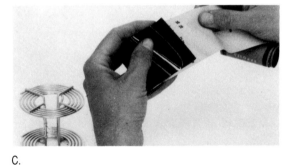

C.

B.

D.

same manner as before, only push it into the clip so that it is securely held in place while you roll the rest of the film onto the reel.

Don't be afraid to touch the outside surface (base side) of the film as you load it onto the reel. Naturally, make sure your hands are clean and free of oil and grease. The emulsion is on the inside surface of the film and should not be touched.

As you are loading the film on the reel, stop and try moving the film back and forth. If it has some play, and moves slightly, then it is going on properly. But if the film seems taunt and has no movement, then it has buckled and gone on unevenly. Uneven loading will cause the film to touch itself and it will not develop in those areas. To alleviate this problem, carefully unroll the film until you are beyond the buckled area and the film has some back-and-forth play on the reel. Then you can load it onto the reel again. If the sprocket holes are bent or broken from problems you had getting it onto the reel, it may be necessary to start over by loading the film from the other end. Once the edges are damaged, it is very hard to get the film onto the reel.

Initially, loading the film onto the reels is frustrating and hard to get used to, but once you get the knack, you will find the loading quick and easy to do. When the film is properly loaded, place it into the tank and put the lighttight lid on the tank. If you are developing one roll of 35mm film in a 16-ounce stainless steel tank that holds two 35mm reels, put the loaded reel on the bottom and an empty reel on the top as a spacer. This positioning will prevent overagitation during the development process. Now you can turn on the lights and do the rest of the process in the light.

Loading Plastic Reels

Plastic reels vary, although most function in a similar manner. They load from the outer part of the reel where small ball bearings catch onto the edges of the film and hold it in place as you advance it onto the reel.

After the film has been removed from its container, insert three or four inches of the film into the reel by pushing it carefully through the entrance slots (the thickest part of the flanges). As you do this, follow the natural curl of the film so that the emulsion side will face toward the core of the reel and be less likely to be scratched and will be easier to load. Take hold of the edges of the reel. With the plastic tank, you should hold the flange (the movable section) in the left hand and the other flange in the right hand. Twist the movable flange forward (away from you) as far as it will go; then twist it back (towards you) as far as it will go. Continue this procedure until the film is wound on the reel.

Figure 10-7

Loading plastic reels.

Plastic reels can be adjusted for either 35mm or 120 film. The film loading procedure is the same for both. First, in total darkness, cut the corners off at the end of the film. This will make it easier to load the film onto the reel.

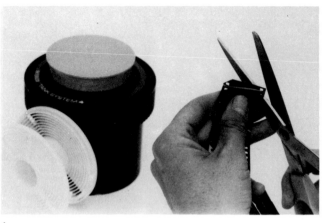

A.

Insert the end of the film into the slot at the outer edge of the reel. Make sure that the two sides of the reel are lined up so that the openings for the slot are opposite each other. Push the film forward until the film catches onto the small ball bearings located on either side of the reel.

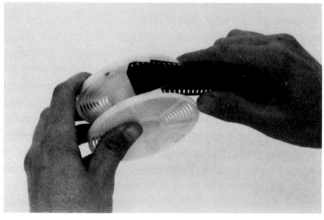

B.

Advance the film forward by a back-and-forth motion of the sides of the reel until the whole roll is loaded onto the reel. Then put the reel into the developing tank, put the lid into place, and turn on the lights to follow through with the chemical steps.

C.

If you are loading 35mm film, this action will stop when the spool reaches the entrance. Cut the film at the edge of the spool and continue winding it onto the reel. If you are using a plastic reel, you will need to use your thumb to push the film forward onto the reel. You can make sure that all the film is wound onto the reel by running your finger around the entrance slots. The edge of the film should be past the entrance.

If the film does not go onto the reel smoothly, do not force it, or you may mar the film permanently. Do not try to pull the film back through the film entrance. Instead, pull off the adjustable flange, remove the film, readjust the reel to the film size, and start again. After all the film is on the reel, place it into the tank, keeping the clear flange on top. Put the lid on the tank by turning it clockwise. The room light may now be turned on since the tank is lighttight.

The Chemicals

The chemicals needed to develop the latent image on film are similar to those used to bring out the latent images in pinhole photographs and photograms. They are (1) the developer, (2) the stop bath, and (3) the fixer, also called hypo. One thing to note: although the chemicals have the same functions, film processing chemicals are different from print processing chemicals.

Developer

The job of the developer is to convert the silver halides (which make up the latent image on the exposed emulsion) to blackened particles of silver that clump together during development to form a visible photographic image. Because the job of the developer is so complex, it contains a mixture of several chemicals. Chemical formulas of the developers on the market today vary. However, most of them contain (1) a solvent, (2) a reducer, (3) an activator, (4) a preservative, and (5) a restrainer. In most, the solvent is water because, in order to work, the other chemicals must be in solution. The reducer causes the actual chemical breakdown of the exposed silver salts. The activator in the developer does two things. First, it renders the developing solution alkaline rather than acidic; and second, it helps the water to soften the gelatin of the film so that the reducer can separate the exposed silver salts. The preservative agent in a developer reduces or retards the oxidizing (combining with air) of the reducers. Without it, reducing agents will deposit rust-colored stains on the film. The job of the restrainer is to control the action of the developing agents, which could attack the unexposed as well as the exposed silver grains, causing a chemical fog on the film.

Many different types of film developers are available. Some developers, such as Kodak D-76, Ilford ID-11, Ethol TEC, and UFG are considered general purpose developers and are used widely for many different types of film. Ideally, it is best to use one that is designed for the type of film you are using. Development times vary, based upon the type of developer, type of film, the dilution, and the temperature of the developer. Always check the data sheets of the film and the developer you are using to ensure that you use the proper time and temperature relationship.

Stop Bath

The next chemical used in film developing is the stop bath, which stops the action of the developer. Water is frequently used as a stop bath for roll-film users and an acidic acid mixture is commonly used with sheet-film development. A mixture of one ounce of a 28 percent acidic acid solution with 32 ounces of water makes a normal stop bath solution and ensures a total stop of all developer action. A plain water stop bath is discarded after use, but the acid stop bath is reusable. A working solution of an acid stop bath will last about a month when stored in a tightly sealed bottle and will treat about 20 rolls of film per quart. Indicator stop baths are available. These change color when the stop bath is exhausted. The stop bath has one other function—to preserve the life of the next chemical, the fixer.

Fixer

Often called *hypo*, fixer removes the unexposed silver deposits from the emulsion and makes the film light-safe and permanent. Use a fixer that contains a hardener, which makes the film emulsion more durable and less likely to be scratched. Fixer is reusable, and regular fixer treats around 25 rolls of film per quart and lasts about a month when stored in full, tightly stoppered bottles. Before reusing the fixer, it is best to test it with *hypo check*, an inexpensive testing solution. A few drops will stay clear when put into usable fixer but will turn milky white if the fixer is exhausted. Another testing method is to use a piece of exposed but unprocessed film, like the film leader that is cut off before you load 35mm film onto the developing reel. Place the piece of film partially into the fixer. If it begins to turn milky and clear within about 2 minutes, then the fixer is okay to reuse. However, if no change occurs, then the fixer should be discarded. *Regular fixer* takes 5 minutes to fix most films, while *rapid fixer* takes 2 to 4 minutes. Kodak T-Max films exhaust the fixer faster and need more time, so to be safe use 10 minutes with regular fixer and 5 minutes with rapid fixer.

Hypo Eliminator

A hypo eliminator is an optional solution, that is, unnecessary, but often used after the fixer to reduce the washing time by neutralizing the fixer. Several brands are available, including Kodak Hypo Clearing Agent and Heico Perma Wash.

Water

Tap water is generally used by most photographers for developing black and white and color films and prints. However, some water supplies contain dirt particles, chemical residues, and algae, which can cause problems. If you are concerned, especially when processing color materials, try using distilled or deionized water for mixing your chemicals. Tap water will work fine for the washing needs of film and prints, although some tap water contains dirt and mineral deposits that may dry into the surface of the emulsion. In this case, a filtering system may be necessary.

Wetting Agent

After the final wash, a wetting agent should be used to reduce the likelihood of streaks and water spots on the film. This is especially a concern if you have hard water. A popular product is Kodak Photo-Flo. A capful in 16 ounces of water will service many rolls of film. This can be used as a standing reusable solution or done in one shot for low volume needs and then discarded.

Mixing the Chemicals

Chemicals are packaged in liquid or powdered forms. Powdered chemicals are generally cheaper but must be mixed with water to make a *stock solution*. Stock solutions are usually the form for storing chemicals. Those chemicals that are packaged as liquids are usually premixed stock solutions. The benefit of premixed liquid stock solutions is convenience.

Most stock solutions must be diluted with water before use. The usable form of the chemical is called a *working solution*. Thus, the working solution is the final form of the chemical prior to use. In general, a stock solution stores for a longer period of time than a working solution. For the best results, always store liquid chemicals in dark, well-filled containers.

Always follow the manufacturer's instructions when mixing photographic chemicals. For example, a popular type of film developer in powdered form is Kodak D-76. The mixing directions read: "Start with 112 fluid ounces (3.32 liters) of water at 125°F (52°C)." If cold water were added instead of hot, the granules that form the developer would not dissolve completely in the water. The result would damage the negative.

Stock solutions of developer can be used in different ways, depending on the type and the brand. Some solutions must be diluted with water while others can be used straight or undiluted. Still others can be used either way to affect the result of the negative. For example, the Kodak developer D-76 can be used straight or can be further diluted with water at a ratio of one part developer to one part water (1:1). The resulting mixture, now the working solution, is called a one-shot solution, and after is it used, it must be discarded.

The ratio for mixing a stock solution to a working solution is important to understand. In the previous example D-76 was mixed 1:1—that is, one part stock solution to one part water. If directions call for mixing a stock solution 1:2 to make a working solution, it means mixing one part stock solution to two parts water. If we need 8 ounces of working solution and the ratio called for 1:3 dilution, we would add 2 ounces of stock solution to 6 ounces of water.

Photographic chemicals must be handled with care, so it is essential that you follow these general rules:

1. Always read labels and follow instructions carefully.
2. Store all chemicals and solutions safely.
3. Avoid skin contact with chemicals whenever possible. If possible, wear rubber gloves.
4. Maintain proper ventilation.
5. Always dispose of used chemicals safely.
6. Call a physician at once should any chemical be swallowed!

The Developing Process

The chemical sequence is as follows: developer, stop bath, and fixer. Then the film must be washed, preferably pretreating it with a hypo eliminator to reduce the washing time. Next the film is treated with a wetting agent, squeegeed, and hung to dry.

Rehearse these steps until you are familiar with them before actually developing a roll of film. The developing process is critical, and a methodical, well-timed approach is important to ensure smooth transitions from step to step.

Preliminary Steps

First, prepare the chemicals by pouring out the needed amounts and checking to make sure that none are exhausted.

Second, take the temperature of the developer and check your data sheets to determine the correct processing time for that film-developer-temperature combination. The recommended temperature for most developers is 68 degrees Fahrenheit, although anywhere between 65 to 75 degrees is usually acceptable. Most advanced photographers prefer to use the same temperature each time to ensure consistent results. A hot or cold water bath can be used to raise or lower the temperature of the developer.

Temperatures of the other chemicals, including the wash water, should be plus or minus 3 degrees to that of the developer. Subjecting the film to drastic changes in temperature can cause the silver particles to clump together, forming an obvious grain pattern. In some cases, drastic temperature changes cause *reticulation*—the physical cracking or wrinkling of the emulsion.

Developer

1. Set the timer for the developer, based upon the time/temperature chart for your film.
2. When you are ready, pour the developer into the tank while holding the tank at an angle to facilitate pouring by allowing the air to escape. Begin timing the developer once it is in the tank.

(list continued on page 222.)

Figure 10-8

Film processing is done in the light. First, pour the developer into a graduate. Be sure to pour the amount needed to fill your developing tank. Then take the developer's temperature to determine the developing time. Either go by a variable time-temperature chart or use a water bath to adjust the developer temperature to the standard 68 degrees, and use the time indicated for that temperature with your film.

A.

Set the timer for the appropriate developing time. Then, with the small center cap off the tank, begin pouring the developer into the tank. Hold the tank at an angle as you pour the chemistry in so that air can escape from the tank. It should take about 10 seconds to fill a normal two-reel 16-ounce tank.

B.

When the tank is full, immediately put the center lid onto the tank. Timing is critical because the film is starting to develop.

C.

D.

As soon as the center lid is in place, give the tank several sharp taps against the palm of your hand to dislodge air bubbles. Otherwise you might end up with *air bells* (light spots on negative film), which are dark circular shapes that float like unidentified flying objects on prints.

E.

Next, agitate the film continuously for 30 seconds, and then set the film down for 30 seconds. Next, agitate the film for 5 seconds and set the tank back down for another 30 seconds. Repeat with 5 seconds of agitation every 30 seconds for the remainder of development time.

F.

The agitation consists of an alternating inversion of the tank for each agitation period. Agitate the film by inverting it first to the right, twisting your wrist as you invert the tank. This will cause the chemistry to move up and down as well as sideways. Then do the same thing, inverting the tank to the left, twisting your wrist in the opposite direction. During a 5-second agitation period, you should be able to invert the tank once each direction. Be careful . . . over- or underagitation can cause uneven film development.

(continued)

During the last 10 seconds of the developing time, quickly pour the developer back into the bottle if it is reusable or dispose of it if it is a one-shot dilution. Immediately move on to the next step, which is the stop bath, and repeat the same procedure.

Pour the chemical into the tank, put the center lid in place, and agitate the film continuously for the first 30 seconds, using the alternating direction, inversion with a twist method. Then set the tank down and get the fixer ready. During the last 10 seconds of the stop bath, pour the stop bath down the drain.

Then pour the fixer into the tank and agitate the tank continuously, as before, for the first 30 seconds. Throughout the fixer time, repeat the same agitation procedure that was done for the developer—after the initial 30 seconds of continuous agitation, alternate by letting the tank sit for 30 seconds, with 5 seconds of agitation every 30 seconds.

After the fixer is poured back into its tank for reuse, take the lid off the tank. The film is now developed and light-safe. Wash the film by placing it under a faucet with a continuous stream of running water for a minimum of 10 minutes. Then immerse the washed film into Photo-Flo for 30 seconds, carefully take it off the reel, squeegee it to reduce water spots, and hang it in a dust-free place to dry.

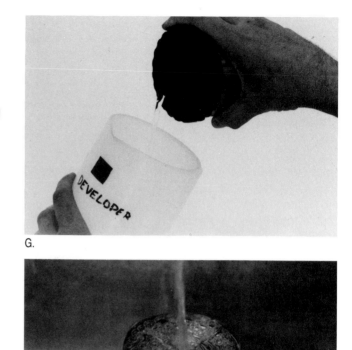

G.

H.

3.   Immediately, after the tank is full, with the cap in place on top of the tank, tap the bottom of the tank against the sink, counter, or your hand. Rapping the tank will release any air bubbles in the developing solution. Air bubbles cause problems because they can adhere to the emulsion, causing *air bells*, tiny clear spots on the negative.

4.   Agitate the tank continuously for the first 30 seconds of the development. Agitation is important and must be done methodically. Inconsistent agitation can cause uneven development as well as changes in contrast and grain structure. To agitate, invert the tank (turn it upside down) while simultaneously twisting your wrist to provide some sideways agitation. Then turn the tank

right side up and do the same inversion with a twist of the wrist in the opposite direction. Continuously repeat this procedure, alternating directions, and inverting the tank with a twist of the wrist for the first 30 seconds of the development time.

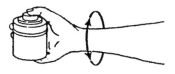

Inversion agitation.

For the remaining time in the developer, agitate the tank 5 seconds out of every 30 seconds. Be careful not to agitate too vigorously. Over agitation can cause problems. An appropriate speed would be to agitate the tank once in each direction for every 5-second agitation period. However, agitation requirements will vary from manufacturer to manufacturer, so it is always wise to check the instructions printed with the film or developer. For T-MAX films, provide initial agitation of 5 to 7 inversion cycles in 5 seconds; that is, extend your arm and vigorously twist your wrist 180 degrees as shown in the accompanying illustration. Then repeat this agitation procedure at 30-second intervals for the rest of the development time.

Many plastic tanks do not have caps on the top, so inversion agitation may not be possible. If a rod is provided with the tank, then agitate by gently turning the rod back and forth. Do not spin the rod like a screw because it will cause overagitation.

5. Prepare the needed amount of stop bath in between agitation cycles.
6. Pour the developer out of the tank approximately 15 seconds before the developing time ends. Use the last 10 to 15 seconds of each chemical step to pour out the chemical.

Stop Bath

1. Tilt the tank and pour the stop bath into the tank as soon as the developer is emptied.
2. Total time for the stop bath is 1 minute. Agitate continuously for the first 30 seconds.
3. In between the agitation and draining the tank, measure out the right amount of fixer to be prepared for the next step.
4. Drain the tank during the last 10 to 15 seconds.

Fixer

1. Tilt the tank and pour the fixer into the tank as soon as the stop bath is emptied.

2. Agitate the tank continuously for the first 30 seconds and for 5 seconds at each subsequent 30 second interval. Most regular fixers work in 5 to 10 minutes, whereas rapid fixers work in 2 to 4 minutes. Remember to allow more time for T-Max films. Check the data sheet for the film and chemicals you are using to determine the optimum time.
3. Pour fixer back into its bottle for reuse. The film is now light-safe, but it is best to finalize the processing before handling because the film is very delicate when wet.

Hypo Eliminator (optional)

1. After fixing, rinse the film in running water for 1 or 2 minutes.
2. Then pour in a hypo eliminator to help facilitate the washing process. Generally this takes about 2 minutes with most brands. Agitate continuously during the first 30 seconds and at 1 minute intervals after that.
3. Pour out the hypo eliminator.

Wash

1. Wash the film by allowing water to run directly into the center of the open developing tank. Keep the film on the reel and in the tank so that all parts are uniformly washed.
2. Empty out the water in the tank manually once a minute to ensure a complete change of water. The temperature of the water should be in the 65° to 75°F range.
3. Wash the film for approximately 15 minutes. If a hypo eliminator was used, wash for 5 minutes.

Wetting Agent

1. A capful of Kodak Photo-Flo can be added to the water already in the tank, or the film reel can be taken out of the tank and placed gently into a separate container of wetting agent.
2. Gently move the reel to make sure that the film is thoroughly coated by the wetting agent, but do not agitate like before.
3. Leave the film in the wetting agent for approximately 30 seconds.

Drying

1. Remove the film reel from the wetting agent.
2. Carefully remove the film from the reel and hang it securely with a film clip to dry in a dust-free place.
3. Squeegee the film to remove excess liquid before drying. For 35mm film use a photo sponge, chamois, or film wipe tissue. The sponge and chamois need to be immersed into the wetting agent and wrung out so that they are not dripping wet before using them to squeegee the film. A film-wipe tissue can be used dry. Fold it over several times and wrap it around both sides of the film at the top. Then gently grasp the tissue on either side of the film, taking care not to apply any pressure to the surface of the film, and slowly move the wipe down the strip of film. If you lose your grip and have to stop midway, it is best to resoak the film in the wetting agent and to begin over again. A similar method is used with the sponge and chamois. (A rubber squeegee works best for film that doesn't have sprocket holes. For sheet film, try using a nonflexible windshield wiper blade like those on antique cars.)
4. Once the film is squeegeed, attach a film clip or clothes pin to the bottom of the film to keep it from curling while drying.
5. After the film is dry, cut it into strips that are 5 or 6 frames long (depending on the film sleeve type) for 35mm and 4 frames for 120 film. Never cut the film into individual negatives because they are too hard to handle and are easily damaged. Store the strips in clear plastic film sleeves in a clean, dry place.

Sheet Film Processing

Large, individual sheets of film are used in view cameras. The developing procedure is basically the same as that for roll film, but because of their size, sheet films have to be processed in open trays or in special sheet film developing tanks and holders.

The Tray Method

The tray method is the simplest and least expensive way to process sheet film. Unfortunately, everything has to be done in complete darkness.

First, arrange three trays in a row. The trays should be one size larger than the size sheet film you need to process. Starting on the left, fill the first tray with developer, the second with stop bath, and the third with fixer. Pour about 1/2 inch of each chemical into the trays. Take the temperature of the developer to determine the length of the development time. After this is known, test the other two chemicals to make sure that they are within a plus or minus 3 degrees of the developer temperature. Set your timer (hopefully it has a luminous dial that glows in the dark), and you are ready to begin.

From this point on you will work in total darkness. When tray processing, most photographers prefer to process one sheet of film at a time, and this is certainly the best way to begin. Should you decide to develop more than one sheet at a time, you will need a larger volume of chemistry in each tray.

Take an exposed sheet of film out of its container and feel for the notched edge of the film. Hold the film in your right hand so that your right forefinger touches the notches, which means that the film is emulsion side up. Now completely immerse the film, emulsion up, into the developer tray. Immediately tap the film against the side of the developer tray to dislodge any air bubbles. Make sure that you always keep one hand dry. Then continuously, but gently, agitate the tray by subtly rocking it back and forth. The film will move from one side to the other as you rock the tray. It is important to keep the film from settling on the bottom of the tray. This could cause uneven development and make it hard to remove the film from the tray without scratching it.

During the last 10 seconds of the development time, lift the film out of the tray and allow the excess developer to drain into the tray. Then transfer the film to the stop bath and continue to provide continuous

Figure 10-9

Sheet film notches.

agitation. To ensure that the developer action is stopped, most photographers use an acid stop bath rather than water when they are developing sheet film. Keep the film in the stop bath for a minimum of 30 seconds, and then drain it for 10 seconds before transferring it to the fixer tray. Handle the film very carefully, touching only the edges, because it is very soft and can scratch very easily when wet. After the film has been in the fixer for several minutes, the room light can be turned on to let you view the negative. However, the film must remain in the fixer for the prescribed time, after which it should be handled as in the final steps of the tank method.

Once you are comfortable with tray processing, you may want to consider processing more than one sheet of film at a time. To do so you will need a larger quantity of chemistry to suspend the film in as your continuously interleave the sheets of film, one on top of the other, throughout the process. This takes practice and should be approached cautiously because it is very easy to damage the film when you are interleaving it.

To interleave sheet film, start with two to four sheets of film, all emulsion side up. Fan them out in your left hand so that you can easily grab them one at a time in the dark. Take the first sheet with your right hand and totally immerse it into the developer. Wait 5 seconds and immerse the second sheet of film. Continue that procedure until all of the film is in the tray. Then grasp the first sheet from the bottom and delicately pull it out to the side and up onto the top of the stack. Gently push it down and immediately reach to get the next sheet from the bottom and lift it to the top. Follow this procedure continuously and uniformly throughout the processing time. Variations in handling and timing can affect the density, contrast, and evenness of your film.

Tank Development for Sheet Film

There are special tanks and film holders designed for developing more than one sheet of film at a time. The tanks are either plastic or stainless steel and come in a variety of sizes to accommodate different quantities and sizes of sheet film. Inexpensive plastic tanks for developing 4x5-inch sheet film will hold between 8 and 12 sheets of film. Stainless steel film holders are used to hold the individual sheets of film. These are available for all common sizes of sheet film.

Four processing tanks are needed: one each for developer, stop bath, fixer, and loaded film holders awaiting processing. The tanks need to be filled so that the chemistry goes over the top of the immersed film holders. Everything needs to be prepared before going dark. The most important thing to remember is to check the developer temperature and determine the development time.

When ready, turn out the lights and load the film into the film holders. These have a lip on the top that flips up, allowing you to slip the film into slots on the sides and the bottom of the film holder. The lips should all be flipped up and the holders all facing the same direction before you turn out the lights. Once the sheet of film is in place, close the top lip to secure it in the holder. Place the loaded holder into the holding tank or another support device and go on to the others. Don't set the loaded holders in a stack on the table. The film is delicate, and it is too easy to scratch it when you are trying to pick up a stack of loose holders in the dark.

Once all of the film holders are loaded, grasp them in the center and remove them from the holding tank. This action will cause them to fan out at the bottom. Push them together with your other hand, start the timer, and immerse them into the developing tank. Immediately

A.

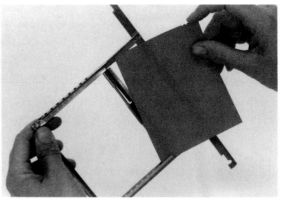

B.

C.

Figure 10-10

Loading sheet film into film holder: Make sure the rack is clean and dry before using it. Open the lid at the top of the rack before going dark. In darkness, remove the film from its lighttight container and find the notches. Holding the film with the notches in your right hand, slip it into the slots on either side of the film rack. Then close the lid at the top of the reel to hold the film in place and begin processing. To save time, process more than one sheet of film at a time. Some small tanks will hold as many as 10 film racks at one time.

tap them up and down several times against the top of the tank to dislodge air bubbles. Then begin agitating continuously for the first 30 seconds and 5 seconds each subsequent 30 seconds for the duration of each processing step.

As always, agitation is extremely important. The following procedure is generally recommended when you are developing sheet film in holders. The top of the film holders sticks out on either side of the processing tanks. With your palms up, put your hands under the part that sticks out on both sides of the tank. Make sure that you have the ends of all of the holders resting in the palms of your hands. Then lift all of the film holders simultaneously, tilting them to the right side of the tank at a 45-degree angle. They should be raised high enough so that they come out of the liquid and rest, momentarily, on the opposite side of the tank. Do not let them slip out of the tank completely or it will be hard to get them back in. The right side of the holders must remain within the confines of the tank. Once the holders are up, immerse

A.

Figure 10-11

The developing tank needs to be filled so that the chemistry is well above the top of the film rack, but no closer than 3/4-inch from the top of the tank. Immerse the film rack into the tank by holding the rack at the top. If you are doing more than one rack, grasp a bottom corner with your other hand to keep the film racks from spreading too wide at the bottom to fit into the tank. Ease the film into the tank and immediately tap it against the top of the tank several times to dislodge air bubbles.

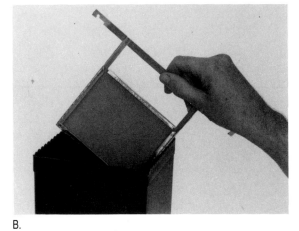

B.

Then agitate the film continuously for 30 seconds by raising it out of the tank at a 45-degree angle so that the bottom of the rack is high enough to be out of the chemistry, but with the edge of the rack resting against the side of the tank. Then lower the rack back into the tank and repeat the procedure by agitating it in the opposite direction. Continue to alternate directions continuously during each agitation period. After the initial 30 seconds of continuous agitation, agitate once each direction every 30 seconds for the duration of each chemical step. Be careful not to raise the film all the way out of the tank; it will be dark, and it may be hard to get the film back into the tank, especially if you are doing more than one rack.

them back into the tank and then reverse the direction. It should take approximately 5 seconds to agitate the film once in each direction.

The rest of the procedure is carried out in a similar manner as for roll film and tray processing. It is best to leave the film in the holders throughout the wash and wetting agent steps. A fifth tank can be used to wash the film in, but it is best to use a wash tank that has small holes in the bottom so the chemical residue drains out the bottom as well as the top. To dry sheet film, remove each sheet from the holder one at a time, and suspend it by a corner from a film clip. When the film is secured, take a rubber squeegee and gently squeegee both sides to alleviate water spots. Then dry the film in a clean, dust-free environment.

Care of Processed Film

Film, regardless of the type, is very delicate. It can be wrinkled, crinkled, and scratched very easily. Scratches on film will appear as black or white marks on a print. To avoid scratches, it is best to handle the film as little as possible. Only handle the edges, for this will also help avoid fingerprints, which are hard to get off and show up in an enlargement. After the film is dry, roll film should be cut into strips and put into clear archival polypropylene or polyethylene film sleeves, which are available at most camera stores. Archival film sleeves are also available for sheet films. The sleeves enable you to handle your film while keeping them free of dust, scratches, and fingerprints. Processed film should be stored in a clean, cool, and dry location. Archival handling and storage of films will be addressed in Chapter 20.

Evaluating Processed Film

Exposure Problems

Once the film is dry, it is time to evaluate your results. To evaluate black and white and color negatives, first look at the overall density. If you can easily see detail in the light and dark areas of your film, then it should be printable. But if your negatives are "dense" or dark, it means that they received too much light and are *overexposed*. Any negatives that are light or "thin" did not receive enough light and are *underexposed*. With positive-image transparency films such as 35mm slides, the opposite is true. Overexposed transparency film is too light, but too dark when underexposed. Slight over- and underexposure does not mean that the film is unprintable. It means that you will have to work harder in the darkroom to end up with what will normally be a compromise result.

If your negative film is completely clear, it indicates that your film was not exposed or else not developed. Check the edges of the film. If the film was not exposed, you will be able to see the manufacturer information and frame numbers along the edge. This means that the film was not loaded into the camera properly, and it never advanced. However, if the manufacturer and frame numbers are missing, this means that the film was not developed. This could be due to exhausted developer or using the fixer first, instead of the developer. If this error occurred with transparency film, it would be completely black.

Negative film that is so dark that you cannot make out any details of the image is radically overexposed, provided there is still a separation between frames and the edges of the film are clear. If the edges of the film and the separation between the frames are dark, it indicates that the film was *fogged*. Fogging is the result of unwanted exposure of the film to light. This can occur from opening the camera back before rewinding the film, by exposing it to light during the processing, or by some other oversight. Once the film is fogged, it is normally unusable.

Your film may reveal other problems that are not processing errors. Fuzzy shapes and clear areas that interfere with the picture may occur because something, such as your finger or the camera strap, covered a portion of the lens when you took the picture. Those with 35mm SLRs may encounter a situation where about a third of each image is missing (the film is clear). This is due to improper flash synchronization. Dark streaks and hexagonal shapes on the film are usually the result of lens flare, which occurs when the camera is pointed directly toward bright lights or the sun.

Processing Problems

If all the steps in the process of development are followed precisely, and if your film was exposed correctly, the result should be a high quality negative or positive that will produce a high quality print. However, mistakes can happen. The following are some of the common problems that occur with film development.

Static Marks
These are lightening-like lines that are caused by static electricity when film is unrolled or rewound too quickly in low humidity.

Figure 10-12

Crescent moons and scratches
from careless film handling.

Crescent Moons

A common problem that occurs when loading roll film onto developing reels is a buckling of the film that causes permanent crescent-shaped creases in the film. This results in dark crescent shapes on the film that appear as light crescent shapes in a print. They are generally caused by not curling the film properly when loading it onto the reel.

Cinch Marks

Cinch marks are vertical parallel lines on the emulsion. They occur from winding the film too tight on the reel or forgetting to press the rewind button on an SLR camera and forcefully rewinding the film into its cassette.

Milky Blotches

Irregular beige or gray-colored blotches that obliterate portions of your film are actually areas of film that are undeveloped and unfixed because

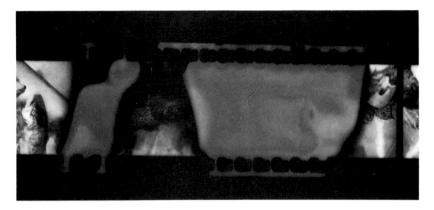

Figure 10-13
Milky blotches.

of improper film loading onto the developing reel. The film needs to be curled as it is put onto the reel so that it rests in between the metal spirals and does not touch itself. If the film is not put on properly, it may buckle and end up touching another portion of itself. Such sections stick together when they get wet and the chemicals can't get in between them.

Air Bells

Air bells are round, nearly clear spots on the film that print as dark spots. They are caused by air bubbles adhering to the surface of the film during the initial stages of development. At the start of the development, sharply tap the film tank or holder against your hand, a table, or the sink to dislodge the air bubbles and alleviate the problem.

Figure 10-14
Air bells.

Figure 10-15

Surge marks.

Agitation and Surge Marks

The purpose of agitation is to move the chemical solution during development so that waste materials are removed and fresh chemistry reaches the emulsion. If the film is not agitated enough, the film will lose contrast and be underdeveloped. If it is agitated too much, the film will gain contrast and be overdeveloped, which is especially evident along the edges of the film. If the agitation is uneven, it can result in blotchy, mottled, uneven development that is very noticeable in pictures containing clear blue skies.

Surge marks occur in between the sprocket holes of 35mm film because of excessive agitation. The developer rushes between the sprocket holes, overdeveloping those areas, while giving less development to the areas under the sprocket holes because they hold back the developer. The result is alternating light and dark areas along the edges of your film. This also occurs along the edges of sheet film that was processed in film hangers, because the excessive agitation causes the developer to "surge" through the holes along the edge of the hanger while being held back between the holes. A methodical, medium-paced agitation procedure that is neither too slow nor too fast will avoid these problems.

Fixer Problems

If you notice that your film has a milky appearance after is has been fixed, then the fixer was either contaminated or exhausted, and your film must be refixed to be light-safe and permanent. This appearance could also be caused by not allowing for enough fixing time. Remember that Kodak T-Max films take more fixing time than most other films. Extending the fixing time beyond what is required can also cause problems because the fixer will start to attack the parts of the image that you want to keep.

Water Spots

Most water spots are caused by hard water leaving residue on the surface of the film when it is drying. Use a wetting agent and squeegee the film before drying to help prevent water spots. Liquid film cleaner and a Q-tip can be used to remove water spots from dry film. To avoid scratching, apply the film cleaner with light pressure. Repeated applications are normally necessary to make the water spot dissolve.

Washing

If the film is not washed and dried properly, two things may go wrong. First, the film may start to discolor and fade in time because some of the fixer is still acting upon it. Second, the film may end up with spots

Figure 10-16
Water spots.

on it. Wash and dry your film carefully and thoroughly. There are no shortcuts in film processing.

Surface Dust

Normal surface dust can be easily removed with a brush, antistatic cloth, or air spray. When dust has adhered to wet film and dried to the surface, it is hard—sometimes impossible—to remove. Try using repeated applications of film cleaner to get it off. The best bet is to avoid the problem by making sure that no dust gets on the film while it is drying.

Manipulation of Contrast

A good negative is essential for a good print. A well-exposed and well-developed negative prints easily, and a poorly exposed or poorly developed negative is difficult to print. Generally, normal film exposure and normal film development produce a printable negative. However, sometimes altering film exposure or development time yields an even better negative.

Contrast is the comparison of tonal values in a negative. Tonal value, or tonal range, is the range of grays in the negative. Thus, contrast refers to the tonal range between highlights and shadow areas. High-contrast subjects have very dark shadows and very bright highlights, such as happens on bright, sunny days. A normally exposed and normally developed negative of a subject taken on a sunny day will have high contrast.

Low-contrast subjects are gray and lack either the very dark shadows or very bright highlights of high-contrast subjects. Lack of contrast often results from cloudy or overcast days. A normally exposed and normally developed negative taken with this type of light will be low in contrast.

Shadow areas of a negative are controlled by the exposure, the amount of light that reaches the film. Highlight areas are also affected by exposure but are controlled primarily by the developing time. Shadows represent areas of little exposure. Keep in mind that dark parts of a subject reflect less light back to the film than bright parts of a subject.

Consequently, shadow areas form much faster on the negative during development than do the highlights. When development begins, all of the values on the film start developing equally. But the shadows, which received the least amount of light, are finished first, while the middle values and highlights continue to develop. During the final stages of the development, the only values on the film that are being actively affected by the developer are the highlight values.

Figure 10-17
Underexposure caused a silhouette effect.

For example, if the normal developing time for a roll of film is 10 minutes, then the shadow areas will form in about half of that time. The other 5 minutes of development primarily influences the highlights. Thus, the longer the development time, the denser the highlights.

Because shadows are determined by exposure, they are not affected a great deal by development time. Therefore, if the film is developed for 15 minutes instead of 10, the highlights rather than the shadows will become denser. This increased development time means a change in the contrast, or the differences between the highlight and shadow densities. Thus, the longer the development time, the greater the contrast of the negative.

Conversely, if the developing time is shortened to 7 minutes instead of 10, the highlight areas become less dense. Since the shadow density

would remain unchanged, the difference between the highlight and shadow density is reduced, and the overall contrast of the negative is decreased. In other words, the shorter the film development time, the lower the contrast of the negative.

Negative contrast can thus be controlled by changing the time the film is in the developer. More time increases the contrast, and less time decreases the contrast. Negative contrast can be altered even more by changing both film exposure and film development. In general, to decrease contrast, overexpose and underdevelop the film. To increase contrast, underexpose and overdevelop the film.

To decrease contrast, a general formula is to overexpose by 100 percent (one *f*-stop) and underdevelop by 20 percent the recommended time. If you are dealing with extreme contrast, try overexposing by two stops and underdeveloping by 40 percent.

To increase contrast, the general formula is to underexpose by one *f*-stop and overdevelop by 50 percent. With extreme cases, try underexposing by two stops and overdeveloping by 100 percent.

Overexposing and underdeveloping are useful when photographing on bright, sunny days. The shadow areas of the subject tend to be quite dark and the highlights quite bright. Thus, overexposing and underdeveloping decrease the contrast. For example, a meter reading made on this type of day may read *f*/6 at 1/500. To overexpose by one stop, use *f*/11 at 1/500 or *f*/16 at 1/250. In the development stage, it is necessary to decrease the highlight density, so underdevelop the film. If the normal development time is 10 minutes, underdevelop by 20 percent and use 8 minutes instead.

Underexposure and overdevelopment are useful when photographing on cloudy or overcast days. This lighting is low in contrast, with an overall gray quality that reveals little or no bright or dark areas. To increase the lack of contrast, underexpose and overdevelop. For example, a meter reading on this type of day may read *f*/5.6 at 1/125. To underexpose by one stop use *f*/8 at 1/125 or *f*/5.6 at 1/250 instead.

To increase the highlight density, overdevelop the film. If normal developing time is 8 minutes, overdevelop by 50 percent and use 12 minutes instead.

These procedures for contrast control (overexposure and underdevelopment to reduce contrast, underexposure and overdevelopment to increase contrast) are the basis of the *Zone System*, which is discussed in more detail in Chapter 19. Remember: If you are using roll film, you will have to alter the exposure/development contrast relationship for the whole roll of film. Sheet film users have an advantage because they can alter the contrast of individual sheets of film. This type of contrast manipulation works best with black and white films, whereas other

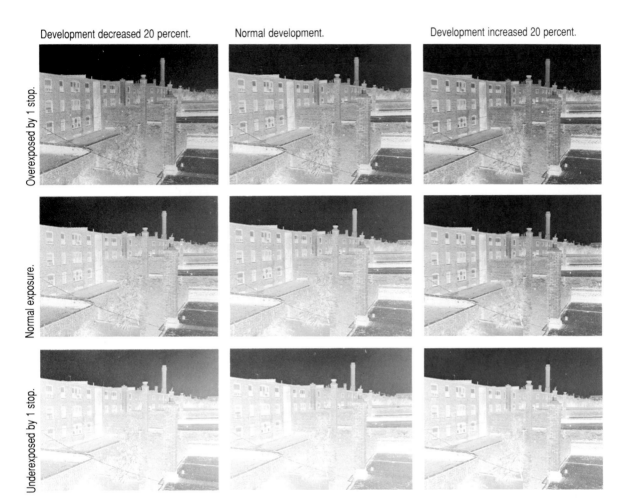

Development decreased 20 percent.   Normal development.   Development increased 20 percent.

Overexposed by 1 stop.

Normal exposure.

Underexposed by 1 stop.

contrast-control methods should be employed with color films. Refer to Chapter 14 on advanced color printmaking. With black and white transparency films, the contrast-control relationships would be opposite of that described for negative films.

Figure 10-18

These negatives show the results of changing the camera exposure and the time of development. The negative in the center received normal exposure and normal development.

Temperature Control

A major factor that affects film density is temperature. The rate of development changes with the temperature of the developer. The developer works faster at higher temperatures and slower at lower temperatures. In other words, warm developers require shorter developing times. Cold developers require longer developing times. For example, a negative being developed in a certain developer may require 10 minutes at 68°F. If, however, the temperature is raised to 75°F, the time would be cut down to 8 minutes. If the time is not adjusted, the result would be an overdeveloped negative.

The time-temperature relationships vary with different black and white film and developer combinations. Color films, discussed in Chapter 12, must be developed at the recommended temperature and no adjustments should be made if you expect normal results. Use an accurate thermometer to measure the temperature of the developer, and make sure that all of the other chemicals are within a plus or minus 3 degree range. Most developers work best at 68°F. Always check the film-developer data sheet to see whether any changes have been made regarding the developing times.

The chart at the right lists the time-temperature adjustments for D-76 developer and some of the more common black and white films by Ilford and Kodak. For other films and developers, check the manufacturers' current recommendations. Please note that this chart is meant to be a reference to the time-temperature relationships and that you should always check the current data for the film and developer combination you are using before relying on this as a guide. D-76 by Kodak is one of the most common and widely used film developers. The chart indicates the time-temperature relationships for using D-76 full strength and diluted 1:1 with water.

Push and Pull Processing

When shooting circumstances do not permit normal exposures because the light is too low or too intense, or if you incorrectly set the film ISO on your exposure meter, you can still salvage your shots by adjusting the film developing time. Underexposed film can be saved by *pushing*, or increasing the development time, whereas, overexposed film can be salvaged by *pulling*, or reducing the development time.

Suppose a situation arises containing the following elements: You are taking pictures at an indoor sporting event such as a basketball game. The film in the camera is ISO 400. A light meter reading was made. The correct exposure would have to be 1/60 at *f*/2. The lens on your camera will not open up any further than *f*/2, but you need to shoot a faster shutter speed to avoid a subject movement that would create a blur. In this case, you would "push" the film or shoot it at a higher ISO rating than is recommended. By changing the ISO, you are

Time-Temperature Adjustment Chart for D-76 Developer

KODAK FILM	Dilution	65°F 18°C	68°F 20°C	70°F 21°C	72°F 22°C	75°F 24°C
Plus-X (125 ISO)	Full Strength	7	6	5.5	5	4.5
	1:1	8	7	6	5	4.5
Tri-X Pan (400 ISO)	Full Strength	10	8	7	6	5
	1:1	13	11	10	9	8
Tri-X Professional (320 ISO)	Full Strength	9	8	7.5	7	6
Verichrome Pan (125 ISO)	Full Strength	8	7	5.5	5	4.5
	1.1	11	9	8	7	6
High Speed INFRARED 2481	Full Strength	NR	14	12	11	10
T-MAX 100 Professional	Full Strength	11.5	10	9	8	6.5
	1:1	14.5	12	11	10	8.5
T-MAX 100 EI 200	Full Strength	10.5	9	8	7	6
T-MAX 100 EI 400	Full Strength	13	11	9.75	8.5	7.5
T-MAX 400 Professional	Full Strength	10	9	8	7.5	6.5
	1:1	14.5	12.5	11	10	9
T-MAX 400 EI 800	Full Strength	9	8	7	6.5	5.5
T-MAX 400 EI 1600	Full Strength	12	10.5	9	8.5	7
T-MAX 3200 EI 1600	Full Strength	NR	NR	10.5	9.5	8.5
T-MAX 3200 EI 3200	Full Strength	NR	NR	13.5	12	11
T-MAX 3200 EI 6400	Full Strength	NR	NR	16	NR	12.5

ILFORD FILM		65°F 18°C	68°F 20°C	70°F 21°C	72°F 22°C	75°F 24°C
PAN-F (ISO 50)	Full Strength	7	6	5.5	5	4.5
	1:1	10	8.5	7.5	6.5	5.5
FP4 PLUS (ISO 125)	Full Strength	6.5	5.5	5	4.5	4
	1:1	9.5	8.5	7.5	6.5	5.5
HP 5 PLUS (ISO 400)	Full Strength	9	7.5	7	6.5	6
	1:1	13	11	10	9	7.5
HP 5 PLUS (ISO 800)	Full Strength	11	9.5	8.5	7.5	6.5
	1:1	16	13	12	11	9
400 DELTA (ISO 400)	Full Strength	7	6	5.5	5	4.5
	1:1	10.5	9	8	7	6

Caution: Times are intended as a guide only. Times shorter than 5 minutes risk uneven development. If you *presoak* your film with water, remember to *add 30 seconds* to D-76.

consistently underexposing by the same amount an entire roll of film. Thus, a roll or sheet of film with a normal ISO of 400 could be taken at an ISO 800, thereby underexposing the film by one stop. It would then be necessary to increase the developing time by push processing.

When you push process film, you are overdeveloping it to compensate for the underexposure. The result will be a printable image, but without the same range of detail as normally exposed and processed film would have. As you have already learned, overdeveloping an underexposed negative will not increase the amount of detail in the shadow areas. It will, however, increase the overall density and, most notably, the highlights. Thus, the contrast will be increased, and the grain will be more apparent.

Pulling or reducing the development time is done to compensate for overexposure. It will also reduce contrast, since a reduction in development time will reduce the density of the middle and highlight values and have minimal effect on the shadow detail.

The following chart is intended as a guide only and applies to both color and black and white films. It is recommended that you run your own tests to determine the best time for you.

The Snip Test

If you're uncertain as to whether your film was properly exposed, a snip test may be the answer. In the dark, cut several inches of exposed film off your roll and develop it normally. You will have to sacrifice several frames from your roll of film, but it is worth the effort if you save the rest of the roll.

Chart of Processing Adjustments: Pushing and Pulling Development Time*

Film ASA	Film Exposure	Change in Developer Time
1600	2 stops underexposed	Increase by 75%
1000	1 1/3 stops underexposed	Increase by 50%
800	1 stop underexposed	Increase by 35%
400	Normal	Use normal time
200	1 stop overexposed	Decrease by 35%
100	2 stops overexposed	Decrease by 50%

* Based on 400 ASA film.

After processing the snip, evaluate the film and determine whether you need to alter the processing time. If it is over- or underexposed, use the preceding chart as a guide for altering the processing.

Developing Black and White Transparencies

Several types of black and white transparency films are available, most of which take special processing. Polaroid makes several varieties that come with a chemistry packet and can be processed by hand with the Polaroid Auto Processor. Agfa recently introduced Scala 200, an excellent black and white transparency film, but it needs special machine processing that is only offered by a handful of labs throughout the country. For those who want to do their own processing with existing darkroom equipment, the Kodak Direct Positive Film Developing Outfit is the best alternative.

This "outfit" is designed for use with Kodak T-MAX 100 Professional Film, which produces excellent fine grain, continuous tone transparencies, and Technical Pan film, which produces high contrast transparencies. The chemistry consists of four chemicals and has a storage life for unused solutions of 8 to 10 weeks, whereas partially used solutions last 6 to 8 weeks. Up to 12 rolls of 36-exposure 35mm film can be processed in a 1-quart outfit. To process the maximum number of rolls, you must extend the processing time of the first developer and redeveloper to compensate for the number of rolls previously processed. Be sure to read the directions that come with the Direct Positive Film Developing Outfit carefully and adhere to them. Agitation and variations in time and temperature will cause you to get inconsistent results.

Chapter 11

Basic Black and White Printmaking

I know few things in the range of science more surprising than the gradual appearance of the picture on the blank sheet.

—William Henry Fox Talbot,
Inventor of the negative positive process

Figure 11-1
The darkroom provides a creative extension for the photographer, who is enabled to add another level of feeling beyond the mechanics of the camera.

Untitled, Sandy Lewis.

For the photographer, making a print is the climax of the creative process that begins with the decision to take a picture. Many photographers enjoy printing as much or more than, the shooting of their images. The print is the final result. It is the ultimate expression of the photographer's vision. Photographic printmaking is highly subjective and enables the photographer to interpret each image creatively. The hands-on involvement and the potential for technical refinement and manipulation beguile many photographers.

A knowledgeable photographic printmaker can correct for shortcomings in the shooting by, for example, emphasizing composition by eliminating part of the image, altering the contrast, subduing unwanted light areas, or making other areas lighter. In the safelight illumination of a

Figure 11-2

The dignified, yet delicate feeling in this full frame photograph was enhanced in printing by means of contrast control and subtle burning in of the landscape. The black border contains and sets off the image. A filed-out negative carrier allowed the clear area surrounding the negative to print as a black border.

Untitled, Chad Lipman.

darkroom, the photographer can make a print that can communicate, motivate, and stimulate the viewer to respond to the essence of the idea initially recorded by the camera.

The chemical process for black and white printmaking is essentially the same as for black and white film development. The enlarger is the photographer's primary tool for transforming the film image, through interpretation, to a finished enlargement. A *contact print* or *proof sheet* transforms the negatives from a roll of film into a recognizable positive form. From the contact print, negatives are selected for enlargement. Enlarging the negative can increase the beauty of the image, or just magnify its deficiencies. Unlike machine printing, hand enlarging gives the photographer control of the results and the potential to raise the quality of the photograph to an artistic level.

The Equipment

Black and white printmaking requires more equipment and materials than film developing. Among those tools are the enlarger, enlarging lens, easel, enlarging timer, processing trays, print tongs, safelights, brush, air spray, print washer, print dyer, print squeegee, and glass. Most of this equipment is also used for color printmaking.

Enlarger

An enlarger is basically a camera in reverse. Rather than absorbing light, the enlarger projects it. The purpose of the enlarger is to increase the size of the film image that is being projected. Thus, from a very small negative, prints can be made to 8×10 inches and even larger.

Enlargers may look menacing, but they are simple to use. A long rail or column holds the enlarger housing or head, that in turn holds a light bulb, an optical system, negative carrier, bellows, and a lens. The rail is attached to a baseboard.

Light from a special enlarger bulb in the head of the enlarger travels through the optical system, the negative, and the lens to project the negative image onto the baseboard. The purpose of an optical system in an enlarger is to spread the light evenly before it reaches the negative. A condenser (one or two glass lenses) or a diffuser (a translucent piece of glass or plastic) is located between the light source and the negative to diffuse the light. Condenser enlargers produce a higher-contrast print than diffusers.

The negative is positioned in the head of the enlarger by means of a negative carrier. Most negative carriers consist of two pieces of metal that fit together and hold a strip of negatives. The carrier has a cutout

The Enlarger.

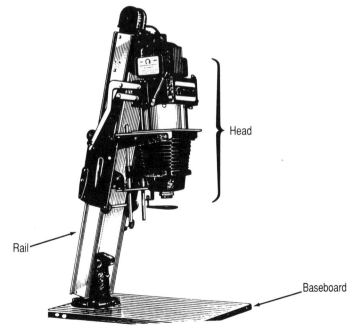

Head

Rail

Baseboard

Diffusion enlarger.
A frosted glass plate scatters the light falling on the negative, causing the enlarger lens to project a softer image. It is important to remember, however, that the bulb used in a condenser enlarger may not be the same type as used in a diffusion enlarger.

Double condenser enlarger.
Condenser lenses collect light and direct it coherently toward the negative and the lens resulting in sharper images with greater contrast than from a diffusion enlarger.

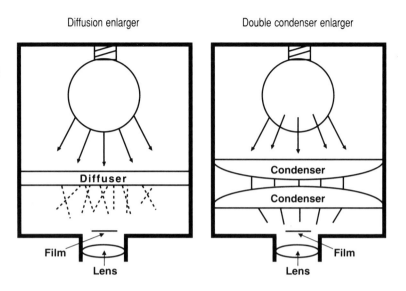

the size of the negative. A few carriers have glass covering the negative to keep it flatter during enlarging. However, glass carriers must be handled carefully to avoid scratching the glass and, harder still, must be kept free of any dust.

In most enlargers, a bellows is located under the negative carrier. A bellows focuses the image. As the bellows expands or contracts, the lens, which is attached to it, moves closer to or farther from the baseboard until the projected image is in focus.

The size of the projected image is controlled by the height of the enlarger above the baseboard. The greater the distance between the baseboard and the lens of the enlarger, the larger the magnification. The size of the projected image changes by raising and lowering the enlarger head on the rail.

Enlarging Lens

All enlargers have lenses. The size of the lens (focal length) depends on the size of the negative being enlarged. Generally, the focal length of the lens on the enlarger matches the normal focal length on the camera for a particular size of film. For instance, the normal size focal length lens for a 35mm camera is 50mm. Thus, a 50mm lens is used on the enlarger. A normal lens for a 2¼×2¼-inch camera is 75mm to 85mm; this lens size would also be used on the enlarger. If a 50mm lens is used to enlarge a 2¼×2¼-inch negative, it might not cover the full

Figure 11-3

Selecting an *f*-stop.

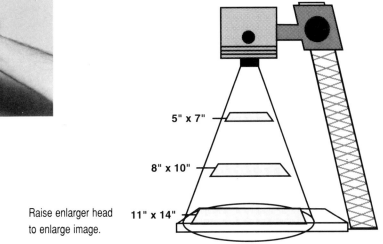

5" x 7"

8" x 10"

Raise enlarger head
to enlarge image.   11" x 14"

area of the negative, but it might cut off the corners of the image. On the other hand, if a 75mm or 80mm lens is used to enlarge a 35mm negative, then it would produce a smaller magnification than a 50mm lens, assuming that the enlarger-to-paper distance is not changed. For small prints, such as wallet size, a 75mm or 80mm lens is needed.

Image brightness is controlled by the iris on the lens. The more the lens is *stopped down*, the less light passes through it. Brightness also decreases as the enlarger is raised to give greater magnification.

Easel

Photographic paper must be kept perfectly flat during the exposure or else one area of the paper will be out of focus while the rest is in focus. Enlarging easels are designed to hold the photo paper completely flat during exposure. Most easels form ¼-inch borders around the image. "Bleed" easels are designed to hold the print without borders. The majority of easels are fixed sizes, but some adjust by movement of thin

Figure 11-4

Enlarging easel.

metal strips to form a mask. They can be masked for various paper sizes, such as 3½×5, 5×7, 8×10, and 11×14-inches. Printing paper is inserted from one end and is slid along the easel guides until it is centered within the mask. The emulsion side of the paper faces up toward the enlarger lens.

Contact Printer

A contact printer holds the film in direct contact with the print paper to make a contact or proof sheet. A piece of glass holds the film in place during exposure.

Timer

A special enlarger timer controls the amount of exposure. Modern electronic timers are extremely accurate and provide exposures from tenths of a second to minutes. They have dimmers for the digital readouts to minimize fogging and an audible exposure option. Older timers have a range from 1 second to 60 seconds. Usually, with both types of timers, there is a manual light switch to turn the enlarger on for focusing. Once the time is set for the period of exposure, a time button is pushed to begin the timing. The timer then automatically turns on the enlarger light and turns it off when the exposure is completed. Although it is not as accurate, a switch on the enlarger line also can be used to turn the enlarger on and off to control the exposure. In this case, check the exposure time with a wristwatch.

Processing Trays

Plastic trays hold the chemicals for print processing. At least four trays are needed. These trays should be a little larger than the paper being used, since it is important that the entire print be immersed in the chemical solution at the same time.

Print Tongs

Use print tongs rather than your hands when moving the print from one tray filled with solution to the next. Tongs help prevent you from getting skin rash or irritation from the chemicals.

Another important reason for keeping your hands out of the chemicals is that you must not contaminate the solutions, especially the developer. While the print will contaminate the stop bath with developer and the fixer with stop bath, it will not immediately ruin those chemicals. However, if the stop or fixer gets into the developer, its capacity to develop prints becomes greatly reduced. Also, contaminated hands can cause fingerprints and stains that ruin photo paper.

Safelights

Because photo paper is sensitive to most colors of light, safelights are used to illuminate the darkroom. Most safelights consist of simple 15- to 25-watt bulbs protected in a housing and covered with a specially colored filter, usually an amber OC or red filter. Safelights should be positioned at least 3 or 4 feet from the enlarger and developer tray.

Brush and Air Spray

Dust is a major problem in the darkroom. Dust will accumulate on a negative and must be cleaned off, or it will show up in the print. To eliminate dust, brush the negative with a soft, camel's hair brush. Canned air is also effective for removing dust, but it is expensive. When using canned air, never tilt it. Always hold it upright, or you will spray a gooey liquid onto your film.

Print Wash

A tray or washer is needed for print washing. In addition, specially made print washers are available. A simple print washer may consist of one large tray with a tray siphon attached.

Print Squeegee

A print squeegee is a flat rubber blade (like a car wiper) or rubber roller. It squeezes excess water off a washed print to help it dry better. A sponge works also. Use the squeegee or sponge on a flat, smooth, surface, such as a piece of glass.

Print Dryer

Prints can be air dried or dried with electric dryers. Fiber-based prints are normally squeegeed and then air dried on fiberglass window screens, or they can be hung by a corner to air dry. Resin coated (RC) prints can be squeegeed and air dried like fiber prints, but they are normally dried with special electric RC print dryers that can be used for either color or black and white. Fiber-based prints take hours to air dry. RC prints air dry in less than an hour and in less than a minute when an electric dryer is used.

Other Accessories

Focusing Magnifier. A magnifier enlarges the projected image to aid focusing. Another type of magnifier, called a grain magnifier, or focuser, enlarges the grain patterns in a negative, allowing for very precise focusing.

Paper Safe. A paper safe is an easily accessible lighttight box that stores the unexposed photo paper. A photo paper box or inner lighttight bag can also be used.

Print Trimmer. Sometimes it is necessary to cut photo paper. A paper trimmer cuts the paper more squarely and accurately than scissors.

Photographic Papers

Photographic paper is classified according to five different qualities: (1) contrast, (2) surface, (3) base type, (4) thickness, and (5) tone.

Contrast

Contrast is the comparison of values (light and dark) in a negative or print. Contrast in a negative is determined by exposure and development. An overexposed or overdeveloped negative is too dark or dense. An underexposed or underdeveloped negative is too thin—it looks flat. In printing, low-contrast prints are gray with few bright or dark areas; high-contrast prints are mostly light and dark with few gray areas.

Photographic paper is usually made in five contrast levels (grades). Graded papers are numbered from one to five, indicating the level of contrast: 1—low contrast, 2—average contrast, 3—slightly high contrast, 4—high contrast, 5—very high contrast.

Eastman Kodak uses a descriptive system to indicate the various contrast levels. This system is primarily for resin coated (RC) paper:

Soft	= 1	Extra hard	= 4
Medium	= 2	Ultra hard	= 5
Hard	= 3		

Another type of enlarging paper, called either *variable-contrast, selective, multigrade,* or *polycontrast* paper, allows for twelve different contrast ranges. Specially designed filters that are placed below the enlarging lens during exposure allow for both subtle and dramatic changes in contrast. Use of variable-contrast paper eliminates the need to buy several different packages of graded paper because one pack of variable

Figure 11-5

A wide range of contrast control is possible with the same negative.

A. This gray, low-contrast print was made with a number 1 variable-contrast printing filter and has no blacks or whites.

B. This high-contrast print was made using a number 5 variable-contrast printing filter and lacks middle tones.

A.

B.

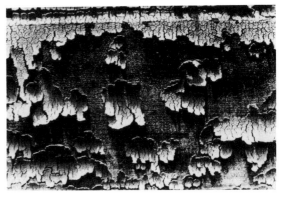

paper allows many more options for control. Variable-contrast filters also permit intermediate contrast levels, such as 1 1/2, which is not available with graded papers. The filters also make it possible to alter the contrast in different parts of the print by selective filtering.

Older variable-contrast filter sets are normally numbered 0, 1/2, 1, 1 1/2, 2, 2 1/2, 3, 3 1/2, 4, 4 1/2, 5, with the lowest number giving the least contrast and the highest number the most. Newer sets have additional filters for even more control. Kodak PolyMax filters now have a–1 and a+5, while Ilford Multigrade filters have a 00 filter. With most filter sets, the exposure does not need to be adjusted, except minimally, for changes between grades below 3 1/2. With grades over 3 1/2, expect to need double or one stop additional exposure each time you go higher in filtration. Handle the filters with care because they damage easily from fingerprints and liquid.

Figure 11-6

The same negative was printed with six out of the twelve variable-contrast filters that are available for black and white contrast control. Note the changes in feeling and the rendition of detail.

Untitled, Edouard de Merlier.

A. Number 0 filter.

B. Number 1 filter.

C. Number 2 filter.

D. Number 3 filter.

E. Number 4 filter.

F. Number 5 filter.

Exposure Factor Table for Image Maginification

Ilford Multigrade Filters	Equivalent	Kodak Filters	Equivalent Polycontrast III RC	Polymax RC
00	199 Y			
0	90 Y	0	103 Y	162 Y
1/2	70 Y			
1	50 Y	1	63 Y	98 Y
1 1/2	30 Y			
2	0 Y	2	13 M	14 M
2 1/2	5 M			
3	25 M	3	26 M	46 M
3 1/2	50 M			
4	80 M	4	54 M	115 M
4 1/2	140 M			
5	199 M	5	109 M	Use a Polymax +5 filter

Enlargers equipped with a dichroic filter head for color can use the built-in filters to vary the contrast in variable-contrast papers. Color enlargers are generally diffusion enlargers and provide a grade less contrast than black and white condenser enlargers, but many photographers like the convenience of using built-in filters. Also, normal variable-contrast filters are used below the lens, which can reduce sharpness. Since color filters are built into the head of the enlarger above the plane of focus (position of the negative), they do not reduce sharpness.

Variable-contrast filter equivalents for dichroic filter heads will vary with new product changes, different equipment, and brands of enlarging papers. To ensure that you are getting the right results, consult the recent data published by the manufacturers of the products you use. Currently the filter equivalents listed above are recommended.

Surface

Surfaces of photographic paper vary. Because photographers have different tastes and produce photographs for many different purposes, Kodak alone offers eleven different paper surfaces. Generally, it is best to buy either an F (glossy), J (high luster), or N (smooth semimatte) surface. These papers do not roughen the texture of the photographic image. The F surface paper is most popular.

Base Type

Photographic papers are available in fiber and resin-coated (RC) types. RC papers are coated on both sides with a very thin layer of clear plastic. They are more convenient to use than fiber-based papers, and they expose more quickly than fiber-based papers. Because RC papers are coated in plastic, they take less time to process, wash, and dry. In addition, they do not curl as much as fiber-based papers during drying.

Because of their convenience, RC papers are especially useful to the beginner or to the person who does not have much time to use the darkroom.

More advanced photographers tend to prefer fiber-based papers for exhibition purposes and fine art collections because the fiber surface is more appealing than the RC surface. Many photographers also believe that fiber-based papers are more permanent than RC papers. Initially, fiber papers were more permanent, but improvements have alleviated the problems and difference in permanence is no longer an issue.

Thickness

RC papers are only available in a medium-weight thickness. Fiber-based papers are available in three thicknesses, or weights: single weight, medium weight, and double weight. Double weight is about twice as thick as single weight and about a third more expensive. However, it is easier to handle, curls less, and is less likely to crease and get crinkles in the emulsion. Double-weight paper is generally used for exhibition purposes and for prints larger than 8×10 inches.

Tone

The tone or color of a photographic paper is described in terms of being warm or neutral (cold). A warm-tone paper is one in which the blacks are brownish. A neutral or cold-tone paper is one in which the blacks are a neutral gray or slightly blue. Neutral papers usually have a purer, cleaner white base, whereas warm-tone papers may have a creamier, off-white base.

Paper developers also affect the tone of a print, and warm-tone and neutral-tone developers are made for the different papers. Most photographers use a universal developer such as Kodak Dektol (D-72) for both types of paper. But some papers, fiber-based in particular, will perform better if used in a developer designed for the tone of that paper. Selectol and Selectol Soft are popular Kodak developers specifically designed for warm-tone papers.

Printmaking Chemicals

The chemicals for processing prints are basically the same as those for film development. However, film developers and fixers are generally stronger and more concentrated than paper developers and fixers, so it is necessary to make sure that you are using chemicals prepared for print developing to get the most out of print materials.

Print developers are either in liquid or powder form. The powder developers must be mixed to produce a concentrated "stock" solution, which is diluted with water for actual use. Liquid developers are already in the stock form and are diluted with water to make a working solution. Check the recommendations for the product you are using because dilutions vary. Developers lose strength and contrast, and they change from a light amber color to a dark brownish color as they get exhausted.

An acid stop bath, made with 1 oz of 28 percent acetic acid to 32 oz of water, is generally used for both RC and fiber-based papers. Indicator stop baths, which change color when they are exhausted, are also available. Most photographers, though, use a fresh batch of stop bath whenever they mix a new batch of developer.

Normally, fixers are also diluted with water to make a working solution. A hardener is incorporated into some fixers and is generally used for fixing films, but is not necessary for most print papers. Many newer RC papers don't recommend the use of a hardener, and fiber prints dry flatter without it. Fixers last longer than the developer and stop bath. Many photographers reuse their fixer for several days. A chemical called HypoChek, which comes in small plastic bottles, is used to check the condition of the fixer. Put a couple drops of HypoChek into the fixer, and if they turn milky, the fixer is exhausted. If the drops stay clear the fixer is okay to use.

For use, each chemical is put into a plastic processing tray. Processing trays holding the chemicals should be positioned in a line, with the developer in the far left tray followed by the stop bath, fixer, and a tray with a water holding bath on the far right. The trays should be filled to a height that provides approximately 1/2 inch of chemistry in each.

Figure 11-7

The chemical sequence for processing black and white prints is normally set up from left to right with the developer first, the stop bath next, then the fixer, and the water holding tray last—before the final wash.

The holding bath, which consists of plain water, is used to rinse excess fixer off the prints and to hold the prints until there are enough to wash. RC prints should not be left in a holding bath for very long because excessive time in water can cause the plastic coating to curl some on the edges.

Prints on fiber-based paper are less likely to be damaged by sitting in the holding bath for lengthy periods. Since fiber-based papers need much longer washing times, prints are generally left in the holding tank until a batch is done and then washed together. Be sure to change the water periodically to minimize the accumulation of spent fixer in the water.

Processing Time

Processing time will vary according to paper, chemistry, and image needs, but the following standard processing times are generally recommended for most materials. For RC papers, the developing time is 1 to 2 minutes, stop bath 30 seconds, fixer 2 minutes, and wash in running water 2 minutes. Fiber-based papers, developing time is 1 to 3 minutes, stop bath 30 seconds, fixer 5 minutes, and final wash 30 minutes to 1 hour. Consistent timing is important, especially for the developer. Pick a time within the suggested range and use it consistently. If tests and subsequent prints vary in development time, the results will vary and be hard to resolve effectively.

Contact Sheets

A contact or proof sheet is generally made before any enlargements are attempted. Contact sheets are made by contact printing a whole roll of film onto a piece of enlarging paper. This sheet allows the photographer to examine each image and decide which to enlarge, whether to crop, and what sort of enlarging problems a particular image may present. Contact sheets also serve as a documentation or visual record of each shot on a roll of film. Photographers who work with larger sheet film negatives often make contact prints, which are the same size as the original negative, rather than enlargements.

To make a contact sheet, first position the enlarger housing near the top of the rail so that it projects a wide circle of light when turned on. Many use this circle of light to expose the contact sheet, but the light is stronger in the center and weaker towards the edges. To get a more even distribution of light, put an empty negative carrier into the enlarger and focus the enlarger so that the edges of the empty carrier are sharp when projected onto the baseboard.

A piece of glass or a contact printer is used to expose the contact sheet. A contact printer consists of a base on which the unexposed paper is placed, emulsion up, with the negatives positioned emulsion down on top of the paper. A piece of glass is positioned so that it can be lowered on top of the film to hold the strips of film and the enlarging

Figure 11-8

A. Contact or proof sheets are made by placing negatives and a piece of unexposed print paper together in a contact printer or under a piece of glass and then exposing them to light from the enlarger.

B. A contact sheet.

Figure 11-9

A test strip can be made to indicate the proper amount of exposure for a contact sheet. Always be sure to make the test strip so that the exposures cut across the film and through each frame. Once the exposure is determined, make a final sheet at one exposure time.

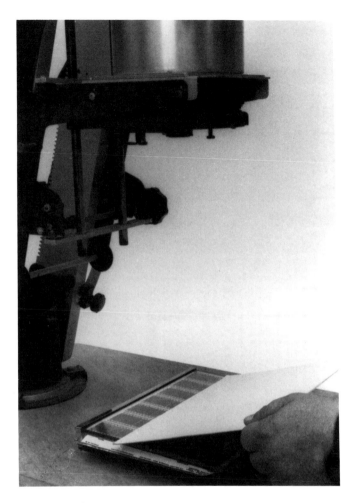

paper in tight contact. When using just a piece of glass, place the unexposed paper, emulsion up, on the enlarger baseboard. Then place the negatives, emulsion down, on top of the paper and cover them with the piece of glass. Because the strips of film tend to curl and are sometimes hard to position, many photographers reduce handling problems by making contact sheets with the film in clear plastic sleeves. Once everything is in position, make an exposure and process the paper. To determine the exposure, a test strip may be necessary. A test strip for a contact sheet is made in the same manner that is used for the enlargement of an individual image. This procedure is discussed in detail in the section Making a Test Strip in this chapter.

Keep in mind that film exposures often vary and that over an entire roll of film, some images may print too light because of overexposure

Mark, Glenn Cannon.

Figure 11-10

Carefully planned sequential shooting enabled Glenn Cannon to use the contact print as a final image. A twelve-exposure roll of 21/4-inch (120) film was used to get a bigger image than from 35mm. The print was developed by putting developer on the surface and moving it around, rather than immersing the whole print into the tray of developer. This gave the painterly edges and kept the outer areas from going black, creating a floating effect. The contact print was made on 11×14-inch paper, rather than 8×10, to give extra space around the image.

and others too dark because of underexposure. A contact sheet shows these discrepancies. The exposure of a contact sheet is based on whatever compromise exposure is needed to reveal the majority of the shots on the roll.

Preparations for Enlargement

Each negative is unique and has its own needs, which the photographer subjectively interprets when making a print. The following ten steps outline the procedure for preparing a negative for enlargement.

1. To reduce dust spots, wipe the film gently with an antistatic cloth before putting it into the negative carrier. Then place the

negative into the negative carrier with the emulsion (dull side) facing down toward the baseboard from its position in the enlarger head. If it is hard to tell which is the dull side, look at the frame numbers and manufacturer data along the edges of the film. When the numbers and words are reading correctly, the emulsion side is facing down. Should you make a print with the emulsion up, the image will be flopped, or backwards.

2. Once the negative is in the carrier, it may need additional cleaning. Even after the use of an antistatic cloth, some dust may still be on the negative. Unless it is removed, it will cause little white spots or lines in the print that have to be spotted out with a brush and liquid dyes. To remove any remaining dust, a camel's hair brush is often recommended, but it may just push the dust around and collect along the edges of the negative carrier. An air spray is normally more effective because it blows the dust off. When using an air spray, be sure to hold it straight up because tilting may cause it to release a gooey liquid onto your film. Should these methods of dust removal not solve the problem, it may be necessary to use a liquid film cleaner and a cotton swab to clean stubborn particles or fingerprints off the film. Take the film out of the negative carrier and dip the cotton swab into the film cleaner. Then gently rub the trouble spot with the wet cotton swab. It may take more than one application to resolve the problem. The film cleaner will evaporate and leave no residue.

   If your negative carrier has glass in the openings, clean all sides of the glass prior to inserting the negative to remove all dust on the glass itself.

3. After all dust is removed, place the negative in the enlarger immediately so that no new dust settles on it. In order to insert the negative carrier on some enlargers, you must raise the lamp housing of the enlarger. Usually the carrier will lock into a tight position, indicating that it is in place. The lamp housing can now be brought back down on the carrier. Always insert the negative with the enlarger light off so that it will not spill into the darkroom.

4. Set the easel for the image size of the print. The image size is the size of the printing paper minus the borders. For example, a 7½×9½-inch size image on an 8x10-inch sheet of photo paper has an ¼-inch border on each side. Some easels are nonadjustable and offer only one standard size.

5. Place the easel on the baseboard of the enlarger.

6. Turn on the safelight and turn off the room lights.

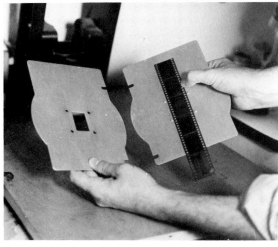

A.

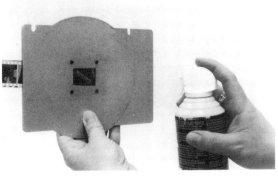

B.

C.

Figure 11-11

Preparing a negative for enlargement. A. Insert the negative into the negative carrier with the emulsion (dull side) down. B. Clean the negative with air spray to remove any loose dust or lint. C. Insert the negative carrier into the enlarger.

7. Turn on the enlarger.
8. Open the aperture on the enlarging lens as wide as possible for easier viewing to size and focus the image.
9. Raise and lower the enlarger head on the vertical rail until the image is the desired size. The position of the easel on the enlarger baseboard needs to be adjusted until the projected image is framed by the easel. Remember, as the head moves up the rail, the projected image becomes larger; as it moves down, the image becomes smaller.
10. Once the size of the image is set, focus the negative by turning the focusing knob on the enlarger until the projected image on the easel looks sharp. If the size changes as you focus, it may be necessary to readjust the height of the enlarger.

To provide a better viewing surface and to compensate for the thickness of the photographic paper, place a sheet of unexposed but previously developed, fixed, and washed printing paper in the enlarging easel during focusing. A magnifier or grain focuser makes the projected image larger, and focusing is more accurate.

Always focus with the lens aperture wide open, and then stop it down to a smaller aperture to make the exposure. This procedure not only makes the image brighter and easier to see initially, it ensures that the image will be sharp. With the lens stopped down, the image can look in focus but be slightly out of focus because of optical distortions that are hard for the eye to distinguish.

Print Exposure

Print exposure times vary with the density of the negative, the size of the enlargement, the type of paper, the chemistry, the developing time, the aperture of the lens, and the enlarger itself. An exposure that is correct on one enlarger may not be correct on another, even if both enlargers are of the same type. Because the variables are many, try to work with the same enlarger and to develop consistent working habits. To ensure the best edge-to-edge optical result, try to use an aperture in the middle of the aperture range, such as f/8 or f/11. Depth of field is not a problem for enlarging because it is a flat surface projection, but some of the less expensive enlarger lenses tend to lose sharpness when used wide open or with very small apertures. However, with a very thin negative, it is better to stop down the lens to a smaller aperture rather than use a very short exposure time. With a dense, overexposed negative, it is better to open up the aperture, rather than use an extremely long exposure time. Generally, try to use exposure times from 5 to 20 seconds. Shorter times may seem advantageous, but they limit the potential for selective exposure controls that you will find important as you gain experience and seek more than machine print results.

Making a Test Strip

A major consideration when you are printing a negative is how dark to make the print. This is a visual judgment based on what feeling you think will best express the subject and the quality of light in the photograph. A light, high key print works with some subjects, whereas a dark, more somber, low key print may suit others better. Most of the time, aim for the exposure that makes the subject seem natural and realistic.

Making a test print or strip is the best way to determine the amount of exposure needed for a particular negative. When you are beginning printmaking, it may be best to use a full sheet of paper to make a test. With experience, however, you will find that a small strip of paper, appropriately placed, will provide enough information for you to determine the right exposure.

The Bridge, San Francisco, Greg Rager.

Figure 11-12

A. A test strip is necessary to determine the exposure each time you make a print because density of negatives varies, and the exposure changes with differences in the height of the enlarger. This test strip was made with the aperture at f/22, and the exposure was set for 5-second increments. The first exposure is the darkest, and the last one the lightest because the paper was uncovered increment by increment, with the last one getting the least amount of light.

B. The exposure for the final print was selected from the test strip. A 15-second exposure at an aperture of f/22 was used.

To make a test strip, first put the negative into the carrier and adjust the enlarger for size and focus. If you are making an 8x10-inch enlargement from a 35mm or 2 1/4-inch negative that is fairly normal in exposure, set the aperture for *f*/8 or *f*/11. Then insert an unexposed piece or strip of enlarging paper into the easel. If you are using a strip of paper, make it about an inch wide and long enough to extend across the image. Place the strip so that it covers the important light and dark portions of the image.

Set the timer for 5 seconds, then cover all but 20 percent of the paper with an opaque sheet of cardboard. Expose the uncovered portion of the paper for 5 seconds. Then move the opaque piece of cardboard down to uncover another 20 percent of the image and make another 5-second exposure. Repeat this procedure until you have gone through five successful exposures of 5 seconds each, uncovering 20 percent more paper each time. For the last exposure, the whole sheet of paper will be uncovered.

Once the print is developed, the result will be a series of strips across it, each exposed for multiples of 5 seconds. The first strip exposed will be the darkest because it received the most light and has a cumulative exposure of 25 seconds. The second strip was exposed for 20 seconds, the third for 15 seconds, the fourth for 10 seconds, and the fifth and last will be the lightest because it was exposed for only 5 seconds. Select the exposure time that seems best. It may be somewhere between the 5-second increments, such as 12 seconds. Then make a full print at that exposure.

Print Processing

The developing process is the same for both test prints and final prints. Processing times that are included here are only suggestions. Always refer to the instruction sheets with photographic paper and chemicals for specific recommendations. Processing temperatures are not as critical for prints as for film. However, try to keep the temperatures of all the chemicals as close to 68°F as possible.

After the exposure, immediately slip the paper into the developer tray, noting the time. Place the paper in the tray either face down or face up for the first few seconds, but turn the paper face up as soon as it is thoroughly wet. The important thing is to get the entire print into the tray quickly. Don't let one end of the sheet hang over the tray while the rest is in the developer. Also, until the paper has been completely saturated, be careful to keep the corners of the print in the developer, as they may tend to curl upward and develop unevenly. Once the print is in the solution, rock the tray gently back and forth. This agitation should not be violent or fast; its purpose is only to keep the solution constantly moving across the emulsion on the paper. Use print tongs occasionally to poke down the corners of the paper. If you do not use tongs, then try not to touch the surface of the print unnecessarily.

It is important to develop consistent and methodical work habits when you are processing prints. RC papers have a normal development time of 1 minute, but they can be developed longer. Fiber-based papers are normally developed in 2 or 3 minutes, with the image appearing after 30 seconds. To get good results and ensure control and repeatability, use a consistent developer time.

Never shorten or increase the development time to make up for a miscalculated exposure. If you remove the print from the developer too soon because it appears to be getting too dark, the result will be a muddy, gray image that lacks contrast. There will be no sharp blacks or whites in the print because the developer was not given enough time to act completely upon the print. If the print comes out too dark, the only way to get the most out of the materials is to reduce the exposure time, not to alter the development time. If the print is too light, increase the exposure rather than increase the developer time. The developer time should remain a constant! The lightness or darkness of a print is controlled by the exposure time and should not be manipulated by varying the developer time.

After the print has been in the developer for the recommended time, hold it by a corner to drain, and then place it into the stop bath. It should remain in the stop bath for 30 seconds, with gentle agitation during the first 10 seconds. Drain the print as before, and then immerse it in the fixer.

Once the print is in the fixer, agitate it for the first 15 to 30 seconds, and then let it soak in the solution for another 30 seconds before

Figure 11-13

A. Mottling can occur when a print is overexposed and pulled from the developer before the developing action is complete. This results in a flat, low contrast print with streaked and blotchy development.

B. The same negative, when properly exposed and developed, produces a print with normal tones and good contrast. Keep the development time constant and adjust the exposure to get the best results.

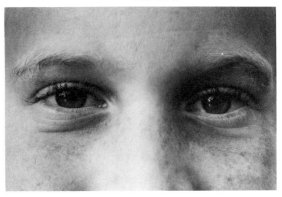

A.

B.

inspecting it in room light. If other prints are in the same tray, agitate them occasionally. The print should remain in the hypo for the time recommended by the manufacturer. Generally, for fiber-based papers, this time is 5 to 10 minutes; for RC papers, 2 minutes. If the print remains in the hypo for too long (more than 10 minutes) the image may absorb hypo in such a way as to resist washing. Eventually, the hypo stains the print. If the print is exposed to white light immediately after immersion in the fixer, it will fog. However, if the print fogs under white light after 2 minutes in the hypo, then the hypo should be replaced because it is no longer working.

To examine the print, turn on the main light, place it in a clean tray, and take it out of the darkroom. The tray will prevent the hypo from dripping. Note that dried fixer is difficult to remove from floors, cabinets, and other surfaces. Also, note that fiber-based prints dry about 10 percent darker.

After the print has been in the fixer for the recommended time, place the test print in the holding bath until it is ready to be washed.

Washing and Drying the Prints

After the print has been in the fixer for the recommended time or in the holding tray, the wash cycle can begin. Prints must be washed sufficiently or they will deteriorate with age. A short water wash of 2 to 4 minutes is recommended for RC papers. However, fiber-based papers absorb more fixer than RC papers, so they require a wash time of one hour. Although a hypo eliminator is not a necessity, using it neutralizes most of the fixer, thereby shortening the washing time. Thus, a hypo eliminator is especially useful for fiber-based papers.

With a hypo eliminator, most manufacturers recommend rinsing fiber-based prints in water for 2 minutes before adding the hypo eliminator. After the water rinse, soak the prints in the eliminator for the recommended time. Directions usually suggest 2 to 4 minutes, with some agitation. Limit the number of prints to fifteen. Washing time is thus cut to 10 minutes for single-weight papers and to 20 minutes for double-weight fiber-based papers.

At the end of the time in hypo eliminator, drain each print briefly, and then place them one at a time in the wash water. When washing either RC or fiber-based papers, use a good print washer that circulates a constant flow of water. An inexpensive washer can be made from an ordinary processing tray with a tray siphon. A siphon is usually a plastic or rubber device that clips onto one side of the tray. It connects to any standard faucet with a rubber hose. Water from the faucet enters the

tray at the top of the siphon, and tray water drains off at the bottom of the siphon. If holes are punctured on the opposite side of the tray, the water will drain even better.

When washing prints, agitate them by hand to keep them from sticking to one another. Again, wash only a few prints at a time to keep the prints from bunching. If a print washer is not available, empty all the water from the tray every 2 minutes during the wash. Continual changes remove any contaminated water. *Never put an unwashed print into a tray of washed prints because to do so will contaminate the washed prints, and they will have to be rewashed.*

Next, dry the washed prints. The simplest way to dry both RC and fiber-based prints is to air dry them. Squeegee them with a rubber squeegee, and then hang them by a corner to dry. The RC prints should dry fine with this method, but the fiber-based prints will curl. To eliminate the curl in fiber-based prints, either flatten them by putting the prints into a heated dry mount press, or stack them face-to-face, and put them under a heavy weight for a day or so. A better way to air dry prints is to put the squeegeed prints onto a fiberglass drying screen (window screens work fine). RC prints should be placed face up on the screens to alleviate surface flaws. Fiber-based prints have a less delicate surface and should be placed face down on the screens to minimize curling. RC prints will air dry within a half hour, but fiber prints will take hours. To accelerate drying, an electric hair dryer can be used.

The quickest and best way to dry RC prints is to use an electric dryer designed for RC papers. The wet prints are placed into the dryer faceup. They are caught by a roller that pulls them into the dryer where hot air is blown over them and they come out dry within 30 seconds. Special electric dryers are also available for fiber-based prints, but few are in use these days because so many photographers have switched to the easier-to-use RC papers. Those who use fiber-based papers generally air dry them or use blotter books that take a couple of days to dry fiber-based prints completely.

Evaluating Contacts and Test Strips

Contact Sheets

The contact sheet provides a convenient means to evaluate shooting and film-processing problems. It can also be used as a visual reference to make cropping and other printing decisions prior to printing. Generally, a contact sheet is given whatever exposure is necessary to make the images visible. Often, lengthy exposure is needed to make overexposed

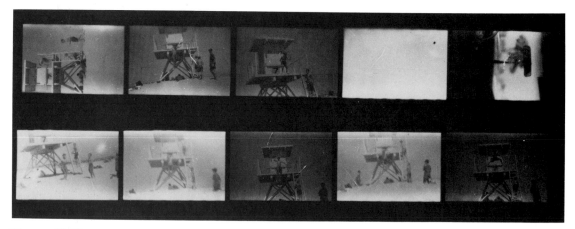

Figure 11-14

Contact sheets provide an excellent means to evaluate shooting and film-processing techniques. This contact sheet shows that the photographer overexposed the film. It is evident because the frame numbers and the clear borders of the film are printed so dark that they have blended into the black background. Normally-exposed and developed film would print so that the frame numbers and sprocket holes along the edges of the film are subtly visible.

negatives visible on a contact. Exposures of such duration cause frame numbers on the edge of the film and the clear areas around each frame to darken and disappear into black background. Contacts made with under-exposed film on the other hand, will be gray overall and lack a black background.

To use a contact to accurately evaluate shooting exposures, the contact needs to be properly exposed and developed. A properly exposed contact sheet will have a black background with the frame numbers readily visible. The clear areas of the film, which surround each frame, will be dark, subtly separating from the black background. If your negatives are properly exposed, they will print normally on a contact sheet exposed in the aforementioned way. If they are too light, then it means that your negatives were overexposed. Too dark means that they were underexposed. Neither means that the negatives are unprintable, but it does indicate exposure problems during shooting and that prints from those negatives will not print as easily and with as much subtle detail as a properly exposed negative.

Test Strips

The processed test print will have a range of five exposures; some may be light and some dark. If all five exposures are either too light or too dark, make another test print. The ideal test print is dark on one end and light at the other. If the entire print is too dark, then shorten the intervals of exposure. If the entire print is too light, then increase the exposure time. Lighter negatives need less exposure time because light passes through them at a more intense level. Denser negatives require more exposure time. An exposure time of more than 60 seconds indicates that a negative is overexposed or overdeveloped. In this case, try opening the *f*-stop on the enlarger lens to shorten the exposure time.

Making an Enlargement

Once a good test print is made, examine it carefully and choose the exposure that looks best. Sometimes, the best exposure falls between two sections of the test print. If a 5-second exposure looks too light and the 10-second exposure looks too dark, use a 7- or 8-second exposure instead.

To begin, place a fresh sheet of photo paper into the easel and expose it for the time chosen. Do not change the *f*-stop setting. Develop the exposed paper for the same time as the test print. To evaluate the quality of this print, consider these factors: (1) exposure and (2) contrast.

1. Print exposure determines the overall brightness of a print. Too much exposure results in a print that has dark shadows and highlights; too little exposure results in a print that leaves the shadows and highlights too light.

    A good test print helps determine correct exposure. However, once the initial print is made, it may need some slight adjustments in exposure. The question that every photographer must ask concerning exposure is, "Is the print too light?"
2. Photographers sometimes confuse exposure with contrast. For instance, after making a test print in which all of the strips are too light, a beginning photographer may change to a lower contrast filter. This is the wrong thing to do. If a test strip is too light, the exposure time should be increased. Then, after a new test, decide whether the print has too much or too little contrast. There is no rule of thumb governing contrast selection. However, if a test print image is still stark white and black after the correct exposure strip and proper length of development, then the contrast is too high. If the strip has an overall gray (muddy) look, then the contrast is too low. The eye is the best judge of proper contrast.

A quality unique to photography is its ability to capture a scene in a complete tonal range. In photography, tonal range is the scale of values from white through a wide variety of grays to black. Tonal range is greatest if the negative has been properly exposed and then printed with a number 1 or 2 filter. Higher contrast filters or high grades of

A. Normal, properly exposed print.

B. Underexposed print, too light, needs more exposure.

C. Overexposed print, too dark, needs less exposure.

Figure 11-15

D. Low contrast print, too flat, needs a higher filter.

E. High contrast print, too contrasty, needs a lower filter.

paper result in a loss of tonal range. This effect may be desirable if the negative has too much of an overall gray look, that is, if it lacks contrast from the original exposure. In other words, the lower the contrast of the paper, the greater the tonal range—the greater the number of gray tones the paper can reproduce. The higher the contrast of the paper, the narrower the tonal range—the fewer the number of gray tones the paper is capable of reproducing.

Print Evaluation

After achieving normal exposure and contrast, look at the print to see whether it is what you want. Does it express your feelings about the subject or just merely show the subject? What would make it better?

Since you can't reshoot it, how can it be improved in the darkroom? Regardless of the subject, the mood of the picture is determined by the print exposure and the contrast. A dark print will be more somber and even mysterious compared with a normally exposed print. The same dark print will evoke different feelings because of differences in contrast. A dark, low-contrast print will seem somber and forbidding compared with a dark, high contrast print, which will seem bold and dramatic, and a light print will have a totally different feeling. Choose an exposure and contrast combination that works best with each individual image. There is no specific guideline to follow, except to make a picture that is expressive.

Cropping

As you study the initial print, also consider the cropping. Most beginners almost always shoot 35mm film and crop their pictures to fit the format of the standard 8x10-inch print paper. The proportion of 35mm film is different from the proportion of photographic print papers, so to maximize the use of the paper, many crop their images to fit. But before automatically cropping the image, consider the cropping you did in the camera when you shot the picture. If you composed the image carefully in the viewfinder of the camera, then cropping may not be necessary. In fact, it may take away from the image.

Always consider how your picture will look full frame, as you shot it. Compare your cropped version to the full frame image on the contact sheet. Which version is better? Maybe more cropping is needed. Ideally, we crop in the camera and shoot the picture the way we want it. But

A. Full frame print from 35mm negative.

Figure 11-16

Variations of the same image.

B. Image cropped to fit 8×10-inch paper format.

C. Image cropped to emphasize a portion of the picture.

we can't always get it the way we want. That is when cropping may be desirable.

To crop out part of the image, raise the enlarger so that the unwanted portion of the negative is outside the area of the print paper. If you have an adjustable easel, you can alter the proportion and shape of the image by adjusting the blades of the easel to fit your cropping needs. But avoid excessive cropping, unless absolutely necessary. The larger the image, the less its sharpness. A cropped image will not be as sharp as a full frame image and will make the grain more obvious. To minimize cropping, learn to crop in the camera.

Other darkroom manipulative processes will be discussed in the next chapter. These techniques can often enhance and improve the result, but they can also be gimmicky. Remember, there is really only one way to make a good photograph, and that is by taking a good photograph. You can make a good photograph look better, but you can't make a bad photograph look good.

Printing Color Negatives on Black and White Paper

Color negatives can be printed on black and white papers by using the same procedure as for printing black and white negatives. However, black and white papers are not very sensitive to colors at the warm end of the spectrum. This is evident from black and white safelights, which are either amber or red. Consequently, black and white prints from

A.   B.

Figure 11-17

A. Color negatives can be printed on normal black and white enlarging papers, but because of the insensitivity of black and white papers to amber and red, the colors do not reproduce as they would with black and white film. B. The proper tones will reproduce when color negatives are printed on Kodak Panalure paper, which is designed to reproduce color negatives in black and white. Note the differences between the two prints.

color negatives may lack contrast, and some of the colors will reproduce lighter or darker than they would normally.

To make the print look more natural, start testing with a number 4 variable-contrast printing filter. This generally makes color negatives look better when printed on a normal variable-contrast black and white paper. To reproduce proper color values in a black and white print, it is necessary to use a special print paper called Panalure. Made by Kodak, this black and white paper is sensitive to all colors and comes in only one contrast grade, number 2. Because of its "panchromatic" light sensitivity, Panalure has to be used in complete darkness or with a number 13 dark amber color safelight. Because of its limitations, Pana-lure is generally only used by professionals. Most find the prints from regular enlarging paper satisfactory.

Printing Problems

A number of things can detract from a well shot image other than the obvious print exposure and contrast considerations. The following are a few of the other problems that may occur in printing.

Out of focus prints have several causes: The negative may not have been properly positioned in the negative carrier; the negative carrier may not have been properly positioned in the enlarger; the negative may have been shot out of focus; the negative may be out of focus in the enlarger; it may pop out of focus due to leaving the enlarger line on too long; or the enlarger may have been bumped or vibrated during the print exposure.

First, always remember to focus the enlarger with the lens aperture wide open and then stop down the lens to make an exposure. If you focus stopped down, the image will be darker and harder to focus. Also, the optics of the lens will make it seem in focus when it isn't. If you are able to focus one side of the image but not the whole image at once, then it means a problem with the negative carrier. Grain will be sharp when a print is made from a negative that was shot out of focus by the *camera*. Grain will be out of focus, however, in a print image not well focused in the *enlarger*. If the enlarger was bumped or had vibrated during the exposure, you may get a double or repeated image.

Fingerprints on a print are either caused by fingerprints on the negative or by handling the paper with fixer on your hands. A dark fingerprint usually means the paper was handled with developer on the hands before exposure. Always keep your hands clean and dry.

Chemical stains are from improper or careless handling of the prints during processing. Often chemical stains occur because people don't wash the chemistry off their hands and/or handle the prints with wet hands. Sometimes a discoloration occurs with black and white prints because they were exposed to light before they were properly fixed. Discoloration can also be due to careless handling during processing and a lack of adequate washing. Even prints that appear okay after processing may start to discolor in time because of inadequate processing. To ensure the longevity of your photographs, be sure to process them properly.

Muddy prints are normally due to a lack of contrast or because a print was overexposed and pulled out of the developer prematurely. Keep the developer time constant, and alter the exposure to control the result.

White spots are usually caused by dirt or lint on the negative. Always clean your negative before making a print. Sometimes water spots show up in prints because of film drying problems. These are readily visible on the negative and can be removed with gentle repeated applications of a liquid film cleaner.

Black marks on a print are usually from scratches or small holes in the film emulsion. Often, they can be alleviated by filling the scratch with oil, which diffuses the light and makes the scratch disappear. The most common approach to this involves first finding the scratch on the film, then getting some "skin oil" on your finger from the side of your nose. Gently rub the skin oil into the scratch and print the image. If this touch-up procedure is done right, the scratch will disappear. For big scratches, try a bottle of Edwal No Scratch, which is used in a similar manner as the skin oil. If that does not work, you may want to try another negative.

Chapter 12

Advanced Black and White Printmaking

The negative is the score, the print is the performance.

—Ansel Adams
Photographer

Figure 12-1

Untitled, Deseree Lyon.

For the serious photographer, seldom is the "straight" print acceptable. Most images need some form of manipulation to achieve a level that resonates the feelings of the photographer. Often this involves simple darkroom procedures, such as the localized lightening and darkening of a print, which are referred to as *dodging* and *burning*. But many photographers go well beyond simple darkroom procedures and use involved techniques such as print flashing, customized developers, bleaching, selenium intensification, and multiple and split contrast printing.

The Fine Print

A photograph is a translation of light into precise tonal relationships that express the photographer's vision of how a subject should be presented in a photograph. Craft and technique are nothing more than means to an end, with the end being a successful and expressive photograph. A negative is merely the starting point, but never the completed version of an image. The print is the only completed photograph.

For several generations, purists have reveled over what has become known as the "fine print aesthetic." Although this sensibility is normally associated with black and white photography, similar attitudes are prevalent among serious color photographers. The core belief is that manipulation of a photograph is bad. But those associated with this aesthetic, such as Ansel Adams, Minor White, Brett Weston, John Sexton, and even photojournalist W. Eugene Smith, are known to be avid manipulators of their images. The distinction, according to Ansel Adams, is that "As long as the final result of the procedure is *photographic*, it is entirely justified. But when a photograph has the "feel" of an etching or a lithograph, or any other graphic medium, it is questionable—just as questionable as a painting that is photographic in character."

With the advent of the computer, photographic manipulation is reaching new levels, yet the basic character of the lens-based photographic image can prevail. The most important consideration for any photographer is to do whatever is necessary to make a successful photographic image, whether it be by traditional means or by electronic

Bowed Tree, Snow and Bridge, Larry Vogel.

Figure 12-2

Control of all aspects of the process (from film selection, camera exposure, and film development to the paper selection, exposure, and processing of the final print) is the key to making a photograph that reproduces delicate detail with a broad contrast range, as in this image.

technology. This chapter will concentrate on traditional darkroom methods to refine black and white printmaking. The zone system and other methods of exposure and contrast control, which are important for those desiring even more control, will be covered in detail in Chapter 19.

Print Papers

Many years ago one of this book's authors (Jerry Burchfield) attended a weekend workshop by renowned photographer Paul Caponigro. While showing his prints, Caponigro stressed that each image had its own particular needs. To determine the needs of an image, Caponigro said he would test each image extensively before making a final print. This meant making test prints on different types and brands of photographic paper with different developer combinations for each. Sometimes he would test a negative on ten different papers before he found the right paper and developer combination for that image.

Most photographers do not explore so fully, but the differences in photographic print papers and developers are worth noting. Of the two main types of photographic print paper, resin-coated (RC) and fiber-based, RC is the newer and more widely used, mainly because it enables quicker and easier printmaking. Both, though, have their own characteristics, and those should be considered when you are making a paper selection. Contrast control is another main deciding factor. Graded papers have their proponents, but variable-contrast paper is constantly improving and taking the market with it.

Fiber-Based Papers

Traditional fiber-based papers are primarily used when the print itself is important as the end product. Fine art photographers are probably the biggest proponents of fiber-based papers, which are also used for black and white portraiture and other commercial applications. For hand coloring, fiber-based papers are preferable because of their diverse surfaces absorbability. RC papers do not absorb the oil paints and they sit on the surface.

Fiber-based papers are available in single-, medium- and double-weight thicknesses. Single- and medium-weight papers were formerly used primarily for commercial purposes, but RC papers have mostly replaced them. Double-weight paper, however, is still widely used for fine art prints and other applications because of its durability and thickness. Fiber-based papers also come in a variety of tones, including some elegant warm tones.

The surfaces of fiber-based papers vary more richly than RC surfaces and range from glossy slick to highly textured. Matte surfaces lend themselves to hand coloring and most portraiture, but many fine art photographers prefer the air-dried glossy surface. Unlike RC papers, glossy fiber-based papers do not dry glossy automatically. They have to be *ferrotyped*, which involves soaking the print in a ferrotype solution and then squeegeeing the wet print face down on a chrome-plated surface, upon which it dries. An air-dried glossy fiber-based print will have a smooth, radiant surface that is unlike any other paper surface, whether fiber-based or RC. The emulsion of fiber-based papers can also be etched (scratched) with a knife or razor blade to remove or reduce black spots and other small, distracting elements in a print.

The same chemicals are used to process fiber and RC papers, but the processing times differ. Fiber-based papers take longer to process, wash, and dry because the paper fibers absorb chemicals. The normal development time for fiber-based papers is 1 to 3 minutes, with many photographers using a 2- or 3-minute development time. The stop bath is 30 seconds, and fixer time is 5 to 10 minutes, depending upon the type of fixer. It takes an hour to thoroughly wash a fiber-based print. If *hypo eliminator* is used, washing time can be reduced to 20 minutes, depending upon the product. To air dry a fiber-based print can take hours, but drying in a blotter book can take several days. Fiber-based prints have a tendency to curl while drying. To eliminate the curl, flatten the prints in a heat press or stack them face to face overnight under a heavy weight.

Resin-Coated Papers

The processing advantage of RC papers derives from the resin coating itself and the reduced thickness of the paper base. The thinner base absorbs less of the chemicals, thereby reducing the time required for processing, washing, and drying. Because of this ease and speed of handling and processing, RC papers dominate black and white and color printing. RC papers are available in medium weight and a variety of surfaces, including glossy, matte, and subtly textured.

Most RC prints are processed by machines. To hand process a black and white RC print, the normal development time is 1 to 2 minutes, with most photographers using 1 minute. The stop bath takes 30 seconds and the fixer 2 minutes. The final wash, with a good flow of running water, is also 2 minutes. It takes about 30 seconds to dry an RC print in most electric dryers, while air drying might take a half hour. To

accelerate air drying, use a hair dryer. Unlike fiber-based prints, RC prints dry flat and do not need any special treatment for a glossy surface.

Graded and Variable-Contrast Papers

Photographers control contrast when shooting through controlled lighting and by altering the exposure-development ratio of the film. (The zone system, which considers these matters, is discussed in Chapter 19). In the darkroom, the simplest way to control contrast is by using either graded or variable-contrast papers. Remember to consider contrast grades and basic methods for using variable-contrast filters. Here, we will cover some of the special refinements possible with graded and variable-contrast papers.

Graded Paper

Both fiber-based and RC papers are available in grades. The contrast grades normally range from a low of 1 to a high of 5. Most fiber-based papers are graded, and some of the specialty fiber-based papers come in only one or two grades. When you are using graded papers, it is necessary to have separate packages of each of the various grades, unless your negatives are extremely consistent.

Variable Development

Graded papers have been around for many years, and photographers have developed different methods to increase control and quality when using them. To get an intermediate grade, such as between a 2 and a 3 paper, photographers vary or alter the developer. Years ago, photographers mixed their chemicals from scratch and could alter the contrast of an image by varying the composition of the developer. Now, most buy prepackaged chemicals, but the contrast of graded papers can still be altered chemically. Use Kodak Dektol and Selectol Soft developers in the following manner to get more out of your prints.

Set up three developer trays. On the left have a normal dilution of Selectol Soft, in the middle use the normal 1 to 2 dilution of Dektol, and on the right use Dektol undiluted. This combination will give you a choice of soft, medium, and hard (contrasty) developers. Use a 3-minute development time. Expose a normal negative and develop the test print in the medium or normal developer. If the contrast looks good, but subtle shadow detail is lost, try developing another test for 1 minute in Selectol Soft and 2 minutes in the medium tray of Dektol diluted 1 to 2. A slight exposure adjustment might be necessary, but this should enable you to retain the shadow detail and have richer contrast than would be possible by going to a lower grade paper. To pump up the contrast, use the undiluted Dektol in the third tray. The potential for altering the retention of detail and contrast by using various combinations of the three developers is tremendous.

Flashing

Another technique for getting intermediate contrast with graded papers is flashing. If your negative prints too flat on a number 2 paper and too contrasty on a number 3, then print it normally on the higher grade paper (in this case the grade 3). Then, with the negative still in the enlarger, take a glassine sleeve (the type used for storing negatives) and hold it under the lens of the enlarger. Reexpose the print through the glassine sleeve for the same amount of time as the initial exposure. The glassine sleeve reduces and diffuses the light, adding an overall gray tone to the print. This additional tone should reduce the contrast about

Untitled, Mark Chamberlain.

Figure 12-3

Print A was exposed on a number 2 graded paper and developed normally for 2 minutes in developer Dektol 1 part diluted in 2 parts water. Print B was exposed the same way, but developed for 2 minutes in Selectol Soft and for 1 minute in the normal developer, Dektol diluted 1 to 2. The highlight and middle values are similar in both photographs, but the difference in the rendition of the dark areas is tremendous.

A.   B.

half a contrast grade. Experimentation will be necessary, however, since every working situation is different.

Variable-Contrast Papers

The prime advantage of variable-contrast papers is that only one pack of paper is necessary, regardless of the contrast need. Developer alterations and flashing do not work as effectively with variable-contrast papers, but the need is less because variable-contrast filters provide half-grade increments.

Variable-contrast papers use varying amounts of green and blue light to alter contrast. The lower-contrast filters are yellow and block blue light, allowing more green light to reach the emulsion. The higher contrast filters are magenta and block green light, allowing more blue light to reach the emulsion. The contrast changes happen by varying the proportions of green and blue light.

Multiple-Contrast Printing

Besides their economic advantage, variable-contrast papers have another important advantage: the ability to allow change of contrast in different areas of the print. For example, you might expose a print with a number 2 1/2 variable-contrast filter and then use a low-contrast number 00 to give additional light to darken a bright, contrasty portion of the print. This manipulation will make it easier to bring out the detail in the bright area of the print without affecting the contrast of the rest of the print. The trick is to "mask" the other portions of the print when using the 00 filter so that only the portion you want altered is affected. How to achieve this control is covered subsequently in this chapter in the discussion of *dodging* and *burning*.

The use of variable-contrast filters to change contrast in different areas of a print is called *multiple-contrast printing*. Lower number filters can be used to reduce contrast and bring out detail in burned-out portions of the print, while higher number filters can be used to deepen the blacks and increase contrast in portions of a print. This manipulation offers the photographer a new level of selective contrast control that is hard to attain with graded papers. It can also be extremely useful when multiple-contrast printing several negatives together, since the negatives may vary in contrast. Naturally, testing will be necessary to determine the right amount of exposure for each filter.

Split-Contrast Printing

With some of the newer variable-contrast papers, such as Ilford Multigrade IV RC Deluxe, it is possible to control contrast by *split-contrast printing*. This is done by exposing a print with a yellow 00 and a magenta 5 filter. For example, if you expose a print for 4 seconds with a 00 filter and for 4 seconds with a 5 filter, the resulting contrast of the print would be approximately a medium, or grade 2, contrast. To get a higher contrast, increase the amount of exposure with the 5 filter. To get a grade 4 contrast, the 5 filter would need about 6.5 seconds of exposure and the 00 filter 1.5 seconds of exposure.

Begin by making a normal test print with a 00 filter that has very light density in the most important highlight areas. Then do a test print with a 5 filter, making sure to get the minimum detail necessary in the blackest area of the image. Next, make a final print by multiply exposing the 00 and 5 filters on one sheet of paper with the exposure times from the tests. The result will be a better contrast range than you would get with the normal use of the filters. To refine the print further, use variations of this technique and selective dodging and burning with the same filters.

Succulent, Greg Rager.

Figure 12-4

Split-contrast printing can heighten and exaggerate delicate details.

Corrective Manipulations

In theory, a well-exposed negative should produce a print with a wide tonal range. However, this is not always the case. Film is capable of recording more subtleties in tone than can be printed. For instance, a light area in your negative may contain some detail, but if the exposure is based on the rest of the negative, that area will turn completely black in the print. If the exposure is timed to hold the detail in that light area, then the print will be too light.

In another negative, the opposite may be true. A dense area of the negative contains detail visible to your eye, but a print based on the overall exposure makes that area completely white in the print. If the exposure is changed to gain back the detail in the dark area of the negative, the rest of the print will be too dark. There are two techniques you can use to change such areas in a print: *burning in* and *dodging*. Burning in will darken an area, and dodging will lighten it.

Burning and dodging can be used to improve almost any image, either black and white or color. Most photographers burn and dodge every image they print. Sometimes burning and dodging are done to correct contrast problems, but often they are used to enhance or emphasize some aspect of the image.

Burning In

To burn in a small portion of a print, you must block out the rest of the picture while allowing light to fall only on the portion of the print you want to darken. Your hands or a piece of opaque mat board can be used to block out (mask) portions of the print while you burn in others. To do this, first expose the print to get a proper overall exposure. Then take a piece of 11×14-inch opaque mat board that is black on one side and white on the other. Cut a small hole about the size of a dime in the middle of it. Hold the mat board, with the white side up, between the lens of the enlarger and the paper. Put your free hand under the hole in the mat board (burn card) to keep light from falling onto the paper. Then, turn on the enlarger light so that the projected image falls onto the white side of the mat board. Keeping your hand in place under the opening, move the mat board until the part of the image that you want to burn in is projected onto the portion of the mat board that has the hole in it. Then move your hand from underneath and let light go through the hole to burn in that portion of the print. As you are burning, move the mat board slightly to blur the edges of

Figure 12-5

Print A is a straight print with no dodging or burning. Print B received the same initial exposure, but the sky and snow were burned in to make the image more dramatic. The photographer used his hands to block part of the image while burning in the other.

A.   B.

the hole so that the increased exposure will blend into the surrounding areas of the image.

Testing will be necessary to determine how much to burn in that portion of the print. Sometimes the initial test strip can provide a guide as to how much additional exposure is needed to burn in a particular area of the image. Use the timer to regulate the time or count to yourself. When burning in, move the mat board closer to the lens to increase the area exposed to the light going through the hole in the mat board, and closer to the paper to reduce the size. To burn in a sky, the edge of the mat board or the edge of your hand can be used to mask the lower portion of the image along the horizon line. Always be sure to move the mask while burning in to keep from getting an obvious line along the edge of the burned-in portion of the image.

Dodging

Dodging an area will lighten it. In other words, keeping light from the area will cause it to print lighter than it normally would. You can make a wand (tool) for dodging by cutting various shapes out of cardboard and fastening them to wires. The wire handles make it possible to dodge out areas near the center of the photograph without blocking out light near the edges. When dodging an area, it is important to keep the tool in constant motion so that the area blends in with the rest of the print.

A.

B.

Figure 12-6

(A) A straight print with no dodging or burning. (B) This print was "overburned." (C) This final version had the proper amount of burning.

C.

Figure 12-7

A. Test strip.

B. Work print.

C. Final print.

A.

B.

C.

Figure 12-8

Print A is a straight print with no dodging or burning. Print B was dodged too much. Print C had the right amount of dodging.

If a large area is to be dodged, your hand, or a piece of opaque mat board can be used to mask off a portion of the light.

Cropping

Cropping an image will not be necessary if you have composed the image carefully in the viewfinder of the camera. However, sometimes cropping is desirable. To crop out unwanted portions of an image, blow up the image in the enlarger so that the unwanted portion of the negative is outside the area of the enlarging paper. You may also move the arms of the print easel (if it is an adjustable type) so that the unwanted image area is masked out.

Never crop your photographs to fit the paper. Cropping is a last resort and should only be used if it makes the image better. The more you crop, the bigger the enlargement, and that reduces sharpness and makes the film grain more obvious. Learn to compose with the camera, and you will become more observant and a better photographer faster.

Vignetting

Vignetting can be used to eliminate a distracting background and accentuate the subject by fading the subject into a white or black background. It can be done with special filters when shooting or while in the darkroom. Vignettes to white are the most common. The procedure can be done while making a print, as follows:

Use a burn card with a small round hole cut in the center. Sawtooth the edges of the hole to make the vignette more subtle. Prior to exposing a final print, hold the burn card under the lens with the white side up. Cover the hole by placing your other hand under the burn card. Turn the timer onto "focus" and position the projected image so that it is located where the hole is in the burn card. Then move your hand so that the image hits the paper through the hole. Gently move the burn card up and down as you count the seconds needed to expose the print. Once the print is exposed, cover the hole with your hand and turn off the timer. The movement of the burn card during the exposure will create a soft edge that fades into a white unexposed background. Be careful not to let any light hit the area to be left white.

Vignetting to black is exactly the opposite procedure. Expose the whole print normally, then use a dodging wand to mask the center of the print while you burn in the outer areas of the print to black.

Diffusion

It is common for photographers to use diffusion filters when they are shooting to soften the detail in an image subtly. This tactic is especially

Figure 12-9

Normal print on left, vignetted print on right.

A. Before diffusion.

B. After diffusion.

Figure 12-10

Diffusion reduces contrasts and softens facial features and skin texture.

true with portrait photographers, who almost always use a number 1 diffusion filter on the camera, as noted in Chapter 9. Diffusion can be part of making a print. On-camera diffusion is permanent, and when done in excess causes a "glow" around anything white in the picture. Darkroom diffusion, however, can always be altered or avoided. Darkroom diffusion done in excess causes a "glow" around anything black in the picture. A single thickness of black sheer nylon hose stretched across an embroidery hoop makes a great darkroom diffuser.

To diffuse an image, hold the nylon-covered hoop in the path of the projected image for a portion of the print exposure. Be sure to move the hoop continually while diffusing the image so that the pattern of the nylon doesn't print. The longer the diffusion, the more obvious it will be. How much diffusion should be used is a decision that is up to you. Do several tests, diffusing the image for different amounts of the overall exposure time. Try tests at 25, 50, 75, and 100 percent of the exposure time and compare the results. Then select the time that looks best to you. The exposure time and contrast will have to be adjusted based on the amount of diffusion. More diffusion causes less exposure and less contrast, which can be corrected by increasing the exposure time and changing to a higher contrast filter or to a higher grade of paper.

Distortion

A less common problem of image making is distortion. For instance, if you photograph a tall building, looking from the ground up, you will get a keystoning effect, with the sides of the building converging towards each other. This is a perspective problem, and usually nothing can be done about it when you are shooting unless you use a view camera or a lens that corrects distortion. It is possible, however, to reduce and sometimes correct distortion when you are enlarging the image. To correct distortion, project the image onto the print easel. Once it is in focus, lift the easel on the normal or larger side of the image, leaving the converging or smaller side of the image on the baseboard. This adjustment will reduce the size of the part of the image that was raised to make it similar in size to the side that was kept on the baseboard. Because the easel is tilted, you will have to adjust the focus and use

Figure 12-11

Distortion correction can be done by raising one side of the easel. Photograph A was printed normally; B was printed with the top of the image being raised slightly; C was printed with the top being raised even more.

A.   B.   C.

depth of field to maintain focus from end to end. Focus on the halfway point of the image, and close down the lens to its smallest aperture to get maximum depth of field. If the easel is raised more than an inch, you may have trouble maintaining focus. Also consider using distortion as a creative option.

Bleaching

Bleaching is a corrective and creative tool that seldom gets attention, but is used by all of the great black and white print makers. It can be used to lighten overexposed film, to correct tonal values in a print, to completely eliminate portions of an image, and to make an image more graphic. Most photographers use bleaching as a last hope corrective tool to lighten part of a print or to bleach out skin blemishes and other disturbing elements. But it can also be a powerful and intriguing means to totally alter the visual character of an image.

Common household bleach products can be used to bleach prints, but Farmer's Reducer is the most controllable and commonly used bleach for reducing black and white prints and film. Small packets of Kodak Farmer's Reducer can be purchased in many photo stores. The active ingredients are potassium ferricyanide and sodium thiosulfate crystals.

Figure 12-12

Photographs A and B illustrate how bleaching can be used to alter a print. Image A is a normal print. In Image B, select areas of the print were lightened by bleaching. The unaffected areas were protected by a covering of rubber cement, which was removed after the bleach was rinsed off. Then the whole print was immersed in water before drying so that the surface would dry evenly. Further bleaching could have reduced these areas to pure white.

A.

B.

When mixed for use, the solution lasts about 15 minutes, which makes it expensive and inconvenient to buy in packet form. However the bulk chemicals are easy to mix and very inexpensive. A 16-ounce quantity will last a lifetime.

To use the packets, follow the instructions that come with them. To make your own bleach, mix a tablespoon of both chemicals with enough water to fill a 5x7-inch photo tray with about a half inch of liquid. Once dissolved, this mixture makes an active solution. If it seems weak, add a little more of the potassium ferricyanide.

A more exact method is shown in the accompanying chart. Be sure to handle the chemicals with care because they are poisonous and can be harmful to the eyes, mouth, and any cuts or skin abrasions.

To bleach part of a print, use a small brush or a cotton swab to reduce that portion of the image. First soak the print in water to soften the emulsion, and then squeegee the surface to keep the bleach from running. Delicately apply the bleach to the part of the print that you wish to lighten. Then rinse the print with running water and squeegee the surface again. Evaluate the result and reapply the bleach if more is needed. Any brown staining that occurs should go away when the bleach is neutralized. When you are done, rinse the print with water and refix and rewash the print. Fixer neutralizes the bleach. Be sure to rinse your brush in fixer and then rinse it with water to keep the bleach from eating up the bristles. Overall print or film reduction can be done by immersing the print or a piece of film into a tray of bleach.

"Pan Pacific" from the *Metropolis* series, Karl Gernot Kuehn.

Figure 12-13

This surreal image of Los Angeles was achieved by the use of several different manipulations of the original photograph. First of all, Kuehn had to shoot very early on a Sunday morning to avoid cars or people in views of the city for his *Metropolis* series. To give the series an apocalyptic look, he made masks to block portions of the picture while he burned-in other areas to make them darker than normal—more somber. Once each print was processed, he selectively bleached areas of the print with Farmer's Reducer to create unusual highlights.

Chemical	Amount	
	U.S. Customary	Metric
Stock Solution A:*†		
Potassium ferricyanide	1.3 oz.	37.5 g
Water to make	16.0 fl. oz.	500.5 mL
Stock Solution B:†		
Sodium thiosulfate (hypo)	17.0 oz.	480.0 g
Water to make	64.0 fl. oz.	2.0 L
Working Solution:		
Stock Solution A	1.0 fl. oz.	30.0 mL
Stock Solution B	4.0 fl. oz.	120.0 mL
Water to make	32.0 fl. oz.	1.0 L

* Less active bleaching results from using half of the recommended amount for Solution A.
† Stock Solution B will keep indefinitely, but Stock Solution A is only good for about six months in a well-sealed, brown-glass bottle. The working solution must be used about 15 minutes after mixing.

Processing for Permanence

All photographs, whether black and white, color, or digital, deteriorate with time. How fast this happens depends on whether they were properly processed, how they were stored, displayed, and the amount of contact with ultraviolet (UV) light. Aside from the fading problems that are due to exposure to UV light, most print deterioration is due to contact gases, acids, and other harmful chemicals commonly found in wood, paints, wrapping papers, cardboard, tapes, and adhesives. To be archivally safe, all storage and framing materials need to be pH neutral. See Chapter 20 for more information.

Properly processed black and white prints are extremely permanent. Special toning procedures can also be used that make black and white prints even more permanent and add to the richness of the tones. Selenium toner is the most common toner used to enhance the permanence of black and white prints. It can be used to add color to prints, but when used for permanence, it is mixed so that it enhances the blacks, adding brilliance to the image without altering the color.

To make a protective selenium toning bath, begin with a one-gallon working solution of Kodak Hypo Clearing Agent or other washing aid such as HEICO Permawash or Orbit bath. Then, add 1 1/2 to 7 ounces of Kodak Rapid Selenium Toner to the clearing agent. The amount of selenium toner determines the amount of the intensification of the blacks in the print. The more toner added, the stronger the intensification and the color shift. Next, add 2 1/2 ounces of Kodak Balanced Alkali to the solution, and mix thoroughly.

Before using the toning bath, be sure to properly fix your prints with a double fixing bath. For the first fixing bath, use a tray of partially used fixer for 3 minutes. Then, use a bath of fresh fixer for 3 minutes. This two-step method gives a more thorough fixing than a normal single bath. Next, rinse the prints in running water for 10 minutes. Then, transfer the prints directly into the selenium toner solution at room temperature, and continuously agitate them for 3 to 5 minutes. After toning, wash the print for the normal wash time. Each gallon of solution provides protective toning and image intensification for fifty 8×10-inch prints. Information on toners to produce colors in black and white is provided in Chapter 16.

Chapter 13

Color Film Processing

Whatever is visible is color, and color is what lies upon what is in its own nature visible.

—Aristotle

Processing color film is similar to processing black and white film. Most color films can be processed by hand with the same equipment that is used to process black and white film. However, most photographers, professional and nonprofessional, rely on professional labs to process color film. Modern color films and their processing chemicals are designed for machine processing. The chemistry is delicate and needs constant adjustment. The inconsistencies of manual handling, along with maintaining the proper chemical balance, have made home processing impractical. Also, there are some color films, such as Kodachrome, which must be processed in special machines because the process is too complex to do by hand. For the best results, color film should be processed promptly after exposure, whether you do it yourself or have it commercially processed. (See Color Gallery B, Plate 13.1.)

There are three types of color processing laboratories, each catering to a different segment of the picture-taking public: the commercial photofinisher, the custom laboratory, and the minilab.

The commercial photofinisher offers the largest number of services at competitive prices. The services offered usually include color negative and color slide development, color prints and enlargements from color negatives and color slides, color slides duplicated from color negatives or from color slides, and color negatives made from color slides and color prints. Most commercial photofinishers produce color prints that range from adequate to good. Minimal correction for color balance is provided by most labs from color negative film.

The custom laboratory generally caters to a more demanding clientele, including professional photographers and serious amateurs who put quality above price. These labs usually include fine color balancing and various corrective manipulations such as cropping, spotting, dodging, and the like.

The minilab is the "fast-food chain" of the photofinishing business. Designed to develop and print a roll of color negative film within an hour, they tend to put speed ahead of other concerns. In general, they do not offer the variety of services available at either commercial or custom labs. Minilabs tend to produce prints of adequate quality designed to meet the need of the average snapshooter.

There are two main types of color film: *color negative film* and *color transparency (positive) film*. Color negative film is often referred to as *print film* and is designed specifically for making color prints. The suffix *-color* is usually used in the name of color negative films and print materials. Common examples are Kodacolor, Fujicolor, and Agfacolor. Color transparency films are positive color images that are primarily designed for projection or viewing with light transmitted through them. However, they are also used for making color prints and are the primary

film used for separation negatives and color lithography. Unlike color negative films, which have an orange color cast, transparency films have natural colors. They suffix *-chrome* is used in the name of most transparency films, such as Fujichrome, Ektachrome, and Agfachrome. Chapter 7 will cover—in more detail—the types and characteristics of color films and chromogenic black and white films that are processed in color chemistry.

Thanks to simplified procedures and processing kits designed for nonprofessional use, anyone with a serious interest in photography can easily process color film and make color prints. Processing color film is time consuming, tedious, and exacting, whereas making color prints can be creatively stimulating. Should you decide to do your own film processing, small-volume kits are manufactured by a host of companies, including, but not limited to, Kodak, Unicolor, Besseler, and Photocolor. The physical preparation, handling, and mechanical aspects of processing film are discussed in detail in Chapter 10 on black and white film development and should be reviewed if you are unfamiliar with those techniques. (See Color Gallery B, Plate 13.2.)

Equipment Needs

The same processing equipment used for black and white film processing can be used for color film processing provided it has been kept clean and uncontaminated. However, new chemical storage containers and mixing equipment should be used to avoid contamination from chemicals absorbed by long-term use. To maintain temperature, it will probably be necessary to use a water bath and a heating element, such as a recirculating heater. Some companies, such as Jobo, manufacture processing equipment that provides for water baths and temperature control. Relatively inexpensive tabletop processors that handle a variety of film formats are also available, and some of them can also be used for processing prints.

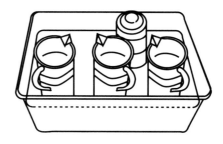

Most important to remember about any type of color processing is: *Be consistent.* Consistency starts with always using the same thermometer and maintaining consistent time, temperature, and agitation procedure. For accuracy, an expensive color thermometer is recommended, but consistency can be maintained with an inexpensive thermometer, provided you use the same one every time.

Chemical Considerations

Follow directions when using color chemistry. The chemistry is more complex than black and white and is frequently improved and altered by the manufacturer. Color chemistry may change because of oxidation and other factors. To get the best results with hand processing, buy only the quantity you plan to use, and mix the chemicals shortly before using. Professional labs reuse their chemistry, but they replenish it to compensate for use. In addition, they constantly test the chemistry and make chemical adjustments to maintain consistent quality. This is impractical, if not impossible, for small-quantity hand processing.

Most manufacturers' instructions suggest increasing the development time to compensate for prior use. While increasing the development time may seem practical, it generally does *not* provide a quality result for color accuracy and longevity. For best results, use fresh chemistry each time you process color film, or take your film to a competent color lab. Avoid the labs that offer discounted low price deals that may compromise quality, resulting in fading, discoloration, and a shorter life for your film.

Processing Color Negative Films

Kodak C-41 process is the worldwide industry standard for processing color negative films. Fuji offers the CN-16 process, Konica CNK-4, and Agfa AP-70, but any color negative film, whether designed for another process or not, can be, and often is, processed in C-41 chemistry. The chemistry is sold in 1-gallon sizes or in Hobby-Pacs for 16-ounce processing tanks. The chemicals include a developer, bleach/fix, and stabilizer.

The Chemicals

Developer. The developer is the most critical step in the C-41 process. It determines the density, contrast, and color balance of the film. It changes the exposed silver compounds in each of the three emulsion layers (red, blue, and green) to metallic silver. A result of this action causes a chemical by-product that activates *dye couplers* in each layer, and these form the image color.

Bleach-fix. The bleach converts the metallic silver to silver bromide, which the fixer dissolves. What remains is a color dye image.

Stabilizer. In the last chemical step, the stabilizer stabilizes the colors to reduce fading. It also contains a wetting agent to help achieve uniform drying.

The C-41 Process

C-41 processing instructions will vary, depending upon the kit and the type of processing equipment used. The following procedure is typical, but refer to the instructions that come with your equipment and chemistry before proceeding.

Processing Considerations

Unlike the processing times and temperatures for black and white films, those for developing color film are standardized. Color negative film

C-41 Process

Step	Temp (° F)	Time (min.)	Agitation
Developer	100± 1/4	3 1/4	First 15 seconds continuous, then 5 seconds every 30 seconds
Bleach-fix	75–105	6 1/2	First 10 seconds, then 5 seconds every 30 seconds

(Remaining steps can be done in normal room light.)

Step	Temp (° F)	Time (min.)	Agitation
Water wash	75–105	3 1/4	Running water, exchange frequently
Stabilizer	75–105	1 1/2	First 15 seconds only
Drying			Drying methods vary; air drying can take an hour or more; heat drying can take 1 to 15 minutes, depending upon the type of dryer.

and color transparency film require different chemistry and must be processed separately for normal results. Otherwise, films of different manufacturers and different ISOs can be processed together in the same tank.

Some manufacturers provide a list of different processing times and temperatures similar in concept to those used for black and white film processing. It is best, however, to be consistent and always use the recommended time and the temperature of 100 degrees. Varying the time and temperature affects contrast and color and may produce less than optimum results.

The processing procedure is essentially the same as for black and white film. Begin timing each solution as you pour it into the tank, and drain the chemistry from the tank during the last 10 seconds of each step.

Agitation and temperature control are very important. A hot water bath is generally the best way to elevate the temperature of the chemicals for processing. It can also be used to maintain the temperature during processing. Keep all of the chemicals in the water bath between steps so that the temperature is constant. To maintain the temperature of a chemical while it is in use, place the developing tank into the water bath between agitation cycles.

Follow the specific instructions of the chemical kit for the agitation procedure. The basic handling will be the same as for black and white, but the timing and sequence may be different. Consistency in agitation is extremely important, since agitation affects the density, contrast, and color of the film. Be sure to tap the tank to remove air bubbles when you are beginning with the developer.

Processing Color Transparency Films

Color transparency films are less forgiving than color negative films. Camera exposures are more critical, extreme contrast ranges are harder to maintain, and color shifts because of lighting problems are hard to correct during printing. Yet transparencies are the preferred type of color film for many professional and advanced nonprofessional photographers because what they see is what they get. Color transparencies are also more permanent than color negatives, have more-permanent print processes available, and are the primary type of film used for color separations and lithographic printing.

Processing color transparencies requires more solutions, takes more time, and is more critical than processing color negatives, but the procedure is similar. Kodak E-6 chemistry is the worldwide industry standard for processing almost all color transparency films except for Kodachrome, Polachrome, and Infrared Ektachrome. The Kodachrome process is delicate and complicated and can be adequately controlled only with expensive machinery. Only a few Kodachrome processing labs exist scattered around the globe, whereas E-6 labs are everywhere, and the process is easy enough to use at home. Polachrome is an instant color transparency film for 35mm slides that comes with its own processing chemistry and must be processed in a special Polaroid Auto Processor. Infrared Ektachrome uses the old E-4 process, which is no longer available. Check to determine where the film can be sent for processing before purchasing.

The Chemicals

E-6 chemistry is marketed by several manufacturers and is available for small quantity use in one-gallon and smaller kit sizes. The chemicals include a first developer, color developer, bleach-fix, and stabilizer.

First Developer. The first developer is critical because it determines the density and contrast of the images on the film. It is a black and white developer that converts the exposed silver halides on each of the three emulsion layers into metallic silver.

Color Developer. The unexposed and undeveloped portions of the film are chemically fogged and converted into metallic silver by the color developer, which also activates the dye couplers in each layer to form color dyes.

Bleach-Fix. The bleach converts the metallic silver to silver bromide, which is dissolved by the fixer. Once the silver is gone, the color dyes remain to form the final image.

Stabilizer. The stabilizer step reduces color fading and provides a wetting agent to ensure uniform drying.

The E-6 Process

E-6 processing instructions will vary, depending upon the kit and the type of processing equipment used. The following procedure is typical, but be sure to refer to the instructions that come with your equipment and chemistry before proceeding. Despite the latitude indicated, it is best to keep all of the chemicals at the same temperature.

E-6 Process

Step	Temp (° F)	Time (min.)	Agitation
First Developer	100± 1/2	6 1/2	Continuous the first 15 seconds, then 5 seconds every 30 seconds
Water Wash	70–110	1 1/4	Exchange water frequently
Color Developer	100± 1/2	6	Continuous the first 15 seconds, then 5 seconds every 30 seconds
Water Wash	70–110	1 1/4	Exchange water frequently
Bleach-Fix	70–110	10	Continuous the first 15 seconds, then 5 seconds every 30 seconds
Final Wash	70–110	5	Exchange water frequently
Stabilizer	70–110	1	Continuous the first 15 seconds
Drying	Drying methods vary; air drying can take an hour or more; heat drying can take 1 to 15 minutes, depending upon the type of dryer		

Processing Procedure

Like color negative films, E-6 films have a standardized processing time and temperature, which means that film of different types and speeds can be processed simultaneously in the same tank. E-6 chemistry is more delicate than C-41 and subject to aging changes that can affect the quality of your results. For the best results, mix what you need when you need it and avoid the reuse formulas suggested by many manufacturers. Although *they* may get an acceptable-looking result, the quality and longevity of your film may suffer. Most professionals have their E-6 film commercially processed by quality custom labs, which can assure quality control. The only advantage to hand processing E-6 film is for a special-effects processing modification that labs can't provide because of their automated equipment.

Timing, agitation, and temperature control are extremely important. Use a hot water bath for temperature control. Immerse the developing tank into the water bath between agitation cycles to maintain the temperature during processing. Do not take shortcuts or compromise on any aspect of the process. Follow the instructions of the chemical kit for specific agitation and handling procedures. Specifics on film processing procedures are provided in Chapter 10.

Processing Problems with Color Films

Aside from inadequate film storage, aging, and improper exposure, many problems that occur with color film processing are like those of black and white film processing. (See Color Gallery B, Plate 13.3 for one such problem.) Chapter 10 covers basic film processing flaws such as air bells, surge marks, and crescent moons. Other problems having to do with color will be immediately evident with transparency films but may not be noticeable with color negative film until after a print is made. Sometimes it is hard to determine the cause of a problem. Errors occur with chemical mixing, storage, handling, solution temperatures, agitation rates, timing, draining, washing, drying, and various combinations of these. The following charts list possible processing problems with C-41 and E-6 chemistry.

C-41 Processing Problems

Problem	Probable Fault
Lack of density	Underexposure, inadequate development
Too dense and too much contrast	Overexposure, overdevelopment weak bleach-fix
Clear film with frame numbers	Film not exposed
Clear film without frame numbers	Developer not used or totally exhausted
Magenta cast	Developer temperature too high, overagitation, overdevelopment
Strange color and/or contrast	Developer contamination, improper development
Surface scum, streaks	Weak or contaminated stabilizer
Green casts in shadow areas of prints	Contaminated developer
Dull image color	Contaminated or exhausted bleach-fix

E-6 Processing Problems

Problem	Probable Fault
Transparencies too dark overall	Underexposure, inadequate first development
Transparencies too light overall	Overexposure, too much first development
Overall color shift	Film not balanced for light source, out of date or improperly stored film, inadequate color development, contaminated chemistry
Whole roll black, except for the frame numbers	Film not advanced in camera, unexposed
Whole roll black, no frame numbers	Chemistry bad, no development
Whole roll clear, no frame numbers	Film fogged, exposed to light, or processed improperly
Overall green cast	Film shot with fluorescent light, or color developer exhausted
Overall yellow cast	Color developer too concentrated or daylight film shot with tungsten light
Yellow highlights	Exhausted fixer
Dull, gray blacks	Contamination, fogging, or overpushed
Mottled, streaked, blotched	Faulty agitation
Subtle cyan cast, weak colors	Color development inadequate
Gray blothces or streaks	Bleach-fix inadequate
Surface scum, streaks	Contaminated or exhausted stabilizer, water residue

Pushing and Pulling Color Films

To obtain the best "normal" results, color film, regardless of the type, should be exposed and processed normally. However, color negative and transparency films can be push processed to compensate for underexposure or to increase contrast and grain. They can also be pulled to compensate for overexposure or to reduce contrast, but pulling is not

Developer Times for Push/Pull Processing Color Negative Films

Camera Exposure	ISO/ASA Film Speed Equivalent			Approximate Change in Developer Time
4 times (2 f-stops) underexposure	400	800	1600	Increase by 75 percent
2 times (1 f-stop) underexposure	200	400	800	Increase by 35 percent
Normal ISO/ASA	**100**	**200**	**400**	**Use normal time***
2 times (1 f-stop) overexposure	50	100	200	Decrease by 30 percent
4 times (2 f-stops) overexposure	25	50	100	Decrease by 50 percent

*Refer to the data sheets accompanying Process C-41 chemicals.

recommended for color negative films because it can result in uncorrectable color shifts and flat, muddy negatives. Custom processing labs generally provide services for pushing and pulling color films for an additional fee.

The results from pushing and pulling will vary with different films. Some are more tolerant than others and adapt easily to processing changes, whereas others have problems. Generally, color transparency films produce better results when pushed and pulled than do color negative films. But color shifts from processing deviations are easier to correct when you are printing with color negatives than with color transparencies. Since films change because of manufacturer modifications, it is best to run tests before relying on pushing or pulling for important shots. If you choose to push or pull your color film, alter the developer time only. All other steps must remain the same.

The following chart suggests the changes for pushing and pulling color films. Be sure to check current film and chemical data sheets for changes in recommendations and data.

Cross-Processing

To get unusual color effects, higher contrast, and increased grain, try *cross-processing*. Process E-6 transparency film in C-41 chemistry and

C-41 color negative film in E-6 chemistry. The results will vary with different films. Also, variations in film exposure, development time, and processing temperature can cause a variety of unique results. With cross-processing, "natural" color is out, and unusual and surreal color is obtainable and predictable with adequate testing to determine the results.

Many professional labs offer cross-processing as a service because it doesn't contaminate the chemistry unless it is done on a large scale. However, you will need to do your own processing for radical deviations from the normal processing procedures. For unusual results, try substituting the first developer of the E-6 process with a black and white developer, then finishing the process with the normal E-6 chemistry.

E-6 color transparency film processed in C-41 produces a color negative image without the "orange mask." This negative image is often visually exciting in itself and may be worth printing as a final image in its negative form. When printed to produce a positive image print, it results in a high contrast image with rich, saturated colors. If the film is exposed and processed normally, the grain structure will be fairly normal, and it will be possible to get natural-looking colors in a print. If the ISO and development procedure are altered, the grain structure will become more apparent and the colors more artificial.

C-41 color negative film processed in E-6 produces a positive image with an orange mask that can have blue shadow areas, depending upon the type of film and the processing procedure. This image can then be printed onto a *Type R* (positive to positive color print paper) and used as a final image. It can also be printed as a distinctive negative image or contact printed onto another piece of film to create a new negative. and cause further alterations through additional cross-processing. (See Color Gallery B, Plates 13.4, 13.5, and 13.6.)

Evaluating Processed Color Film

It is impossible to judge the color by looking at a color negative because of its overall orange cast and the reversed colors. However, density and exposure problems can be determined in the same manner as you would with black and white negatives. If a negative is dark overall and the detail hard to distinguish, it was probably overexposed and will be hard to print, especially in the highlight areas. A light negative, conversely, was probably underexposed. Underexposed color negatives are much less likely to print will than underexposed black and white negatives

because of the limited contrast variations possible with color print papers. (See Color Gallery B, Plates 13.7, 13.8, and 13.9.)

Color transparencies are far easier to evaluate because what you see is what you get. Overexposed transparencies are too light, and washed-out highlights lacking in detail are impossible to reclaim because you can't put back what is not there. Underexposed transparencies are too dark, but they may be salvageable in printing or they can be lightened one to three *f*-stops by making duplicate transparencies with increased exposures. In general, it is better to have a transparency underexposed, rather than overexposed. For printing, a normal exposure is best, whereas slides made for projection look richer if they are slightly underexposed. Color can be evaluated by looking at the transparency on a light box or by holding it over a sheet of white paper in a well-illuminated room. For an accurate evaluation of color, you need to view the transparency with light that is balanced for 5000K. Chapters 7 and 18 address film, light, and color balance in more detail.

Color Gallery B

List of Plates

continued on next page

continued from previous page

Suyen, Michael Weschler.

Plate 13.1

This fashion image was pushed and *cross-processed* to get the high key and unusual color effects. Kodak Ektapress 100 color negative film was shot at ISO 80 and push processed 1 3/4 stops in E-6 transparency chemistry.

Plate 13.2

On the Beach: *Positive/Negative*, Jerry Burchfield.

Color transparency films are positive color images and are used for separation negatives.

Plate 13.3
This transparency faded rapidly
and lost most of its color because
of inadequate film processing.

Plate 13.4

Color film has three color-sensitive layers, one for each of the three primary colors of light. This tricolor exposure was made by triple exposing the film through the primary color filters red, blue, and green. Natural color resulted when nothing moved. The artificial color of the moving subjects was determined by when the subject moved within the exposure sequence. For instance, a person would be magenta if standing still during the red and blue exposure, but moving during the green exposure.

Tricolor Beach, Jim Nordstrom.

Plate 13.5

A Fuji panoramic camera and 2 1/4-inch color negative film reproduced a wide range of delicate tonalities and detail in this coastal view.

Shell Cove, Tom Lamb.

Plate 13.6

Use of Ektachrome infrared film helped produce the surreal color in this photograph. Color relationships change through the use of color filters in the shooting of infrared film. Experiment to see what results you can get.

Afterlife, Jerry Burchfield.

Plate 13.7

Be a Good Citizen, Judith Taggart.

The result of properly-processed color film is accurate color and a
quality image.

Plate 13.8

Low-light shooting is often impossible because of long exposures and the lack of a tripod. Intentionally underexposing the film, however, and push-processing to compensate, can make it possible to still get the shot.

Sante Fe Night, Boyd Jaynes.

Trees in the High Sierras, Jerry Burchfield.

Plate 13.9

Cross-processing was used to get the high contrast and artificial coloration for this photograph. E-6 transparency film was exposed and processed normally in C-41 chemistry to produce a different, yet almost natural-looking effect.

Lily Pads, Justin Courter.

Plate 14.1

This photograph is quite beautiful and evocative, an excellent example of *effective* color. The artificiality of the color in this photograph is due to the time of day and the natural lighting conditions when the picture was shot.

Plate 14.2

Shot late at night from a hotel
room window, this image uses
color to capture the feeling of
night in a big city. Contrasting
warm and cool colors heighten
the impact.

Hot Hot, Clayton Spada.

Plate 14.3

Color wheel.

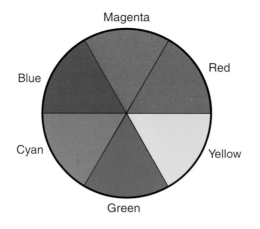

A. Full-color

Suburban Soft Drinks, Mark Chamberlain.

Plate 14.4

As shown, a full-color image (A) can be separated into the yellow dye image, the magenta dye image, and the cyan dye image—the three colors that combine to produce the final image.

B. Yellow

C. Magenta

D. Cyan

Plate 14.5

A color ringaround was made with a four-image test print easel, as shown on the next page. A portion of a larger image (the lighthouse) was selected for testing because it had a variation in values and colors. The test print easel was repositioned between exposures to repeat the same portion of the image in each quadrant. Four different initial filtrations were used, each 20 degrees different from the other. The lower left image was selected as the closest to natural color. A correction was made from that, and the image was subsequently printed.

Color ringaround.

Plate 14.6

A. When any two primary color filters are put togther, they absorb the color that each transmits—creating black.

B. When the three primary colors—red, blue, and green—are projected in equal parts and overlap, they create white light. When any two overlap in equal parts, they create the complement of the third.

A.

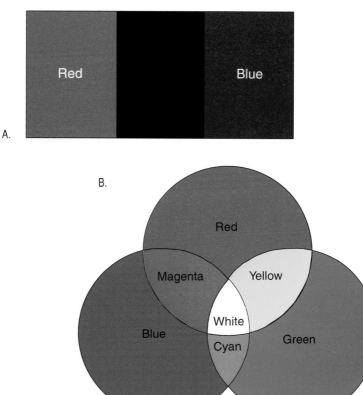

B.

Plate 14.7

This image of a car shows two common drum processing flaws. The two vertical streaks resulted because the drum was not thoroughly dried before use and water drops ran down the print. The three dark semicircles along the top were light leaks caused by the improper placement of an end-cap light baffle.

A.

B.

Plate 14.8

Filters are used to produce proper
color balance in color prints. They
can also be used to create
artificial color. In fact, as shown,
you can make a sunset any color
you want simply by changing the
filters.

C.

Plate 14.9

Color Combinations.

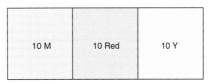

20 Y + 20 M + 20 C = 20 degrees of neutral density or gray with the exposure affected by +100%

10 M	10 Red	10 Y

10 M + 10 Y = 10 red with the exposure affected by +25%

10 M	20 M	10 M

10 M + 10 M = 20 magenta with the exposure affected by +50%

Plate 14.10

(A) Too often, people get lazy when making test prints and don't reposition the easel to repeat the same portion of the image in each test. As this image indicates, it would be impossible to make an accurate filter correction without having the boy in each test. The upper left quadrant is very different from the upper right quadrant, and both are different from the one with the boy in it.

Brian at Maui, Jerry Burchfield.

(B) When you are using the test print easel, it is also important to select a portion of the image that has a full range of values from light to dark and a variety of the important colors. This small test print provides all the information that is needed because it includes all of the important elements in the picture and is a better choice than any of the other images in the four quadrants of the larger picture.

Plate 14.11

Ringaround exposure and filtration test.
Each quadrant has a different filtration and an exposure test strip showing 7-, 14- and 21-second exposures. The filtration in the upper left quadrant is 60Y 40M, the upper right quadrant is 60Y 20M, the lower left quadrant is 40Y 40M, and the lower right quadrant is 40Y 20M.

Plate 14.12

A color contact sheet (above) can be a time saver. It can help keep track of what you shot, provide cropping references, and be a exposure and filtration guide. Some of these shots are ready to print as is but others need exposure and filtration corrections.

Plate 14.13

This distinctive image (*Metamorphosis*) was made by printing the leaf directly onto a piece of 16×20-inch Ilfochrome Classic paper without camera or film. Type R print materials lend themselves to the direct printing and creation of photograms because they can reproduce a positive image with natural colors and detail unlike anything possible with a camera.

Metamorphosis V, Paula Martin.

A.

B.

Plate 14.14

The print on the top left (A) was made with the normal contrast Ilfochrome Classic paper and lost detail in the highlights. The print on the bottom right (B) was made with the low contrast Ilfochrome Classic and has a much better retention of detail in the highlights.

In the Shadow with the Cloud, Jerry Burchfield.

Plate 14.15

When this 35mm slide image is projected, subtle detail is visible in the boy's face and the other shadow areas. But when it is printed, the shadows go black, with no detail. To get a more accurate feeling for how a transparency will print, hold it about 10 inches above a white background in a well-lit room. The contrast range and the amount of detail you see indicate how it will print.

Plate 14.16

This image was shot on Polapan, a black and white 35mm instant slide film by Polaroid. It was printed on Ilfochrome Classic and given its distinctive color cast by filtering during printing. Black and white images, negative or positive, can be printed on Type R materials and filtered to achieve natural or artificial monochromatic hues.

Dreaming, Diane Edwards.

Sibling Sunrise, Fritz Cramp Smith.

Plate 15.1

This totally manufactured photograph started as an idea, and each part was created separately and later combined together with elaborate masking techniques into a five-element photo composite. The children were photographed in a room watching TV, the beach scene was a natural setting, and the sky was made by liquifying a plastic material that was then photographed. Over 20 pieces of film were used to get it onto one final piece of 4 x 5-inch transparency film. Today, we have the option of using the traditional darkroom method Smith used, or combining the images together on a computer.

Plate 15.2

A. This image uses warm and cool contrast to heighten feeling and visually separate the statue from the church. Attention focuses on the cool-colored statue in the foreground, but the vibrant yellow church in the background comes forward aggressively.

B. The warm color harmony in this image and the position of the statue unify foreground and background. The statue seems to become a structural element of the church.

From the Church Series, Greg Phillips.

Bank of America, Mark Chamberlain.

Plate 15.3

Although monochromatic, this image vibrates with color as it contrasts the dark natural form of the tree with the golden glow of the rigid constructed environment. The yellow and red lines in the street symbolize barriers to be overcome before one can gain access to the riches implied by the glowing bank building.

Plate 15.4

This image suggests a primal forming of matter or the molten
insides of a volcano. In actuality, it is an extreme closeup of crystals,
shot with a microscope attachment. Hastings created the color
artificially, using polarized light.

Untitled, Gordon Hastings.

Plate 15.5

The warm color of the tungsten-lit window display contrasts with the green glow of the fluorescent lights of the gas station to make an ordinary scene emotive and dramatic.

Lip Service, Mark Chamberlain.

Plate 15.6

Selective filtration was necessary to correct the green bias that had occurred in this transparency image (A) because of aging and chemical problems. To reduce the green, a 20 magenta filter was used as a dodging tool during the exposure. As shown in B, the green was effectively neutralized, but the dodged area was a little light because of the density of the magenta filter. For a final print, additional burn-in exposure through the magenta filter would be needed to make the density more uniform.

A. Normative filtering.

B. Selective filtering.

Plate 15.7

A. The top photograph is a straight, unaltered image printed on Ilfochrome Classic paper.

B. Ilfochrome Transparent Retouching Dyes as used on the bottom print intensify color and add impact.

Plate 15.8

The total bleach—bleaching all three layers of Ilfochrome prints—was used to create the border and bring out abstract detail and color in the surreal image on the next page.

Untitled, Jerry Burchfield.

Chapter 14

Basic Color Printmaking

The only possible rival to sound as a vehicle of pure emotion is color.

—Hugh Randolph Haweis
Clergyman and theological writer

The basic equipment, techniques, and costs are similar for both color and black and white printmaking. The main difference is the need to control and manipulate color. Everything else is essentially the same. Initially, most photographers are taught to print black and white photographs and hesitate to print color because it seems too complicated and confusing. But color processes have been simplified tremendously over the years, and most are easy to work with and do not require extensive investments in new equipment. A few minor additions to the darkroom are all that is necessary to produce beautiful, professional quality color prints. (see Color Gallery B, Plate 14.1.)

It is generally best to have a competent professional lab handle your color film processing, but color printing is subjective, and a lab may not interpret the image the way you want. When you make your own color prints, you have creative control. Most photographers seek *accurate* color prints, which means that they try to make the color as natural and as close to the reality of the subject as possible. Others, however, are more concerned with a color print that is *effective*, whether the color is accurate or not. Initially, it is best to learn how to make accurate color prints because this discipline forces you to learn how to evaluate, correct, and control your results. Ultimately, accurate color is seldom a necessity—photographs that effectively use color are *far* more important. (See Color Gallery B, Plate 14.2.)

Color Prints: Types and Processes

Today many different processes and types of color prints are in use. Two earlier processes, carbro printing and dye transfer, are classic but complicated color processes still used by a handful of photographers because of the beautiful results. Other specialty and novelty color processes also exist, but most color prints are made with one of two basic methods: *negative-to-positive* or the *positive-to-positive*. The negative-to-positive method is commonly called the Type C process and uses orangish color negatives, often referred to as print film, to make positive image color prints. The negative-to-positive process, which is currently based on Kodak RA 4 chemistry, uses a chromogenic dye-coupler process similar to that used for most color film development. It is inexpensive, easy to use, and very forgiving, making it the most commonly used color print material.

The other basic color print processing method, positive-to-positive, is referred to as Type R (reversal). It uses a positive image color transparency (slide) to make positive image color prints. Reversal print processes are like reversal film processes (transparency/slide films), in that they start as a negative image and are chemically reversed during processing to a positive image. The most widely used Type R papers are based on Kodak R-3000 chemistry, which is a *chromogenic dye-coupler reversal process*. Ilfochrome is an exception; it uses a *dye destruction* process called P-30 and produces prints with more saturation and permanence than any of the other color print products currently in common use. Inexpensive, machine-made Type R prints are generally contrasty, lack subtlety, and don't have the color quality of comparable prints made from color negatives. Type R products have improved tremendously in recent years, however, and with hand printing, they can produce prints that are beautiful, sharper than prints from negatives, and more deeply saturated in color. Many photographers prefer to make prints from color transparencies because they have the transparency as a color reference, whereas negatives provide no direct reference.

Tricolor Printing and White Light

Color film and print emulsions are delicate and vary in color and light sensitivity from one batch to the next. An *emulsion number* is printed on all color film and print products to indicate the emulsion batch used to make that particular product. Film emulsions are generally close enough so that emulsion changes are not a problem for most shooters, but color print papers vary considerably from batch to batch. Chemistry also varies from batch to batch and as it ages. Changing the enlarger light bulb also affects the color, as do differences in the color of light during the shooting of the pictures. These factors, coupled with diverse working conditions, procedures, and equipment, make it necessary for color printers to continually correct and alter the color by filtering the light when they are printing.

Two filtering methods are used to control the color balance of a print: the *white light*, or *subtractive*, exposure method and the *tricolor*, or *additive*, exposure method. Both methods require that color filters be used during the enlarging process. Unlike black and white variable contrast printing filters, color printing filters have no effect on contrast; they affect only color and exposure. Contrast needs to be controlled during the shooting. By filtering the light while making an enlargement, the photographer can correct for the differences in materials and circumstances to achieve the desired color balance in a print.

To use color filters effectively, it is important to understand how the white light and tricolor exposure methods work. First, the primary colors of light differ from the primary colors of pigments (paint). White light, whether sunlight or artificial light, is composed of three primary colors:

red, blue, and green. The primary colors of pigments are red, blue, and yellow. Because most people learn to work with pigments in their childhood, the difference in the primary colors of light and of pigments creates confusion when they start learning about color photography. The color wheel (See Color Gallery B, Plate 14.3) shows the primary colors of light—red, green, and blue—and their respective complements, cyan, magenta, and yellow.

Like color film, color print materials have three light sensitive color layers, one for each of the three primary colors of white light. When a color print is exposed, each of the primary color layers responds to its own color of light. Later, when the film is processed, a negative, or opposite, color result occurs. The red-sensitive layer forms a cyan image, the blue-sensitive layer forms a yellow image, and the green-sensitive layer forms a magenta image. Cyan, yellow, and magenta are the opposites, or complements, of the primary colors, red, blue, and green. The cyan, yellow, and magenta color layers combine, one on top of the other, to produce a full color photographic image.

Tricolor Filtering

Red, blue, and green, the primary or pure colors of light, transmit their own color while absorbing all other colors. When any two primary filters are put together, they absorb the color that each transmits, creating black. No light can get through. However, when red, blue, and green are projected individually, so that they overlap in equal parts, they create white light.

When any two primary colors overlap because of projection, the complementary, or opposite, colors are produced. Red and green create yellow, which is the complement or opposite of the primary color blue. Red and blue create magenta, which is the complement of the primary color green. Blue and green in turn create cyan, which is the complement of the primary color red. Because of the way that primary colors are added together to create other colors, they are referred to as *additive* colors.

When you are making prints with the primary, or additive, color filters, three separate exposures have to be made, one for each of the three primary colors. Each filter has to be exposed and tested individually because the filters create black when they are placed together. This exposure method is called the *tricolor*, or *additive*, printing method. It is primarily used in computerized printing machines and color copiers. Because of its complexity, the tricolor method is seldom used for hand printing.

White Light Filtering

The complementary colors—cyan, yellow, and magenta—are made from the combination of equal parts of two of the three primary additive colors. The missing, or third, primary color is always the opposite of the complementary color that was formed by the other two primary colors. For instance, yellow is made by combining equal parts of red and green light together. Blue, the third and missing primary color, is the opposite color of yellow.

Because cyan, yellow, and magenta are the opposites of the primaries, they can be overlapped, and light will pass through them. This is how a color image is formed with color film and color print materials. The red, blue, and green sensitive layers of color films and papers respond to their color of light when exposed. These layers change color during development to form their complementary colors, which then overlap to form a full color image. This means that it is possible to transmit light through more than one complementary color filter at a time and to make color prints with just one exposure.

During printing, the complementary filters actually subtract the light of the primary color that is their complement. For example, a yellow filter subtracts blue light from the image projected by the enlarger. Consequently, by adding or subtracting yellow filtration, we can control the amount of yellow or blue light that exposes the print. This exposure method is called the *white light*, or *subtractive*, printing method and is the method used for most hand printing. Because of the practicality and popularity of the white light printing method, we will concentrate on that method for both negative-to-positive and positive-to-postitive printmaking. (See Color Gallery B, Plate 14.4.)

Color Printmaking Equipment

Most black and white darkrooms can easily be adapted for color print-making. The equipment needed to produce color prints is the same for printing both color negatives and color transparencies. The following is a list of the basic color printing equipment needed to make color prints with an existing, well-equipped black and white darkroom.

Enlarger and color printing filters
Voltage stabilizer
Enlarging lens
Test print easel
Exposure devices and color analyzers

Kodak Color Print Viewing Filters
Cotton and rubber gloves
Color safelights
Chemical mixing implements and storage containers
Processing equipment
Print drying equipment

For more complete information on darkroom equipment, refer to Chapter 11 on black and white printmaking.

Enlargers and Color Printing Filters

Any enlarger can be used to make color prints. Most black and white enlargers use incandescent light bulbs and *condensers* to direct and provide even distribution of light. Some black and white printmakers use *cold-light heads* on their enlargers. Cold-light heads use fluorescent tubes and provide a more subtle contrast range than does a condenser head, but they are impractical for color printing because of the fluorescent light source. *Dichroic color heads* generally use a *diffusion* system, which reduces the contrast from a condenser enlarger by approximately one contrast grade. The diffusion system also uses the longer lasting and more stable quartz lights, mixes the colored light evenly, and minimizes the effects of grain, scratches, and other film imperfections.

Color printing (CP) filters can be used with black and white enlargers by placing the filters between the light bulb and the condenser. Most black and white enlargers have an opening for this purpose; if yours does not, then you will have to use the filters below the lens.

Dichroic color heads have built-in filters and a diffusion light chamber, which softens contrast and makes film scratches less noticeable. Filter changes are made by adjusting colored dials and can be made in any increment.

If you already own a black and white enlarger, the most affordable approach is to begin by purchasing a set of *color printing* (CP) filters to fit your enlarger. CP filters control color and should not be used below the lens like variable-contrast black and white filters because they lack the optical quality needed for use below the lens. Most enlargers have

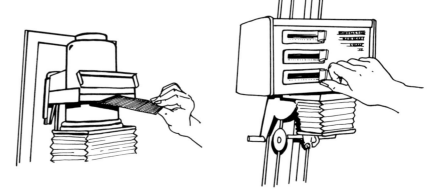

an opening for the placement of CP filters between the light bulb and the condensers. When placed there, filter imperfections and flaws from handling will be diffused out because they are above the plane of focus. The more expensive and optically purer *color compensating* (CC) filters, which are normally used for on-camera filtering, can be purchased for use below the lens.

Later, should you decide that you do enough color printing to justify the extra expense, a dichroic color head can be purchased to fit your enlarger. Dichroic color heads provide more refinement and are easier to use because the filters are built into the head of the enlarger and can be changed by simply adjusting a dial. Color heads can also be used for making black and white variable-contrast prints by dialing in the dichroic filter combinations that are the equivalent to the black and white variable-contrast filters. Further information on the filter combinations needed for black and white printing with a color head is provided in Chapter 11. A few enlargers are designed to suit the needs of those who do extensive printing of both black and white and color by enabling them to switch from a condenser to a diffusion system by making a simple adjustment on the enlarger. However, most photographers who use a dichroic color head find that it works well for black and white too.

Voltage Stabilizer

Fluctuations in electric currents can adversely affect exposure and color by altering the density of the print and the color temperature of the light. Although not a necessity, voltage stabilizers or regulators detect current changes and adjust for them to keep the current constant. Some are built into color enlarging systems, while others can be purchased as a separate item. The need varies depending upon the fluctuations in power where you live.

Enlarging Lens

Most modern enlarging lenses work equally well for black and white and color. Inexpensive lenses may have less sharpness and can cause a light falloff around the edges of an image. For richer color and sharper prints, try *apochromatic* lenses. Also, transparency printing will be easier if you have a fast lens with a maximum aperture of $f/2.8$ or more.

BUILDING A TEST PRINT EASEL

Supplies: Three 10 x 12-inch pieces of smooth mat board that is white on one side and black on the other.

Equipment: A mat knife, metal-edged ruler, pencil, tape, glue, and a piece of 8 x 10-inch photo paper.

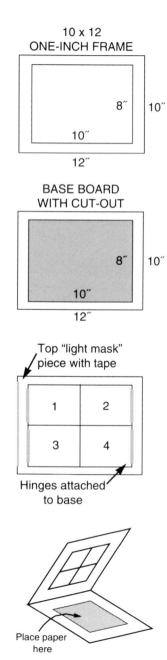

10 x 12
ONE-INCH FRAME

8″ 10″

10″

12″

BASE BOARD
WITH CUT-OUT

8″ 10″

10″

12″

Top "light mask"
piece with tape

| 1 | 2 |
| 3 | 4 |

Hinges attached
to base

Place paper
here

Procedure:

1. Center an 8 x 10-inch print on a piece of white mat board and draw a pencil line around the print.
2. Cut out the center of this piece of board using the metal-edged ruler and mat knife with the pencil line being your guide. Be careful and make clean straight cuts.
3. Place the outer cut-out piece on top of the black side of one of the remaining two pieces of 10 x 12-inch mat board. Then either glue or tape it to the top of the black piece of board. This will be the base of the easel and the cutout will serve as your means to position the print while working in the dark.
4. Next, center the 8 x 10-inch print on top of the white side of the remaining 10 x 12-inch board and draw a pencil line around the print. Cut out the outlined area as before.
5. Then cut this piece into four equal pieces that will be 4 x 5 inches each. These will be the exposure windows (masks) that you lift up to expose different parts of the print. Keep them together as you cut them.
6. Next, reassemble the piece that was cut in steps 4 and 5 with the white side up. Per the third illustration, hinge the 4 x 5-inch pieces to the cut-out piece by taping the top edge of 1 and 2 and the bottom edges of 3 and 4. Then hinge the whole piece to the base piece by taping them together along the top edge. Now you can lift the top piece that serves as a light mask, and place the photo paper in position under it.
7. Then make tape handles for each of the 4 x 5-inch pieces.

After completing step 7, you will be ready to use the test easel. When you begin printing, lift the top section and insert a piece of unexposed paper into the easel. Cover it by lowering the top piece. The image can then be projected down onto the top of the easel to position it in the first 4 x 5-inch section. When ready, lift the first section and make the test exposure. Then reposition the easel to expose the second section, and so on.

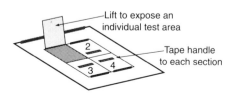

Lift to expose an
individual test area

Tape handle
to each section

2

3 4

Test Print Easel

Color printing is less immediate and more time-consuming than black and white printing. To maximize materials and time, it is best to minimize the variables, develop consistent work habits, and do multiple testing. Processing color prints is the most time-consuming part of the printmaking process. Most experienced printers do multiple tests of the same or different images on the same piece of paper to maximize their results with each processing run. A commercially made multiple exposure test print easel can be purchased, or you can make your own. Both are designed so that once the paper is in place, masks cover it so that it is relatively light safe, thus making it easy to switch images, focus, reposition, crop, and change filtration without removing the paper. When all is ready, a mask covering a portion of the paper can be lifted and a test exposure made. Once that portion of the paper is exposed, it is covered, and the next exposure is readied. The easel is repositioned and, when ready, another mask is lifted to expose another portion of the paper. See Color Gallery B, Plate 14.5.

To build your own test print easel, refer to the directions on page 318.

Exposure Devices and Color Analyzers

The most difficult thing to learn about color printing is how to evaluate a test print and make the proper correction to get a final print to look the way you want it. Almost everyone seeks a formula or some special device that will make color and exposure correction easier and more predictable. Inexpensive, nonelectronic calculators have been made for amateur use. These use a grid or matrix system. Professional labs rely on expensive electronic color analyzers, which read the density and color of a negative or transparency and recommend a print exposure and filter combination (filter pack). Affordable analyzer units are available for individuals, but for the small-volume user, nonelectronic calculators and color analyzers are more trouble than they are worth.

The inexpensive nonelectronic calculators enable you to expose through a matrix device and then compare the result with a printed matrix the manufacturer supplies. Unfortunately, the results are based on a subjective interpretation, and it takes experience to be able to get anything more than passable results. With experience you can get better results just as fast by evaluating tests of the actual image. You will also learn how to make color judgments based upon what works for the image, rather than accepting the solution given by some standard formula.

To use a color analyzer, the first thing you have to do is make a good print the traditional way, by trial and error. Color analyzers are then programmed with these results, and subsequent prints are evaluated according to the programmed result. This works fine provided you use the same type of subject, film, and light. It is also important that you don't change enlargers, paper batches, chemistry, or the light bulb. Any change in the variables means that you have to retest your original programmed image by trial and error and then reprogram the analyzer. Most photographers find it necessary to have a number of different programs for different shooting situations and have to reprogram the analyzer frequently. Consequently, color analyzers are impractical for the small-volume or occasional color printer.

Exposure monitors are worth considering. They measure exposure only and determine exposure changes that are due to variations in enlarger height, image density, or changes in filtration. Ilford makes an inexpensive exposure monitor that can provide accurate results when used properly with black and white or either of the two main color processes.

Kodak Color Print Viewing Filters

Viewing filters are used to help determine whether a print has a color problem, which color is causing the problem, and how to correct for it. They come in a kit form and are inexpensive. The kit includes six filter cards, one for each of the six colors used to control light: red, blue, green, cyan, yellow, and magenta. Each filter card has three filters with varying densities of a particular color. These densities are listed as 10, 20, and 40 and correspond to the filter densities used in color printing. One side of the card is black and gives the filtration information needed to make corrections for printing color transparencies. The other side is white and provides filtration information needed to make corrections for printing color negatives.

There are two ways to use these filters. The first method is to use the filters to determine whether a test print has a color problem and, if so, determine what color is causing the problem. This is done by laying the print on a white background in a well-illuminated room. (*Never view a print on a light box because the back lighting bleeds through and makes accurate judgments impossible.*) Then select filters with colors that seem to be similar to what you think is the problem color. For instance, if the print appears to be too reddish, it may be too red, or it may be too magenta. Often it is hard to tell, especially if the problem

Kodak Color Print Viewing Filters

Figure 14-1

If you are unsure about a color correction, lay several viewing filters on a white background next to the print. The resulting comparison should make it more obvious as to which color is causing a problem.

Then take the filter that is the complement of the problem color and view the print through it. Hold it above the print and flick it back and forth to see the difference the filter makes. If the change seems appropriate, make a filter pack adjustment based on the suggested filtration change printed on the viewing filters.

is subtle. Take the red and magenta filter cards and lay them next to the print on top of the white background. With the filters lying next to the print, it will be obvious as to which color is causing the problem. If this procedure doesn't do it, try combining filters of varying densities, because often the problem is due to a combination of colors. (See Color Gallery B, Plate 14.6.)

Next, after the problem color has been identified, pick up the filter card containing the color that is the *complement*, or *opposite*, of the color that is the problem. Hold this card 5 to 10 inches above the print and look through it, going from one density to the next, to see what affect it has on the color of the print. Flick it back and forth, so that you see the print without the filter and then with it. If you examine the print through the filter very long, your eyes will adapt, and you may not sense the degree of change needed to alleviate the problem. Don't place the filter on top of the print, for it will dominate the color. It must be held above the print to show a more accurate relationship. Remember that the filters are merely indicators and how effective they are depends upon how you interpret them. Prints that are way off, almost monochromatic, should not be viewed with the filters, only images that are fairly close can be helped by viewing with the filters. Also, do not worry about the white areas; they will pick up the color of the filter. Look at the print overall and concentrate on how the neutral colors (black, gray, and the shadow areas of white) are affected.

Once you determine the color and density that seem to make the print look better, refer to the information written below that filter window. It will give you a suggested filtration change. The effectiveness of that change is dependent upon your interpretation of the problem. Normally, though, the viewing filters are quite helpful.

Cotton and Rubber Gloves

Most professional printers wear white cotton or nylon gloves when handling film and prints in the darkroom and when matting and framing. These reduce fingerprint problems and can be purchased at photography stores or beauty supply stores. For darkroom work, it works best to wear a glove on one hand, keeping the other hand free to handle things other than film and print paper.

For safety and health reasons, wear plastic or rubber gloves when you are mixing and handling chemistry. Color chemicals, while safe for normal handling, are more complex than black and white chemicals and should be treated with caution. Over time, repeated contact might cause skin irritations or other problems.

Color Safelights

Color print materials are sensitive to all colors of light and should be handled in total darkness or for limited time with color safelights. If you have existing black and white safelights in your darkroom, replacement filters that are safe for color can be purchased. Use a #13 dark amber filter with a 7 1/2 watt bulb no closer than 4 feet from your paper. Limit safelight exposure to no more than 1 minute to avoid fogging. Papers such as Ilfochrome, which instruct users to work in total darkness, can be used with color safelights, but caution is necessary. Never expose film to color safelights; it is much too sensitive and will definitely become fogged.

Small color and black and white safelights are available that can be used by hand like very dim flashlights. Most come with a strap or string to wear around you neck when you are printing. They are handy for finding misplaced items when the paper is out, but they need to be used minimally to avoid fogging.

Chemical Mixing Implements and Storage Containers

Color chemicals are very sensitive and easily contaminated. It is best to buy new chemical mixing equipment and storage containers, rather than cleaning and recycling previously used containers. Most inexpensive equipment is made from plastic, which absorbs chemistry, and no amount of cleaning will completely eliminate prior chemical residue.

A safe approach is to have separate mixing containers, stirring rods, graduates, funnels, and storage containers for each chemical. Storage containers need to have floating lids or be the collapsible type to minimize aging that results from oxidation. Carefully check the mixing and storage instructions for individual chemicals because they vary, and their longevity is dependent upon how you handle and store them.

For health and safety reasons, wear plastic or rubber gloves and work in a well-ventilated environment when mixing and handling chemistry. When mixing powdered chemistry, wear a respirator to avoid breathing airborne particles. A less expensive method is to buy containers with lids, such as thermos containers. Per instructions, fill them partially with water and then cut off the top of the chemical packet and immerse the cut end under the water. The powder will spill into the water and not be airborne. Remove the empty packet and put the lid on the container. Shake the container until the powder is thoroughly dissolved and mixed. To dispose of used chemistry, follow the guidelines provided by the manufacturer.

Processing Equipment

Processing color prints is time-consuming and more exacting than black and white print processing. Slight variations in time, temperature, agitation, and handling can cause color and density shifts that defy normal color correction logic. Tray processing color prints is impractical because of the difficulties in maintaining consistent timing, handling, and temperature control in the dim light of color safelights. But there are easy, safe, consistent, and inexpensive ways to process color prints. The most popular means for small-volume use is plastic *drums* or *tubes*. Larger-volume users may find small tabletop autoprocessors a good choice, and professional labs use expensive, totally automated processing machinery.

Drum Processors

Color print processing became practical for home darkrooms in the mid-1970s because of simplified chemical processes and the introduction of the *drum* and *tube* processors. These consisted of small, lighttight plastic cylinders that work much like film developing tanks. In the dark, exposed prints are loaded into the drum, with the emulsion facing in, towards the center of the drum. A lighttight end cap is put on, and the rest of the processing is done in the light by pouring chemicals in and out through a light baffle in the end caps. The print is agitated by rolling it on a counter top or placing it on an electric motorized base that rotates it.

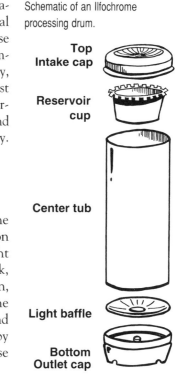

Schematic of an Ilfochrome processing drum.

Top Intake cap

Reservoir cup

Center tub

Light baffle

Bottom Outlet cap

Figure 14-2

Color print processing in a processing drum—4 steps. (A). Hold the drum upright when you pour the chemistry. (B) Begin continuous agitation immediately after you turn the drum on its side. Rolling the drum back and forth on a tabletop is sufficient, provided you are consistent with the agitation. (C) A motorized base is easier to use and ensures consistent action. (D) During the last 10 seconds of each processing step, hold the drum vertically over a graduate to drain the used chemical as you pour in the next. Pouring should take 10 seconds. Then immediately begin the agitation again.

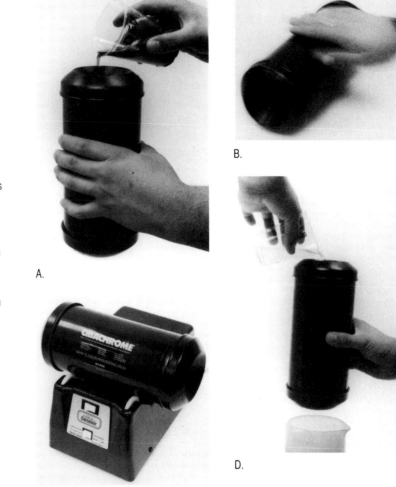

A.

B.

C.

D.

Processing drums are made to process most popular print sizes, from 8x10-inches through 30x40-inches. The amount of chemicals needed to adequately process a print is based on the size of the tube. An 8x10-inch drum uses 3 oz of chemistry, an 11x14-inches drum uses 6 oz, a 16x20-inch drum uses 12 oz, a 20x24-inch drum uses 18 oz, and a 30x40-inch drum uses 45 oz. Some manufacturers indicate that a smaller quantity of chemistry is adequate, but often the desire to economize leads to inadequate coverage of the print.

Drums need to be completely dry and chemical free before use to avoid contamination and streaked prints. The best design features a drum with a smooth interior, a chemical intake cap, and a chemical outlet cap. The smooth interior insures even processing, while the intake and outlet caps allow you to pour fresh chemistry in one end while used chemistry drains out the other.

The drum is held vertically while the chemistry is poured into the intake cap, which has an interior cup that holds the chemistry until the drum is turned onto its side. Begin agitation by rolling the drum the moment it is put in a horizontal position. The chemistry will drain out of the intake reservoir cup, through baffles, and cover the surface of the print. The drum must be level and the agitation constant to evenly cover the print with chemistry. During the last 10 seconds of each processing step, the drum is held vertically over a plastic graduate, and the chemistry for the next step is poured in while the old chemistry drains out the bottom into the graduate. (See Color Gallery B, Plate 14.7.)

The biggest problem with drum processing is inconsistency. Changes in temperature, timing, agitation, and careless chemical handling lead to changes in color and density. To ensure consistency and the best quality, it is preferable to use fresh chemistry for each processing run, rather than reusing the chemistry. It is also best to always use the same processing time and temperature. Shortcuts, although tempting, usually lead to inferior and inconsistent results. Several manufacturers, such as Jobo, make drum processing systems that include water bath heating systems and other options to make drum processing more consistent. But with a little care, excellent color prints can be made with drum processors and a minimum of accessories.

Automatic Processors

Professional labs use large automated processors that replenish the chemistry to compensate for use. To ensure consistency, technicians run periodic tests and adjust the chemistry to keep it in line. A large volume of processing makes this approach practical.

For limited-volume users, small automated tabletop processors are available. These self-contained units control the time, temperature, and agitation of the prints. Most of the newer products are adjustable and designed to function with a variety of different color and black and white processes. Some use one-shot chemistry, and others have replenishment systems, but most use a depletion system whereby you process a certain quantity of prints until the chemistry is exhausted. A few models have washer and dryer modules that can be purchased separately, but most leave that as an extra step to do by hand.

When maintained properly, automated tabletop processors provide more consistency than most people are able to produce by hand with a drum. But more important, they free you from having to handle the chemistry constantly and enable you to work on something else rather than spend time standing over a drum. Tabletop processors vary in size, with the most common size taking paper that is 16 inches wide or smaller. Since paper is available in long rolls, these processors make it possible to do long prints, which is impossible to do in a tube and extremely costly to have a professional lab produce.

Print Drying Equipment

The majority of popular color print materials are all resin coated (RC), except for a couple of polyester-based color print products by Ilford and Fuji. This fact makes print drying easy and essentially the same as drying black and white RC prints. Normal RC print dryers work equally well with RC black and white and color prints. Polyester-based prints, like fiber-based black and white prints, can be run through an RC dryer to squeegee off the surface liquid, but they will not be dry. Nor should they be run through a second time because the partially dry prints have a tendency to stick to the entry roller and wrap around it, thus destroying the print. Either squeegee the polyester-based prints by hand, or run them through the dryer once and then air dry them. To air dry, place the squeegeed prints emulsion up on a drying screen. A hair dryer can be used to accelerate the drying process.

If an RC print dryer is not available, and you are reluctant to squeegee the prints by hand for fear of damaging the delicate surface, hang them up by a corner to drip dry. Should you get water spots, try a little Photo-Flo in the water.

Color Negative Printing

Almost all color negative print papers are resin coated. There are no fiber-based color print papers. Ilfocolor Classic Deluxe Glossy Print Material has a polyester base like that of the Ilfochrome color transparency print paper. Print paper surfaces include glossy, semimatte (also called luster and pearl), and matte. Contrast choices are limited to two basic choices, medium contrast and low contrast. The difference is generally no more than the equivalent of a half grade with black and white paper. To get higher contrast, try a glossy paper like Ilfocolor, which gives the illusion of more contrast, or get it in the shooting. There are no variable-contrast color printing papers.

Each package of color print paper has an emulsion number printed on it. This indicates the particular batch of paper that you are using. Color papers vary in color sensitivity from emulsion batch to emulsion batch. To reduce the need for retesting each time you get a new package of paper, consider buying color paper in larger quantities and storing it in the refrigerator until you need it. Refrigeration keeps the paper stable. After removing it from the refrigerator, allow enough time for the paper to come up to room temperature before opening it. Otherwise, condensation might build up inside the package and leave water spots on the print paper.

Printing color negatives is similar to printing black and white negatives. In addition to your normal darkroom equipment, you will need a color head or a CP filter kit, a test print easel, color safelights, a cotton glove, a processing drum, RA 4 chemistry, and a data sheet to record your test and printing information.

Print Record Data Sheet

Because of the many variables and the time it takes to process color prints, it is to your advantage to test and process several images at a time. Doing so makes it possible to finalize one image while saving time by moving ahead and testing new images. To keep track of your progress, it is important to keep a record of each test and final result that you make. These records serve as references for current and future printing needs. Without writing down your data, you will forget or confuse some of the information, making it impossible to accurately make a correction in exposure and color.

Before each exposure, be sure to record the following data: *the name of the subject, the date, enlarger height, f-stop, exposure time, and filtration.* Recording the enlarger height makes it easy to quickly switch negatives and get them back to the same position as before. Most enlargers have height measurements indicated along the vertical rail of the enlarger. Differences in enlarger height, which come from guessing, result in differences in exposure and the need for more testing. After the print is exposed and processed, refer to the data sheet to determine the proper corrections. Write the corrected data down and make a new test. Keep a running log of the changes made with each image. Should you go too far, you can refer to the past data and backtrack. This information also serves as a record of your most current *working filter pack*, which is the filtration you start with the next time you print. It can also be helpful to record dodging and burning information.

Use the following sample print record data sheet as a model.

Print Record Data Sheet

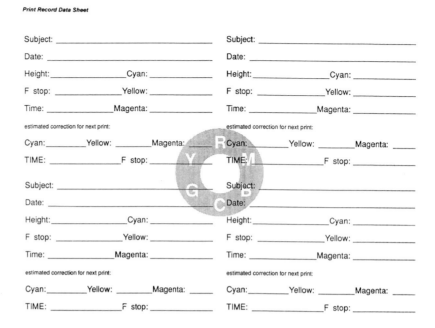

Subject: _____	Subject: _____
Date: _____	Date: _____
Height: _____Cyan: _____	Height: _____Cyan: _____
F stop: _____Yellow: _____	F stop: _____Yellow: _____
Time: _____Magenta: _____	Time: _____Magenta: _____
estimated correction for next print:	estimated correction for next print:
Cyan:_____Yellow: _____Magenta: _____	Cyan:_____Yellow: _____Magenta: _____
TIME: _____F stop: _____	TIME: _____F stop: _____
Subject: _____	Subject: _____
Date: _____	Date: _____
Height: _____Cyan: _____	Height: _____Cyan: _____
F stop: _____Yellow: _____	F stop: _____Yellow: _____
Time: _____Magenta: _____	Time: _____Magenta: _____
estimated correction for next print:	estimated correction for next print:
Cyan:_____Yellow: _____Magenta: _____	Cyan:_____Yellow: _____Magenta: _____
TIME: _____F stop: _____	TIME: _____F stop: _____

What to Print

Begin by selecting several different color negatives that you would like to enlarge. Choose negatives that have already been printed so that you can use the existing prints as a reference for comparing your results. Make sure that the negatives are normally exposed and have a variety of obvious and easy-to-distinguish colors, such as a person standing next to a red car on green grass with a blue sky background. Initially, it is best to avoid sunsets and other subjective color situations. Images with distinctly different colors are easier to evaluate and color correct.

Select one negative for the initial testing. Once that image is "in the ballpark," you can begin testing the other images. The results from your first negative will serve as a working exposure and filtration, which can be used as the starting point for testing other negatives. Ultimately, you need to test several images with each processing run. Unlike with black and white processing, it is wasteful to work on one image at a time. Color processing is much more time-consuming, making the results less immediate. A multiple exposure test print easel makes it easy to test several images at one time on a single sheet of paper, which saves both time and paper.

Filtration

The filters for the single exposure *white light* printing method consist of cyan, yellow, and magenta. Cyan is the opposite of red, yellow is the opposite of blue, and green is the opposite of magenta. The filters act in the following manner:

Filter	Color Absorbed	Colors Transmitted
Cyan	Red	Green + Blue
Yellow	Blue	Green + Red
Magenta	Green	Red + Blue

The effect of a filter (the proportion of a color that a filter subtracts) depends upon the density of the filter. Filter densities are referred to as degrees and are designated by number. Higher number filters are denser in color and have more effect on the color of the print. Most dichroic color heads have a filtration range from 0 to 190, which enables you to make adjustments as subtle as one degree at a time.

CP filter kits, which come in several sizes to fit different enlargers, normally have a filtration range from 2 1/2 to 50 degrees, but the filters can be stacked together to get higher degrees of filtration. The kits contain a UV filter and cyan, yellow, and magenta filters in the following densities: 2 1/2, 5, 10, 20, 30, 40, and 50. Some kits contain several high-number red filters that can be used to supplement yellow and magenta filters when high filtrations are needed, because a 50 red is equal to a 50 yellow plus a 50 magenta filter.

How Much to Change the Filters

5 degrees or less	is like "fine tuning" and has a *subtle* effect in a print.
10 degrees	will cause a *slight*, but noticeable, change in a print.
20 degrees	is a *moderate*, but very obvious, change in a print.
30 degrees or more	is a *big* change and causes an extreme difference in a print.

To reduce diffusion and maximize sharpness and contrast, always use as few filters as possible to make your *filter pack* (the combination of filters used to make a color print). To get 50 degrees of yellow filtration, use a single 50Y filter rather than a 20Y and 30Y. The *UV filter* always goes on the bottom of the filter pack because it should always be used. Next, place the larger number filters; put the smaller number filters on top because they are the most likely to get changed.

Filtration and Exposure

It is impossible to judge color accurately with an over- or underexposed test print. Consequently, initial testing must determine exposure as well as filtration. The awkward part is that exposure varies with changes in filtration. Yellow filtration has little effect on exposure, but a plus or minus 10-degree change in cyan or magenta filtration will cause a plus or minus 25 percent change in exposure. Should you subtract 20 degrees of magenta filtration, you need to make an exposure compensation that is equivalent to a 50 percent or 1/2 stop reduction in exposure. This is because each 10-degree change in magenta or cyan filtration affects exposure by approximately 25 percent. (See Color Gallery B, Plates 14.8 and 14.9.)

How the Filters Control Color

Every color within the visible spectrum is controllable by adding or subtracting varying amounts of cyan, yellow, and magenta filtration. Adding or subtracting cyan filtration controls the amount or balance between cyan and red in a print; adding and subtracting yellow controls the amount of yellow and blue; and adding and subtracting magenta controls the amount of magenta and green. Generally, filters are always needed to get a proper color balance, but occasionally some Type R papers print properly without filtration. But such an occurrence is unusual, and it is unheard of with color negative materials.

A point to remember is that there is no specific amount of filtration that is correct. Filtration varies and cannot be judged by looking at the projected image on the baseboard. You have to make a test print and evaluate it. Then use whatever density and combination of filters you need to get the result that you want. You may find yourself using a high filtration or a low filtration. You will probably need to use two filters, but don't worry if it takes only one filter or no filters. What works is what matters. *But never use three filters!*

Three filters, in equal parts, produce neutral density, or gray. For instance, with a filter pack of 30Y, 20M, and 20C, you actually have 20 degrees of gray neutral density that is doing nothing but increasing your exposure time. Only 10 degrees of yellow filtration is all that is

Filtration Changes to Correct Color

Excess Print Color		Filter Corrections
Too yellow	add yellow	or subtract magenta & cyan
Too magenta	add magenta	or subtract yellow & cyan
Too cyan	subtract yellow & magenta	or add cyan
Too blue	subtract yellow	or add magenta & cyan
Too green	subtract magenta	or add yellow & cyan
Too red	add yellow & magenta	or subtract cyan

left to affect the color of your print. Fortunately, we can control all of the color relationships with just two filters.

A combination of yellow and magenta filtration is normally used when printing color negative materials. Adding or subtracting yellow filtration controls the amount of yellow and blue in a print. Adding or subtracting magenta filtration controls the amount of magenta and green. To control cyan and red, add or subtract equal parts of yellow and magenta.

To understand these relationships better, refer back to the color wheel and note that yellow and magenta are located on either side of red. This means that together, in equal parts, yellow and magenta create red. For a visual example, test this and other color relationships with the viewing filters by placing them in combination with each other on a white paper background.

Make the adjustment that is the simplest, based on the filters in your filter pack.

When adding or subtracting two colors to affect a third, always change equal parts of each.

The amount of filtration density needed to make a color correction will vary from image to image. Use the Kodak Color Print Viewing Filters to help make a determination.

Starting Filtrations and Color Ringarounds

Because of the differences in color papers and emulsion batches, most manufacturers do not provide starting filtration information. Their working environment is different from yours; therefore, suggested starting filtration is seldom correct. To get a close estimate, it is best to pick a negative with easy-to-distinguish color relationships and to make several tests with it, using different filtrations and exposures. We call this procedure a *color ringaround*, and it is necessary to do this only when you first start printing in a new facility or when you haven't printed for a long time. The ringaround will provide an approximate exposure and *working filtration*. Once the working filtration is refined, you use that whenever you begin testing a new image. It is not necessary to do another color ringaround. That is only needed when you start up with no prior working filtration to use as a reference.

Color negative print materials generally need yellow and magenta filtration. The yellow filtration is normally about 20 degrees more than the magenta filtration. A ringaround filtration test consists of a series of separate exposures, using different filtrations with the same image. For testing, use the test print easel and begin with a four-exposure ringaround using the following filtrations as a starting point.

80Y	40M
60Y	40M
40Y	20M
20Y	20M

Consider each section of the test print easel as a quadrant. *Do your tests with the enlarger at the height you plan to use for the final print and select a portion of the image to test.* Make sure that the portion of the image you test includes important subject matter, values from light to dark, and as much variety as possible in color. *Between each exposure, cover all of the quadrants and reposition the test easel so that the same portion of the image is used in each quadrant.* If you fail to reposition the easel, you will have different areas of the image in each quadrant, and often these areas differ so much that you can't make a good enough comparison to determine a proper filtration.

Exposing a Ringaround, Test Print 1

Since the ringaround is an initial test and the exposure needed is still unknown, it will be necessary to do an exposure test strip in each of the four quadrants. This will also make up for exposure variations that are due to differences in filtration. If you plan to make an 8x10-inch print from a 35mm color negative, try an aperture of *f*/8 or *f*/11 and set the timer for 5 seconds. Position the test easel, and set your filtration for your first exposure in quadrant 1. In the dark, open the mask and cover all but about a third of the open area with an opaque material

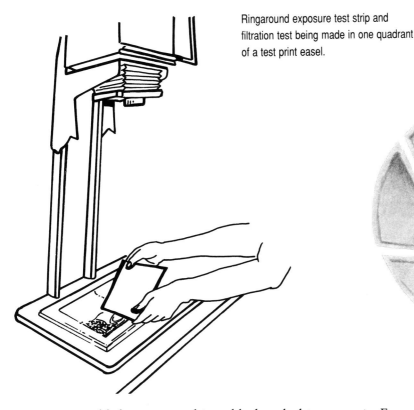

Ringaround exposure test strip and filtration test being made in one quadrant of a test print easel.

just as you would if you were making a black and white test strip. Expose the uncovered portion of the paper for 5 seconds and then uncover another third of the image. Make another 5-second exposure, and then uncover all of quadrant 1 for the third and final exposure. This will give you an exposure test stip within that quadrant that has exposures of 5, 10, and 15 seconds. One of those should be close.

Next, cover quadrant 1 and turn on the enlarger light so that you can reposition the easel to get the same portion of the picture in quadrant 2. Change filtration and do the same exposure procedure for quadrant 2. Continue that procedure for quadrants 3 and 4. You will be ready to process the ringaround once all four quadrants are exposed with different filtrations and exposure test strips in each quadrant.

Evaluating the Ringaround

After processing your ringaround, evaluate the dry print in a room with good illumination. It is important to dry the print before evaluating because it has a bluish color bias that is in the dark areas when wet. It is equally important that you use the same viewing light to evaluate your prints. Don't use daylight because the color of the light will vary from day to day and at different times of the day. Professionals view prints with 5000 K light. Some add a weak tungsten light for a little extra warmth. Most fine art photographers evaluate prints with tungsten light sources because that is the type of light most often used in galleries and museums.

Examine the quadrants and select the one that seems to have the most natural color. If you have an existing machine print of that image, compare it with your test print. Determine the color corrections before deciding upon the exposure because changes in the filtration will affect the exposure. Use the print viewing filters to help you decide whether there is a color problem and how to correct for it. Be sure to use the white side of the viewing filters when printing color negatives, because the "black" side is for color transparencies.

For example, in the ringaround image in Figure 14-12, the upper left quadrant has the most natural color. Yet it doesn't seem quite right. There seems to be a slight reddish bias in the shadows of the white sails, and the foliage in the background is red, not green. When viewed through a cyan viewing filter (the complement of red), the red bias lessens, and the color seems more natural. The middle filter, which indicates a 10-degree change, worked the best.

With negative print materials, whatever we want to do to the print, we do the opposite in the filter pack. To make a filtration change that will reduce the red in the print (making it more cyan), we have to add red to the filter pack. The filters in the filter pack are yellow and magenta; when they are added together in equal parts, they make red. In this case, the existing filter pack of 60Y 40M would be changed to 70Y 50M. (See Color Gallery B, Plates 14.10 and 14.11.)

Once the filtration is decided, you can determine the exposure. Look at the exposure variations in the same quadrant. In our example, the best exposure is the lightest one, which was for 5 seconds. Because we decided to increase the magenta filtration by 10 degrees, we need to add 25 percent to the exposure time. This will result in an exposure of 6.25 seconds at the same aperture used previously.

Exposing Test Print 2

At this point, the temptation is to go ahead and make a full print. But it is best to do a second test to make sure that the filter and exposure corrections produce the desired results. To maximize time and paper, pick three additional negatives to test with your retest of the initial image. This will enable you to use one piece of paper and get a refined test of the first image and starting tests with three new images.

Expose the initial image in quadrant 1, using the corrected filtration and exposure. Then use the remaining three quadrants to expose a test for each of the three additional negatives. To test the new images, use the same filtration that was used for the second test of your first image in quadrant 1. This is your *working filtration* and is what you will use as a starting point for subsequent tests. However, should you decide after this test that the working filtration needs to be changed, then the changed filtration becomes your working filtration. In other words, the working filtration that you start new testing with is whatever filtration worked best the last time you printed. There is no need to do another ringaround.

The exposure for the tests of the new images will be the same if they are similar in density to the prior image and the enlargements are from the same height. However, a test strip exposure like the one you initially did with the color ringaround will be necessary if the density of any of the three new images is different or if the enlarger is moved to a different height.

After processing this test, evaluate the first image and the three new images. You will probably be close enough to make a full print of the first image, but you may need to do additional testing with the other three. Should that be the case, make the appropriate color and exposure corrections for the three new images and pick a fourth image to fill the vacant quadrant. That way, as you finish one, you will be working ahead towards the next.

If you have an 11x14-inch drum insert to use with your 8x10-inch drum caps, two prints will fit into it because the insert drums are normally 16 inches long. This convenience will enable you to save time by processing a final print and a new test print at the same time. Just remember that you will need to use 6 oz. of chemistry with the larger tube.

To ensure consistency and accuracy, try to allow enough time to do final prints of the tested images during the same printing session. If this is not feasible, then the next time you come back to print, start by making a test of each image, using the corrected working filter packs from your last printing session. Do not make a full print based on a prior session's results without retesting, because time can change the chemicals, and a color shift may result. A quick initial test will put you into the ballpark, and you can move on from there.

The Final Print

Always evaluate tests and full prints when they are dry, in a well-lit room. Use a light source that is the same type as that under which the prints will be viewed. For easy viewing and normal brilliance, make the print as light as possible without sacrificing detail in the highlights. Although accuracy in color is technically commendable, try to use the color effectively. If this means that the color is inaccurate, so be it. Dodging and burning are effective means to heighten the feeling in an image. Use them as you need them. Color dyes are available for spotting color prints. Ilford makes an inexpensive dye kit designed for Ilfochrome, which is also usable with other color materials. Procedures for dye retouching and image enhancement will be covered in Chapter 15.

Remember: Think of color as form. Color is a design element to be used within the picture. A good color photograph is more than just a reproduction of what appeared before the camera: It is the subjective *interpretation* of the photographer.

Making Color Contact Sheets

Color contact sheets are very useful, both as an archive and as a means to test many negatives at one time. Except for the filtration, color contact sheets are made in the same manner as black and white contact sheets. Raise the enlarger to a height that you commonly use to make enlargements. Put an empty negative carrier into the head of the enlarger, turn on the enlarger light and adjust the focus until the edges of the empty negative carrier are sharp on the baseboard. This provides uniform light and extends the bellows as they would be for an enlargement.

Stop down the lens to $f/8$ or $f/11$ and use a filtration that is your most current working filtration. When ready, go dark and position the negatives emulsion down on the unexposed color print paper. To establish an exposure, do a test strip at 5-second increments. After processing, evaluate the test contact for color and exposure. Make the appropriate corrections, and then make a final contact sheet. Next time, you won't need to do an exposure test. The exposure will be the same if your negatives are similarly exposed and you use the same procedure, including the same enlarger height.

Do not expect all of the negatives on the contact to come out with the right color. Most likely, they were shot under differing circumstances with varied lighting. Any that are correct could be enlarged with no additional testing, provided you use the same enlarger height, exposure, and filtration that were used to make the contact. Corrections can be made from the contact for off-color images and save testing time. (See Color Gallery, Plate 14.12.)

Processing Color Negative Prints

Color negative prints are processed in RA 4 chemistry. A methodical and consistent approach to the processing procedure is essential if you hope to get controlled results. Automatic processing machines provide consistency, but tray processing does not because temperature control is too hard to maintain. Drum processing can be consistent but often isn't, and that leads to problems. Time, temperature, agitation, and cleanliness are important factors to control. Inconsistency and a lack of control lead to shifts in color, density, and contrast.

Drum Processing Equipment

You will need chemical storage containers; a processing drum; motor base; thermometer; five small, clear plastic drinking cups; water bath tray; final wash tray; towel; and means to dry the prints. If you don't have a motor base, agitate continuously during processing by rolling the drum on a countertop. Premark the plastic cups with a waterproof marker. Designate a cup for each step, and mark them to indicate 3 oz. of chemistry for 8x10-inch prints and 6 oz. for 11x14-inch prints.

The RA 4 Process

RA 4 chemistry is available in kit form for home darkroom use and larger quantities for professional applications. It is supplied by several manufacturers. Processing instructions for RA 4 chemistry vary with the kit and the type of processing. RA 4 is a fast process, and the recommended processing temperature is 95°F plus or minus 1/2 degree in the developer. It is designed for machine use, and it is hard to control in drum processing. The chart on the next page lists the normal RA 4 processing temperature and times and a modified version that reduces problems and is easier to use with drum processing.

Step	Normal Temp. °F	Time	Modified Temp. °F	Time
Prewet	95±2	30 sec.	80±2	60 sec.
Developer	95±1/2	45 sec.	80±1/2	90 sec.
Stop Bath	95±2	30 sec.	80±2	60 sec.
Wash	95±2	30 sec.	80±2	60 sec.
Bleach-Fix	95±2	45 sec.	80±2	90 sec.
Wash in Drum	75–95	30 sec.	68–75	30 sec.
Final Wash in Tray	75–95	90 sec.	68–75	180 sec.
Total Time		4 1/2 min.		9 min.
Drying		Varies, depending upon the method used.		

Note:
Rinse all equipment both before and after use.
Drums must be completely dry to avoid water spots and streaks on prints.
Keep chemicals up to temperature with a water bath.
Preset timer for each step.
Allow 10 seconds of drain time at the end of each step.
Drain chemicals together into a graduate and dispose according to manufacturer's recommendations.

RA 4 Processing Procedure

1. In the darkroom, *load the exposed print* into the processing drum. Make sure that the emulsion side is facing towards the center of the drum. To avoid light leaks, make sure that the end caps are assembled and attached properly.

2. In the light *prepare the chemistry.* To process an 8x10-inch print, fill each cup with 3 oz. of its designated chemical (including the water prewet and wash cups). Put the cups in a water bath to bring them to the proper temperature. To speed up the process, keep your chemical storage containers in a water bath. Then it won't take as long to bring the cup quantities up to temperature. The most critical temperatures are the prewet and the developer. The other steps will have more latitude.

3. Preset the timer for the first step, and begin pouring in the *prewet* while keeping the drum vertical. The prewet brings the print up to temperature and prepares the emulsion so that the developer reacts evenly. It should take no more than 10 seconds to fill the drum. When filled, place the drum on the motor base, or agitate it by hand, rolling it back and forth on a countertop.

4. Begin draining the drum during the last 10 seconds of the pre-wet by holding it vertically over a graduate or bucket. At the same time, pour the *developer* into the intake end of the processing drum. It should take no more than 10 seconds. When the drum is filled, immediately begin the agitation. The developer converts the silver halide on each color layer into metallic silver and determines the density, contrast, and color balance of the print.

5. Drain the developer into the same graduate and pour in the *stop bath* during the last 10 seconds of the development. Agitate immediately after. The stop bath stops the development and extends the life of the bleach-fix. There is a strong likelihood of streaking if a stop bath is not used. If your kit lacks a stop bath, use an acedic acid stop bath like the one you use for black and white processing.

6. Follow the same procedure with the *wash* step. This step extends the life of the bleach-fix. Without it you may get color shifts, stains, and dull colors.

7. Follow the same procedure with the *bleach-fix*. The bleach-fix must be fresh and not contaminated; otherwise, you will get inferior, dull, off-color results. It makes the dyes permanent and bleaches out the metallic silver. The print is light-safe after this step.

8. Drain the bleach-fix and pour in 3 oz. of water for a *wash in the drum*. This will rinse the bleach-fix out of the drum. The print will not get adequately washed on both sides while in the drum. Do the final wash in a tray with running water.

Figure 14-3

A. Prepare all of the chemicals ahead of time and bring them up to temperature in a water bath.
B. Take the outlet or exit end off the drum to remove the print. Once the end cap is off, place the drum under a faucet and fill it so that it overflows with running water. The print will float above the surface of the drum and be easy to pull out.

9. After the final drum wash, drain the water out into the graduate as before, and take off the outlet or exit end cap. The wet RC print will tend to stick to the plastic drum, and the delicate surface may get damaged if you try to *pull the print out* by hand. Place the drum under a faucet and turn on the water so that it pours into the exit end and overflows. The print will float freely up above the edges of the drum, making it easy to pull out without damage.

10. Do the *final wash in a tray* with running water. For the final wash, cold tap water is fine, but increase the time if the water is below 68°F. The final wash removes all residual chemistry and is critical for long-term print stability.

11. Color prints can be *dried* in RC dryers, hung by a corner and air dried, or squeegeed and air dried on a drying screen or with a hair dryer. Polyester-based prints such as Ilfocolor will not dry in an RC dryer and will need to be air dried in one of the aforementioned manners.

Color Transparency Printing

The procedure for printing color transparencies, whether 35mm slides or 8×10-inch chromes, is similar to that used for printing color negatives. But because transparency printing is a *postive-to-positive* process, exposure and filtration are exactly opposite of that used for color negative printing. To make a print lighter, expose it to more light. To make it darker, expose it to less light. Think of the paper as being black and that you have to expose it to light to make it lighter. The unexposed borders of negative image prints are white, while the unexposed borders of positive image prints are black. Burning-in makes that portion of a print lighter, because burning-in exposes it to more light. Dodging darkens a print because dodging reduces the amount of light hitting the dodged area. Logically, this approach is easier to understand, but it is confusing for many because it is the opposite of everything you learned with black and white and color negatives.

Color filtration is also more logical with transparencies, but it is the opposite of that used for color negative printing. With the negative process, to subtract yellow from the print, you must add yellow to the filter pack. While with transparencies, to subtract yellow from the print, you subtract it from the filter pack. Initially, the differences in the process can be confusing, but with experience you will learn how to differentiate. The chemical process is also different, but the basic processing procedure is the same. Like the negative process, transparency printing will involve the need for consistency, multiple testing, and keeping printing data sheets on each image. (See Color Gallery B, Plate 14.13.)

The equipment that you will need is the same as for printing color negatives. Exposure and filtration are different as is the chemical procedure, but the processing is similar to that for color negatives. Color safelights are safe to use for limited periods, despite contrary statements about using Ilfochrome only in complete darkness. To be safe, test your safelights for fogging by placing an unexposed piece of paper under the safelights for varying durations of time. For comparison purposes, partially cover the paper so that one part receives no light. After processing, check the results to see whether and at what amount of time the safelights caused the paper to lighten. Results will indicate how much "safe" time you have. To make the safelights weaker, use a smaller watt bulb or move them farther from your working area.

Many photographers prefer to shoot and print transparencies because what you see is what you get. A transparency is a final image, not an intermediate step like a color negative. But they are less forgiving than color negatives, in both the shooting and the printing. Exposure is much more critical and contrast is harder to control, especially with printing.

Transparency Print Processes

Print processes for transparencies are commonly called Type R, which stands for *reversal* process. Most Type R processes use chromogenic dye couplers that are built into the paper and are formed during developing in a manner similar to that of the E 6 film process. During development a negative monochromatic silver image is formed. In subsequent steps the negative image is chemically reversed to a color positive. The industry standard is the Kodak R-3000 process. Several manufacturers, including Kodak and Fuji, make chemicals and printing paper that are R-3000 compatible. Most inexpensive and custom Type R prints are made with the R-3000 print process. All R-3000 print materials are RC and come in the same basic glossy and matte surfaces available for color negative printing. The exception is a glossy polyester-based print paper by Fuji.

For the utmost in quality and permanence, many photographers use the Ilfochrome process. Known for rich, saturated color, Ilfochrome classic has a unique super-glossy polyester base. It is the sharpest and most permanent color print process readily available for home darkroom and professional use. Ilfochrome is also available in less expensive RC glossy and pearl (matte) surfaces. These have the same dye structure and color characteristics as the more noted Classic polyester-based glossy paper. Ilford also makes low and normal (high) contrast Ilfochrome, but these are not available in consumer packages and may need to be specially ordered.

Unlike the commonly used chromogenic dye coupler systems that form dyes during development, Ilfochrome uses a dye destruction process and more stable azo dyes that are built into the paper. P-30P is the Ilfochrome process currently available for small-volume use. It is a powdered chemical designed for use in drums and small automated tabletop processors.

Contrast control has always been a problem with reversal printing. For many years photographers made internegatives from transparencies and printed them on color negative paper to control contrast. Today, however, Type R materials are much better and internegatives are seldom used. For problem situations, photographers and many labs make contrast masks specifically to reduce contrast. (See Color Gallery B, Plate 14.14.)

Selecting a Transparency to Print

The easiest transparencies to print are those that are exposed normally. Underexposed transparencies, while beautiful when projected, have an excessive dye buildup in the low values, which increases the overall contrast and makes them harder to print. This condition can lead to extremely long exposures with extensive dodging and burning. Overexposed transparencies lack detail in the highlights, and it is impossible to put back what is not there. Efforts to do so normally end up resulting in prints with muddy highlights.

To determine how a transparency will print, look through it while holding it about 10 inches above a piece of white paper in a well-illuminated room. The image will be easy to print if you can easily discern the full range of contrast and see the necessary detail in the shadows. The transparency will be hard to print if the shadows are too dark and you can see into them only by viewing the transparency when it is illuminated from behind by a room light. If you have an underexposed transparency that you need to print, you can make it easier to print by getting a duplicate made. A transparency can be lightened several f-stops by duplicating, with no noticeable loss in quality.

Filtration for Printing Color

The same basic printing procedures and the same cyan, yellow, and magenta filters are used to print color transparencies and color negatives.

As stated earlier, the difference is that the corrections for transparency printing are opposite those used for color negative printing. The density variations in filtration have the same effect on color and exposure as they do on color negative materials. Refer to the section on color negative filtration for specifics on those relationships. The following is a color correction chart to be used for printing color transparencies.

If the print is too	Add	or Subtract
Blue	Yellow	Blue (magenta & cyan)
Yellow	Blue (magenta & cyan)	Yellow
Green	Magenta	Green (yellow & cyan)
Magenta	Green (yellow & cyan)	Magenta
Cyan	Red (yellow & magenta)	Cyan
Red	Cyan	Red (yellow & magenta)

To evaluate prints from transparencies, do not use a light box. Place the print on a white background in a well-illuminated room. Hold the transparency adjacent to the print and about 10 inches above the white background, being careful not to cast a shadow onto the background. This approach will provide the same intensity, color balance, and type of light for both. Use a loop to view the transparency when comparing it to the print. Use the black side of the Kodak Color Print Viewing Filters and make the corrections that they indicate. In practice, cutting Kodak's recommendations in half seems to work best for Ilfochrome, while their recommended corrections are fine for R-3000 materials. Remember to dry prints before evaluating them. R-3000 prints will have a bluish cast in the shadows when wet, and Ilfochrome prints will have a reddish cast overall. (See Color Gallery B, Plate 14.16.)

Starting Filtrations, Exposures, and Color Ringarounds

Filtrations for Type R processes are generally lower than those for color negatives. Often they are around the threshold of zero and sometimes consist of cyan in combination with either magenta or yellow. Remember never to use all three filters at once because they neutralize each other and create gray. Two, one, or no filters may be okay, but never three at once.

Most R-3000 materials do not indicate a starting filter pack, but Ilfochrome has a starting filter pack printed on each package. Unfortunately, the manufacturer's suggested filtration is seldom accurate because the working environment there is different from yours. The best way to start is with a color ringaround using four different filtrations on one image as was suggested in the section on color negatives. For exposure with a 35mm slide projected to an 8x10-inch print size, try *f*/8 with 7-second test strips. Remember that the darkest test exposure received the least exposure and the lightest one received the most. Ilfochrome normally takes more exposure than other print materials.

Once you have established a working filter pack, begin testing several images on one piece of paper. There should be no need to do any more ringarounds. For more specifics, refer to this procedure in the section on printing color negatives.

If a manufacturer's suggested filter pack is available, use it in place of one of the four following suggested ringaround exposures. If not, try the following: 40Y 20M, 20Y 20M, 20Y 0M, and 0Y 0M. Then use the previously given guidelines to make corrections after the test is processed. Once you are in line with a *working filter pack*, filtration will be closer from image to image than it was with color negatives, thus lessening the need for testing. A consistent processing procedure and accurate record keeping are essential, and the same print data sheet recommended earlier will work for printing transparencies.

Making Contact Sheets

Contact sheets can be made with color transparencies in the same manner that was used for contact printing color negatives. Establish a working filter pack and do an exposure test at 7-second increments. Ilford makes an excellent 35mm slide contact print easel that enables you to contact print 35 mounted color slides onto one piece of 8x10-inch paper.

Processing Color Transparencies

The R-3000 and P-30P processes can be used at varied times and temperatures, but it is better to avoid shortcuts and use the processes at their recommended times and temperatures. Follow the mixing and handling instructions described earlier in this chapter and those given by the manufacturer. The procedure for drum processing outlined earlier also pertains to Type R processes.

Ilfochrome instructions indicate that the chemistry can be reused by saving a portion and mixing it with fresh chemistry. While this will work, it is not recommended for those expecting optimum control and consistent results. Be sure to drain all of the used chemistry into a single graduate or bucket. Ilfochrome chemistry will self-neutralize when mixed together. It can also be neutralized with baking soda. Dispose of the chemistry according to the manufacturer's recommendations. Be careful when handling wet Ilfochrome prints, because the surface is extremely delicate.

Dye Chrome Research Co. makes K-2 chemistry that can also be used to process Ilfochrome. The K-2 process uses two bleach steps instead of one, a dye bleach and a silver bleach. This separation allows you to vary the image contrast by altering the dye-bleach time. A shorter dye-bleach time reduces contrast, and a longer time increases contrast.

The R-3000 Process

Step	Time (at 100°F)
Prewet	1 min. ±1 degree
First Developer	1 1/2 min. ±1 degree
Wash	1 min. ±2 degrees
Color Developer	2 min. ±1 degree
Wash	1 min. ±2 degrees
Bleach-Fix	1 1/2 min ±1 degree
Wash in Drum	30 sec. ±5 degrees
Final Wash in Tray	2 1/2 min. ±5 degrees
Total Time	11 min.
Drying	Varies depending upon the method used.

The Ilfochrome P-30P Process

Step	Time (at 75°F)
Prewet	1 min. ±2 degrees
Developer	3 min. ±1 degree
Wash	1 min. ±2 degrees
Bleach	3 min. ±1 degrees
Wash	1 min. ±2 degrees
Fixer	3 min. ±1 degree
Wash in Drum	30 sec. ±5 degrees
Final Wash in Tray	3 min. ±5 degrees
Total Time	15 min., 30 sec.
Drying	Varies depending upon the method used.

Chapter 15

Advanced Color Photography

When considering, with reference to color, the objects that constitute the world, it is quickly noted that these fleeting appearances, which so readily appear and disappear through certain angles of those objects, are not accidental but are dependent upon definite laws.

—Johann Wolfgang Von Goethe
Poet, dramatist

Color photography is subjective. The quality, intensity, and color of light illuminating the subject vary, depending upon the circumstances that day. The relationship of the subject to neighboring colors affects our perception of color and influences our response to the subject. Actually, our perception of color is seldom as it is in the physical world.

Many people prefer color to black and white photographs. This is perhaps due to the tendency to consider photographs as surrogates of reality, so therefore color photographs look more "real." Good photographers use this predilection to their advantage by understanding that the human perception of color is relative and that color can be used to influence a viewer. (See Color Gallery B, Plate 15.1.)

Color and Perception

Warm and *cool* are terms frequently used to describe colors. Reds, yellows, and oranges are considered warm colors, while blues, greens, and violets are deemed cool. Red is a vibrant, advancing color associated with fire, blood, death, importance, and royalty. Red is also capable of raising blood pressure, promoting anger, exciting aggression, and causing dizziness. Yellow is considered stimulating, happy, optimistic, and innovative, but it can also promote aggression. Orange suggests friendship and warmth but can stimulate at a high level, comparably to red and yellow. Pink can be vibrant yet can also tranquilize and suggest calm. Brown though warm, comfortable, and earthy, is also associated with depression, fatigue, and a loss of depth perception.

The effects of cool colors are different. Blue reminds us of clear skies and calm seas, and can help reduce stress and blood pressure and soothe emotions. Green can vary, depending upon whether it is a warm or a cool green. Many consider green a calming color—quiet, refreshing, healthy—nature's color. Violet, although less calming than blue, is still restful but is also considered elegant, mysterious, and, to some, depressing.

White generally makes people feel colder, isolated, and increases depth perception. It can be either warm or cool depending upon the tint. Black and gray decrease depth perception, encourage fatigue and depression, and may evoke feelings of foreboding and mystery.

The most effective uses of color balance warm with cool and light with dark. This kind of balance provides visual variety that involves a viewer. People react more favorably towards photographs that have variations in color and contrast than they do to a monochromatic scene with limited light and dark contrast.

Color contrast occurs when colors that are opposite on the color wheel appear adjacent to each other. Contrast also occurs when the primary colors—red, blue, and green—are next to each other. This effect is heightened because of the human eye's limited ability to perceive different wavelengths of light simultaneously. Every color of light has a different wavelength, with cool colors having short wavelengths and warm colors having longer wavelengths. When red and blue are next to each other, the eye cannot focus on them simultaneously. Our flexible iris moves back and forth, perceiving contrast so that colors appear to vibrate when stared at long enough.

Color harmony results with a mixture of colors that are related to each other, such as with a combination of yellow, orange, and brown. A photograph with harmonious colors has less contrast and a more placid feeling than a photograph with contrasting colors. Harmonious relationships are soothing and easy to respond to, but they are generally less involving. (See Color Gallery B, Plate 15.2.)

Hue, Saturation, and Luminance

Color has three distinct qualities that are important to note. *Hue* is the name of the color, such as red or blue, and refers to the specific wavelength that is that color. *Saturation*, or *chroma*, is the vividness or purity of a hue. Bold, vibrant hues, such as pure red lipstick, are considered saturated. Pink, which consists of red and white mixed together, has a low saturation. *Luminance*, or *value*, refers to the lightness or darkness of a hue. Sometimes a photograph is referred to as high key. This means that it is very luminous and has light colors of low saturation. A low key photograph is dark and somber with little luminance and color saturation. These terms are used to describe colors, whether in the form of pigment or light.

Thinking in Color

Photographs have their own reality, and photographic materials react to color differently than do the human eye and brain. The success of a color photograph depends upon how well the photographer understands and controls the variables that affect the picture. No magic formula provides the answer. You learn by doing, and success comes with experience. There is no industry standard that says this is proper color and a good color photograph. Everyone perceives color differently, and color materials vary in their color sensitivity. Some films emphasize warm colors, and others emphasize blue and green. Consequently, it is important for persons serious about photography to work with the materials to develop their own sensitivity. It is the only way to understand the characteristics, potentials, and limitations of the medium as well.

Most people who are comfortable with black and white photography have learned to create compositions that use the light and dark areas of a picture as *forms*. These considerations also apply to color photography, but with one important addition: think of *color* as form. Regardless of what you are shooting, do not make the picture unless the color and the light are working effectively in the picture. Light and color relationships are extremely important and make the difference between another shot to languish in the files and an image that is worth showing. You have to learn to think in color. (See Color Gallery B, Plate 15.3.)

Controlling the Technical Variables

Photographers need to be aware of the contrast range when they are shooting because contrast control is more limited with color materials than with black and white. Color films cannot be altered with variations in exposure and development as effectively as can black and white films. Color print papers vary only about one contrast grade, versus the wide range possible with black and white papers. This limitation means that you have to become a more perceptive, knowledgeable, and better shooter to use color materials effectively.

When shooting, consider the quality and type of light. Determine what it will do to the color and look of the photograph. If the light is contrasty, consider using shadows as forms. Let them go black. Let the highlights burn out to white. Otherwise, to hold the detail in a print, you will have to use reflectors and supplemental lighting, or do contrast masking when printing. Both of these options get involved.

You can simplify things when you are shooting by making a concerted effort to visualize how the subject will look in a print. Before you aim the camera, ask yourself the following: What is it about this subject that interests me? Why am I shooting a picture of it? How can I express my feelings in the picture?

If you decide to take the picture, then ask yourself the following: Is the composition good? Should I change the camera position? Am I including too much or too little? What should I crop out? What about the background? What lens should I use? Do I have the right type of film? How much depth of field do I need? Is motion a concern? What shutter speed should I use? Is the lighting good? Does it work with the subject? Does it work with the composition? What about the shadows? What about the highlights? Is there too much contrast? Should I meter from the camera or spot meter the high and low values? Do I want the shadows to go dark? Should I expose normally or underexpose for more drama? Should I overexpose the picture? What about bracketing? Should I use fill flash or a reflector?

These are a few of the questions that need to be considered anytime you take a picture in black and white or color. A new camera, even with fantastic electronic options, will not make your pictures better. You will still need to consider these questions every time you seriously attempt to photograph. In time, if you shoot enough, you will learn to deal with these factors almost instantaneously.

To make effective color pictures, you need to ask yourself even more questions: What about the colors? Do they contrast? Do they harmonize? Do they lead you through the print to the centers of interest? Do the "forms" created by the colors work with the "forms" created by the light? Or do they conflict? What about the color of the light? Will it affect the overall color balance? Will it change the look of the photograph? Will it change the feeling of the photograph? Does the color work with the subject? What about the background color? Do I have the right type of film for this light? Should I use a filter to change or enhance the color? Will I have trouble printing this or can a lab do it? And finally, how will this look as a photograph?

Shooting the picture and making a print are separate events tied together by a mutual need: the need to make an effective photograph. To make effective pictures, you need to have control when you are shooting and in the darkroom. Advanced photography is not about new equipment or special techniques. It is about understanding how things will look in a photograph and knowing how to make them happen. (See Color Gallery B, Plate 15.4.)

Darkroom Practices

Consistency, control, and cleanliness are the three most important concerns when it comes to darkroom practices. A consistent and methodical approach to darkroom work reduces the variables and makes it easier to determine and solve problems. Keep methodical records of print data for future reference. Such information can save time and materials. The people who seem to have the most problems with color printing and advanced photographic methods are those who don't keep track of what they are doing.

Consistency leads to control, which in turn can lead to a successful result. Control comes with time and experience. Do not expect to become a master color printer immediately. Many beginners, who are satisfied with their black and white work, get impatient with color. They are used to the immediacy of watching a black and white print appear in the developer tray. They are used to Polaroid and one hour photo stores and want immediate gratification. But it takes time to make good color prints, and you must develop your understanding of color. Because we are all familiar with color, we expect more from it than we do from black and white.

To have control, you have to have cleanliness. Dust is an obvious problem and shows up as spots on your prints. Contaminating your color chemistry is only too easy: A drop of an alien chemical in the developer or bleach can cause major color problems. Therefore, always rinse everything you use with fresh running water. Use separate containers, graduates, funnels, and mixing implements for each chemical. Never use a water bath to rinse your thermometer when you are checking chemical temperatures. Avoid contamination. Always thoroughly dry all components of a processing drum before using it. A wet drum can cause streaks on a print.

Chemical contamination is normally more evident in the borders of a print than it is in the image area. Color negative materials should have white borders, and Type R materials should have black borders. If the borders have the slightest hint of a color cast, it indicates chemical contamination or aged paper. Ilfochrome papers get a green cast if they are aged and haven't been stored in a refrigerator. All of the manufacturers publish information indicating how to identify contamination and other problems with their products. To avoid problems, keep color materials in cool, dry storage areas and be wary of contamination.

Selective Filtration

Mixed lighting is not a problem with black and white photography, but it can be with color. Reflected light can also cause problems because it is subtle and we may not notice it. Our eyes and mind adapt to light

and see color naturally, even if reflected or artificial lighting cause unnatural color. The kelvin temperature of light varies, both outdoors and with artificial lights. The results may be an image with several different color casts. Such variation can add beneficial impact to a picture, especially if the photographer exercised control over the light and the color possibilities. Variations in kelvin temperature, if light sources are mixed, can also lead to visual conflicts and detract from the picture.

Selective filtration is useful for altering the color of a portion of the print. Normally in printing, the filtration affects the color of the whole print. But dodging and burning techniques combined with color filters can selectively alter the color in portions of a print. Such techniques can also help correct color photographs that have partially deteriorated from aging or other problems.

Burning-in with a different filtration can be done by changing the filter pack in the head of the enlarger, as long as you are careful not to bump it and cause a double image. But dodging with filters has to be done with supplementary filters, and in many cases it is easier to use them for burning-in too. Ideally, color compensating (CC) filters should be used when you are selectively filtering portions of a print under the lens with dodging and burning techniques. But because of their cost, you may find it more practical to buy another CP filter kit and use it to make your selective filtering tools for dodging and burning. The difference in quality will be minimal because you will only be using the CP filters under the lens for portions of the overall exposure.

Testing will be necessary to determine exposure and how much filtration is needed to selectively dodge or burn a portion of a print. Begin by trying a 20 degree filter. (See Plates 15.5 and 15.6, Gallery B.)

Dye Enhancement

Color prints can be enhanced or altered by adding dyes to them in a manner similar to hand coloring black and white prints. Often considered a retouching technique, dye enhancement can also be used as another creative alternative to make an image more distinctive. Dye enhancement can be done in large, plain areas of a print as well as in small, highly detailed portions. With Ilfochrome, the dyes are added while the prints are wet. With most other processes, the dyes are added when the prints are dry.

With Kodak, Fuji, and other chromogenic dye-coupler print materials, use the Kodak Retouching Colors. These dyes have a wax-like consistency a little harder than that of shoe polish. To apply the dye, use a piece of dry cotton or a cotton swab. Breathe onto the cake of dye before rubbing the cotton into it. With the dye on the cotton, apply it to the surface of the print by rubbing it onto the intended area. Do not get the dye wet, because this will prematurely, and permanently, adhere the dye to the print. Smooth the dye onto the print surface with the cotton so that it blends naturally with the image. At this point the dye can be removed with a reducer (in the dye kit) or with a clean piece of cotton. When the dye on the print is ready, set the dye by breathing on the print or by directing steam toward it. When set, the dye will be permanently absorbed into the emulsion and will no longer sit on the surface. If you want a more saturated color, apply several coats of dye, setting the dye after each application. Subtle color biases can often be neutralized by applying a dye of the complementary color.

The approach with Ilfochrome prints differs slightly. The dye is applied while the print is wet. Use Ilfochrome Transparent Retouching Dyes, which have the same basic dye structure as the print dyes and are as permanent. (See Color Gallery B, Plate 15.7.)

Start by wetting the print in a tray of water, squeegee off the surface liquid, and apply the dyes with cotton balls or swabs. Apply them with caution because the dyes set upon contact. With practice, however, you will find that it is easy to blend them. A spray bottle can be used to keep the print wet. Apply some dye to the print, give it a light spray, squeegee, and then add more dye as needed. To apply an even color to a large area, such as a sky, it is better to not squeegee the print, because the wet surface dilutes the dye and makes it easier to smoothly blend the dye over a large area. Should you get dye in the wrong areas or apply too much dye, you can remove most of it by resoaking the print in water. Once the dye is properly applied, squeegee and dry the print. The dye is absorbed into the emulsion, and when the print is dry, it is no longer visible on the surface of the print.

Both of these methods can be useful to enhance or save marginal prints. You can add a little color to a person's cheeks, intensify a blue sky, accent a particular color, or radically change the look of a picture. Sometimes a little dye enhancement is a much better option than redoing a print.

Dye Bleaching

Photographers seldom consider the creative option of bleaching color prints. This is partly due to the fact that chromogenic dye-coupler prints do not bleach easily or effectively. But Ilfochrome is easy to bleach,

Dye Bleach Formulas

Cibachrome Yellow-Dye Bleach*

Chemical	Amount
N, N-dimethyl-formamide	2 volumes
Water	1 volume

*Mix to make a stock solution, which will keep for several months.

Cibachrome Magenta-Dye Bleach*

| Chemical | Amount | |
	U.S. Customary	Metric
Solution A:		
Chloramine T	0.5 oz.	15.0 g
Water	32.0 fl. oz.	1.0 l
Solution B:		
Acetic acid (10% solution)	any	any
Solution C:		
Sodium bisulfite	0.3 oz.	10.0 g
Water	32.0 fl. oz.	1.0 l

*Each solution should be mixed and stored separately in plastic-capped glass bottles for a longer life. The individual solutions will keep for several months. Once used, they should be discarded.

Cibachrome Cyan-Dye Bleach*

| Chemical | Amount | |
	U.S. Customary	Metric
Sodium dithionite	0.1 oz.	3.0 g
Sodium bicarbonate	0.1 oz.	3.0 g
Water	32.0 fl. oz.	1.0 l

*Prepare only for immediate use. Once mixed the solution lasts approximately 8 hours.

Total Bleach for all Cibachrome Dyes*

Chemical	Amount	
	U.S. Customary	Metric
Solution A:		
Potassium permanganate	0.25 oz.	8.0 g
Distilled water	16.0 fl. oz.	500.0 ml
Solution B:		
Water	32.0 fl. oz.	1.0 l
Sulfuric acid (2-normal)**	2.0 fl. oz.	56.0 ml
or		
Water	11.0 fl. oz.	340.0 ml
Sulfuric acid (concentrated)**	.75 fl. oz.	20.0 ml
Solution C:		
Sodium sulfite	0.3 oz.	10.0 g
or		
Potassium metabisulfite	0.3 oz.	10.0 g
Water	16.0 fl. oz.	500.0 ml

*For use, mix equal parts of solutions A and B. Solution C is used separately to remove yellow/brown stains. The stock solutions keep for several months, while the mixed solution only keeps for approximately 8 hours.

Never add water to the acid, for it can spatter the acid. Always add the acid to the water. **Be very cautious with sulfuric acid**. It is highly corrosive. Avoid all contact with skin, and store in a polyethylene bottle. If you are unable to get the weaker 2N solution, mix it from the more concentrated solution.

and Ilford has published bleaching formulas for each of the individual dye layers, as well as a total bleach that removes all of the dyes. The total bleach is also used to bleach out black dust spots on prints so that spotting dyes can be applied.

Selective Dye Bleaching of Ilfochrome Prints

To reduce yellow in specific areas of a print, apply the *yellow-dye bleach* with either a nylon brush or a cotton ball or swab. Allow the bleach to remain on the print for 1 1/2 to 8 minutes. For overall yellow reduction, immerse the print completely in the bleach. After bleaching, wash the print for 10 minutes in running water, and then dry it. To determine the proper amount of bleaching time, experiment on scrap prints. Avoid prolonged bleaching because it may affect the magenta dye layer.

The working solution for *magenta-dye bleaching* is made by adding a few drops of solution B to solution A. The amount of solution A depends on how much you think you need to do the job. Unless you plan to immerse the whole print, mix a small amount. For normal retouching applications, 2 to 3 oz. should be enough. Add drops of solution B until the solution turns milky. The amount of solution B varies with the volume of solution A. Apply the working solution to the print surface until the desired bleaching occurs.

Rinse the print in running water for 30 seconds. Next, immerse the print into Solution C for 2 minutes. Finally, wash the print for 10 minutes and then dry it. A yellowish stain may result in the white areas of the print. To remove the stain, immerse the print in the following solution until the yellow stain disappears: 10 volumes of hydrogen peroxide (3%) and 1 volume of ammonia (10%). Then wash the print for 10 minutes and dry it. This solution keeps just one day, so discard it after use.

For bleaching small cyan areas of a print, use the undiluted *cyan-dye bleach* solution. It normally takes 2 to 3 minutes to completely bleach out all of the cyan dye. To reduce the entire print, immerse it in a tray of bleach. To slow the bleaching action, lower the concentration by diluting the bleach 1:1 with water. After bleaching, wash the print for 10 minutes, and then dry it. (See Color Gallery B, Plate 15.8.)

Total Dye Bleaching

To bleach all three dye layers, make a working solution of the *total dye bleach* by mixing equal parts of solutions A and B. Apply it to small areas of the print with a nylon brush or cotton swab. Use only a small amount of bleach, and be careful to apply it only where needed. After about a minute, rinse the bleach off with a spray or running water and squeegee the print. Examine it to see whether more bleaching is necessary. The bleached area should be white if it is completely bleached. However, it may have a yellow-brown stain from the bleach. This stain can be removed by applying solution C or P30 fixer to the spot for 10 to 20 seconds. Avoid prolonged applications of solution C or the fixer because either may discolor the print. This step is necessary because, in addition to removing any staining, it also neutralizes the bleach.

After neutralizing the bleach, determine whether another application is needed. If not, wash the print for 10 minutes in running water and dry as usual. The total bleach exhausts within an hour, so mix what you need and discard the rest upon completion.

To reduce the whole print, immerse it completely into the bleach. Large areas can be selectively bleached in a tray by masking the parts that are to remain normal with photomaskoid or rubber cement. Leave this protective mask on the print while it is in the bleach. After the bleaching is completed, neutralize and wash the print. Then carefully rub off the rubberish mask and rewash the whole print so that the surface dries uniformly.

Chapter 16

Photo-Chemical Image Manipulations

The material of the artist lies not within himself nor in the fabrications of his imagination, but in the world around him.

—Paul Strand
Photographer

One advantage of doing your own film processing and printing is the opportunity to explore many different paths: it can open the door to another world of your own creation. This opportunity exists especially for those whose darkroom experience extends beyond the basics. With today's technology, anyone can take a technically okay photograph. Many feel this a blessing, but others find that images straight from the camera are often lacking. They discover that the darkroom not only offers an opportunity to refine their photographs but also offers a step beyond the limits of the camera's view of reality.

Specialty darkroom processes and techniques vary from methods to improve the straight camera image to procedures that alter and abstract photographs. The computer has become an excellent tool for combining, altering, and retouching photographs. Some see the computer as a "lightroom" technology that will make the darkroom obsolete. Computer software options provide tremendous creative freedom and quick-fix solutions for imitating famous artists' styles and techniques. With the click of a mouse, you can change a color, get a canvas texture, or create another painterly effect. Most of these digital options were previously produced by hand, using photo-chemical methods. Surprisingly, many of these digital options can still be done quicker, easier, and better by hand, whereas others benefit from the capabilities of the computer. (See Color Gallery C, Plate 16.1.)

This diversity of options offers a tremendous advantage for photographers, but to take full advantage of these choices, photographers need to be aware of both the darkroom and the computer. The biggest difference between the two is that photo-chemical darkroom work is a physical, get-your-hands-wet activity, whereas digital work involves pressing keys or clicking a mouse. This chapter explores creative options that are possible with photo-chemical materials in the light and in the darkroom. The next chapter explores the digital possibilities. It is important to involve yourself with both to understand the possibilities and to develop your feeling for the materials.

Lightroom Image Manipulations

There are many ways to heighten the impact of a photograph. When the camera work is done, it does not mean that the potential for creative expression is over. For many it has just begun. Most postcamera work is done in the darkroom, but there are lightroom activities other than the digital options that also offer creative potential.

Polaroid Time-Zero Manipulations

Noted for the instant picture, Polaroid became popular with photographic artists when it introduced the SX-70 camera in the 1970s. The pictures popped out of the front of the camera and the jewel-like colors formed as you looked at them. The emulsion was self-contained within the picture packet.

Shortly after the SX-70 was introduced, New York artist Lucas Samaras had an exhibition of manipulated SX-70 Polaroids. Samaras was the first to manipulate Polaroids by moving the emulsion around during the development, and he opened the door to a new wave of photographic possibilities. The SX-70 is no longer around, but *Time-Zero, Spectra High Definition*, and *600 Plus* films respond to similar manipulation. Time-Zero is easier to work with because it has an emulsion that remains pliable longer, allowing the photographer more time to work with the image. Chapter 7 provides a visual example.

Before altering the picture, wait about 15 seconds or until the outlines of the image start to appear. The portions of the image you choose to alter, the amount of pressure applied, and the tools you use to move the emulsion will determine the final look of the photograph. Blunt objects such as dental tools, ceramic tools, wood burnishers, kitchen utensils, and even fingernails can be used to move the emulsion without cutting through the plastic covering. Some photographers heat the prints to keep the emulsion pliable longer, whereas others freeze recently developed images to save them for future manipulation.

This type of Polaroid print can also be altered later, after the emulsion has hardened. Take a knife or razor and delicately cut open three sides of the back of the image so that the back can be separated from the front of the packet. Portions of the emulsion can then be scraped off to produce drawing effects, add words, or completely clear the plastic covering for collaging other images into the picture. The back can then be resealed, and the photograph will look like an unusual but normal Polaroid print. (See Color Gallery C, Plate 16.2.)

Altering Emulsions

Films and prints can also undergo creative emulsion alterations. Before the introduction of resin coated (RC) prints, etching or carefully scratching off layers of the emulsion was a quick and practical way to retouch fiber-based color and black and white prints. Because of their plastic coating, RC prints cannot be etched like fiber prints, and the technique has become a lost art since RC paper has become so popular. But creative applications can be used with any of the print materials, and each will result in its own characteristics.

Etching and cutting can be done to produce a variety of diverse results on any type of photographic paper. RC prints can be delicately cut so that the emulsion is slit, but not the paper backing. The emulsion can then be peeled from the paper backing to isolate a subject, remove a background, or add words or some design element. The paper backing is very white and textured, which contrasts with the smooth plastic surface of an RC print.

Sandpaper, wire brushes, and other abrasive tools can create interesting effects, especially when you leave part of the image intact. Scratching and drawing on film can also lead to one-of-a-kind images. Experiment with film and prints when they are wet too. The same tools will produce very different results.

Image Transfers

Transfer processes enable the artist to move an existing photograph onto another surface, altering its texture and visual impact. Artists such as Robert Rauschenberg, Darryl Curran, and Robert Heinecken did extensive work with magazine image transfers in the 60s and 70s. In recent years, image transfers with Polaroid and laser prints have been extremely popular.

Polacolor image transfers can be fully rendered with soft painterly qualities or partially rendered with a look similar to that of deteriorating fresco paintings. Peel-a-part Polacolor films such as 669, 59, 559, or 809 work best. These films are available in a variety of sizes from 3 1/4x4 1/4-inches to 20x24-inches. The film can be exposed directly in a Polaroid camera, or by projecting a transparency onto it from an enlarger. There are also several instant slide printers on the market, such as the Vivitar Instant Slide Printer and the Daylab Slide Printer. Once exposed, the Polaroid negative can be transferred to either a wet or a dry receptor material. The most popular of these materials is 90 lb. Watercolor papers such as Arches and BFK, which are available in cold- and hot-press surfaces. Cold-press paper surfaces have more texture and produce a more impressionistic look than do the smooth hot-press papers.

The transfer process itself is simple. Prepare your receptor paper ahead of time by soaking it in water, and then blot off the surface water with a paper towel. Next, expose the film and pull it through the processing rollers. Wait about 10 seconds, and peel the film apart. Set the positive print aside and place the negative facedown on the receptor paper as quickly as possible. Use a roller to rub the negative into contact with the paper. Start at the center and work out in each direction with the roller. Wait 1 to 2 minutes (experiment to determine what works best for you), and peel the negative from the receptor paper. Polaroid transfers have a tendency to come out a little cyan. To counteract that, try exposing the film with 20 degrees of red filtration.

Laser transfers work a little differently. The biggest advantage of the laser print is that 8 1/2x11-inch prints are inexpensive to make and are larger than the normal sized Polaroid prints. Most stationary stores and copy centers have laser printers that function like copy machines, making laser prints from flat art and transparencies. To end up with a normal print, have the image flopped when you make the laser print. Otherwise you will get a reversed image with the transfer. The look of a laser transfer print is similar to a Polaroid transfer, but different. Watercolor papers work well as receptors, but rice paper, homemade papers, and even cloth can be used. (See Color Gallery C, Plate 16.3.)

To make a laser print transfer, soak the receptor paper with a lacquer thinner such as MEK to loosen the image. Be sure to work in a well-ventilated area to minimize any ill affects from the lacquer thinner. Let the surface liquid drain off the receptor paper, and then lay the paper flat on a tabletop. Then place the laser print facedown, in contact with the receptor paper. When contact is made, rub the back of the print with the under side of a spoon bowl, your hand, or another suitable implement. The tool you use, the amount of pressure, and the type of movements you make will determine the amount of transfer and the look of the final print. You have 10 to 15 seconds to transfer the image before the lacquer thinner dries.

For more control, the transfer can be done in sections rather than all at once. Tape a dry laser print facedown onto a dry piece of watercolor paper. Begin in one area and use a paint brush to coat the back of the laser print with the MEK lacquer thinner so that it is thoroughly wet, but also so that the liquid is not running. Then, using the underside of a spoon bowl, rub the back of the print to transfer that portion. To check on the amount of transfer, carefully lift a corner of the print. Rewet that portion of the laser print and do more to the transfer if needed. When you are ready to move to another area of the print, repeat the process. Continue the procedure until the whole image is transferred. With practice you will gain a feel for the technique. To add more than one image, let the paper dry after the first transfer. Then repeat the process and transfer another image on top of the first one.

Polaroid Emulsion Lifts

Emulsion lifts are another creative innovation with Polacolor print films. This procedure involves actually lifting the Polacolor emulsion from its normal paper backing and transferring it to another surface. Virtually any surface can be used, including paper, cloth, wood, ceramic, tile, glass, and sheet metal. Naturally, some surfaces work better than others because the emulsion is delicate and hard to handle when being transferred and gets brittle when dry.

The process itself is easy to do. Expose and process a sheet of Polaroid 669, 59, 559, or 809 film and let it dry 8 to 24 hours, or force dry it with a hair dryer. To prevent the backing paper from dissolving when it is wet, attach a piece of contact paper to it. Heat a tray of tap water to 160°F and fill a separate tray with cold water. The hot water is very important, because a lower temperature does not work effectively. If you are transferring the image to paper, wet the paper and squeegee the surface before transferring the Polaroid emulsion. Immerse the Polacolor print faceup into the tray of hot water for several minutes. Carefully remove the print from the hot water and place it into the cold-water tray. Gently push the emulsion from the edges of the print towards the center. Carefully lift the emulsion, pulling it away from the paper backing, and let it float in the water. To make it easier to lift the emulsion out of the water, try slipping a piece of waxed paper under the emulsion while it floats in the cold-water tray. The waxed paper is an optional step, and experimentation will be necessary. You may want to practice a few times.

While the image is floating, flip the emulsion over so that it will transfer facing normally. You can also move the emulsion around to stretch it out naturally or to bunch it up into an abstraction. When you get it positioned the way you want, gently lift the waxed paper and let the emulsion rest on it as you raise it out of the water. You may have to adjust the shape again by gently moving the emulsion with your fingers or by reimmersing it in the water. When satisfied, place the wet emulsion in contact with the receptor material by flipping it over so that the waxed paper is on top. Rub the image with your fingers to make it adhere to the receptor material and gently lift off the waxed paper. Straighten and smooth the emulsion as needed once the waxed paper is removed. A rubber roller, or brayer, can be used to help smooth and adhere the emulsion. Let dry, and subsequently flatten in a dry-mount press if you wish. After drying, coat the emulsion with a protective spray such as McDonald's Pro-tecta-cote to keep the emulsion from flaking. (See Color Gallery C, Plate 16.4.)

Hand Coloring Film and Prints

The art of hand coloring black and white film and prints goes back to the early days of photography. It is easy to do and also an effective way to create a nostalgic feeling or a contemporary innovation that is different from ordinary print color. Hand coloring is normally done with transparent oil paints, such as Marshall Photo Oils, which allow the photographic image to show through the coloring. But film and color prints can also be colored. Opaque oils, acrylics, felt pens, spray paint, pastels, and colored pencils are among the materials used to add color to photographs. With most materials, experimentation is the best teacher. However, because of the popularity of coloring black and white prints with transparent oil colors, the following basic procedure is suggested as a starting point.

It is best to use a fiber-based paper with a slight texture, or tooth, for hand coloring and to avoid glossy papers. RC papers can be used, but the pigments are not absorbed and sit on the surface, taking an exceeding long time to dry. A *precoat spray* is available at photo stores for giving RC papers a little tooth so that the pigments will look more natural, but the results still don't compare to what is possible with fiber prints. The exception is P-Max Art RC paper by Kodak, which has a specially designed RC surface for hand coloring with oils, dyes, pastels, and pencils. Fiber-based papers such as Agfa Portriga Rapid 118, Kodak Polyfiber double weight G, and Kodak Ektalure G provide excellent results.

To ensure permanence and control of the coloring thoroughly wash and dry the prints before coloring. Brown toning is frequently done prior to coloring to give skin tones a more natural look. Sometimes photographers will use a blue toner or other color toner prior to toning to create a particular look. It can also be helpful to make prints slightly lighter than normal to compensate for the additional density from the hand coloring. (See Color Gallery C, Plate 16.5.)

Oil colors are applied to dry prints by hand with cotton balls and cotton tipped swabs. Because of the transparency of the oils, the photo image shows through, providing a natural looking shading. This factor makes a knowledge of drawing techniques unnecessary since you are merely blending the colors onto the structure of the printed image. You can overrun the outlines of a subject and easily remove the color later. In fact, it is easy to remove all of the color and start over if necessary.

Begin by squeezing out a small amount of the needed colors onto a plate or glass palette. Color large areas first, using cotton balls and a rotary motion. Apply the color darker than needed and then blend in the color until it looks natural. Use cotton swabs and small brushes for detail work in small areas. Buy long-fiber cotton and make your own cotton swabs, using tooth picks. That way you can vary the size and not have stray cotton fibers sticking out. Remove colors before they dry by moistening a piece of cotton with Marlene or PM Solution, both of which come with Marshall Oil Color Kits. Once coloring is completed, it can take two to three days for an oil-colored print to dry completely. Additional color can be added after the print is dry to increase saturation or add other effects. Color pencils and pastels can also be applied to finish the print. When the print surface is thoroughly dry and completed, use a lacquer spray such as McDonald's Pro-tecta-cote or a varnish to preserve the coloring.

Color prints and film can also be colored or altered. Dye enhancement techniques with color prints was discussed in Chapter 15. But transparent oils, opaque paints, pencils, and pastels can also be used on color prints. Many artists paint directly on photographs, totally covering the photographic image, whereas others keep part of it to provide contrast with the painterly effects. Numerous options are available. Film can be scratched, painted, and drawn upon with ink, felt-tip pens, or other materials and then printed. (See Color Gallery C, Plates 16.6 and 16.7.)

Toning Black and White Prints

Chemical toning of black and white prints is used to enhance, add color, and improve the permanence of photographic images. Various types of toners are available at most photography stores. Brownish toners such as sepia and selenium have always been the most popular toners, but there are other toners to produce red, blue, green, and even yellow prints. Substances such as coffee, tea, and food-coloring dyes can also be used to tone prints. However, these items tone the paper fiber, whereas commercial toners react with the emulsion, are more permanent, and provide a more natural look.

Make sure you thoroughly fix and wash your prints before toning to ensure longevity and avoid staining. A slightly darker than normal print is generally best since most toners bleach the print, lightening it up to 10 percent. Dry prints need to be soaked in water before toning. Carefully read and follow the instructions packed with the toner you use. Results will vary with different papers and dilutions of the toners. It is always possible to deviate from the manufacturer's instructions later, once you have a feeling for the procedure and type of the results you want.

Sepia Toner

Various brown toners are available. Many are one-solution toners, some of which are only good for one usage. The most popular sepia toner is a two-solution process that can be used repeatedly and lasts for months. Prints are initially bleached, then rinsed, and finally toned with the sepia process. Variations in the amount of bleaching can result in shades of brown varying from chocolate, with a short bleaching time, to yellow brown, requiring a long bleaching time. The age of the bleach also affects the color, while the toner only tones to a certain point, based upon the amount of bleaching. Be sure to give prints a final wash in the usual manner after the toning bath. The main disadvantage of sepia toners is that they have a strong odor.

Selenium Toning and Permanence

The permanence of all black and white prints is enhanced with selenium toner, which changes the metallic silver to a more durable metal. Selenium is a one-solution toner diluted with water to make a working solution. Variations in toning time and the amount of dilution change the effect of the toner. For a strong, purplish-brown color, try a dilution of 1 part toner to 3 parts water. Weaker solutions such as 1:20, 1:30, or 1:40 produce deeper browns but get progressively subtler as the dilution increases. Regardless of the dilution, selenium toner makes the dark areas of a print darker, adding an extra richness to the print. Photographers concerned with a *fine print aesthetic* tone for permanence use a weak solution of selenium toner so that the color effect is not obvious.

Toning procedures can be varied, but the basic procedure is as follows: Thoroughly process and wash prints, wet prints that have been dried before toning them, tone for 3 minutes at the dilution of choice, and wash and dry in the normal manner.

Split toning is also done with selenium toner, producing a seductive warm-cool color relationship that subtly expands the tonal range and extends the depth of the photograph. Effects vary with different papers, but it works best with Kodak Azo paper. Try Kodak Selectol developer diluted 1:1 at a temperature of 23–25°C. Lower temperatures negate the split effect and result in an overall brown cast. Tap water generally works better than distilled water. A thorough two-bath fixing (3 minutes in each of two different fixing baths) is necessary. After the second fixing bath, transfer the print directly into a toner-clearing bath for 4

minutes. The toner-clearing bath is made with 70 ml selenium toner, 30 ml Perma Wash, and 20 g Kodalk or sodium metaborate to 1 l (liter) of water.

Should stains occur, separate the toner-clearing bath into two separate steps. First clear the print for 5 minutes in a solution made from 30 ml Perma Wash and 20 g Kodalk to 1 l of water. Then use a toning solution of 70 ml selenium and 1 l of water. The split in color should occur in 4 or more minutes. The blacks intensify first, then the print goes dull overall, and slowly the dark areas begin to turn brown as it splits. When the result seems good, transfer the print immediately into a water bath to examine it. Return it to the toner if you desire more toning. Wash fiber-based prints after toning for 20 minutes. RC prints should be washed for 10 minutes. Dry in the normal manner.

Color Toners

Edwal makes a popular line of color toners in brown, red, blue, green, and yellow. The 4 oz. bottles can be diluted to make a 64 oz. solution. Stronger concentrations of toner eat the silver away, causing a semireversal effect. The normal toning time is 4 to 10 minutes, and varying the time alters the result.

Use caution when opening the bottle. Inside the cap is a small plastic container filled with orangish crystals. Dump this material into the bottle and put the lid back in place. Shake the bottle to dissolve the crystals. The contents are now active and ready to dilute to a working strength. The working solution lasts for only about an hour, so plan ahead and have lots of prints ready to tone. Intermediate colors can be produced by partially toning the print in one color and partially in another. Don't mix the colors. Check the instructions packed with the toners before using, and be careful—the toners stain clothing.

Masking for Partial and Multiple Color Toning

Masking part of a print with rubber cement or a liquid frisket, or masking material, enables you to partially tone a print or tone it with differing colors. Apply the liquid mask with a brush to a dry print in the areas you want to protect from the toner. Thoroughly coat the area so that there are no breaks in the mask. Immerse the print into the toner, being careful not to disturb the masked area. Once the print is toned, remove it and rinse it with water. Carefully pull off or rub off the mask and rewash the print so that it has a uniform surface when drying. To add a second color, mask the part that was previously colored and tone the untoned portion. (See Color Gallery C, Plate 16.8.)

Bleaching Black and White Prints

Most photographers use bleaching as a corrective tool to lighten part of a print or to bleach out skin blemishes and dark spots in a picture. But bleaching can also be a powerful and intriguing visual tool for altering the impact of an image and has been used readily by purists such as Ansel Adams and W. Eugene Smith. Household bleaches will work to some extent. But for real control, try Farmer's Reducer. It is the most popular professional photographic bleach used with black and white film and prints.

Farmer's Reducer is easy to work with and can be bought in small packets produced by Kodak, or as individual chemicals. Potassium ferricyanide is the active ingredient in Farmer's Reducer. It changes the metallic silver of a print into a silver salt that dissolves in hypo. The second ingredient is sodium thiosulfate crystals, which are pure hypo without the other ingredients in normal fixer. The sodium thiosulfate ensures that the silver salts dissolve.

To use the bleach, mix equal parts of both chemicals with water. This working solution goes bad within 15 to 30 minutes, so only mix what you need. For small-volume work, mix a teaspoon of each chemical with two cups of water. To make a stronger solution, change the dilution or add more potassium ferricyanide. The bleach will work faster on a wet print. Before bleaching, soak the print in water, and then squeegee the surface to keep the bleach from running. To bleach out small black spots in a print, apply the solution locally with a brush. A weak solution applied selectively to dark areas of a print or film will lighten them and provide accents. Reduce a whole print or piece of film by immersing it completely into a weak bleach solution. Experimentation is necessary to master your technique. Be sure to practice with scrap materials and work slowly. You can always apply more bleach, but if you overbleach first, there is no turning back.

You can evaluate the progress of the bleach by rinsing the print with water. If more bleach is needed, squeegee the print and apply more. The bleach may leave a brownish stain, but this will go away when the bleach is neutralized. After you have completed the bleaching, briefly rinse the print in water, and then immerse it in normal fixer for 5 minutes to neutralize the bleach. After refixing, wash and dry the prints or film as usual.

Darkroom Image Manipulations

The darkroom provides unlimited creative potential despite the arrival of computer technology and will remain important in image making. Commercial needs for darkrooms may lessen, but the hands-on interaction with light, chemicals, and the diverse array of light-sensitive materials in the darkroom will continue to offer vital and dynamic visual opportunities.

Paper Negatives

One of the oldest and least expensive methods for retouching, altering, adding texture to and softening an image is the paper negative. The paper negative is also a quick and easy method for making negative image prints or positive prints from paper negative images made with a pinhole camera. To make a paper negative, simply contact print an existing positive image photographic print, emulsion to emulsion, with a piece of unexposed photographic paper. Determine the exposure by doing a test strip. The resulting negative print is often quite exciting. The paper negative can, in turn, also be retouched and contact printed again to produce an improved positive print. When working with paper negatives, think of each stage as a new generation. The positive print made from a film negative is the first generation. The paper negative made from the first generation positive print is the second generation. If a positive print is subsequently made from the paper negative, it would be the third generation.

With each generation, the texture and thickness of the print paper will subtly change the appearance of the image, softening it and adding texture. In addition, with each generation, contrast subtly increases.

Two Faced, Jerry Burchfield.

Figure 16-1

A. A filed-out negative carrier enabled the black border around this image. Farmer's Reducer bleached the shirt to white.
B. Positive print A served as a paper negative contact printed to create this negative print. Paper negatives are easy to retouch for corrective or creative needs. Light areas in the negative print could be darkened with dyes and pencils, and those areas would disappear if another positive print were made.

The contrast can be heightened to produce a look similar to that achieved with high contrast litho film. Several generations are necessary. Each generation will lose detail that would normally be retained by making a print with a number 5 variable-contrast filter. For this effect, begin by using a number 3 or 4 filter to make the first-generation positive. Continue to use the same filter for each subsequent generation. If you want to maintain more detail in the image, begin with a low filter such as a number 1, and build up contrast by going to a higher number filter with each generation. As always, experimentation will be necessary.

Retouching can be done on any of the print generations. Pencils work well on most papers and are easy to blend in, whereas dyes or pigments may be the best option for some needs. Dark spots in a positive image print can be lightened or completely removed by retouching them on the paper negative. Because the values are reversed, the dark spots will be light on the negative print. They can be darkened to match the surrounding areas by drawing on the print, and they will completely disappear with the next-generation positive print.

To get maximum sharpness with paper negatives, use RC papers or single-weight fiber-based papers. RC papers have little paper fiber compared to fiber-based prints and produce sharper results with minimal textural effects. To maximize the textural possibilities, use double weight fiber-based textured paper, such as Kodak Ektalure X.

A normal glass contact printer will work fine for making paper negatives, although a vacuum easel ensures maximum contact. Wet contacts work well with RC prints and speed up the back-and-forth, one-generation-to-the-next process. Take a dry piece of unexposed photographic paper and lay it emulsion up on a flat surface. Place your first-generation positive image print, while wet, emulsion down, on top of the unexposed photo paper. Then squeegee the wet and dry print together, forcing out the air and liquid between them. Then make an exposure through the back of the first-generation print. Because of their plastic surface, the wet and dry print will maintain excellent contact.

Texture Effects

Many oil paintings have an obvious surface texture, whereas photographs have a smooth or only subtly textured surface. Photographers have imitated the textural surface of paintings by adding transparent painterly textures to print surfaces or by actually mounting prints onto canvas. However, successful textural approaches occur when photographs maintain their integrity as photographs and texture is printed into the photographic image.

Mother and Child, Mark Chamberlain.

Figure 16-2

This print was made by sandwiching a piece of lens cleaning tissue with a black and white negative. The texture is large because it was enlarged with the negative. To get a smaller and darker textural pattern, contact print the texture material with the print paper but leave it in contact for only a portion of the exposure.

The natural grain of film can be accentuated to create a textural quality that is uniquely photographic as discussed in Chapter 7. Many photographers shoot textured subjects such as sand or peeling paint and sandwich or double print the texture into the image. Other types of texture can be printed into an image by using textured paper, fabric, or commercially made texture screens. These materials can either be contact printed with the print paper or sandwiched with the negative and enlarged. Textured substances, such as cheesecloth, will create a strong, white pattern of texture that competes with the image if you have the material in contact with the paper for the whole exposure time. To get a more subtle effect, leave the material in contact for just a portion of the exposure.

Bracket towards underexposure when shooting textured subjects to combine in printing with other images. A textural negative underexposed one *f*-stop will add texture, but without overwhelming the subject the way a normally exposed textural negative would. Also consider the

Barbara, P. W. Derby.   A.   B.   C.

Figure 16-3

A. A black and white print from a normally exposed negative.

B. A close-up of wet beach sand from a normally exposed negative.

C. For this highly textured print, the negatives for A and B were sandwiched together.

enlargement ratio of the textured negative. It is generally better to shoot a finely detailed texture pattern that won't visually compete, upon enlargement, with another image.

Commercial texture screens are made on film and can be purchased at photography stores that cater to professionals. They come in a variety of patterns and are designed to have a subtle effect on images. The least expensive approach is to buy texture screens that are the same size as your film and can be sandwiched with your original for printing. Large texture screens are also made for contact printing, but they are more expensive and work best with vacuum easels.

One sheet film has a built-in texture pattern: Kodak Autoscreen Ortho 2563. This can be used with a red safelight (ortho films are not sensitive to red) and printed on as on photo paper. Designed for lithographic printing, it will automatically produce a dot pattern like the dot patterns of magazine and newspaper photos. Autoscreen reproduces images with a continuous tone (normal film is continuous tone because it has a full range of tones), but with a dot screen or pattern. Photographers use this film for special effects or as a base film for photo silk screen printing. Refer to the manufacturer for more information on Autoscreen film.

Multiple Image Printing

The single image frequently limits the statement you make, but combining images can let you delve into innovative and unusual areas. There are many ways to create multiple image photographs. The simplest method is by making multiple exposures in your camera. Unfortunately, many cameras are designed to prevent making multiple exposures. Also, you are stuck with any multiple exposures made with your camera. Multiple image printing in the darkroom, however, gives you the freedom to make revisions, variations, and refinements until you are satisfied. The computer provides similar freedom for multiple image photography, but the difference in the working methods can generate different results.

Sandwiching Images

Sandwiching is a simple method to combine two photographs into one image. By putting two transparencies or negatives in contact together, you make a single image that can be printed, viewed, or projected. The disadvantage to sandwiching is that you can't alter the size and placement relationships of the two images. They work together as they

Codri, Ana Luisa Johnson.

Figure 16-4

Two separate negatives from the same shooting session were multiple printed, with one receiving less exposure than the other.

are, whereas printing multiple images allows you to vary the sizes and positioning of the separate images.

If you plan to sandwich images together, underexpose each image by one-half f-stop when shooting so that the combined densities will be fairly normal. Otherwise the sandwich will be too dense and hard to print. Vary the exposures to emphasize one image more than the other. Try a normal or a slight underexposure for the main image and underexpose the secondary image by a half or one full f-stop. Sandwiching works well with black and white films and color transparencies, but it is not advisable to sandwich color negatives because of the increased orange mask density. When sandwiching 35mm slides, take them out of their mounts to maintain focus for both images. To maximize sharpness, use a glass negative carrier.

Multiple Printing

Multiple printing combines two or more photographic images onto one piece of paper with separate exposures for each. This procedure enables you to emphasize one image more than another and to create visual relationships impossible in a single-image or sandwiched photograph. Techniques vary considerably because each image combination has its own needs but are essentially the same for both black and white and color. Regardless of the process used, each image must be individually tested for exposure, contrast, and filtration. With black and white materials, a variable-contrast paper permits you to print negatives of varying contrasts on the same piece of paper.

Photographers who consistently work with multiple images tend to tailor their shooting to that end. Preplanning during shooting makes the job in the darkroom or with the computer much easier. Backgrounds are an extremely important consideration. To print a picture of an object floating in the sky, use a white background with black and white or color negatives and a black background with positive transparencies. The white background will be dark in the negative and will not expose that area of the print, making it possible to print in another image. A black background will not expose that portion of the paper when you are printing transparencies.

When working with landscapes, try to shoot neutral foregrounds and backgrounds. Doing so will make it easy to drop out the unimportant neutral part of the picture and blend it with another image. The type of neutral ground, light or dark, textured or smooth, depends on the images you plan to combine together and whether you are using positive

or negative film. The important thing is to consider these variables when you are shooting and to plan ahead.

Photo Composites

A photo composite is an industry term for a photograph that consists of several images seamlessly combined together. There are many approaches to making composites, most are technically involved, and many have been taken over by the computer. A simple approach to photo composites is to put several 35mm negatives together in a 4x5-inch glass negative carrier and enlarge them all at once. Another approach would be to make an opaque mask from a piece of mat board, with cutout windows for contact printing separate negatives simultaneously on one sheet of paper. A similar type of cutout mask could be placed on top of the print paper and images enlarged one at a time into the separate windows of the mask. Simply cover all but the one being exposed, and then switch to the next one. For a visual reference to this approach, refer to Color Gallery C, Plate 16.9.

A more involved approach is necessary when you want to combine a hard-edged object seamlessly into another photographic environment without overlapping the images. This is normally done with pin-registered positive and negative litho film masks that block one part of the picture while the other is being printed. High contrast litho film will be discussed later in this chapter.

Image-Blending Techniques

Blending is a term used to describe the faultless combination of one image into another without its being obvious that a blend was done. Unlike the hard-edge masking approaches discussed in the section on photo composites, blending involves soft-edge combinations of neutral textural elements that subtly overlap while maintaining a natural look.

The approach is similar to the multiple-image filter masks for camera use discussed in Chapter 9. It involves blocking portions of a print during enlarging by holding a dodging wand or other masking device under the enlarger lens. Unlike normal dodging, the mask does not have to move. If the mask is 2 or more inches under the lens, the distance will cause the mask to have a soft graduated edge when printed. The type, shape, and position of the masking device depend upon the images that are being combined together. (See Color Gallery C, Plate 16.10.)

Blending One Image Into Another

A dodging wand and a burn-in card can be used to blend one image into another. Each image needs to be separately enlarged; the size and positioning need to be determined in relation to each other. First, project each negative individually onto a white piece of paper in the easel. Make a positioning sketch of each image when projecting it by drawing an outline of the image on the piece of paper. Then test each for exposure and contrast.

For example, when printing the first image, use the dodging wand to keep the portion in which the second image goes from being exposed. The wand must be continuously moved to produce a soft edge and to keep the wire from showing. Keep the wand in place for the whole exposure so that no light will hit that portion of the print. After the exposure, the partially exposed print paper should be removed from the

Figure 16-5

Congestion, Jerry Burchfield.

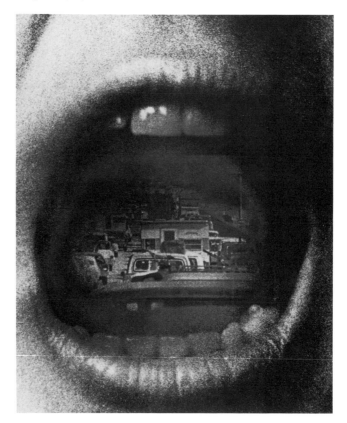

easel to a light safe box and the positioning sketch should be put back into the easel. See Figure 16.5 as an example of image blending.

Next, place the second negative in the enlarger, focus it, and project it onto the positioning sketch. Move the easel so that the second image lines up with the positioning indicated by the sketch. Stop the lens down and set the timer. Remove the positioning sketch from the easel and place the partially exposed print back into the easel. A burn card can then be held under the enlarger lens to block the already exposed portion of the print while letting the second image project through the opening in the card to expose the unexposed portion of the print. Jiggle the burn card during the exposure to blur the edges of the image. No light should be allowed to hit the previously exposed portions of the print. Dodging and burning are done so that the blurred "soft" edges overlap and blend together, making it appear that the two images belong together.

Blending Foreground and Background Images

You can blend foreground and background images together by using the filter holder found below the lens of most enlargers. Again, it will be necessary to test each image separately and to make a sketch to use as a sizing and positioning guide. To mask off the top portion of the print, place a small piece of black cardboard on the filter holder under

B.

Figure 16-6

A. Variable-contrast filter holder located under the lens.

B. Filter holder with black cardboard mask covering half the opening.

C. Mask switched to cover the other half for exposing the second image. The masks were positioned so that the soft edges of the images overlap slightly.

A.

C.

A. *Road Cut*, Jerry Burchfield.

B.

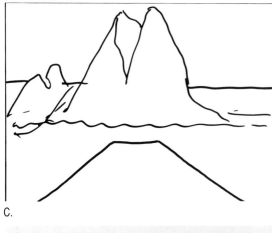

C.

D.

E.

F.

Figure 16-7

A. This is a straight print of a road cut.

B. This is a straight print of the end of a road.

C. This drawing was made by projecting the negatives for A and B onto the paper. It is used for sizing and positioning the two images for multiple printing.

D. A small cardboard mask was placed on the filter holder under the enlarger lens to block the lower part of the image.

E. The mask was repositioned to block the upper portion of this image. The mask is positioned with both exposures so that the soft, diffused edges of the two images will overlap about 1/2 inch into each other.

F. When properly exposed and overlapped, the two images blend into each other, looking perfectly natural.

the lens. Because the filter holder is several inches below the lens, the piece of cardboard will create a soft, out-of-focus edge when the bottom portion of the picture is printed.

Switch the cardboard mask to cover the bottom portion of the print when you are printing the negative for the top portion of the picture. The two images will blend together if the masks were positioned so that the images overlapped slightly and if the portions of the two images that join have similar densities and textural qualities. It will take some testing and positioning adjustments to get it right, but once you get used to the procedure, it will be easy. Refer to the image sequence in Figure 16.17 to get a better feeling for how the procedure works.

High Contrast Effects

The ability to alter contrast gives photographers another means to heighten the impact of their images. Color materials are limited to a fairly normal contrast range, and photographers increase the contrast with lighting or cross-processing as discussed in Chapter 13. Normal black and white films are continuous tone and panchromatic, meaning that they reproduce a wide range of tones and are sensitive to all colors of light.

Litho films, the most commonly used high contrast films, are not sensitive to all the colors of light. They are orthochromatic, meaning that they do not record red light and can be used in the darkroom with a red safelight. When processed in the normal A & B litho developer, litho films have no gray tones. They reproduce all values as pure black and white, simplifying photographs by increasing their graphic qualities while reducing their realism.

Designed for the graphic arts and lithographic printing, litho films are used by photographers for high contrast effects, masking, posterization, and many nonsilver alternative processes, such as Van Dyke, cyanotype, photo silkscreen, and gum bichromate printing. Since litho film was not designed for normal camera shooting, it has a slow film speed of approximately ISO 6. It is easy to use in the darkroom with red safelights. Handle it as if it were enlarging paper. Litho films are made by most major film manufacturers and are available in sheet film sizes. Most camera stores carry 4x5-inch litho film in 50-sheet boxes. High contrast roll films are covered in Chapter 7.

You can expose an existing black and white negative directly onto a piece of litho film in the darkroom. Color transparencies and negatives can also be exposed onto litho film, but they work best with panchromatic litho film because ordinary litho film isn't sensitive to red. Pan-

chromatic litho film is a special order item and may be hard to find. To determine the amount of exposure, a test strip will be necessary just as with any other printing material.

Develop litho film in a high contrast litho developer. Most litho developers have two parts, A and B, which keep for months separately. To make a working solution, mix equal parts of A and B together. Mix only what you need because it goes bad within an hour. Tray processing is the easiest method to use. Develop the litho film for 3 minutes at room temperature (not below 68°F) with continuous but gentle agitation. When initially immersing the film, tap it against the side of the developing tray to dislodge air bubbles. The film should look thoroughly developed after 2 minutes, but develop it for 3 minutes to get a pure black. Use water as a stop bath because an acid stop bath can cause pinholes in the black areas. Fix, wash, and dry as normal. During fixing, the film will have a milky appearance on the emulsion side for the first couple of minutes. Once this clears, the film is light-safe but still needs additional fixing time to be permanent.

Properly exposed and processed, litho film will not have any middle values, just black and clear film. The black should be opaque enough to prevent any light from coming through, even when held next to a light bulb. Overexposed and overdeveloped films will have a slight overall fog and less sharpness because the black areas bleed around the edges.

The first-generation litho from your original black and white negative will be a film positive. To arrive at a final positive image high contrast print, contact print the litho film positive onto another piece of litho film. A litho negative will result. Some detail will be lost in each generation, and retouching can be done to simplify the image by using a paint called *opaque*. Opaque, available in photo supply stores, comes in red and black and can be painted directly onto the film to remove distracting elements. Do not use the red opaque if you plan to use your lithos to print color. The litho negative can be used to make a final print. Retouching simplifies the image and increases its graphic impact.

Other Applications of Litho Films

Litho films are used for title slides and to print words into images. Dyed various colors with Edwal toners, they can be used in light box displays and other specialty applications. Sandwiching a piece of litho film with a piece of tinfoil behind it creates a look similar to a tintype. Posterization, a complicated multiple step process that is easily done on the computer, can also be done with litho films. They also solarize extremely

A.

B.

Untitled, DeeDee Perkins.

Figure 16-8

Line images can be made by sandwiching a litho negative and litho positive together. The first image (A) was made from the film positive that resulted when the sandwiched litho positive and negative were printed onto a piece of litho film. The second image (B) was made from a litho negative that was made from the film positive used to print the first image.

well and can be used to make bas-relief images. Bas-reliefs have a combination two- and three-dimensional look. They are usually made by combining a normal continuous tone negative with a litho negative and putting the two slightly out of register.

Continuous tone negatives can be made with litho film by developing it in a normal developer such as Dektol, a developer used for black and white prints. This development procedure retains more detail in a high contrast image. Develop your first-generation litho positive in Dektol diluted one part developer to three parts water. The resulting film positive will be a continuous tone image, but with more contrast and grain than normal. Use the continuous tone film positive for making the litho negative and you will end up with a final image that has much more detail than if you used only litho developer. To retain even more detail, you can dilute the Dektol further and make subsequent generations in Dektol, slowly decreasing the dilution with each generation. This processing procedure will allow you to retain tremendous detail as you slowly build the contrast and make a final negative in litho developer.

Line images can be made with the litho films by sandwiching a litho positive and negative together in perfect register and contact printing

them onto another piece of litho film. When the two pieces of film are sandwiched together and viewed directly, no light should come through the film. But when they are viewed at an angle, you will be able to see thin outlines of your subject. Use a glass easel (two pieces of glass will work) to hold the litho positive, negative, and unexposed litho film in contact during your exposure. With the enlarger as a light source, position the glass easel under the lens of the enlarger. Tilt the easel at a 45-degree angle facing the enlarger, and make a 5-second exposure at f/8. Then lift the right side of the easel to a 45-degree angle and make another 5-second exposure. Repeat this procedure until you have made four separate 5-second exposures with the easel elevated on all four sides. Develop the film normally in litho developer.

If you expose properly, you will have black lines defining your image on an otherwise clear piece of film, similar to Figure 16.8(A). This positive line image can then be printed to produce a negative image print like Figure 16.8(B). The film with the positive line image can also be contact printed onto another piece of litho film to produce a negative line image on film. When the negative line image is printed, a positive line image print will result.

The Sabattier Effect

Another unusual darkroom effect that produces a negative and positive on the same piece of film or paper is the Sabattier effect. Obscured by a kind of mystery, the Sabattier effect is a darkroom technique that is unpredictable for the novice, but great when it turns out. Many people confuse solarization with the Sabattier effect because both techniques produce similar results. However, true solarization is coupled by extreme exposure, approximately 1,000 times the amount needed to produce a normal contrast negative.

Solarization, like the Sabattier effect, will produce a reversal of the image, both negative and positive on the film. This used to occur quite frequently in long exposures taken at night. The street lights in a scene would be so overexposed that they would reverse and produce a positive image in the negative. With today's films, however, solarization is nearly impossible to obtain.

The Sabattier effect will produce both a negative and positive image on the same film or photo paper. The effect is achieved, however, by reexposing the film during the development stage rather than by overexposure. In effect, when reexposure occurs, the already developed image acts as a negative through which the rest of the light-sensitive silver in the film or paper is exposed. This results in some reversal of the image. If your reexposure is long enough, the resulting positive will develop to a greater density than that of the original negative image.

The Sabattier effect produces a narrow line of low density, called a Mackie line, between the highlight and shadow areas. The Mackie line occurs because the shadow areas, which have already been exposed, are not that affected by the reexposure. The bright areas, however, still contain many sensitive silver crystals and thus respond to the reexposure. The bright areas therefore turn gray, but usually remain somewhat lighter than the shadow areas. The silver bromide along the highlight and shadow boundaries retards the development, forming a more or less clear line—the Mackie line.

The Sabattier effect can be produced on both black and white and color film and print papers. The process is simple and basically the same, regardless of the photographic material used. The light from the enlarger can be used, but it is better to avoid bringing wet prints over to the enlarger. Instead, attach a light with a 7 1/2 watt light bulb to your timer and place it about 4 feet from the developing tray. The hardest part of the Sabattier effect is determining the length of the reexposure time and achieving repeatability. Establishing a consistent procedure and minimizing the variable are a big help.

These are some of the variables that will affect the results: (1) the initial enlarger exposure, (2) the length of development time before the reexposure, (3) the length and intensity of the reexposure, (4) the length of the development time after the reexposure, (5) the developer dilution, and (6) the type of film or paper being used. The results tend to be more dramatic with images that have distinct contrast and value differences. Also, used developer is generally better than fresh because it contains some waste products that make the Mackie lines more distinct. A special developer called *Solarol* is available at many photo stores and is designed to enhance the technique. (See Color Gallery C, Plates 16.11 and 16.12.)

In general, if the reversal effects are too much, reduce the reexposure time, develop the film or print paper longer before doing the reexposure, or increase the amount of the initial enlarger exposure of the print. To obtain more reversal, increase the reexposure time, make the reexposure earlier in the development stage, or decrease the amount of the initial enlarger exposure. The reexposure is normally done about one-half to three-quarters of the way through the development time. Stop agitating the print about 20 seconds before the reexposure to let the print and chemicals settle. After the reexposure, let the print continue developing for 1 minute without agitation. Avoid pulling the print out of the developer prematurely. This results in a lack of control and mottled, uneven development. If the print goes dark too fast, reduce the amount of the reexposure rather than cutting short the redevelopment time.

Most photographers arrive at their own approach to using the Sabattier effect, and many variations are possible. The following steps can serve as a general guideline for producing the Sabattier effect with most photo materials.

1. Use an image with good contrast, differing values, and distinct forms.
2. Make a test strip and determine a normal exposure for the image. Make the contrast slightly higher than normal if the print is a black and white.
3. Make a normal print per your test results.
4. Develop the print, emulsion up, for 50 to 75 percent of its normal development time.
5. Stop agitation during the last 10 to 20 seconds before the reexposure and let the print settle to the bottom of the tray.
6. Reexpose the paper to a small amount of white light while it is in the developer tray. Use a timer for repeatability.
7. After the reexposure, let the print redevelop for 1 minute. Agitation is optional—many feel the Mackie lines will be stronger if you don't agitate.
8. Then continue with the normal chemical steps.

Try variations with all but the redevelopment. Also try using a pinlite and achieving the effect in selected areas of a print while the rest is left normal. For more predictable results, test strips can be made. First make a normal print. Then make a series of test strip exposures on a new sheet of paper at 2-second increments. Process the test for one half the normal developing time. Then rinse with water and squeegee the surface. Next reexpose the print to white light, doing another series of 2-second test strip exposures at right angles to the previous series of test exposures. Finish by redeveloping the print for 1 minute. The test strip will show a wide variety of effects. The differences in the amount of reversal will be obvious, and the necessary amount of initial exposure and reexposure will be easy to determine.

Color Sabattier Effects

To produce the Sabattier effect in color, use the same basic procedures given for black and white materials. Both negative and positive color processes can be used, but the positive processes produce less dramatic results because they get lighter with the reexposure and redevelopment. To effectively use positive processes, make the prints much darker than normal so that they end up a normal density. Also, to control the results, it will be necessary to tray develop the color materials because it is hard to reexpose a print evenly while it is in a processing drum.

The color effects can be quite dramatic. Filters or colored gels are used to control the color during the reexposure. With color negative materials, use filters that are the complement of the color you want in the print. With positive materials, use filters of the same color that you want in the print. Experimentation will be necessary to determine exposure and the effect of the filters. (See Color Gallery C, Plates 16.12 and 16.13.)

Duotone Solarization and Chemical Drawing

Duotone solarization is essentially a chemical deviation of the Sabattier effect that produces colors in black and white prints. Gold, brown, orange, green, blue, and even reds can be achieved in combination with normal black and white tones. The results will vary with different print papers and developers, and experimentation is definitely necessary. But the process is controllable. The colors occur because of a chemical reaction that takes place when a developer-laden print, which has come into brief contact with the acid stop bath and the fixer, is reexposed to light while the developer is still active. This chemical mixture causes the silver to change abnormally and produces the colors.

Use the following procedure as a general guideline, and then develop your own methods:

1. Use full strength undiluted Dektol developer, an acetic acid stop bath, fixer diluted 1 to 6, normal fixer, and a 150-watt lightbulb.
2. Expose your black and white negative normally onto a high con-trast graded paper such as Kodabromide Number 5.
3. Develop the print until the image starts to appear.
4. Transfer the print, without draining, into the acid stop bath for 1 second. The stop bath should be 28 percent acetic acid diluted 1 to 32.
5. Without draining, transfer the print into the tray of diluted fixer for 1 second.
6. Remove the print, without draining, from the diluted fixer and place it on a flat surface and expose it to the light for 15 to 30

seconds. The light acts as a catalyst and exposes the partially stopped and fixed print while the developer continues to alter the silver halides. This chemical reaction causes the color. Tilt the print and let the chemistry run; this will cause a flowing effect in the image. To keep a more uniform surface, squeegee the print before reexposing it.

7. Fix in the normal fixer and wash and dry normally. The color will change when the print is fixed. With experience you will be able to anticipate the change and work accordingly.

Liquid Light

If you want to print a black and white image onto another surface such as wood, metal, cloth, rock, plastic, or ceramic, try *Liquid Light*. This is a liquid emulsion that you can brush onto another surface and then process like any black and white print paper. Contrast is controlled by your choice of developer. It is available at many better-equipped photo stores and is easy to use. Read the manufacturer's instructions for specifics.

Chapter 17

Digital Imaging

Of course, there will always be those who look only at technique, who ask "how," while others of a more curious nature will ask "why." Personally, I have always preferred inspiration to information.

—Man Ray
Artist

Figure 17-1

This image was created digitally by laying objects and pictures on the bed of a *flatbed scanner*, in much the same way as for making a photogram, and might well be called a "scanogram." The drop shadow and sky background were added, using effects applied from within Adobe Photoshop. See Color Gallery C, Plate 17.1.

Self Portrait or Vacation, Robert Johnson.

Photography has changed very little over time. Despite improvements in equipment and the many different processes that have evolved over the years, the fundamental characteristics are the same. Photography, regardless of the process, utilizes light, light-sensitive materials, and chemical processes to make images visible and permanent. New technologies, however, are adding a new dimension to the practice of photography.

It has been said that "digital imaging" will change the future of the medium. For those who are unaware, digital imaging has arrived, and it is changing photography's present. Digital imaging has already profoundly changed the way photographic images can be created, processed, and printed. Regardless of the branch of photography, computer technologies are making their presence and influence felt.

This chapter will focus on many of the changes that emerging technologies are bringing to photography. Technological changes are occurring so fast that it is impractical to provide detailed information on specific computer systems and software. Instead, we will discuss some of the possibilities and limitations offered by digital imaging and explore ways in which it may be applied.

What Is a Digital Image?

Traditional photographs, whether color or black and white, are *analog*, or *continuous tone*, images. They consist of grain structures, and reveal a smooth transition from light to dark and from one color to the next. Digital images consist of *pixels* with tonal and color transitions that occur in abrupt increments or steps. The digital world occurs inside a computer, and a pixel could be referred as a *picture element*.

Hardware

To create and process digital images, a computer is the essential element. It facilitates image creation, manipulation, and modification, but it cannot do the job unassisted. The computer needs to be connected to an input or digitizing device and an output or image printer/recorder. A storage or memory system, either inside the computer or joined to it, is also necessary. The input/digitizing device provides a means to introduce (*scan*) an image into the computer. The output device is the means to produce a hard copy or print of the image. The memory serves to store and allow access to the image.

The computer consists of a case or shell that houses electronics that can perform complex calculations at high speeds. To operate the computer, the following accessories are required: (1) a keyboard for giving directions (input) to the CPU (central processing unit); (2) a monitor—a televisionlike screen—to display (output) information; (3) a pointer—a mouse, or stylus—that, when moved by hand, produces a change in position and direction on the monitor; (4) a disk drive; a *hard disk drive* is inside the computer and stores *software* (programs) and information or projects that you have created; computers also have disk drives, used for loading and unloading software and image files onto or off the hard disk; (5) peripherals—the name for other pieces of hardware that connect to the computer and make working with images possible; they include scanners, video and digital cameras, CD-ROM drives, modems, printers, film recorders, and external memory devices.

Platforms

Computers used for most digital imaging are either Macintosh (Mac), IBM, or IBM-compatibles—referred to as microcomputers or personal computers (PCs). *High-end* computer work stations, such as Sun Microsystems, Hewlett-Packard, Siemens, and Silicon Graphics, work on their

own *platforms* and are capable of producing extremely complex manipu-lations and high quality images. Whether the platform is Mac, IBM, or one of the other high-end platforms, the heart of the computer's ability to store and process digital images is its memory.

Memory

Computers have two types of memory. The first can be made permanent and is found on the hard drive, floppy diskettes, optical drives, and such things as tape backup. The second is called random-access memory, or RAM, and is an electronic memory that facilitates all of the tasks the computer may perform. RAM is required to contain the part of the software in use (such as Photoshop, Live Picture, Painter, Color Studio, and so forth.) It also contains whatever information you generate or bring in from the hard drive, and the computer's operating system. The amount of RAM is a major factor in determining the size, speed, complexity, amount of manipulation, and other modifications possible with photographic images. The larger the amount of RAM, the more potential for a higher quality, more detailed final result. Likewise, a large hard drive (permanent memory) allows for the storage of larger images and more complex software (processing instructions). The mini-mum memory requirements for digital imaging on a PC is 250 MB (megabytes) hard drive and 20 to 32 MB of RAM.

Peripherals

Input Devices

Digital images can be created from within the computer, but most originate from without in the form of a photograph, drawing, or other two-dimensional representation. These sources are made digital by a peripheral called an input device, which include filmless digital cameras and scanners.

Digital Cameras

There are two common types of digital cameras, both of which use electronic circuits, or *chips*, to capture an image. (1) *Still video cameras* record an image in the traditional analog form and make it digital by a "frame grabber" within the computer. (2) *Digital cameras* capture an

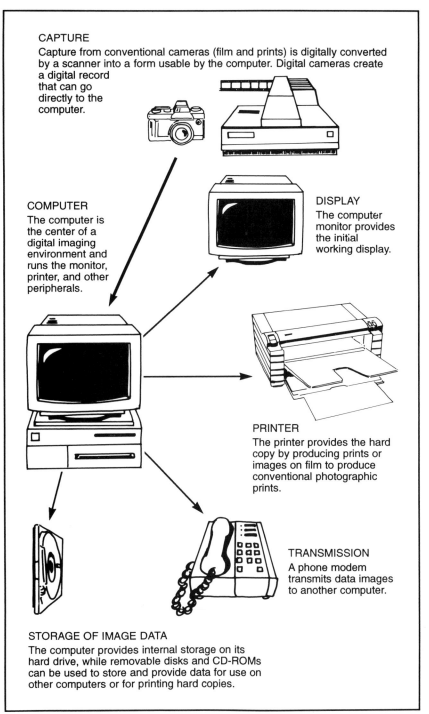

CAPTURE
Capture from conventional cameras (film and prints) is digitally converted by a scanner into a form usable by the computer. Digital cameras create a digital record that can go directly to the computer.

COMPUTER
The computer is the center of a digital imaging environment and runs the monitor, printer, and other peripherals.

DISPLAY
The computer monitor provides the initial working display.

PRINTER
The printer provides the hard copy by producing prints or images on film to produce conventional photographic prints.

TRANSMISSION
A phone modem transmits data images to another computer.

STORAGE OF IMAGE DATA
The computer provides internal storage on its hard drive, while removable disks and CD-ROMs can be used to store and provide data for use on other computers or for printing hard copies.

Figure 17-2

Electronic Imaging System. This diagram shows possible workflow for electronic imaging from input (digitizing), to editing, through output (printing or film recording). The CPU (central processing unit) and software facilitate or coordinate the process with the attached peripherals.

Figure 17-3
Digital cameras.

image directly in digital form. With digital cameras, the image can be transmitted directly to the computer or stored within the camera's memory until transfer to the computer is convenient.

The main advantage of filmless digital cameras is that the image is viewable at the instant of exposure, and it can be instantly modified or transmitted via satellite or telephone line throughout the world. The developing process and the time required for handling traditional film based photographs is no longer required. Instant access is part of the digital difference.

Scanners

Scanners provide the most common means of getting an image into the computer because conventional photographic prints and films are usually the origin of digital images. Scanners are used to digitize existing photographic images, whether film or print. In effect, scanners function as an *interface* between traditional photographic processes and computers. An existing print, negative, or transparency, whether black and white or color, is converted to a digital image when scanned by a CCD (charge-coupled device) or PMT (photomultiplier tube). Once scanned, the resulting digital image is transferred to the computer and stored on the hard drive, a floppy disk, or a photo CD. The three most common scanner types used in digital imaging are film scanners, flatbed scanners, and drum scanners.

Film scanners work with photographic films but not with other media. They capture and digitize an image by scanning photographic negatives or transparencies. Many, such as the Nikon Coolscan, handle only 35mm film. Others, such as the Leaf, accommodate film up to 4x5 inches.

Flatbed scanners digitize photographic prints, drawings, illustrations, or any other flat (two-dimensional) art. Some flatbed scanners have the capacity to scan small and low-profile three-dimensional objects. Others can be adapted to scan photographic negatives and transparencies, but scanners specifically designed for film yield better results.

Drum scanners produce the highest quality scans of both flat art (prints, drawings, etc.) and film materials. They have the capacity to capture a wider dynamic range of colors and tonalities. Because of their cost, which can range from $10,000 to several million dollars, drum scanners are usually found only in large corporations or service bureaus (data processing services).

Resolution

Images can be scanned at different *resolutions*, or *dots per inch (DPI)*. A high number of dots per inch means that there will be more detail in the digital image. As of this writing, scanners can create images of higher resolution than digital cameras, which makes them the preferred input device for most situations. However, when speed or on-location image capture is required, a digital or filmless camera is preferable. Factors that affect the resolution of scanned digital images include the medium to which the final image will be printed (see output devices), the print size, and the computer's ability to store and process large image files.

Photographs can also be scanned to an intermediate medium such as Kodak Photo CD. Various types of photo CDs allow for the storage of images at several different resolutions, depending upon user need. The higher the resolution, the smaller the quantity of images that can be stored. Images on photo CD can be read by the computer and transferred to its internal memory (hard drive) via a CD-ROM drive.

Output Devices

Disks and Drives

Digital images are output from a computer for storage, transmission to another computer, display, or printing of a hard copy of the picture. *Storage devices* provide a means to keep an image for later use. The hard

drive and the floppy diskette are most common means used to store digital information. The hard drive, depending on its size, can store large image files, but the floppy diskette (1.4 MB capacity) is too limited in capacity and not practical for digital imaging applications.

Rewritable drives, such as *Bernoulli* or *Syquest*, can store files of 44 MB or more and allow for transport of the information to other locations. *Iomega Zip drive* uses disks approximately the size of a 3 1/2-inch floppy diskette. The storage capacity is 100 MB, or about the same storage capacity as 70 of the 1.4 MB floppy disks. Consequently, the Zip drive is a practical and economical storage option for most desktop photo-imaging applications.

CD-ROM, which means compact disc read-only memory, is an economical means to store large amounts of data. CD-ROMs are frequently used for archiving information by museums, libraries, and businesses and are replacing earlier means of archiving, such as microfiche. But unlike other disks, CD-ROMs can have their information written only once. The data can be read again and again, but they cannot be changed. Kodak Photo CDs are compatible with most CD-ROM drives.

Magneto-optical drives are available in different sizes and storage capacities. Like CD-ROMs, they can store large amounts of data. Unlike CD-ROMs, they are rewritable.

Kodak Photo CDs are designed specifically for digital image information. They can hold a large number of photographic images, each in several different resolutions. They can also hold audio information and have become an increasingly popular means for portfolio presentation by professional photographers and businesses.

Film Recorders

Film recorders offer the option of outputting or copying a digital image onto conventional photographic film. Basically, a film recorder is a box containing an internal computer monitor with a camera to photograph the image on the internal monitor. The internal monitor is black and white and has a higher-resolution than the color monitors used with most computers. The image to be recorded is separated into red, green, and blue color channels. Each color channel is displayed separately on the internal monitor, and each is photographed by the camera through the corresponding RGB filter onto one frame of color film. The three superimposed "separations" produce a full-color image on the film.

High quality, high resolution film recorders are quite expensive. However, they produce a digital output onto traditional photographic film that is, at least to the naked eye, identical to an original analog or continuous-tone film image.

As digital imaging gains acceptance and becomes more economically practical, the necessity to output to film may diminish substantially, especially when other types of reproduction and hard-copy printing options become more prevalent.

Printers

Printers are the most common means of outputting digital information (data) to hard copy. They are used to produce invoices, letters, and other common business correspondence. In terms of digital imaging, printers are used to make comps (comprehensives), proofs, and images for display, sale, or portfolio presentation. There are several kinds of printers useful for digital imaging. The following lists and briefly describes a few of the more common types of printers available.

Inkjet printers spray droplets of ink from a group of nozzles onto paper, forming the image from the dried "dots" of ink. Some, such as the Iris Printer, provide exquisite quality and allow for the use of a variety of different types of papers to print on, such as fine watercolor paper. This capability provides a welcome alternative for photography, which has traditionally been limited to only a few variations in types of paper and surfaces.

Figure 17-4

The Fargo dye sublimation printer outputs continuous-tone digital prints similar to traditional photographic prints from color negatives.

Electrostatic printers are essentially like photocopy machines. Laser printers are the most common type of electrostatic printer and are often attached directly to a desktop computer system.

Dye sublimation printers use colored ribbons to generate images. These ribbons, when placed over the paper, are heated until the pigments within the ribbons are converted to a gas. The gas is then absorbed by a polyester coating on the paper and the image is formed. Dye sublimation printers are capable of producing a continuous tone or analog image on a substrate (paper) similar in appearance, weight, and texture to a conventional color photographic print. The quality is so similar that it is often hard to distinguish the difference.

Thermal wax transfer printers produce an image by heat embossing thin, colored ribbons of wax onto a paper substrate.

Image setters combine the technologies of computer printers and commercial photographic printers. The data or image is exposed directly onto photosensitive film or paper and then chemically processed.

All of the printers named above can print in color, black and white, or halftone dots (gray scale). Some are capable of printing in all three modes. Most printers attached to desktop imaging systems print on 8.5x11-inch paper, but can print up to 11x17-inches. Most will print on plain paper and on special transparent film, whereas others require coated stock. High-ended devices such as Iris Printers can print on a variety of surfaces, including archival etching and watercolor papers.

Archival Considerations

Whether an image is archival or permanent, is an issue often discussed in reference to conventional photography. In digital imaging, all of the

Figure 17-5
Typical desktop imaging system, including CPU, keyboard, mouse, and monitor.

information is not yet in. The best estimates are that most storage devices will last anywhere from ten years to several decades. Since the technology changes rapidly, and image transfer is relatively simple, prolonging the life of a digital image may be less difficult than with traditional media by simply transferring it to whatever new storage system is appropriate. An advantage of digital archiving over traditional means is that there is no loss of information or visual quality when transferring digitally.

Once an image is printed, however, it becomes part of the "real world" as a printed object and is subject to the same physical limitations as other conventional photographic prints, paintings, or drawings. For the commercial industry this is not an issue because images have a short-term usefulness, but for the fine arts archival quality is an important consideration. The industry is aware of this issue and is striving to make more permanent dyes and inks. As of this writing, ink dyes similar in permanence to those used in Ilfochrome are being explored for use in Iris Printers.

Software and Image Processing

The computer and its peripheral equipment have the tools to perform many complex image adjustments and image editing functions. Almost any image one can imagine may be created within the digital imaging environment. However, the computer and peripherals do not know what the tasks should be or how to perform them. They need instructions to know what to do and how to do it. The way we communicate and provide instructions with a computer system is through the software or programs we install in it. Digital imaging software provides an environment within the computer system where a variety of operations may be performed on a photograph. The software also facilitates the interface between the user and system hardware. Once the user decides what editing or manipulations should be used on a particular image, the user then gives the system the required instructions through the software.

Illustration programs provide a blank paper or canvas where an image may be generated from scratch, using drawing and painting tools such as pencils, paint brushes, air brushes, erasers, and so on. Common illustration programs are Adobe Illustrator, Corel Draw, and Aldus Freehand.

Paint programs are more appropriately called image or photo editing programs. They contain tools and instructions for simple adjustments or complex manipulations of visual images. Although these programs can be used to create images from scratch, they are designed mainly for

Figure 17-6

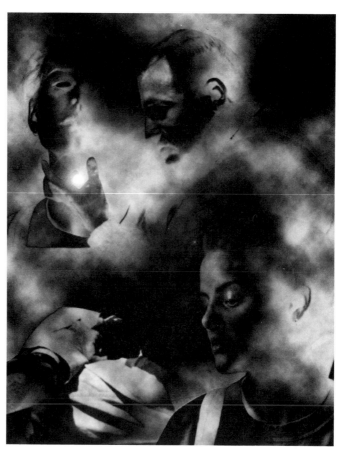

Diana, Ana Luisa Johnson. (See Color Gallery C, Plate 17.2.)

modifying existing images that have been inputted into the system. Most often they are used for the modification and manipulation of photographs. Common paint programs applicable for photographers are Photoshop, Photostyler (now discontinued), Picture Publisher, Live Picture, and Color Studio.

Digital Darkrooms

Systems for electronic photo imaging are often referred to as digital darkrooms or digital studios. They give the user the ability to perform multiple and complex modifications to a photographic image in one small workstation.

The screen layout of different imaging programs varies, but most have similar elements and operating procedures. Elements usually in a

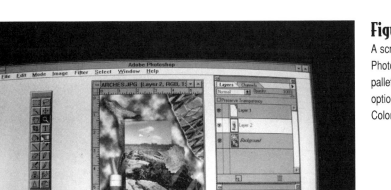

Figure 17-7

A screen capture from Adobe Photoshop, showing the floating pallets for tools, layers, tool options, and color selection. (See Color Gallery C, Plate 17.3.)

program's visual display include drop or pull-down menus found across the top of the screen. Pallets that float in the work area are also common and can be shown or hidden by the user. Floating pallets routinely include (1) a tools pallet, which contains drawing, painting, and selection tools; (2) a color pallet for selecting foreground and background colors to be applied by the drawing and painting tools; (3) a brush pallet for adjusting the brush size and the configuration of the drawing and painting tools; and (4) a layers pallet, which shows all of the layers within an image and their relationship to one another.

Most imaging programs allow the user to make common darkroom adjustments to a photographic image, whether black and white or color, negative or positive. These adjustments include contrast control, color correction, and density changes. Special effects such as creating a negative or positive, adding texture, solarization, or posterization, are also possible. The computer system can apply these effects and adjustments to an image with great precision and high speed generally impossible by hand in a chemical darkroom. The complexity and magnitude of the desired effect or adjustment can also be precisely controlled.

In addition to basic darkroom effects, two-dimensional and three-dimensional effects can also be applied to an image. These include ripple, wave, scratch, pinch, punch, and motion-blurs, among others. It is also easy to scale (resize) and rotate or flip an image horizontally and vertically.

Digital Retouching

Imaging programs also provide painting and drawing tools that allow the user to create images from scratch or apply nonphotographic effects to existing images. Cloning or duplicating one area of an image to another may also be accomplished with the painting tools. This cloning tool is particularly effective in retouching photographs.

The most powerful tools in most paint programs are those for masking, selecting, and creating layers.

Masking allows one or more areas of an image to be effectively isolated from the rest of the image. Special effects or adjustments can then be applied to the masked area(s) only. This feature is useful when color, density, or contrast needs to be changed in small parts of an image. Any of the available tools or filters can be used in the active area created by masks without affecting other areas of the image.

Selection tools are similar to masks but allow the selected area(s) to be resized, flipped, or even moved to another area of the image. They

Figure 17-8

Photographs showing simple effects created digitally: (A) original image, (B) solarization, (C) negative, (D) pinch, (E) punch, (F) shear, (G) wave, (H) posterization, and (I) difference clouds. (See Color Gallery C, Plate 17.4.)

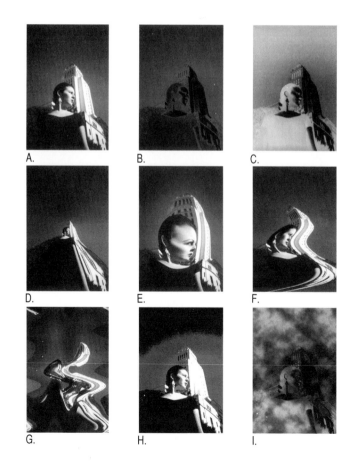

A.   B.   C.

D.   E.   F.

G.   H.   I.

A. Before

B. After

Digital restoration, Bob Brooks.

Figure 17-9
Digital imaging software offers many tools that are useful in photo retouching and restoration of old photographs. Some of the tools used in the restoration shown here are clone, blur, smudge, paint brush, color balance, brightness, and contrast. (Original photographer unknown.) (See Color Gallery C, Plate 17.5.)

also make it possible to move the selected area(s) to an entirely separate image. Selection tools facilitate the making of composite images from multiple sources.

Layering is a new and powerful feature available in most desktop imaging software. Layers, like masks and selections, allow the application of effects to limited areas of an image. What makes layering different is that it is an effect that can be applied to one layer with no effect on the other layers in an image. Also, that effect can be changed at any later time without affecting the rest of the image. Image layers are like playing cards, in that their order, from top to bottom, may be changed or shuffled. Elements within layers can be modified countless times without the need to reselect that area of the image. In other words, the user does not have to make one decision or step final before moving on to the next. Multiple changes may be made to each layer and the results compared before the look of the image is finalized. This flexibility makes complicated image composites and manipulations much easier and quicker to work on.

Digital Imaging Applications

Digital imaging consists of image capture, which means taking the picture and making an image digital, along with image editing and manipulation. Many areas of photography use and benefit from one or both ends of this technology.

Figure 17-10

Top row: Three faces as scanned into the computer. Bottom row: Composites created digitally using cut, paste, and clone tools, among others. (See Color Gallery C, Plate 17.6.)

Photojournalists primarily use image capture, whereby an image taken with a digital camera can be sent by phone or satellite directly and instantly to a newspaper or magazine office anywhere in the world. This technology eliminates the time required for physical transport and chemical processing and reduces human handling.

Illustrators can create "realities" that never before existed by means of composite images. Picture elements from different sources seamlessly combined express the illustrator's vision. In many cases, composites eliminate the need for hiring a photographer to shoot new images because a "new" image can be created by compositing and manipulating existing images.

Retouchers can use digital painting tools to restore damaged areas of an old photograph or eliminate unwanted components, such as distracting reflections or blemishes, with seamless results and a finesse that only the very skilled are capable of by hand. Today, digital retouching has almost completely replaced traditional hand methods.

Commercial photographers can capture and edit images digitally for use in catalogs, brochures, advertisements, and numerous other media. The advantage for the commercial shooter is that exposure, color control, contrast, focus, and perspective can be controlled within the computer. In addition, color separations can be made and the image prepared

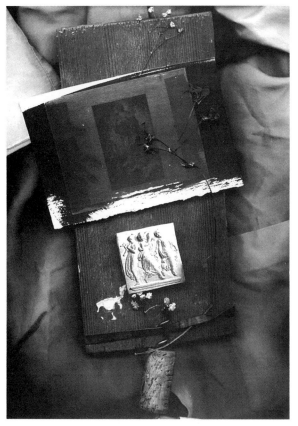

Musings, Darryl Curran.

Figure 17-11

This image, created without a camera, was composed on the bed of a custom made flatbed scanner at Nash Editions. The digital image data were then printed on archival paper on an Iris printer. (See Color Gallery C, Plate 17.7.)

for press by photographers in their computers. This gives them a level of control they previously only dreamed about.

Portrait photographers benefit by being able to provide instant proofs to subjects immediately after the sitting. They have the option of showing variations in both poses and backgrounds that can be applied to final images.

Forensic photographers can digitally enhance photomicrographs, allowing them to see features and detect anomalies previously not visible.

Fine arts photographers have a whole new array of creative image-making tools at their disposal. The freedom associated with the fine arts enables photographers to explore countless possibilities and hybrid combinations of new and traditional technologies.

Snapshooters and serious nonprofessional photographers will, however, probably find digital imaging impractical until the costs of the technology make digital cameras more accessible. Once digital imaging becomes economically practical, the multimedia and interactive possibilities have the potential to create new levels of involvement for the average consumer, just as video did a few years ago.

The digital image is limited only by one's imagination. The greatest advantage of this emerging technology is its versatility. Many studio and darkroom functions can be performed with desktop imaging systems merely by the touch of a finger.

Ethical Considerations

Do photographs tell the truth? Can they accurately represent reality? Are they objective? Do they show bias? Can they be manipulated?

The View, Robert Johnson.

Figure 17-12

A. Original black and white image scanned on a Microtek flatbed scanner from a gelatin silver print. B. The composite image. Additional images were scanned from prints, and color was added in the software application. Cut, paste, scale, and sharpen applications were also used. (See Color Gallery C, Plate 17.8.)

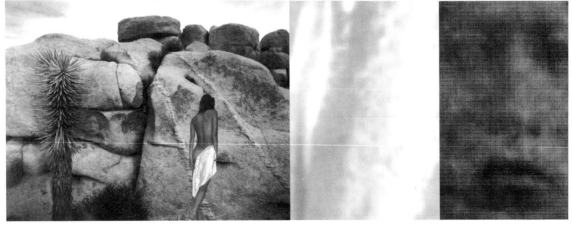

Should they be manipulated? The answer to these questions could all be yes, but a better or more accurate answer would be, sometimes.

Photographs are often used as evidence in legal cases as institutionalized representations of fact. Journalists use photographs to add interest and credibility to their stories. In the fields of journalism and the law, society has been led to trust the veracity of photographic images. The wide use of photographs in these areas is dependent upon the public's willingness to believe what they see in a photographic image. This willingness to believe probably stems from the notion that photographs must be objective representations of reality because they are recorded with a mechanical device, the camera. However, one must remember that the camera is controlled by a human being. The images it produces are subject to the decisions and biases of the photographer.

Advertisers also use our willingness to believe what we see in photographs. Fortunately, most people are more skeptical of the motives of advertising because they know that the intent is to sell by persuasion. Still, people want to believe that the products, shown in a photograph, will look that way when they get them home.

It is more accurate to say, photographs, instead of showing the truth, present a convincing illusion of what is truthful or real.

Digital imaging allows rapid, complex, and precise alterations of photographic images. When skillfully done, the alterations in photographs can be undetectable, resulting in a *new original*. The photograph is no longer what it was, and this new original can be reproduced countless times or changed again and again without apparent loss in quality, resulting in *another* new original.

The question, "Should a photograph be manipulated?," and, if so, "When should it be manipulated?," take on new levels of meaning when digital technologies are considered. Remember that almost any image alteration or manipulation "do-able" by computer can also be done with traditional camera and darkroom techniques. Photographers have always

Flying in Circles, Michael Johnson.

Figure 17-13

Multiple sources in Aldus Photostyler produced this image printed on an Iris ink jet printer to an original size of 10x30 inches. (See Color Gallery C, Plate 17.9.)

manipulated their images: some, simply by deciding on one point of view over another, others by deciding what to include and exclude from the frame. Dodging and burning are forms of manipulation, as is contrast control, yet even purists think of them as basic darkroom techniques. No, manipulation of photographs is not new—it is just harder to detect when done digitally.

Should photographers manipulate their images? The answer depends upon the context in which the photograph is to be used and the intent of the photographer. We *hope* that journalists will use only minor image modifications (dodging, burning, color correction, contrast control) in an effort to communicate directly and honestly. We must expect embellishment of photographs from advertisers, however, since they will go to whatever lengths they can afford to promote a product or service. In contrast to journalists, artists often create works of a personally expressive nature and may greatly alter reality to tender the creative vision.

Image Appropriation and Copyright Law

Legal controversy surrounds digital imaging because of its ability to appropriate (steal) someone else's picture for one's own use. Copyright law clearly prohibits such appropriation without permission. Digital technology, though, can easily alter an image beyond recognition. If someone appropriates the image of another and drastically alters it, does it then become the property of the one who alters it? If the appropriated image is used only as a small part of a large picture, has the context been changed enough so as not to be a violation of copyright laws? The courts are still trying to decide these issues. As a general rule, it is improper to take someone else's work and use it without permission. It likely is also illegal, and engaging in this practice could land one in court.

Digital imaging is here, however, and it will continue to affect and change the practice of all areas of photography. Although it brings new possibilities for creativity to the medium, it does not diminish the expressive potential of traditional photographic processes.

Color Gallery C

List of Plates

continued on next page

continued from previous page

What's the Point? Sandy Lewis.

Plate 16.1

Duo-tone solarization was used to
bring the color out in this black
and white print.

Untitled, Ken Vallens.

Plate 16.2

The emulsion of this Time-Zero Polaroid print was selectively moved
and altered as the image was developing. Later, the back of the
print was cut open and the emulsion scraped off the upper portion of
the image, leaving that area clear. Then separate images of the sky
and the monkey were positioned in the clear areas, with the
remaining original Polaroid image layered on top to form a
composite picture. The back of the print was taped shut, and the
resulting image looks like a very unusual Polaroid.

Plate 16.3

This Polaroid transfer is from a 35mm color slide that was enlarged onto Polaroid 669 film with a Vivitar Instant Slide Printer. After developing for 10 seconds, the film was pulled apart and the negative laid facedown on a piece of wet watercolor paper. A roller helped ensure firm contact, and the film was allowed to develop an additional minute. Then the negative was peeled from the watercolor paper and the resulting print completed. The abstract cyan shapes occurred because not all of the emulsion transferred. Sometimes this accident can ruin an image, but in this case it adds a surreal effect.

The Johnson Cottage, Jerry Burchfield.

Untitled, Diane Edwards.

Plate 16.4

Emulsion lifts are another alteration possible with Polaroid films that allow a photographer to change the feeling of an image by changing its shape and putting it onto another surface. This image was made from a 35mm color slide that was enlarged onto Polaroid 669 film. The film was developed normally, and the print left unaltered for 8 hours. Then the emulsion was soaked off and lifted onto a water color paper.

Roatan, Bay Islands, Honduras, Karen Schulman.

Plate 16.5

Hand coloring black and white photographs with transparent oils has been popular since the early days of photography. Karen Schulman, who is well-known for her hand-coloring work, left part of this image black and white to provide an unaltered photographic feeling to contrast with the coloring.

Plate 16.6

Acrylic and opaque oil paints can also be used to alter the look of a
photograph. Patricia Whiteside Phillips paints directly onto color
prints, combining the natural character and surface of the
photograph with the texture and qualities of a painting.

Light in the Darkness, Greg Phillips.

Plate 16.7

This heavily manipulated color image began as a black and white original shot on 4x5-inch Polaroid Type 55 positive and negative film. After development, the negative was rinsed in water and placed inside a plastic baggie to dry. The baggie stuck to the negative, leaving permanent marks on the film. Subsequently various tools, including a knife, razor blade, and ice pick were used to scratch and draw into the film. Color retouching dyes were then added to the altered negative, and the film was subsequently enlarged onto color negative print paper.

Black and White Duck, Kevin Starr.

Dancers, P. W. Derby.

Egyptians, John C. Hesketh.

Plate 16.10

On the streets of New Orleans, Hesketh shot separate images from the same vantage point over a period of time to record the movement and energy of Mardi Gras. The separate color negatives are composite printed together onto one sheet of paper. Masks cover one part of the paper while another is exposed.

Plate 16.8

This print on the top left was toned brown with sepia toner. Rubber cement used as a mask was painted over the duck to keep it black and white. After the toning was complete, the rubber cement was rubbed off, and the whole print was rinsed so that it would dry with an even surface.

Plate 16.9

Red and blue Edwal toners give this black and white print on the bottom left its color. Rubber cement applied to the center figure kept it black and white. The rubber cement was put on without masking the figure exactly, to suggest movement. Concentrated solutions of the toner "ate" the silver, causing an artificial tonal effect. The print was put into blue toner first for several minutes, then into the red toner for several minutes, and finally back into the blue toner.

Plate 16.11

A. This photo-composite image started with a pen and ink drawing of a fish, which was photographed with 4x5-inch transparency film. Pin-registered positive and negative litho masks were made from the fish transparency.

B. A positive and negative litho masks were also made for the telephone pole and wires image. The litho masks were then used in contact with the various transparencies—the fish, the telephone wires, and the neighborhood scene—to allow Smith to print one part without exposing the other.

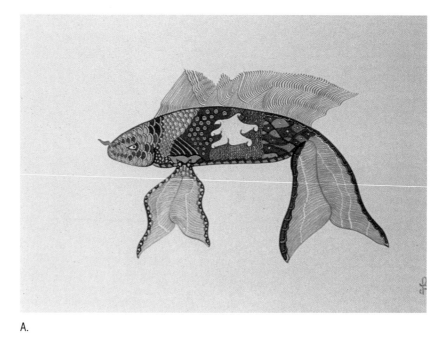

A.

Neighborhood Watch, Fritz Cramp Smith.

B.

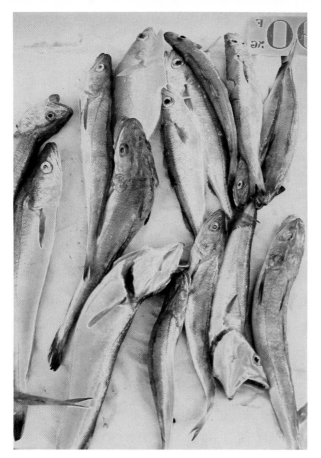

Fish at Market (French Fish), Diane Edwards.

Plate 16.12

A color negative was printed and the print solarized while tray-processed. A magenta filter was used over the solarizing light to get the green effect.

Plate 16.13

Vogel created a dramatic color background by chemically painting a piece of light-sensitive photo paper while in the light. Later, after fixing, washing, and drying the print, he used India ink and an air spray to create the dark horizon line and the silhouetted tree shapes directly on the surface of the print.

View from the Other Side, Larry Vogel.

Plate 17.1

This image was created digitally by laying objects and pictures on the bed of a *flatbed scanner*, in much the same way as for making a photogram, and might well be called a "scanogram." The drop shadow and sky background were added, using effects applied from within Adobe Photoshop.

Self Portrait or Vacation, Robert Johnson.

Plate 17.2

A photo composite of camera images that were scanned and then combined using Photoshop.

Diana, Ana Luisa Johnson.

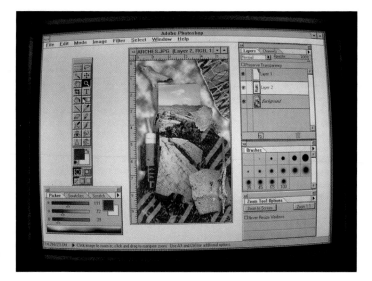

Plate 17.3

A screen capture from Adobe Photoshop, showing the floating pallets for tools, layers, tool options, and color selection.

C–16

Plate 17.4

Photographs showing simple effects created digitally: (A) original image, (B) solarization, (C) negative, (D) pinch, (E) punch, (F) shear, (G) wave, (H) posterization, and (I) difference clouds.

A. Before

B. After

Plate 17.5
Digital imaging software offers many tools that are useful in photo retouching and restoration of old photographs. Some of the tools used in the restoration shown here are clone, blur, smudge, paint brush, color balance, brightness, and contrast. (Original photographer unknown.)

Digital restoration, Bob Brooks.

Plate 17.6

Top row: Three faces as scanned into the computer. Bottom row: Composites created digitally using cut, paste, and clone tools, among others.

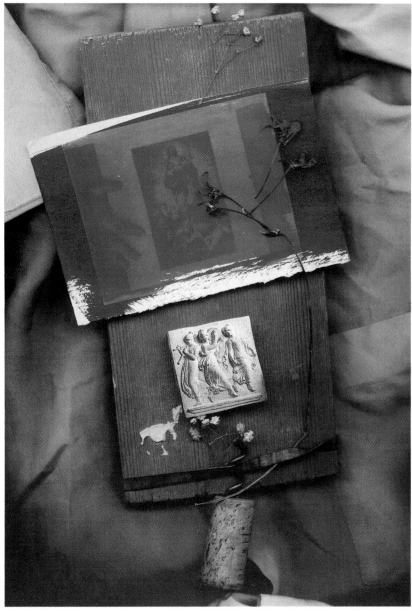

Plate 17.7

This image, created without a camera, was composed on the bed of a custom made flatbed scanner at Nash Editions. The digital image data were then printed on archival paper on an Iris printer.

Musings, Darryl Curran.

A.

Plate 17.8

A. Original black and white image scanned on a Microtek flatbed scanner from a gelatin silver print.
B. The composite image. Additional images were scanned from prints, and color was added in the software application.

B.

The View, Robert Johnson.

Flying in Circles, Michael Johnson.

Plate 17.9

Multiple sources in Aldus
Photostyler produced this image
printed on an Iris ink jet printer to
an original size of 10 x 30 inches.

Untitled, Julian Vasquez.

Plate 18.1

Vasquez made this image by
painting with light, the primary tool
of photography. Walking through
the picture and lighting the
subject, but unable to see what
the camera was recording, he
relied on his experience and
feelings to light the subject and
provide enough exposure for the
transparency film over a 20-
minute period.

Plate 18.2
Silhouette.
Untitled, Boyd Jaynes.

Plate 18.3

Directional-diffused lighting.

The Studio, Jerry Burchfield.

Plate 18.4

A. The color of light changes with time of day and can radically change the look and feeling of a photograph. This photograph was shot in the middle of the day, when the light source was directly overhead.

B. This photograph was shot in the late afternoon from a similar vantage point, but the quality of light is warmer and more dramatic.

Grand Canyon, Jerry Burchfield.

Plate 18.5

A change in camera position resulted in two distinctively different
photographs of the same subject. Shot moments apart, image A
took advantage of late afternoon direct sunlight to make the cross

stand out against the cloud-speckled sky. In Image B, taken
form the other side, the sun behind the cross created a radiant
glow around a silhouette.

Untitled, Greg Phillips.

Plate 18.6

At twilight, there is a brief period when the intensities of natural and artificial lights are in balance. This balance provides wonderful opportunities for mixed-light effects that are especially effective in color. Note the green glow of the fluorescents from inside the cafe, while the tungsten lights of the automobiles have the normal yellow-red color cast, and the neon lights record naturally. *Hot Spot*, Jerry Burchfield.

Plate 18.7

Tungsten film shot in daylight will give an overall blue cast because of the extra blue that is built into the film to provide a natural coloration with the yellow-red tungsten light. It is an easy way to get monochromatic blue casts. To get a monochromatic red cast, try using Kodak Ektachrome Underwater color slide film. It has extra red built into the film to give more natural color underwater.

Untitled, Jerry Burchfield.

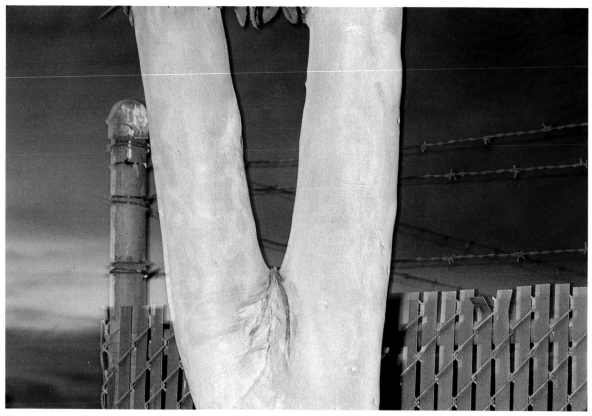

Untitled, Robert Bell.

Plate 18.8

Flash illuminated the backlit tree and fence, while a long hand-held exposure captured the rapidly darkening red sky. The resulting artificial look heightens the anthropomorphic symbolism.

A.

Plate 18.9

A long hand-held exposure heightened the sense of motion in both photographs. Exposure A was short enough so that Larson could hold the camera steady and retain a natural feeling. B received a much longer exposure, causing the sky wheel to become more abstracted.

B.

Sky Wheel, Harold Larson.

Using Flash, Jerry Burchfield.

Plate 18.10

Flash on a camera is primarily used for snapshots. It causes harsh light, redeye (reflection from within the eye), glare on reflective surfaces such as foreheads, and distracting background shadows. Use a sync cord and hold the flash off camera to get more interesting lighting and to avoid the aforementioned effects.

Chapter 18

Light and Lighting

Light, to the accomplished photographer, is as much an actuality as a substance like rock or flesh.

—Ansel Adams
Photographer

Light makes photography possible. When light is recorded on film, an image forms. Regardless of the subject, consider the light and how it functions within the picture every time you make an exposure. Light not only illuminates the subject and exposes the film, it also determines the look and feeling of a photograph. Form, depth, dimension, texture, contrast, and color are dependent upon the type and quality of light. Whether an image is abstract or realistic depends on the photographer's control of light. By controlling light, the photographer is free to determine the expression within a photograph. Learning to see photographically means learning about light, both natural and artificial. If you learn to use natural light effectively, you will easily learn how to use artificial lights in a studio because the basic principles are the same. You will begin to use light and shadow to communicate and establish interrelationships of patterns and forms within the boundaries of photographs; to realize the potential of photography as art. (See Color Gallery C, Plate 18.1.)

Natural Light

The way a subject appears to us, and to the film, is directly influenced by the quality of the light that is illuminating it. When a light condition changes a scene, the photographer, if aware of that change, may see a range of new possibilities, even if it is a scene that is quite familiar.

Untitled, Dee Dee Perkins.

Figure 18-1

Side light.

Light, then, is never stable: It changes from second to second, minute to minute, hour to hour. The photographers who are aware of and sensitive to these ever-changing conditions will not only be able to see a more exciting world, they can photograph it.

Depending upon where light is coming from, it has differing pictorial qualities. Light can be classed as side light, front light, top light, back light, diffused light, and directional-diffused light.

Side light occurs when light hits the subject from one angle. The light source is focused on the subject, creating a hard-edged effect that may leave the shadow areas devoid of details. In a portrait, this effect may be dramatic. Often, a clear, bright, sunny day, either early in the morning or late in the afternoon, will produce a sidelighted quality, leaving a highlighted area surrounded by dark shadows.

Front light strikes the subject directly, from the same position as the camera and the photographer. The sun is behind the photographer in a front-lighted situation. Almost all shadows will fall behind the subject and generally will not be visible in the photograph. Since shadows are necessary to reveal the three-dimensional qualities and surface textures of objects, most subjects will have a flat look in frontlighting.

Back lighting is light that comes from behind the subject and toward the camera. Back lighting can produce dramatic photographs, but you should avoid getting the direct sun in your picture, unless it is masked by a tree, cloud, or other object. Transparent and semitransparent objects such as ice formations, flower petals, and clouds, can result in dramatic photographs if they are back lighted.

Barbara, Jerry Burchfield.

Figure 18-2
Back lighting.

A *silhouette* is created when the subject is underexposed because of a great difference in brightness between the subject and background. The classic silhouette is essentially a back-lighted photograph that is metered for the background as opposed to the subject, or it is achieved by averaging several light-meter readings. A person standing in front of a window will make a silhouette if the meter reading is based solely on the background. (See Color Gallery C, Plate 18.2.)

Directional-diffused light has some of the quality of sidelight, in addition to light that has been scattered or diffused. While a directional-diffused quality of light appears to come from one direction, it also includes shadow areas that are softer and less hard-edged than sidelight. Details in the shadow areas of direct-diffused images can be seen and reproduced as shades of gray, rather than as a mass of black.

Diffused light scatters itself over the entire subject from all directions. Diffused light is rather difficult to achieve indoors because most indoor illuminations come from a single light source, fluorescents being the exception. Outdoors, however, diffused light can usually be achieved by photographing on a heavily overcast day, or in open shade.

One source of a direct-diffused light can be a photograph taken next to a window. The direct light source is, of course, the light shining

Untitled, Barbara Kurk.

Figure 18-3
Diffused lighting.

through the window. The light then will hit the subject and the walls near the subject. Thus, the shadow area receives some light. Another source of direct-diffused light is found outdoors on a moderately overcast day. (See Color Gallery C, Plates 18.3, 18.4, and 18.5.)

Color and Light

In black and white photography, the color of the light falling on the subject is usually unimportant. This is not true in color photography, where subtle differences in illumination are accurately recorded on the film and can produce effects that even the eye will not see when you are taking a photograph. The eye is fooled because the brain remembers what the color ought to look like and compensates for different kinds of illumination. Color film, on the other hand, sees color as it is and only as it is. For example, to most people, a white dress looks much the same in daylight as in household light. But house lamps have more red wavelengths and fewer blue wavelengths than daylight. Color film will record these differences and produce a yellowish image of a white dress. To prevent this variation and to render color as the eyes see it, manufacturers make different kinds of color film, each balanced for a specific kind of light.

Matching Color Films to Light

For true color, you should select a type of film based on the kind of light in which you will take photographs. Sometimes, as in existing-light photography, choice is not possible, because daylight and artificial light may be present at the same time. If the photographer is seeking to capture a mood, then less-than-perfect color is often acceptable. But if color rendition is critical, as in commercial photography, then the photographer must take steps to balance light and film.

To match the varying colors of light, two kinds of color film are made—daylight and tungsten. Daylight film has a color temperature of 5500K and is balanced to give natural colors when shot outdoors with midday sun and flash. In the morning and afternoon, the color of the light is warmer, so the color film will record a warm cast. On overcast days, the color of the light is bluer, and daylight color film records colors with a slight blue cast. With the exception of electronic flash, most artificial lights record on daylight film with an unnatural color.

Figure 18-4

A typical studio portrait setup with studio strobes, a softbox providing diffused light, and a silver reflector to fill the shadows.

The Studio, Greg Phillips.

Incandescent lightbulbs (tungsten lights) record a yellow-red color, while fluorescents record with a greenish cast.

Tungsten film has a color temperature of 3200K. It has extra blue filtration built into it so that colors will look more natural when shot with the yellow-red incandescent lights. When shot in daylight or with flash, tungsten film records everything with a blue cast. This is because the daylight color is bluer than tungsten light. With fluorescent lights, everything still comes out green. More information on color films, color temperature and light is provided in Chapter 7. (See Color Gallery C, Plates 18.6, 18.7, and 18.8.)

Filters to Match Color Film to the Light

Suppose you have a half-finished roll of tungsten color film in your camera. You want to shoot some pictures outdoors, but you don't want your images to have a bluish cast. What should you do? The answer is that you should use a filter—in this case, an 80B conversion filter. Three kinds of filters are made to balance the Kelvin temperature of the light with the film being used. These are conversion filters, light-balancing filters, and color-compensating filters, and all are discussed in Chapter 9.

Color Film and Mixed Light Sources

Balancing color film to the light source is often complicated by the presence of several light sources of incompatible color quality. For example, a subject might be illuminated by daylight from a window on one side and on the other side by light from a table lamp. Balancing the film for daylight makes it incompatible for use with the artificial light; balancing the film for the table lamp makes it incompatible for use with daylight.

Several solutions deal with the problem of mixed light sources. The easiest is simply to eliminate the light source you don't want—for example, turn off the table lamp so that only daylight illuminates the subject. Or, you might choose to close the curtains and move the subject away from the widow, illuminating the subject with only light from the table lamp.

You may also decide to use the dominant light source. Thus, if one light source is stronger or brighter than another, first choose the film or filtration for that light source, and then compose the picture to exclude as much of the area illuminated by the other source.

Sometimes mixed lighting will be of equal proportions, so light of different color temperatures will affect the scene equally. Thus, if the photographer balances the film for daylight, the portion of the scene under artificial light will be rendered warm, or yellow-orange. Conversely, if the photographer balances the film for artificial light, the daylight area of the scene will be rendered cool, or blue. It is up to the photographer to decide which area of the scene is more important and balance the film to the light accordingly. However, if the scene includes a person, it is usually best to err on the side of warmth, since most people find a warm skin-tone rendition pleasing.

Existing-Light Photography

Illumination can be added to a scene with the use of artificial light sources such as photo flash, electronic flash, or floodlights. However, once light is added, the picture no longer possesses one of the inherent qualities of photography—the natural feeling of an unplanned moment. Existing-light photography—picture-taking in available light—allows the photographer an endless array of photographic possibilities. They range from a photograph taken with a single candle to a brilliantly sunlit view of the Grand Canyon. The term *existing light*, however, has come to mean pictures taken at low light levels. Usually, these are

indoor scenes with a variety of light sources, such as candles, lightbulbs, window light, and stage lighting like that at rock concerts. Taking pictures in available light requires certain equipment. The camera lens should be reasonably fast, at least $f/2.8$. If a slower lens is used, the shutter speed required for a correct exposure would be so long that, with a handheld exposure, the picture would be blurred. For the same reason, the film should also be fast, ISO 400 or better. Two other equipment items should be considered for existing-light photography, especially for very dimly illuminated subjects such as night scenes. These are a tripod and a cable release. When you are taking pictures at shutter speeds slower than 1/30th of a second, any movement of the camera will cause blurry images. Since it is hard to hold the camera perfectly still this long, you should use the tripod to support the camera as you shoot. Assuming that the tripod is on a solid, vibration-free surface, you can eliminate blurred images. A cable release is a flexible cord that enables the photographer to trip the shutter button as the camera rests on the tripod. Some cable releases have locks that, with the camera on the B setting, will keep the shutter open as long as the photographer wishes. Some newer cameras have electronic cable releases that serve the same functions.

Exposure Considerations

Illumination in existing-light photography is, unfortunately, often very contrasty. For example, the light around the bulb of a street light is very bright; a few feet away that illumination stops, and total darkness begins. Consequently, exposure literally becomes "a shot in the dark."

You will often want to use exiting light for pictures of people. However, you may find yourself in light so low that your exposure meter doesn't seem to work. In that case, use a white card for your reading, rather than the person's face. The correct exposure will be about $2\frac{1}{2}$ times the exposure indicated on the card. For example, at a shutter speed of 1/60 second, you might get a reading of $f/8$ off the white card. You would then open your lens $2\frac{1}{2}$ f-stops to a setting halfway between $f/4$ and $f/2.8$. However, it is still preferable to take your reading directly from the subject's face.

Another situation for existing light is concerts or plays. Although the stage lights are often very bright, they are directed at only a few people, while the rest of the stage is dark. It is important to avoid the dark areas on the stage when you are calculating exposure. You will tend to overexpose such pictures because the dark areas combined with the spotlight areas tell the meter that there is less light on the stage than actually exists. Be sure that you always expose for the area in the spotlight. It is best, if possible, to walk up to the stage and take a meter reading off your hand. Use that meter reading no matter where you are sitting when you actually shoot the picture. However, if this is impossible, point the meter toward the stage from where you are seated and then close the lens down by at least one f-stop. Remember that meter reading takes into account the dark areas and so is based in part upon a lack of light, while actually there is a great deal of light on stage.

In general, avoid overall readings when photographing at concerts. The meter will respond to the dark areas surrounding the performers and cause them to be overexposed. Meter for the spotlit subjects.

If you are uncertain about your exposure, the best thing to do with existing light is to *bracket* the exposure one f-stop over and one f-stop under. In other words, if the correct exposure is 1/30 second at f/5.6, take another picture at 1/30 at f/8 and one more at 1/30 at f/4. Doing so should compensate for any error in your judgement of the exposure.

Because existing-light photography requires a film with a high ISO number, grain may be a problem. To minimize this effect, try not to overexpose your negatives. Overexposure coupled with a high ISO film will result in large clumps of grain in the photo, making the image appear less sharp.

Shutter speeds for existing-light photography are generally slow. When possible, use a tripod and cable release. If your subjects move during a slow exposure time, the image will blur. Some subject movement can add interesting effects to a photograph. Camera movement, though, usually ruins the picture.

Existing-light photography usually requires that the f-stop be open wide, so depth of field is not very great. You must focus the shot carefully. (It is best to focus on the eyes when you are photographing people.)

The chart on the next 2 pages provides general exposure guidelines for the subjects listed. However, it is only a guide, because lighting situations vary. Exposure bracketing is recommended. The chart is based on a film speed of ISO 400. If the film you are using is faster, shorten the exposure time. If the film you are using is slower than 400, then you must increase the exposure.

Existing-light photography offers many photographic possibilities. Pictures taken in available light look natural and candid. However, there are times when existing-light photography is just not possible or acceptable. Sometimes there is not enough light illuminating the subject, or the subjects cannot be seen to their best advantage in the existing light. Maybe there is too much contrast, or the color of the light may be wrong for the film you are using. Whatever the reasons, you also need to know how to use artificial light sources.

Existing Light Exposure Guidelines (based on ISO 400)

OUTDOORS AT NIGHT

Fairs, amusement parks	1/30 sec *f*/2.8
Amusement park rides—light patterns	1 sec *f*/16
Fireworks—displays on the ground	1/60 sec *f*/4
Fireworks—aerial displays (Keep shutter open on Bulb or Time for several bursts.)	*f*/16
Lightning (Keep shutter open on Bulb or Time for one or two streaks of lightning.)	*f*/11
Burning buildings, campfires, bonfires	1/60 sec *f*/4
Subjects by campfires, bonfires	1/30 sec *f*/2
Night football, baseball, racetracks	1/125 sec *f*/2.8
Moonlit landscapes	8 sec *f*/2
Snow scenes	4 sec *f*/2
Brightly lighted downtown street scenes (Wet streets add interesting reflections.)	1/60 sec *f*/2.8
Brightly-lighted nightclub or theater districts	1/60 sec *f*/4
Neon signs	1/125 sec *f*/4
Store windows	1/60 sec *f*/4
Subjects lighted by street lights	1/15 sec *f*/2
Floodlighted buildings, fountains, monuments	1/15 sec *f*/2
Skyline—distant view of lighted buildings at night	1 sec *f*/2.8
Skyline—10 minutes after sunset	1/60 sec *f*/5.6

INDOORS IN PUBLIC PLACES

Basketball, hockey, bowling	1/125 sec f/2
Boxing, wrestling	1/250 sec f/2
Stage shows—Average	1/60 sec f/2.8
Bright	1/125 sec f/4
Circuses—Floodlighted acts	1/60 sec f/2.8
Spotlighted acts (carbon-arc)	1/250 sec f/2.8
Ice Shows—Floodlighted acts	1/125 sec f/2.8
Spotlighted acts (carbon-arc)	1/250 sec f/2.8
Interiors with bright fluorescent light	1/60 sec f/4
School—stage and auditorium	1/30 sec f/2

AT HOME

Home interiors at night—Areas with average light	1/30 sec f/2
Areas with bright light	1/30 sec f/2.8
Candlelit close-ups	1/15 sec f/2
Indoor and outdoor holiday lighting at night, Christmas trees	1/15 sec f/2

Artificial Lighting

Two kinds of artificial light sources are used for photography: *instantaneous* and *continuous*. Instantaneous light sources include all the varieties of flashbulbs and electronic flash or strobe. Continuous light sources are photo floodlights, quartz halogen lights, HMI lights, and any other light that remains on after the exposure has been made. In the early days of photography, flash powder was used for artificial illumination. It was a compound of chemicals that, when ignited, produced a bright flash and clouds of smoke. It often caused burned hands, singed hair, and occasionally a good house fire. Flash powder was replaced by much safer flashbulbs, which were used for many years. Today, electronic flash is the main source of instantaneous light, whether in a small built-in camera flash or a big studio strobe unit. Electronic flash is excellent for freezing action because of its fast speed. Color balanced for daylight, it can easily be shot in conjunction with daylight for a natural look.

Continuous light sources have been essentially the same for many years. Incandescent photofloods have given way to quartz halogen lights, which are the most popular continuous light source used by photographers. Both photofloods and quartz halogen lights have a tungsten color temperature of 3200K. A more recent continuous light addition, used primarily by professional photographers because of its expense, is the metal halide medium arc lamp, or HMI. These lights provide a continuous, flicker-free, daylight-balanced light that has more power per watt than a quartz light, yet produces less heat. These lights are considered excellent for balancing with daylight and for video, movie film, and digital photography.

Electronic Flash

Flash is normally used to illuminate a subject in a low light condition, but it has much more potential than that. Since it is color balanced with daylight, electronic flash can be used as a fill to lighten shadows in sunlight and to increase interior illumination to balance with exterior light. It is an excellent tool for stopping action because the duration of most flash exposures is faster than most camera shutter speeds. Another advantage is that electronic flash is not a hot light source like photofloods or quartz halogen lights. It will not melt ice cream or cause a portrait subject to break into a sweat. For the knowledgeable user, a small electronic flash can add emphasis to subjects in daylight without looking as if shot with flash. Small electronic flash units can also create special lighting effects that most people associate with large studio flash units.

Most snapshot cameras and the more sophisticated electronic 35mm SLRs have a built-in electronic flash. Many such flashes function automatically and work well for snapshots. Most newer models are designed with an "anti-redeye" function that most users appreciate because it is hard to avoid "redeye" with a direct, on-camera flash. Redeye is caused by the flash going directly into the eyes of the subject and bouncing off the interior of the eye socket straight back into the camera. To avoid redeye with normal flashes, either shoot with the flash off to the side or about one foot above the camera lens so that the light will bounce back at an angle and not into the lens. If you are limited to using the on-camera flash, then shoot the subject at an angle rather than straight on. Follow this advice to avoid glare when you are shooting reflective subjects and backgrounds.

For those who desire to use flash for more than snapshots and simple direct illumination, you need to consider a supplemental flash that can be used both on and off the camera. For convenience and versatility, it is best to have a flash that has automatic features but can also be used manually. Another important feature to consider is a flash that has variable power. This capability will enable you to have more control of depth of field and to use fill flash more effectively. Also, the flash will recycle faster when shot on reduced power. The amount of power you need depends upon the type of shooting you are going to do. Most flash units are designed to function well within a 5-to-30-foot range, which is fine for most needs. But if you plan on shooting high school football games at night, you are going to need a much more powerful flash to illuminate the action when it is 50 or 60 feet away.

When buying an electronic flash, make sure that it has an adjustable head so that you can bounce the light off another surface for a diffused effect. Also, most flashes are designed to give the proper coverage for a normal lens but do not provide adequate coverage for other focal lengths. Attachments are available to help alleviate this deficiency, and many newer flashes have adjustable telescoping heads. Some flashes are dedicated to work with specific camera systems and function with a through-the-lens (TTL) automatic exposure system. Most of these work well and are definitely worth considering. However, no matter how good an automatic system might be, it is important to have manual functions and to learn how to use them, because certain situations will need manual control. Also, you will need to use manual functions should you ever work with studio strobes (the terms *flash* and *strobe* are interchangeable).

The biggest limitation and often the most confusing aspect to using electronic flash is that normal exposure meters cannot be used with flash. Special flash meters are necessary. Fortunately, most of the better handheld meters provide readings for normal ambient light and for flash. TTL flash systems also provide auto exposure capabilities, which is a definite advantage. Most other flashes have exposure data indicated on the body of the flash.

An electronic flash unit consists of a battery (sometimes rechargeable), a capacitor, and a flash tube. The battery sends electricity to the capacitor, where it is stored. When the energy is released, it produces a bright, split-second flash in the flash tube (about 1/10,000 second). Unlike the flashbulb, the flash tube is reusable for thousands of flashes.

Some electronic flash units are more powerful than others. These produce more light and allow the photographer to take pictures at a greater distance or with a smaller lens opening for greater depth of field. Other variables in electronic flash units are rechargeable batteries, AC power supplies, variable-angle flash brackets, and a variety of automatic features that will be explained later in this chapter.

Color Film and Flash

The Kelvin temperature of most electronic flash units is very close to that of daylight, so that, in general, no filter is required for using Daylight film with electronic flash. However, electronic flash units do vary, and some may produce pictures that are consistently too bluish. To absorb the excess blue, use a No. 81B yellowish filter over the camera lens and increase the exposure by ⅓ stop.

To use electronic flash with Tungsten film (3200K), you would need to use a No. 85B conversion filter over the lens. Type A film (3400K) would require a No. 85 filter. Either filter requires an exposure increase of 2/3 stop.

Electronic Flash Exposure Types

Manual Electronic Flash Exposure

The first step in using a manual electronic flash unit is to be certain that the proper synchronization is used. If your camera has a choice of settings, such as M, MP, and X, use the X setting for electronic flash. The others are for flashbulbs.

With electronic flash, the burst of light peaks very fast. When the shutter button is pressed, and before it is fully opened, the flash must reach its peak. If the peak occurs after or before the shutter is fully opened, part of the picture will be dark. Shutter speed selection for the X synchronization will depend on the type of shutter in your camera. In a single-lens reflex camera with a focal plane shutter, the speed is often synchronized at 1/60 second. The focal plane shutter travels horizontally across the film, but it exposes the entire piece of film only at a speed of 1/60 second or lower. At faster speeds, part of the film would be covered during the short burst of light from the flash unit. If a third or fourth of your photograph is nothing but a black rectangle, you can be almost certain it was caused by a shutter speed too fast for the flash synchronization.

Some single-lens reflex cameras have metal shutters that travel up and down instead of sideways. Most of these are synchronized at 1/125 second. Many newer electronic cameras are synchronized at even higher shutter speeds, some as fast as 1/4000 second.

If yours is a rangefinder camera or a "compact 35" with a between-the-lens shutter, then speed selection may not matter. Check your instruction manual to find which shutter speed should be used or X synchronization.

Makers of electronic flash units provide guide numbers for determining correct exposures. You simply divide the distance from your subject into the appropriate guide number and set the lens aperture.

After selecting the correct aperture, turn on the flash unit. There should be a ready light, usually on the back of your flash unit, that will indicate when the flash unit has built up enough power to take a picture. Many cameras need to be set to ON or MANUAL and have the frame counter at 1 before the flash will fire. Check your camera instruction manual. Now take your flash picture. Do not take another picture until the ready light comes on again, indicating the flash has recycled and is ready again.

In addition to a guide number, many manufacturers of electronic flash units rate them in terms of BCPS (bulb-candlepower-seconds), a scientific unit of light measurement useful in comparing the output of different units. The higher the BCPS rating, the more powerful the unit.

Many electronic flash units are equipped with dials that automatically calculate exposure without the need of guide numbers. In the illustration, notice that the ISO indicator is pointing at 100. The distance scale is marked off in feet. If the flash-to-subject distance is 10 feet, the number above 10 is 8. The *f*-stop, is, therefore, *f*/8. If the flash-to-subject distance is 15 feet, then, according to the dial, the *f*-stop would be *f*/4. Such dials facilitate calculating exposures.

Some manufacturers of electronic flash units unfortunately assign guide numbers that are too high. If you rely on these numbers, you will constantly have underexposed negatives. Should this happen, you may want to use a larger lens opening than the one recommended by the flash unit (probably one-half to one full stop). This adjustment will require some testing. However, once you know how much to open your lens, it becomes a matter of routine because the amount of light doesn't vary from flash to flash.

Automatic Electronic Flash Exposure

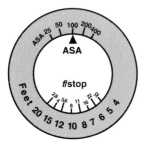

Flash calculator.

Exposure calculation is simplified with the use of an automatic flash. Invented by Honeywell Photographic in 1965, the automatic flash emits a pulse of light controlled by a light sensor. The sensor responds to the pulse of light reflected from the subject. When enough light for a correct exposure has been received, the flash is electronically turned off. A thyristor automatic flash is an energy-saving device that controls the capacitor so as to release only the energy needed to produce the light required. A thyristor unit will thus have a faster recycling time.

Many automatic flash units have the light sensor built into the flash head. This will put the sensor in line with the flash-to-subject axis. These units are intended to be mounted in an accessory clip, or shoe, on top of the camera. These units are not intended to be used for bounce-flash in the automatic mode. Some automatic flash units can be used on automatic for bounce-flash because the sensor is separate from the flash head.

Bounce flash is a technique of bouncing the light from the flash off a bright, reflective surface onto the subject. Bounce flash often gives a softer light with less contrast between shadows and highlights.

With an automatic flash, the flash calculator on the back of the unit will tell the photographer what aperture to use with a particular film speed. As long as the flash is used within the distance "seen" by the sensor, the *f*-stop will remain constant. Exposure that is determined by the sensor is based on the assumption that an average subject reflects approximately 18 percent of the incident light. Thus, it is important to remember that unusually bright subjects may be underexposed, whereas dark subjects may be overexposed. Also, the sensor reads a narrow angle of view. If the subject is placed off to the side of the frame, the sensor may not read any of the light reflected by the subject.

Consult your instruction book to determine the angle of view of the sensor and the beam spread. Beam spread is the angle at which light spreads once it leaves your electronic flash unit. The angle of the beam must match the angle of view of your camera lens. If you are using a 50mm lens with a 35mm camera, the beam spread from the electronic flash will match the angle of the lens. If a shorter focal length lens is used, the beam spread of the electronic flash unit might not be wide enough to cover the angle of the lens. In this case the edges of the photograph will be slightly underexposed. If a longer than normal focal length lens is used, then the beam spread of the electronic flash unit will be wider than the angel of view of the lens. Much of the light will be wasted because it falls outside the picture area as seen through the lens. In both cases, special attachments may be available to enlarge or reduce the beam spread of the electronic flash unit.

To take a picture with automatic electronic flash, you must first set the proper ISO film speed on the dial of the unit. Many automatic flash units have several distance ranges within which a specific aperture may be used to take a picture. Typical ranges found on automatic flash are 2 to 11 feet; 3 to 20 feet; 4 to 30 feet; and 5 to 45 feet. Each of these ranges is color coded on the exposure calculator dial, and each has a corresponding aperture for a correct exposure. The flash unit itself must be set for a distance range by setting a color-coded dial, usually found on the remote sensing device. Once you have done this, select the shutter speed synchronized for the electronic flash on your camera. This speed is often indicated by a different colored number on the shutter speed dial. If you are using a newer camera, do not set the shutter to aperture priority, shutter priority, or program mode. If you do not feel comfortable estimating the distance to your subject, focus on the subject and read the distance on the lens scale as a double check. Check your instruction manual to be certain you are reading the flash exposure scale correctly. The biggest cause of incorrectly exposed flash pictures is photographing outside the correct distance range.

Often, your subject will be positioned so that more than one combination could be used. For example, if your subject is ten feet away and you are using an automatic unit, you might choose the 2-to-11 foot range with a smaller aperture, which would increase depth of field. You might also choose the 3-to-20, 4-to-30, or the 5-to-45 range with correspondingly larger apertures. All of these could be used. Your decision may be affected by the aperture necessary for each range. However, it would normally not be wise to select the 5 to 45 foot range because your unit will be generating far more light than is necessary for an object only ten feet away. In this long-distance mode, the unit will take

Figure 18-5

Bounce flash is an effective way to illuminate a subject with soft, diffused light. Since a ceiling or appropriate wall may not be available, many photographers use a bounce card to provide subtle bounce light as a fill light.

much longer to recycle, and the batteries will be depleted sooner. This factor needs to be considered as well.

Once the proper settings have been made, switch on the flash and wait for the ready light to come on. As with manual flash, many cameras may not function with automatic electronic flash unless the camera is set to ON and the film counter is at 1 or higher.

Once you have taken the picture, you may notice another light on the back of your flash unit. This is a confidence light, and it will come on if the subject has received enough light. The confidence light will also come on if the subject has received too much light, so it is only a guard against underexposure. If the light does not come on, move closer to the subject or select a distance range that allows you to use a larger aperture. Not all flash units have a confidence light.

Dedicated Electronic Flash Exposure

As the name might imply, a dedicated flash is one designed for a specific camera or series of cameras. To work, the unit is attached by a specially designed hot shoe on top of the camera. By attaching a dedicated flash unit to an aperture-priority camera, the user need not worry about flash synchronization because the circuitry built inside the camera automatically selects the correct shutter speed.

Because dedicated flash units are designed for specific cameras, you must use one that is made for your camera. All camera manufacturers produce dedicated flash units. In addition, most independent manufacturers also produce dedicated flash units, although they generally must be used with a module or adapter to ensure dedication.

To take a picture with a dedicated flash unit, you may need to set the film's ISO number on the camera and on the unit. Some cameras with DX coding automatically set the ISO number. Next, mount the flash on the camera. If the flash unit is to be used off the camera—mounted on an L bracket, for example—you will need a special cord called a synchronization, or PC, cord. Be sure that you have the proper cord for your dedicated flash system, or a remote electronic flash controller.

You may now set the camera to either aperture priority or the program mode (P). With the latter, the camera will set both the aperture and shutter speed for you. Whichever mode you choose, the camera will select the properly synchronized shutter speed when the flash is turned on.

If your dedicated flash system does not have a sensor in the camera (non–through-the-lens flash) and you have chosen the shutter priority, then you must select the proper aperture. If you have selected the program mode (P), the camera will select the aperture automatically. Be sure you are shooting within the proper distance range for your flash unit. Check your instruction manual for this information.

Figure 18-6

Minolta Maxxum 9xi with Maxxum AF Flash 5400xi and Wireless Remote Flash Controller.

Dedicated TTL Electronic Flash Exposure

Through-the-lens (TTL) dedicated electronic flash operates in a manner similar to the regular dedicated electronic flash. The difference is that the light-sensing unit is located inside the camera. The light reaching the film is measured after it has passed through the lens (TTL). The sensor performs the same function as the sensor on a regular automatic electronic flash unit. Both kinds of units measure the amount of light present during the flash exposure, and they shut down the unit when enough light for a proper exposure has been emitted. In the TTL system, the measuring device inside the camera is located near the film plane and actually reads the light off the film itself. For this reason, this type of unit is also referred to as an off-the-film (OTF) electronic flash. The advantage of this system is that the amount of light actually reaching the film is measured, not the amount of light reaching the flash unit. In some situations, these may be different. For example, if you have decided to move the flash unit off the camera, the flash unit could be closer to or farther away from the subject than the camera is. Thus, the sensor in the flash unit will receive more or less light than the film in your camera, and the photograph will be over- or underexposed. As long as a TTL unit is used properly, neither can happen because the sensor always reads the light reaching the film. Another situation in which a TTL system will produce more accurate exposures is when lens filters are used. These filters absorb light and therefore change the exposure. Since a TTL system measures light after it has passed through the lens, the light will be automatically adjusted for a correct exposure. If you are using a longer or shorter focal length lens than is normal for your camera, or a zoom lens, some exposure correction may be necessary. Again, with the TTL system, the sensor in the camera automatically corrects these problems.

TTL units may be used for close-up photography (within 1 foot of your subject). The TTL sensor will give an accurate exposure as long as very small apertures such as $f/11$ and $f/16$ are used. Consult your instruction manual for specifics.

Electronic Flash Features

Some other features, besides automation, are worth investigating. They include power, power source, recycling time, portability, energy requirements, and trends.

Power. In general, the greater the power, the more desirable the unit. The more powerful the unit, the greater the flash distance becomes.

More power also allows for the use of smaller apertures. On the negative side, added power costs more and involves a physically larger unit.

Power Source. Most popular flash units today are powered by batteries, usually size AA. In most cases, these are alkaline batteries and drain quickly and must be discarded. Some units have nickel-cadmium batteries, which can be recharged. A few use standard AC current.

Recycling Time. The time it takes a flash unit to reach full power after firing is called recycling time. This varies anywhere from less than 1 second to 10 seconds or more. As battery power drains, recycling time increases.

Portability. Larger units generally have more power and faster recycling times. This is because most larger units can use external power sources, called battery packs, which carry more powerful batteries (like 510 volts). However, those battery packs must be carried separately, usually over the shoulder.

Energy Requirements. The majority of flash units made today feature an energy-saving circuitry, called a thyristor, which both prolongs the life of the battery and shortens the recycling time. A thyristor acts as a governor controlling the flow of power from the battery to the capacitor, where the power is stored.

A second energy-saving device found on more expensive units is a power-reduction switch. This switch allows the flash to be used at fractions of the maximum power of the unit. For example, some units offer energy reductions of $\frac{1}{2}$ power, $\frac{1}{4}$ power, and $\frac{1}{16}$ power. Saving power is especially useful for close-up photography, where overexposure can become a problem.

Trends. With the advent of the microprocessor (microchip), flash units have become more sophisticated. For example, calculator dials on the backs of most units will be replaced with liquid crystal displays (LCDs). In addition, computerized circuitry allows for more auto ranges (such as eight *f*-stops instead of the usual three or four). More expensive units offer interchangeable flash heads, thus allowing for more creative uses of the flash. Finally, features such as the audible indicator will replace the ready light.

Special Purpose Flash Units

A *ringflash* is an electronic flash unit that surrounds the lens of a camera. It procures a soft, shadowless illumination that is useful for photographing recessed areas. Many dentists use ringflash to make photographic records of dental work because the light can be directed into the mouth. Thus, it is useful for close-up photography.

A *stroboscopic flash* produces a series of rapid-sequence flashes in a brief interval. Many stroboscopic units can be set to flash up to 50 times a second at a duration of at least 1/10,000 second each. Such a unit enables a photographer to show progressive stages of motion on a single exposure. Thus, professional photographers use it quite often for time and motion studies, or for special effects in advertising.

Generally, when a stroboscope is used, the camera is mounted on a tripod and set at B (bulb), or 1 second. The subject is in front of a dark background and moves while the shutter is open and the flash is being fired. The result is frozen motion: each movement of that subject fixed each time the flash fires.

Using Flash

Flash can usually be used in the same ways as natural light. Flash units are commonly attached to the camera, giving you the advantages of both speed and convenience. You need not hold or aim the flash separately. This is convenient for photographing action, such as sports events. Calculating exposure is usually more accurate because the camera and flash are the same distance from the subject. However, there are some disadvantages to having the flash attached to the camera. The major one is that the picture may have a washed-out background and probably a harsh shadow behind the subject. Another disadvantage is that the subject will have little or no modeling. For an object to look three-dimensional, there must be both shadows and highlights. One way to avoid this is to keep the flash above and slightly to one side of the subject. Remove the flash unit from the camera and either attach it to an L bracket or hold it in your free hand. (See Color Gallery C, Plates 18.9 and 18.10.)

Bouncing the light is another way to soften it. This is done by aiming the flash at a surface that will reflect the light back onto the subject, such as a white ceiling or wall. Bounce light, however, reduces the amount of light on your subject, and so you must increase the exposure. One rule is to open the lens two stops. A more accurate way is to measure the flash to the reflecting surface and from the surface to the subject. Divide the total into the guide number to determine exposure. Remember that bounce light works only in a small, bright area and that dark colors absorb light while light colors reflect it.

When using automatic units for bounce flash, you must be able to aim the sensor at the subject while the flash head is directed at an angle to the subject—for example, toward the ceiling. If this cannot be done, you must use your automatic unit in the manual mode.

Figure 18-7

A. Direct flash.

B. Off-camera flash.

C. Bounce flash.

Bounce flash with automatic and dedicated units may produce under-exposed pictures because the flash-to-subject distance may be too long and require more power than the unit can deliver. In addition, much light is scattered and absorbed by the bounce surface. If you have a choice of several apertures, always use the largest for bounce flash with an automatic or dedicated electronic unit. A film with a high ISO rating will also help. Finally, if your flash unit has a confidence light, it will tell you when your bounce light picture is underexposed.

Using Fill Flash

Flash can be used to lighten (fill) dark shadows caused by bright sunlight or to add light to a backlit subject. If executed properly, it will not look as if a flash was used. Everything will look natural, but the lighting ratio (the *f*-stop range between shadows and highlights) will be reduced to an easily printable range. To use fill flash effectively, it is important to understand that you will be simultaneously balancing two separate exposures. One exposure is for the ambient or natural light, the lightness and darkness of which is controlled by the aperture and shutter speed. The other exposure is for the flash. The lightness and darkness of the flash exposure are determined by the power of the flash. Ambient light and flash work in conjunction with each other, but each has to be determined separately to determine a proper working exposure that functions for both.

Flash exposure is also affected by the distance of the flash to the subject and the lens's *f*-stop. Shutter speed has no effect on the flash exposure, it only affects the ambient exposure. Most 35mm cameras

Figure 18-8

A. No fill.   B. Normal fill.   C. Bright fill.

have to use a specific flash sync shutter speed or slower to ensure that the shutter will be completely open when the flash goes off. Although most other types of cameras have leaf shutters built into the lens and can be used with flash at any shutter speed, be sure to read your flash and camera manual thoroughly to make the most of the options they offer. With these principles in mind, the following explains the procedure for determining flash-fill exposures with a TTL flash and camera system.

Fill Flash with TTL Systems

1. Set the ambient exposure first by metering the subject in the normal manner with your through-the-lens or hand-held meter. Make sure that the shutter speed is at your flash sync speed or slower.
2. Decide upon the amount of fill light you want. A regular full-flash exposure will overpower the ambient light and look like an ordinary flash shot. To get a more natural effect, the flash exposure needs to be less than normal. For half the normal flash intensity, set your flash exposure dial for 1 EV of flash compensation; for a one-third fill, set it at 1½ EV; for one-quarter fill, set it at 2 EV. If your autoflash unit doesn't have variable settings, use the system it indicates to reduce flash output, or use the flash manually.
3. Take the picture, bracketing until experience enables you to be sure of the results.

Fill Flash with Non-TTL Autoflash Units

To use fill flash with non-TTL autoflash units, try the following:

1. Take a normal meter reading for the ambient light and set the aperture and shutter speed accordingly. Make sure that the shutter speed is at the flash sync speed or slower.
2. Next, set the aperture selection on your autoflash as follows: For one-half the flash power, set the aperture selection on the flash at one stop open from the camera aperture. For example, if the camera aperture is $f/11$, set the flash for $f/8$. For one-third flash power, set the flash a stop and a half open. For one-quarter flash power, set the flash two stops open.
3. Leave the camera settings as they were, and shoot the picture.

Should you find that the needed autoflash setting is not available, adjust your shutter speed to shift the ambient exposure to an equivalent setting that will provide a workable autoflash aperture setting. Should this not be possible due to shutter speed limitations, reduce the flash to subject distance or switch to a slower film.

Fill Flash with Manual Flash Units

Manual fill flash is a little more confusing, and the easiest way to figure it out is with a flash meter. But without a flash meter, try the following:

1. Determine the flash-to-subject distance, and look at the exposure dial on your flash for the *f*-stop needed at that distance. Then stop the *f*-stop down one time to reduce the flash exposure in half so that it will look more natural in relation to the daylight.
2. Take an ambient meter reading and determine the shutter speed needed at that *f*-stop for a normal ambient exposure. This determination will provide the proper ambient exposure but cause underexposure of the flash so that it will function as a fill and not be overtly evident. If the shutter speed is faster than your flash sync speed, you will have to increase the power of the flash by moving it closer to the subject or using a higher power if it has variable power settings. The increased flash output will enable you to use a higher *f*-stop for the flash and a slower shutter speed (the sync speed or slower), keeping the ambient exposure the same. For example, if the initial exposure setting was *f*/11 at 1/250 second, twice as much flash output will enable you to use *f*/16 at 1/125 second and get a proper flash exposure and the same ambient exposure. This setting will be fine, provided your flash sync speed is 1/125. If the sync speed is slower, you will have to make further adjustments. A slower film or a neutral density filter might help.
3. Shoot the picture but bracket until you become comfortable with the procedure.

Studio Strobe Units

Electronic flash has been the main lighting source for professional photographers for many years, especially for color photography. Studio strobes, as they are called, have all of the attributes of small flashes and then some. Most strobe units come with a separate power pack that can be used for at least four light heads. This power source gives you the opportunity to use multiple lights at differing powers with a diverse array of lighting accessories, such as snoots, barn doors, different reflector sizes, diffusers, umbrellas, and soft boxes—all of which change the quality, quantity, and look of the light you use.

Studio strobes have one other important feature that small strobes do not—modeling lights. These are tungsten-balanced continuous lights that allow you to see what the strobe flash will do. With small strobes you have to guess, but with studio strobes you arrange the light and see exactly what you get.

Most photographers use a flash meter or Polaroid to help determine exposure. Studio strobes have no automatic features, you have to know how to control light manually to use them. Their advantage is that they offer tremendous versatility, power, and control. Aside from the exposure and the specific attributes of flash, the way the lights are used in the studio is basically the same as for continuous light sources.

Continuous Light Sources

Continuous light sources are those that provide a steady flow of artificial illumination. A flashlight, for instance, gives a steady flow of light, although it is not normally bright enough for photography. Certain types of lightbulbs have been designed for photographic purposes. Called photofloods, they provide an even, steady light that is bright enough for taking pictures. The light from photoflood bulbs must be directed. This can be done with either reflectors or reflector floods. Reflectors direct the light so that it travels at a certain angle. Generally, the larger the reflector, the more area the light will cover. Usually, the smaller the reflector, the more concentrated the light will be. A large reflector with a 12-inch radius, for instance, would be used to light a large area such as a room. Reflector floodlights are photoflood bulbs with built-in reflectors. This type of light source provides a concentrated light beam. Reflector floods are useful when the light is to be directed on a small area, such as the face. Both types of bulbs must be mounted in a light socket. A clamp and cord set provide a socket as well as a clamp to fasten the unit on a chair or other support. The bulb can also be fastened on an adjustable light stand, which can be lowered and raised like a camera tripod.

Reflectors and bulbs give you an effective way to control light. A typical lighting setup in a professional studio may use as many as seven different lights at different angles. These give a more controlled light

Figure 18-9

Strobe light is used with umbrella and reflector to fill shadows.

than daylight. However, many successful portraits can be taken using one to three lights.

Try this exercise to practice different lighting techniques. Use a Number 2 photoflood lamp, which uses 500 watts of light (a Number 1 lamp uses 250 watts). Attach the bulb to a clamp or light stand with an 8–12-inch reflector. (You can also use a reflector flood alone.) Ask a friend to model in front of a white wall or screen. Set the camera about 3 to 5 feet from the head. The image of the head should fill the viewfinder. This distance should not vary with each photograph. There should be no lights in the room except the photo lamp. *Shot 1*—place the light as near the camera as possible, aimed squarely at the subject. *Shot 2*—place the light on the left side of the subject at a 45-degree angle to the camera-subject line. *Shot 3*—same position as number 2, but raise the light to shine down on the subject at a 20-degree angle. *Shot 4*—same position, but lower the light to beam up at the subject. *Shot 5*—place the light so that it beams directly down on the subject's forehead. *Shot 6*—place the light directly below the subject's face, aiming

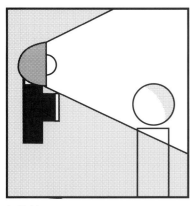

1. Light source near camera.

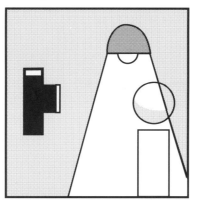

2. 45 degrees to the left.

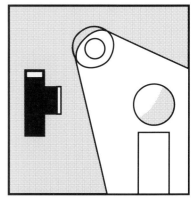

3. Same as 2 but 20 degrees higher.

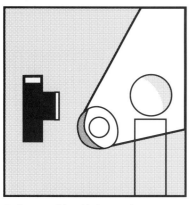

4. Same as 2 but 20 degrees lower.

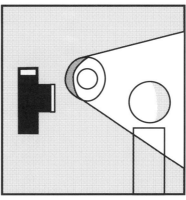

5. Straight down.

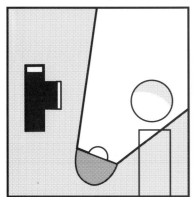

6. Straight up.

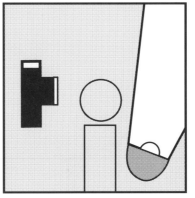

7. Light on background.

up toward the chin. *Shot 7*—aim the light behind the subject onto the white background.

After the photos have been developed and printed, compare them. The first photo will show the subject well-lighted without shadows. However, the features will appear flat. Shot 2 will be a high-contrast rendering of the subject, with deep shadows beside the nose and mouth. Shot 3 will show the subject with deep shadows under both eyes and underneath the mouth. In Shot 4, the face will look somewhat strange because the shadows fall upward. Shot 5 will have extreme shadows under the eyes and mouth. Shot 6 will make the subject look scary and grotesque. Shot 7 will produce a silhouette.

Multiple Lighting

After you have done the above exercises, you may want to experiment with more than one light, especially for portraits of people. When a second light is used, that light is called a *fill*. The first light source then becomes the *main*. The general purpose of the fill light is to add some light to the shadow area. It in effect will reduce the harsh contrasts between the dark and light areas. Thus, a more direct-diffused quality of light is achieved.

The simplest and most effective way to add a fill light is to use a reflector to bounce the main light back to the subject and to the area where it's needed most. One way to make a reflector is to use a piece of stiff cardboard about 16x20-inches, with a white surface on one side. On the other side, attach some crumpled aluminum foil that has been smoothed flat. Tape the corners of the foil to the other side of the board.

The white side will give a soft, even illumination, which works well for portraits. The aluminum foil side reflects a harder light that will be more direct.

Another possible solution to a fill light is to use a second light. The second light is normally half as powerful as the main light. This can be achieved by having the lights the same distance from the subject but using a fill-light bulb that is half as powerful as the main light bulb. If the bulbs are the same intensity, move the fill light farther back until it is half as powerful as the main light. This would normally be twice as far from the subject as the main light.

Create modeling (the shadowing of the subject that brings out form) with the main light. Position it (with the fill light off) so that you get the effect you desire. Then place the fill light close to the camera so that it provides an overall front light. The fill light will add one light value to the overall picture. If the main light is twice as strong, it will add two light values to the portion of the subject it is illuminating. The

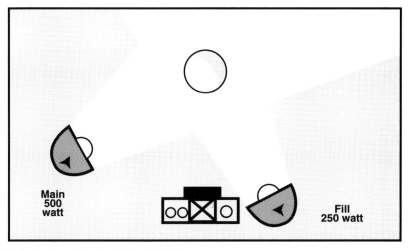

Portrait set-up with main light and fill light.

shadows will only get one value, which is from the fill light. The highlights will get three light values, one from the shadows and two from the main light. The resulting three-to-one lighting ratio has a one *f*-stop difference in exposure from highlight to shadow and is the most common lighting ratio used for most studio portraiture.

Lighting, of course can get more complicated than using just two lights. Regardless, try to keep the setup simple. Begin with the main light and add other lights only for fill and accents. Think of the procedure as building with light. You need to begin with a good foundation and everything else needs to be carefully considered in relation to that foundation. Often, less light is more. It doesn't matter whether you use strobes or continuous light sources such as photofloods or quartz halogen lights—the basic techniques are the same.

Here are some other variables to consider: (1) the number of lights needed; (2) angles of light in relationship to the subject; (3) distance between lights and subject; (4) the size of the reflector used; and (5) the color and value of the background. One other variable is most important—the subject. Lighting should not make everybody look alike. The lighting should fit the personality of the subject rather than the photographer's convenience in setting up. The inexpensive color portrait that is frequently advertised in newspapers and magazines employs the same type of lighting for each person being photographed. This setup, of course, cuts down on costs, but approximately two million other babies have been photographed exactly the same way. The resulting photograph is scarcely unique.

Figure 18-10
Studio strobes and a softbox lit this human-interest portrait of a father and son.

Father and Son, Greg Phillips.

The following diagrams illustrate combinations using four lights. Each lighting setup highlights a different characteristic of the subject. Portrait photographers would probably arrange the lights in a manner similar to the illustrations. Remember, though, that the goal of the commercial photographer is to produce a standardized representation of the subject. After all, most people don't want to pay money for a portrait that makes them look ugly.

Many other types of lighting relationships and techniques are used by commercial photographers. This section presents only some of the basic considerations and approaches. The equipment options are also much more varied than we have been able to represent here. Snoots are lighting attachments that funnel the light into a small circle, like that of a flashlight beam, to accent a small part of the picture. Barn doors are another attachment for the front of the light that can be adjusted to block the light from a portion of the picture. Diffusers soften the light, as do umbrellas and soft boxes. Umbrellas are attached to a

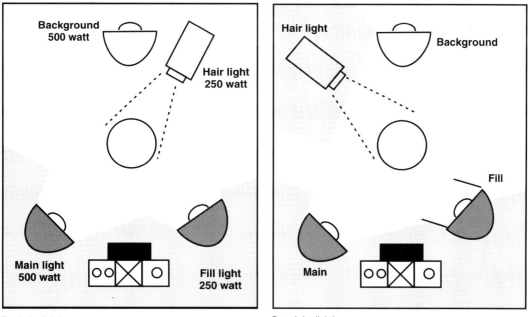

Back rim lighting.   Broad rim lighting.

light stand and pointed towards the subject. The light is aimed into the umbrella and bounces back to envelop the subject with soft light.

Soft boxes fit onto the front of the light fixture, and the light is beamed into the box. The sides of the soft box bounce the light around and out through the flat, translucent white front. Owing to problems with heat buildup, soft boxes are used only with strobes, which are cooler than most continuous light sources. But special fans must be used with the strobes because of heat buildup from the modeling lights. Soft boxes vary in size, from small ones that fit onto the front of small camera flashes to big studio models often as big as 4x8 feet. They make directional-diffused light and overall diffused light very easy to achieve and have become quite popular. Consequently, many photographers are returning to more traditional lighting techniques.

Copying

Copying is the photographic recording of a subject that exists in either two dimensions (paintings, drawings, or other photographs) or three dimensions (any object that has depth to it). For our purposes, however, we will limit copying to subjects that are essentially two-dimensional.

The best lighting arrangement for copying is to use two photoflood lamps, placed at a 45-degree angle on either side of the subject. If the subject being copied is larger than 11x14 inches, a second light can be added to each side. The distance between the light source and the subject should be far enough apart to flood the surface with a strong intensity of light. It should be even across the entire subject so that the edges are not brighter than the center of the subject. One way to check this is with the use of an exposure meter. If it measures differently from one edge to another, you know your lights are uneven. Another technique is to hold a pencil perpendicular to the copy at its center, in line with the optical axis of the lens, and then compare the shadows cast by the pencil stem. If the shadows are of equal intensity and the length is the same on both sides of the stem, the lighting is balanced.

With a large subject, such as a painting, this standard setup can be altered by arranging the lights at a more oblique angle and directing them so that they illuminate the subject from edge to edge. This illumination will help bring out the brush stroke and texture of the painting.

The size of the reflector used will also alter the illumination. A bullet reflector, which is generally about 4 inches in diameter, will not distribute the light at as wide of an angle as would a 12-inch reflector. Thus, for very small subjects, use a small reflector; for large subjects, use a reflector with a large diameter.

Subjects that are covered with glass will sometimes cause a glare. Changing the angle of the lamps might eliminate this drawback. Should this method fail, you may need to use a polarizing filter on both the lens and the reflectors. Polarizing filters are sold in large sheets to fit over reflectors, but must be positioned at least one foot from the light to keep from getting too hot.

By far and away, the easiest method for exposure determination for copying is with the use of an 18 percent gray card (Kodak Neutral Test Card). This card can be used for determining the exposure for both black and white and color films. To use it, place the card on the same plane as the subject that is to be copied, and take a normal reflected light reading. If you are using a handheld meter, be careful not to cast a shadow over the card by getting your arm in the way of the lamps.

Exposure Calculations for Other Lighting

When reading the meter for a subject illuminated by artificial light, it is usually best to average several readings. In other words, take an exposure reading from various areas of the subject, such as hair, face,

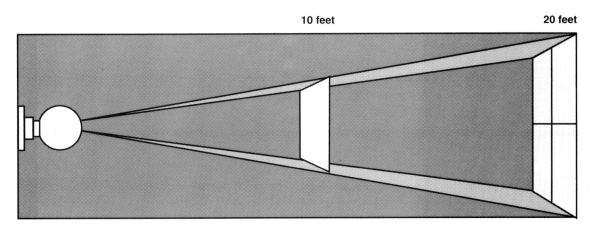

10 feet   **20 feet**

clothes, and shadow areas, and then find the average exposure. If the subject is to be silhouetted on purpose, then read the background area only.

Light incidence is four times more intense at 10 feet than at 20 feet.

One fact about the behavior of light is important to know when you are using artificial light. The intensity of light falls off rapidly as the distance between the light source and subject is increased. In mathematical terms, the illumination of a surface is inversely proportional to the square of the distance between the light source and the illuminated surface. If you double the distance between the subject and the light source, the light becomes only one-fourth as bright. For example, if the correct reading were 1/125 second at *f*/11 with the light 10 feet from the subject, moving the light back to 20 feet (twice the distance) would mean the exposure should be increased to 1/125 second at *f*/5.6. The closer the light is to the subject, the more light the subject will reflect, thus requiring a shorter exposure time. The longer the distance between the subject and light source, the less intense the light will be. Less light will be reflected, and the exposure will have to be longer.

Whatever kind of light you choose for your photographs, artificial or natural, learn to control it to achieve the effects you want.

Chapter 19

Advanced Shooting and Exposure Techniques

Through analysis and evaluation of the facts he has collected, the photographer evolves his concept of the subject he wishes to depict. At this moment, his integrity is put to the test.

—Andreas Feininger
Photographer

No formula or specific guideline can tell you how to make an effective picture. Value judgments are subjective and vary from one individual to another. Most important is to learn to *visualize your subject as a photograph.* Visualization involves technical considerations and aesthetic concerns. Ultimately, good photographers develop an intuitive sense that enables them to decide how they want a subject to look in a picture. That visualization determines the technical decisions that make the photograph a reality.

In the beginning, most people rely on *postvisualization* to determine the final look of their pictures. They respond to a subject or circumstance by using a conventional exposure and the most convenient means to take the picture. Later, they select the image that seems to work the best and rely on darkroom manipulations to get a satisfactory print.

Conor, Judith Taggart.

Figure 19-1

Now, with the advent of digital imaging, a new generation of image makers is relying on postvisualization as the key to their success.

Experienced photographers have learned to think in terms of photographic possibilities. They understand how to record a subject as literally as possible and how to radically depart from reality. They make decisions before exposing their film. They learn to *previsualize* and see a subject as it would appear in a photograph, whether it is traditional or digital. This process leads to a personalization of the photograph and decisions that provide the photographer with more control and a higher level of aesthetic and technical quality. Even those who rely on postvisualization as the culmination of their creative decision making use previsualization when generating the visual materials that they will reconstitute later.

If personal expression and interpretation are the goals of a photographer, then understanding photographic technique and knowing how to use it are essential. Otherwise, their creative potential is limited. When the film is exposed, the basic characteristics of that particular photograph are established and not easily changed. To control those characteristics,

Cat and Fish Tail, Ron Leighton.

Figure 19-2

Previsualization means more than just a technical understanding of how a subject will look in a photograph. It also means having an idea about what you want in the picture. Regardless of whether the subject represents a candid situation or a staged one, knowing the what and why leads to decisions that produce sound results.

photographers need to make a decision about the look of a photograph before they expose the film.

The Zone System

Advanced shooting and exposure techniques vary, depending upon the needs of the situation. There are many different methods and approaches to the refinement and control of shooting and exposure. The *Zone System*, one of the best known methods for photographic image control, was refined by Ansel Adams and Fred Archer in the 1940s. It is based on the premise that photographers needed an easily understandable method for applying the principles of sensitometry (the science of exposure and development) to the creative process. The Zone System pro-

Figure 19-3

Using the Zone System enabled Woods to increase contrast and create a dramatic and abstract rendition of his subject.

Marsh Grass, Alaska, John Charles Woods.

vides a means to interpret the tonal values in a scene and a method to control those values photographically to make the picture the way it was envisioned. Most importantly, the Zone System teaches photographers to previsualize and to think about what it is they are making.

Film responds to the light that the camera sees. The subject of a picture is recorded as a particular light value or a combination of values. Variations in brightness, from light to dark, are referred to as the contrast range of the picture. Our eyes enable us to see a broad range of contrast, whereas film records a much smaller range. Photographic print materials, both black and white and color, record even less. Controlling contrast to reproduce the subject as envisioned is essential, regardless of the type of photography. Whether the end product is a photographic print, lithographic reproduction, or digital output, contrast control is important.

Contrast control is the essence of the Zone System, the knowledge and use of which will enable you to accurately control metering, film exposure, film development, and ultimately, the look of the final print. A black and white photograph consists of gray tones. Through variations in the film exposure and development, you can control the contrast range of these gray tones. This rule of thumb has guided photographers for years: *To increase or expand contrast, underexpose and overdevelop; to reduce or compress contrast, overexpose and underdevelop.* The Zone System is a systematic means of control. With it you can evaluate the light values of the subject and determine the necessary film exposure and development to get the value relationship you want in a print.

The Zone System breaks down the continuous gray scale of a black and white photograph into ten generalized areas of brightness or exposure zones, with each zone one *f*-stop apart. The basic relationships also apply to color. Each zone is a specific shade of gray and numbering ranges from 0 to IX. The zones form three main groups: low values—Zones 0, I, II, III; middle values—Zones IV, V, VI; and high values—Zones VII, VIII, IX. Pure black is zone 0, and the whitest white the paper can produce is Zone IX. The following is a list of zones and the gray values they represent:

Zone 0: The maximum black possible with a specific photo paper.

Zone I: The first perceivable tone above maximum black. No texture or detail is visible.

Zone II: A very dark gray that is nearly black and contains barely noticeable detail and texture.

Zone III: A very dark gray similar to grays found in dark shadows, with a delicate rendition of texture and detail.

Zone IV: A dark gray midtone, with a full, easy-to-distinguish rendition of texture and detail.

Zone V: Middle gray, with 18 percent light reflectance, the value meters are calibrated to give.

Zone VI: A light gray midtone, with a full, easy-to-distinguish rendition of texture and detail.

Zone VII: A very light gray, with a full but delicate rendition of texture and detail.

Zone VIII: A bright white with very subtle texture and detail, if any. The last distinguishable tone before the maximum white of the paper.

Zone IX: The maximum white possible with a specific photo paper.

Abandoned Station, Jerry Burchfield.

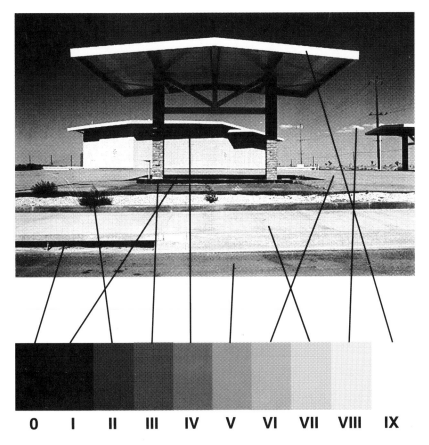

Figure 19-4

The Zone System divides the continuous tonal scale of a black and white photograph into ten tonal zones, beginning with Zone 0, the maximum black possible with the materials, to Zone IX, the maximum white possible.

0   I   II   III   IV   V   VI   VII   VIII   IX

The Zone System has been primarily associated with large format cameras and black and white landscape photography. The system was an integral part of the so called *fine print aesthetic*, which was championed by photographers such as Ansel Adams and Minor White, and has been carried on by contemporaries such as John Sexton, John Charles Woods, and Larry Vogel. The principles, however, apply to all aspects of photography.

Using Light Meters and Contrast Control

Light or exposure meters measure light. Reflected meters are the most common and are the type built into 35mm camera systems. They are also the easiest type of meter to use with the zone system because they read the light that is reflected from the subject, which allows the photographer to relate directly to the specific light values of the subject.

Figure 19-5

A normal meter reading was taken for this scene. Because of the fairly even balance between the light and dark values, the overall averaging meter reading was inadequate. In this case, better detail and a richer print would have resulted if the exposure had been based on producing a Zone VII in the white areas.

Untitled, Jerry Burchfield.

Light meters, whether manual or automatic, read any uniform tone as a Zone V or middle gray, regardless of whether the subject is black, white, or some value in between. Consequently, with black and white film, if you took a meter reading from a black dog and exposed, developed, and printed the film normally, you would get a picture of a middle gray dog. The same would happen with a white dog—you would end up with a print showing a middle gray dog.

Naturally, you can make a print from either negative that will show the dog as black or white simply by reducing or increasing the exposure. But this would result in a loss of detail and a poor rendition of the dog. Using variable-contrast filters or changing the contrast grade of the paper will help make the pictures look more natural, but they will still lack the detail and subtlety that should be there.

To get a negative that is easy to print, with a broad range of tones and good detail overall, use the logic of the zone system. When you meter the black dog, reduce the exposure by two f-stops from the meter indication. Underexposing the film will put the tonal value at a Zone III, which is a very dark gray, almost black, with a delicate rendition of detail and texture—a value like that you would expect to find in dark shadows. For the white dog, increase the exposure two f-stops from the meter reading to a Zone VII. The consequent overexposure of the film will produce a very light gray with a full but delicate, rendition of texture and detail.

When an exposure adjustment is made to alter a value relationship, the other values in the scene are also altered. They will be affected in the same proportion as the black dog and the white dog. In some cases, this proportional change will be fine. But in others, the decrease or increase in the overall relationship of tonal values may not work. The change might be all right for the dog, but not the neighborhood.

For instance: If a normal (Zone V) spot meter reading off the hair of the black dog indicates an exposure of f/5.6 at 1/125 second, you would need to reduce the exposure two f-stops to get a Zone III, which would produce a more natural tonal rendition of the black dog. Highlight values in the neighborhood around the dog would be reduced from Zones VII and VIII to Zones V and VI. This change would reduce the overall contrast, making the print darker and more low key. If that is okay, great. But if you want a Zone III dog and a Zone VII highlight value, then you have a problem.

Sometimes you get lucky. If the light values of the overall scene are split evenly with a similar amount of dark and light values, then a normal overall reading of the scene might be fine. It would indicate an exposure in the middle and the various zones should fall naturally

Figure 19-6

Careful control of lighting and exposure maintained delicate textural detail in both the light and dark values in this photograph.

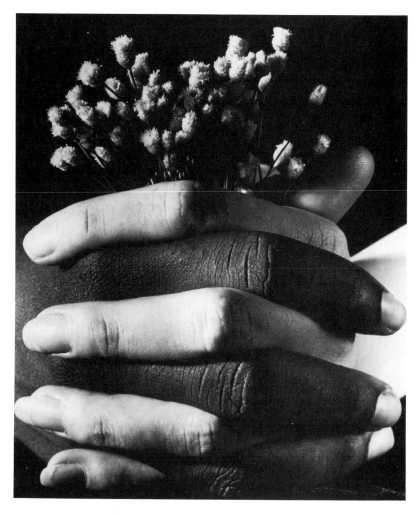

Untitled, Lisa Herndon.

into place. But if a dark or light value predominates, then an overall reading wouldn't work, regardless of whether you used a manual or an automatic metering system. The meter would be overly influenced by a dominant value, throwing the overall value relationships out of sync. In that case, another simple solution would be to meter from a middle gray Zone V value in the scene or from a gray card. This approach would also place the exposure in the middle so that the values would fall naturally on the Zone tonal scale.

Another common approach to the problem would be to take a meter reading of the dog, a Zone III value, and a meter reading of the most important Zone VII highlight value. Then pick an exposure that is in the middle. If the light values are fairly normal, then the relationships should work out fine. For example: Unless the light changed, the meter reading of the black dog should be the same, $f/5.6$ at 1/125 second. The meter reading of the Zone VII highlight value should be $f/22$ at 1/125, since Zone III and Zone VII are four f-stops apart on the Zone scale. If you shot each subject at the exposures indicated by the meter and did no manipulation in the printing, both would come out a middle gray Zone V. To get a normal Zone III rendition of the black dog, you need $f/11$, which is two stops less exposure than the meter indicated. To get the right exposure for the Zone VII highlight value, you need two stops more exposure, which would also be $f/11$.

Unfortunately, circumstances aren't always that easy to deal with. The contrast (f-stop) range between the Zone III reading and the Zone VII reading may be more or less than the four f-stop range that falls naturally on the scale. Should that be the case, then a compromise exposure can be used, but it will mean a compromise in quality too. If you choose an exposure in the middle, then both extremes will suffer. A better option is to select an exposure that ensures you will get the detail you need in the most important part of the picture—then deal with the other areas in the printing. With negative films, choose an exposure that favors the shadows. This ensures detail in the low values, overexposed highlights can be handled with variable-contrast filters and burning-in during printing. With positive transparency films, expose for the highlights and print for the shadows, since overexposed highlights burn out and lose all detail with transparency films. In either case, you will have a compromise exposure that is hard to deal with in the darkroom, and a compromise print.

To get a better result, you have several options. Try using a reflector or adding supplemental lighting to get the value relationships into a workable range. If neither is possible, then go further with the Zone System and use film characteristics to get the contrast range where you want it.

Tonal Placement and Fall

A light meter produces a suggested exposure that is based on a Zone V, or middle gray tonal value. Opening the lens aperture one stop or slowing the shutter speed one stop will increase the exposure by one stop (+1) more than the normal exposure. Stopping the lens down one stop or going to a one-stop faster shutter speed will reduce the exposure one stop (−1) less than normal. A +1 increase in exposure changes the

Zone System value placement from a Zone V to a Zone VI, whereas a −1 reduction in exposure changes the value placement from a Zone V to a Zone IV. A +2 increase in exposure would be what we suggested previously to get a better exposure for the white dog.

When shooting, consider the light values of the subject you are shooting. If you see a Zone V value that you would like to make a Zone III to add drama to the picture, then *place* that value on Zone III by reducing the exposure two *f*-stops (−2). In another shot, should you have a Zone IV value that you would like to place at a Zone VII, you will have to increase the exposure by three *f*-stops (+3). Thus, subject tones can be placed by controlling film exposure.

After *placing* the Zone III low value, you need to determine the contrast range of the subject and its printability. To do this you need to know where the Zone VII fully detailed light value *falls*. If it falls within the normal four-stop range between the Zone III value and itself, then it is okay and should get normal development. If it falls too high, say with five stops of difference, then the contrast is too much, and the print value will be too light. To get the image into a printable range, it needs to have the contrast reduced one stop. If it falls too low, then the subject has less contrast than normal and you will get a flat print. To increase the contrast, you need to increase the film development.

Controlling Contrast

Film exposure combined with development time determines the contrast range of the subject. Increasing development time increases the contrast, whereas reducing the development time lessens the contrast. To know whether a development adjustment is necessary, you must first meter the important, fully detailed dark value in the scene and adjust the exposure to *place* it on a Zone III. Then find the *fall* of the fully detailed light value in the scene and determine whether it falls within the normal contrast range. If so, shoot the picture and develop it normally. For easy identification, refer to normal development as N.

Figure 19-7

Diffused natural lighting provided the rich detail and full range of tones in this photograph. Careful metering and the use of zone system controls helped to ensure these results.

Bunker Hill Rooming House, Los Angeles, CA, David F. Drake.

If the light value falls too high, say one stop beyond a four *f*-stop range, then you need to reduce the development by one stop, which is referred to as N–1 (N minus 1) development. If it falls too low, for instance, one stop below a four *f*-stop range, then you need to expand or increase the development by one stop, which is referred to as N+1 (N plus 1) development.

For specific information on developing time adjustments, it is recommended you consult one of the many guides on the Zone System, such as those listed in the bibliography at the end of this chapter. Then do your own testing to determine the proper approach for you and your working methods.

Zone Tonal Control with Roll Film

It is easy to control individual shots when you are using single sheets of film in a view camera. But Zone System controls can help roll film users provided they expose and process the whole roll in one way. Otherwise, they may have to cut the film in darkness to process one part one way and another part differently. Given the lack of individual frame control with roll film, it would be wise to bracket your shots to provide some assurance of success.

When shooting, make notes on each shot. First, meter the important dark tone in the picture, the one that should be a Zone III value. Then adjust the exposure to place it on a Zone III value. Next, meter the important light tone, which is normally a Zone VII, and see where it falls. Later, when you are ready to process the film, refer to your notes to assess the predominant exposure pattern. Then make any plus or minus film development decisions, basing them on what would be beneficial overall.

Zone Tonal Control with Color

Zone System exposure and development variations for contrast control work best with black and white film. Color films do not respond well to alterations in exposure and development for contrast control. But the principles of controlling the contrast range still apply to color and in many respects are much more critical.

With color negative films, find the fully detailed dark value and take a normal meter reading. Then adjust the exposure to *place* it on a Zone III. Next, you need to determine the *fall* of the fully detailed highlight value to establish the contrast range. Since development adjustments are not applicable, you either live with what you've got and struggle to make it work in the darkroom, or adjust the lighting to modify the contrast range.

Positive image transparency films present more of a problem than color negative films because exposures are much more critical with positive films. Overexposure causes an irreplaceable loss of detail in the highlights. Therefore, it is best to base exposure on the fully detailed light tone and use the fall of the dark tone to determine the contrast range. To modify the contrast range, use reflectors or supplemental lighting.

Zone System Testing

The practical use of the Zone System, beyond the basic applications previously discussed, is dependent upon extensive testing and works best with black and white film because exposure and development alterations do not work well with color materials.

Zone System testing must be done with the specific materials, methods, and working environment that you use. Change the type or speed of film, print paper, developer, or enlarger, and the tests are no longer valid and need to be redone. The tests determine the following: 1) the minimum film exposure needed to produce the first useful print density, 2) a normal film development time, 3) variations in film development time to control the contrast range through expansion and contraction, and 4) a standard printing time for the papers you use. Increasing the development time expands the contrast range. Reducing development time decreases the contrast range or compacts.

Testing results in a personal *working film speed* and a *normal developing time* (referred to as N) for that specific film. Both are very important because the manufacturer's suggested ISO and film development time are seldom the best choices. Most working professionals determine their own working film speed and normal developing time based on trial and error. The Zone System testing gets results much faster.

Once established, the working film speed and normal development time are then used for all normal shooting, provided the luminance range of the subject falls normally within the nine-stop range of the Zone System. Variations in the contrast range may be necessary if they do not fall into a normal relationship with the zone scale. Also, you may need to vary the range should you desire to personalize a photograph and expose it so that it expresses your visualization of the subject.

The testing and calibration procedures for the Zone System are complicated and extensive. However, the basic principles of the Zone System—understanding tonal relationships, contrast range, metering to determine contrast range, and basic approaches to control contrast—apply, regardless of the level of photographic endeavor. For further information on these procedures and Zone System testing, you may refer to the following handbooks: *The Zone System Craftbook* by John Charles Woods (Brown & Benchmark), *Beyond the Zone System* by Phil Davis (Brown), *The Practical Zone System* by Chris Johnson (Butterworth-Heinemann) and *The Zone System Manual* by Minor White (Morgan & Morgan).

Chapter 20

Finishing, Presentation, and Storage

It's the small things that are hard to do.

—John B. Flannagan
Sculptor

Figure 20-1

Presentation has a big impact. The black border surrounding the image is part of the photographic print, made possible by use of a filed-out negative carrier. It suggests looking *into* the photograph, as if through a window.

Untitled, Lisa Herndon.

Once your creative energy is spent and your prints are made, it is time to consider the finishing touches. Seldom is a print so clean that it doesn't need spotting. While dye enhancement gives most color prints an extra edge, the method and quality of presentation are also important. Matting and framing finish the print and give it a final context. Professionalism is expected in the presentation as much as in any other aspect of the work. If you want people to respect your work, you must respect it yourself. "Finish fetish" is a label that was used to describe the work of some Los Angeles artists in the 1960s. But the term is still relevant. A properly finished and cleanly presented photograph will have more impact than a loose print with bent corners, fingerprints, and dust spots.

The materials you use to finish, mount, mat, frame, and store your work are also important. Many materials in common use contain acids and other ingredients that are harmful to photographs. People in the field know the difference and expect anyone who is serious to use the more professional archival materials for presentation and storage. Not only will archival materials protect and extend the life of your work, they will look better too.

Spotting Black and White and Color Prints

Regardless of how careful we are, prints usually need to be spotted. Dust, scratches, water spots, and fingerprints cause white spots on prints. Film cleaner, antistatic cloths, air spray, and cotton gloves are all helpful, but inevitably some touch-up will be necessary. Spotting is the simple touch-up work that photographers do on their prints. Retouching is far more involved work and generally needs a specialist's touch. Fiber-based and matte prints of any type are the easiest to spot, and glossy surfaces are the hardest.

Black spots on prints occur from dust inside the camera or film holder, scratches on the film, air bells, or other handling problems. They are harder to remove. Most can be etched off of fiber-based prints with a sharp razor or knife. RC prints, however, can't be etched because of their plastic surface. Bleaching is the only way to remove black spots from RC and color prints. (Dye bleaching of color prints is discussed in Chapter 15, and bleaching of black and white prints with Farmer's Reducer is covered in Chapter 16.) If bleaching is not feasible, retouch the film and remake the print, or cover the spot with a white paint and then add the appropriate color dye to match the surrounding print tonality.

Figure 20-2

The thin black line surrounding the image provides framing that unifies the pictorial elements. The direction of the main figure's gaze and the triangle of bright light on the upper right would normally lead viewers' attention out of the picture, but the outline keeps attention focused on relationships within the frame. A filed-out negative carrier and a four-blade adjustable easel helped produce the delicate black edge.

Untitled, Jim Koch.

Photographic Preservation

You can increase the life of your photographs by considering a few basic conservation techniques. These techniques involve controlling the environment and materials used for the presentation and storage of your photographs. Most adhesives, tapes, rubber bands, paints, papers, wood, cardboard, mat board, plastics, and painted metals are harmful to photographic prints and films. Extremes in temperature, humidity, and prolonged contact with ultraviolet light sources cause substantial damage.

Store your negatives, transparencies, and prints in your normal living environment where conditions are fairly constant. Avoid attics and basements where temperature and humidity fluctuate and control is limited or nonexistent. If feasible, keep the relative humidity at 50 percent or below, and maintain temperatures at 70°F or below. Also avoid displaying your work in direct sunlight or under fluorescent illumination. Both are strong ultraviolet light sources and cause photographs to fade, yellow, and become brittle. They are especially harmful to color photographs, for which incandescent light is best. If ultraviolet light sources are impossible to avoid, use ultraviolet-filtering materials over windows, fluorescent tubes, and frame glass, or plexiglass with a UV inhibitor built in. Air purity is also a problem in urban areas. Chemical fumes and airborne particles can damage photographs over time.

Keep photographs contained in sealed frames, metal cabinets, and archivally safe boxes. Store them away from paint, paint fumes, plywood, cleaning supplies, and wood, which produces potentially harmful gases.

The materials used to store, mat, and frame photographs are important to consider. To be archivally safe, use materials that are chemically safe for photographs. Archival quality mat boards, mounting materials and storage materials are the most important. Most photo stores do not sell them, but they are available at art supply stores. There are also several mail-order companies that sell archival materials at very competitive prices and have excellent catalogues explaining and illustrating various archival products. These sources include *Light Impressions*, 439 Monroe Ave, P.O. Box 940, Rochester, NY 14603; *University Products*, P.O. Box 101, S. Canal St., Holyoke, MA 01041; and *Maine Photographic Resource*, 2 Central St., Rockport, ME 04856.

Archival mat boards are designed to protect photographs from damaging acids, lignins, and chemical migration. The pH level is kept high enough to resist fading, discoloration, and the embrittlement of the mat board itself. The preferred board for museum and professional use is often called museum or rag board. It is made from 100 percent cotton fibers and is available in two-ply and four-ply thicknesses. Museum board is available with approximately 3 percent calcium carbonate to serve as a buffer against chemical migration or in a nonbuffered form, which is best for chromogenic color prints, dye transfer prints, and albumen prints.

The same type of considerations apply to tapes and adhesives. They need to be acid free and manufactured not to react with other chemicals; they must also not stain, bleed through, or yellow and get brittle with age. Protective slip sheets, barrier papers, corrugated backing boards, storage envelopes, and sleeves should all be made with archival materials. Plastic enclosures should be made from polyester, polypropylene, tiacetate, and polyethylene because they are all chemically stable and pH neutral. Avoid polyvinyl chloride (PVC) because it is not stable and has plasticizers that cause deterioration. For years, film sleeves, slide sleeves, print sleeves, and photo albums were made with harmful materials. Fortunately, most manufacturers have switched to more permanent materials, but caution should still be exercised.

Presentation Considerations

Traditionally, photographs are presented in a simple, straightforward manner that sets the image off without distracting from it. Today, photographers seem less interested in conformity and more interested

Figure 20-3

Marshutz wanted to do more than just make portraits of ex-gang members. He wanted to tell their story in their own words. To achieve this unique style of presentation, he came up with a wooden box, approximately 20x24x3-inches, and covered it with stucco and graffiti. Within each piece of the series, he mounted an 8x10-inch photograph of the subject, a small motion-activated speaker, and a recording of the subject's story of life as a gang member.

"Lefty" from *The Gang Series*, Roger Marshutz.

in presentations that fit the specific context of the work. Often this means that the photographs may be large or have an unconventional size. In such cases, special matting and framing have become a necessity. Consider the following when deciding upon a method of presentation: your intent, the content of your work, the context it will be seen in, the audience, the size of the work, the print process, archival needs, protection, portability, handling, practicality, cost, salability, and, most of all, whether your work will look right.

White mats have been the preferred color for the presentation of photographs because they set the photograph off from its surroundings without distracting from it. Color mats, whether beige, brown, black, or pink affect the way viewers responds to the photograph. People who use color mats and frames do so for decorative purposes, such as to match the couch, the drapes, or some secondary color in a picture. Remember, though, that colors evoke associations and emotions that may have nothing to do with your photograph. Consequently, the type of framing and matting *are* important considerations and can make or break a photograph. Also important is how your photographs function as a group. It is generally best to choose a presentation that will let the photographs function individually as well as in a collection. This is a

A.

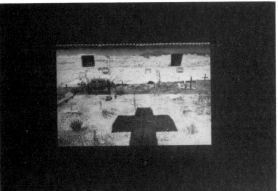

Figure 20-4
The feeling of a photograph changes with the color and value of the mat and frame surrounding it. White mats are used most often because they tend not to impact a viewer's response to a picture, while black or other colors cause a definite mood change.

major consideration, especially important should you have an opportunity to exhibit your work.

Permanent Print Mounting Techniques

After a print has been spotted, it is ready for the final stages of presentation—mounting onto a stiff support. The most common methods are dry mounting with a heat press, cold mounting, laminating, and wet mounting.

Dry Mounting

Dry mounting is a surface mounting technique that is done with a resin-impregnated tissue and heat press. Dry-mount tissue is placed between the print and the mounting board. When the materials are pressed with even heat in the dry-mount press, the resin melts, adhering the print to the mount board. Both RC and fiber-based prints can be dry mounted. This method may be used for color prints too, with the exception of the polyester-based Ilfochrome Classic Deluxe, which does not respond well to heat mounting. With RC papers, use a temperature between 180 and 200°F, and keep the print in the press for 10 to 20 seconds. Fiber-based papers will need 30 to 40 seconds to adhere. Check the manufacturer's instructions for the particular product you are using to ensure a quality result.

The first step before trimming your print is to attach the dry-mount tissue to the back of the print with a hot tacking iron. To begin, place

Figure 20-5

Becerra's color light-painting techniques allow him to explore the relationships of cultures past and present on an intensely personal level. Framing and total presentation of the work relate to the cultural context of his pictures. Failing to find satisfactory commercially made frames, Becerra designed his own, which echo the strong Mexican tradition of craftsmanship with metal and tin.

The Gods That Haunt Me, Raymundo Becerra.

the print face down on a clean, flat surface and lay a sheet of dry-mount tissue on it, aligning at least two edges. Take the tacking iron and place it on the tissue in the center of the print. Apply gentle pressure, moving the tacking iron slightly for several seconds until a portion of the tissue about the size of a nickel adheres to the back of the print.

Then, trim the tissue and the print simultaneously, getting rid of the white borders and any other extraneous part of the photograph. Trim with a paper cutter or a metal straight edge and a razor blade or knife. Make sure that the print and backing come out even on all four sides. Otherwise, problems may occur in the mounting if they are trimmed unevenly.

Once the print is trimmed, position it on the mat board. Normally, it is best to leave a 3- to 4-inch–wide border around the print, depending upon the size of the print. For prints 16x20 inches and larger, consider an even wider border. Many photographers prefer to have the top and sides even, with a little more space at the bottom. There is no set rule. Look at other work to get a better feeling for what will work best with your images. After positioning the print, make some light pencil marks as a reference to ensure that the print doesn't slip out of place. Then lift a corner of the print, leaving the dry-mount tissue in contact with the mounting board. Make sure that the print is still positioned properly, take the tacking iron and, with an outward motion, attach that corner of the tissue to the mounting board. Do this to all four sides, making sure that the tacking iron never touches the print or the surface of the mounting board. The tacking iron can damage RC prints and leave marks on the mounting board.

Figure 20-6
Matted print with borders.

The photograph is now ready to be inserted into the press. Place the board, print side up, onto the pad of the press and cover the face of the print with a large, clean sheet of paper. Cover the *entire surface* of the photograph with paper because the print must *never* touch the heated metal of the press. The time that the press remains closed on the print will depend on the weight of the board, the press being used, the thickness of the cover sheet, and the type of tissue. Check the instructions on the tissue package and experiment a little. Generally, though, the time is between 15 and 30 seconds.

Another popular method of mounting is called bleed mounting. With this method, the white borders of the board are trimmed so that the edges of the board and the print are even. After the print is mounted in the usual way, the borders of the board are cut off, using a metal straightedge (ruler) and a mat knife. Be sure you have a sharp blade, or your cut will be ragged. Do not attempt to cut through both the print and board in one stroke. Rather, use a series of light strokes until the excess border is separated. Don't try to pull apart a partially cut board—it will leave an unsightly rough edge.

Problems that frequently occur with dry mounting are dirt particles on the metal plate of the mounting press, dirt particles under the mounted print, air bubbles, overheating (which melts RC surfaces), and the tissue not adhering.

Dirt is the easiest problem to take care of. Keep the platen (metal plate) of the mounting press clean and free of dirt particles. Dirt particles on the platen will cause indentations in the surface of your print. If you are using a community or school press and cannot be sure that the platen is free of dirt particles, try using a piece of mat board as a cover sheet. This will mean that you need to leave the print in the press

Figure 20-7

The dry mounting process.

(A) Use the tacking iron with light pressure to attach the dry-mount tissue to the back of the print. The area attached needs to be no bigger than a nickel.

(B) Trim the borders off the print once the tissue and print are attached. Make sure they are trimmed evenly.

(C) Position the print face-up on the mounting board. While holding the print in position, lift one corner of it and use the tacking iron to attach the corner of the tissue to the backing board. Repeat this procedure until all four corners of the tissue are tacked to the mounting board.

(D) Then place the mounting board with the attached tissue and print into the mounting press. Make sure that a cover sheet is on top of the print to protect it from direct contact with the hot platen of the press.

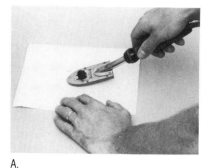

A.

B.

C.

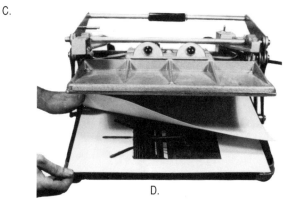

D.

longer, but the mat board, rather than your print, will absorb the surface indentations. Heat the mounting board in the press before using it to expel moisture. Specks of dirt trapped under the print after it's been mounted appear as little lumps in the surface. These can be avoided by keeping the print and the working area clean.

Air bubbles appear as blisters on the print. They are usually caused by moisture in the board. If the problem occurs often, place the bare mounting board in the press for several seconds before tacking the photograph into place. This step will remove the moisture from the board and should alleviate the problem. Always time how long the print is in the press. Too much heat can melt RC prints and shorten the life of fiber-based prints. It can also cause the tissue not to stick or the edges of the print to curl up.

Cold Mounting

Adhesives for cold mounting prints have improved tremendously in recent years. Many are considered permanent and safe alternatives to hot press mounting. Cold mounting is also a good alternative for mounting the polyester-based Ilfochrome Classic Deluxe glossy prints, which do not respond well to hot press mounting. Exercise caution, however, and only use those products that indicate they are safe for the *long-term* mounting of photographs. Many products are good only for *short-term* needs, and some, such as rubber cement, are extremely harmful to photographs.

The four most common types of cold-mounting are spray adhesives, transfer adhesives, two-sided adhesive sheets, and laminating.

Spray adhesives are better used for short-term rather than long-term needs. Use them in a well-ventilated environment and hold the spray about 10 inches above the back of the print paper. Coat it evenly in one direction and then again from another direction. Let the adhesive sit momentarily to become tacky, and then lift the print and place it on to the mounting board. Start in the center of the print and use a roller or your hand to burnish it down securely and force out any air pockets. (A piece of acid-free paper should be placed on top of the print prior to pressing down on it, especially by hand.)

Transfer adhesives are attached to a carrier sheet. The print is positioned on top of the carrier sheet in contact with the adhesive. When the print is lifted, the adhesive comes with it and the print can then be attached to the mount board. Many of these adhesives are positionable, which means they do not adhere until pressure is applied, making it possible to adjust the positioning.

Two-sided adhesive sheets have adhesive on both sides of a carrier sheet. A cover sheet is removed and the print is positioned onto one side of the adhesive sheet and pressed down to ensure a firm contact. This "sandwich" is then positioned onto the mounting board, and the cover sheet on the bottom side of the adhesive sheet is pulled out so that the adhesive will have contact with the mounting board. Even pressure is applied from the center out, to ensure firm and lasting contact.

Laminating requires costly special equipment and uses very thin, crystal clear adhesive sheets to attach a print to a support board between

Laguna Open, Damon Nicholson.

Figure 20-8

To heighten the action in this photograph, Nicholson made several extra prints, cut them into strips, and then mounted them together—in sequence. To mount the strips, he used a positionable transfer adhesive, making it easy to handle the separate strips of paper.

layers of transparent materials. It is mainly a service offered by professional labs and is used widely in the commercial industry. Laminating is also the most practical way to mount large prints. It is considered a safe and permanent procedure and provides a protective surface coating for prints. A variety of laminates with differing surface characteristics are available. Some include a UV (ultraviolet) inhibitor to reduce fading of color materials.

Wet Mounting

Mural prints were traditionally mounted with liquid glues until laminating became a more practical method. Today, liquid adhesives are seldom used, but they remain an approach worth considering because wet mounting of large prints is far less expensive than laminating. The

The Tell, Mark Chamberlain and Jerry Burchfield.

Figure 20-9

Wet mounting with white glue on plywood panels was used for this outdoor photo mural consisting of over 100,000 individual photographs. Color and black and white images were collaged to form metaphorical references to change. Because of daily assault by sunlight and ocean air, the color images faded to an overall yellow cast during the 8 months the mural was exhibited outside. The black and white images stayed basically the same.

disadvantage is messiness, and RC prints do not adhere well. For wet mounting, it is best to use a plastic, metal, or wood mounting board because mat board will not be solid enough. Techniques requiring print borders big enough to wrap around the back of the support board work well because they hold better. Most glues are bad for photographs, but some white glues, wheat paste, and bookbinding glues are safe. Investigate the glues available at your local art supply store or refer to the mail-order outlets previously mentioned in this chapter.

Nonpermanent Mounting Techniques and Overmatting

Most museums and serious collectors prefer nonpermanent print mounting techniques and window overmats. They find permanent mounts a problem because mats get abused and add to storage problems. If a print is removable, the mat can be replaced if it gets damaged, or it can be reused for another print. Most nonpermanent mounting techniques either use photo corners or hinge prints with archival tape. Window overmats are used to hide corners and tape, as well as to provide a finished, professional look. Not only do overmats look better than a plain surface mount, they also provide surface protection. The cutout window creates an air space between print surface and frame glass that insulates the print and precludes possible damage from direct contact with the glass.

Hinge Mounting

Archival linen tape or rice paper and glue are used for hinge mounting of photographs. For 16×20-inch prints or smaller, use T type hinges. Cut four pieces of tape or rice paper about 1 inch long. Attach two of them to the back of the print, at the top, on both sides, so that about half to three-fourths of the tape is sticking up above the top edge of the print. Turn the print faceup and position it on to the backing board. Then, take the two remaining pieces of tape and tape the pieces that stick up from the back of the print to the backing board. The window overmat, which is hinged at the top with linen tape to the backing board, will hold the rest of the print flat. The weight of large prints may in time cause the print to warp where hinged. Even weight distribution is needed. To avoid the problem of uneven distribution, use tape wide enough to make one continuous hinge all the way across the top of the print.

Using Photo Corners

Commercial photo corners are available, some of which are archival, but many photographers make their own photo corners from pH-neutral paper, such as museum barrier paper. Cut narrow strips of paper about 1 to 2 inches long. The width depends upon the widths of the print borders. A half-inch-wide photo corner gives good support, but the print borders and overmat have to be planned with that width in mind. The strips of paper are folded over, as illustrated, and placed over the corners of the print. Then pieces of linen tape are used to attach the photo corner to the backing board. For prints 16×20-inches and larger, use a T hinge at the top center of the print to ensure that it does not slip out of the photo corners when handled. The corners are then covered by the window overmat.

Window Overmats

A window overmat provides a finished professional look while providing extra protection to the print surface. Sometimes artists add a second overmat, with the window cut slightly larger than the first to add visual depth to the presentation. Special decorative cuts are also done, but most of the time a straight cut with a beveled edge is enough. If you are using museum board, make sure that you get a four-ply board to have enough thickness.

Paying to have mats cut gets expensive, and professional mat cutters are too high priced to be warranted for occasional use. Several inexpensive hand mat cutters can do an excellent job, however. Available at most art supply stores, the two most common brands are Dexter and Logan. Additional supplies include a metal straightedge, fine sandpaper, a burnishing bone, and lots of extra blades. A single blade is good for about two 8x10-inch windows. Then it needs to be replaced to avoid rough edges. Follow the instructions that come with the mat cutter and practice on scrap board before trying good board. Practice will bring mastery.

Framing Considerations

Traditionally, photographers have used simple, unadorned frames, in contrast to painters who sometimes use elaborate framing. A frame is a part of the piece and will influence viewer reaction to the work. Print sales are always better when artwork is framed. People like to see the work in a finished form.

Frames also protect the work. For maximum protection, a print should be framed under glass or plexiglass and be sealed in the back

Figure 20-10

A Logan mat cutter and a metal straightedge are being used here to cut a beveled window overmat.

to keep out dust and air contamination. Overmats should be used to keep prints from having direct contact with the glass or plexi. Some frames are available with spacers or setbacks for bleed mounts or prints hinged to float in the frame. The spacers and setbacks provide an air space between the print and the glass. Avoid nonglare glass. In theory it is good, but in actuality it mutes the print and changes its appearance and impact.

The frame should work with the picture, but there are no set rules. Since the 1980s, when photography became more prominent in contemporary art, framing of photographs has become more sophisticated. This does not mean that it has to be expensive or imitative of styles used for painting, it just means that framing must be considered a part of the work. Homemade options still can work provided that they extend—rather than limit—the life of the work.

Storage and Care of Film and Prints

To preserve your film and prints, whether they be family records or important artworks, you need to follow the basic considerations discussed throughout this chapter. Unexposed photographic materials will lose contrast, speed, and color over time unless they are refrigerated. Processed film and prints will also change unless properly cared for. Archival materials should be used for storage. Heat, moisture, and UV light should be avoided.

Unexposed films should remain in their original packages until ready to use. Many films come supplied in vapor-tight packaging that protects the film against humidity. However, vapor-tight packaging is not heat proof. For most films during the summer heat, with temperatures over 75°F (24°C) for extended periods, refrigeration is recommended, provided the film remains sealed in its vapor-tight package. To avoid condensation on the cold film, remove it from the refrigerator 1½ hours before you plan to use it.

Unexposed film should be used well before the expiration date printed on the package. This is especially important for high-speed color and black and white films.

Airport X-ray machines can fog unprocessed film when the radiation level is high or when the film receives several low-level doses. The effect of this exposure is cumulative. These X rays are particularly damaging to high-speed films. Although alternatives are not possible in all airports, passengers can usually avoid this problem by hand-carrying their film and loaded cameras and requesting a visual rather than an X-ray inspection. Carry the film in a clear plastic bag to help simplify the inspection. Also, containers that shield film from X rays are available in most photo supply stores. Film that has been processed, however, is not affected by airport X rays. In any case, never put unprocessed film into baggage that you are not carrying on the plane because the machines used to X-ray that type of baggage are stronger than the other type.

If the vapor-tight film package has been opened, the film is no longer protected from the effects of humidity or harmful gases. Thus, use the film and process it promptly after the package has been opened. Do not store opened packages of film in damp basements, refrigerators, or freezers, where the humidity is high.

Storage and Care of Processed Color Film and Prints

Unlike the images of most black and white photographs, which are composed of metallic silver, the images in color photographs are formed by dyes. Time will cause an alteration in all dyes so that, in effect, no color print, negative, or slide is truly permanent. Nevertheless, precautions can be taken to extend their life. First, store processed color films and color prints in a dark, dry, cool place. Never store processed films or prints in damp basements or in hot attics. Places with a humidity between 30 and 50 percent and a temperature of 70°F (21°C) or below are satisfactory. However, avoid relative humidty below 30 percent because brittleness of the photographic paper may occur. High humidity, above 60 percent, should also be avoided since this may promote the growth of fungus.

Color slides and negatives can be stored in metal file boxes and drawers, which will help prevent light from causing deterioration of the dyes. Do not use wood or plastic file boxes because these materials may contain substances that are harmful over the long term.

Color slides are intended for projection. However, the light and heat of high-wattage lamps can shorten the life of the color and even cause warping of the slide mount. Therefore, avoid projecting a slide for over a minute. Slides that are frequently projected should be glass-mounted to prevent warping.

Color prints can be stored in archival boxes or photo albums. Make sure that the materials used to make the album are recommended for archival storage. Many of the inexpensive "magnetic" type albums do not meet this requirement. Remember: It's important to keep the album in rooms free of contaminants and out of direct sunlight, where temperatures and humidity are within the recommended levels discussed earlier.

Chapter 21

A History of Photography

Today everything exists to end in a photograph.

—Susan Sontag

Writer

Photography, though based on a natural phenomenon, is not natural—it had to be invented. Its evolution over hundreds of years was much like assembling a jigsaw puzzle—one person would make a small discovery, and years later another would build upon that discovery. Eventually all the pieces fit together. Today, photography is so ingrained in our culture that it is surprising it took so long to evolve.

The First Camera

No one knows who constructed the first camera, referred to as the *camera obscura*, a Latin phrase meaning dark chamber. The principle of the camera obscura was known to the Arabian scholar, Ibn Al Haitham before 1038. In its basic form, the camera obscura was literally

Pepper No. 30, Edward Weston, 1930.

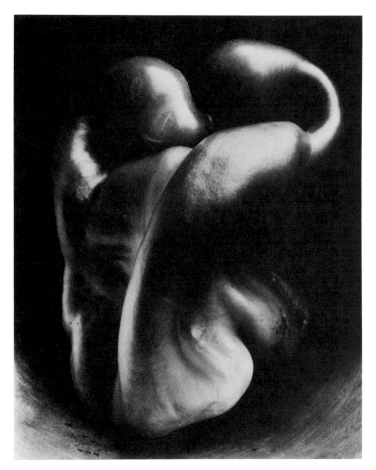

Figure 21-1

The work of Edward Weston exemplifies the purest tradition of straight photography. Mainly using an 8x10 view camera and contact printing his images by means of a light bulb hanging from the ceiling, he produced some of the most important photography of the twentieth century. His interest in discovering the essence of things through photography resulted in photographs that transcended subject matter.

Camera obscura.

a dark chamber or room. Light passing through a small hole at one end of the room formed an image on the opposite wall. This image was not sharp because no lenses were attached to the opening in the wall. What was noted, however, was that the smaller the hole, the sharper the image (as in pinhole photography). In 1558, Giovanni Pattista della Porta described the camera obscura at length. He was also the first to suggest that the camera obscura be used as a guide for drawing, and it is for this idea that he is remembered. The application of lenses to the camera obscura (by 1550) increased both the sharpness and brightness of the image and led to further investigations into design and construction.

As interest in the camera obscura grew, the chamber became a box and its size diminished until, finally, it became more or less portable. Artists and architects could use it in rendering perspective correctly. In 1676, the first "reflect" camera appeared—one in which the image was reflected onto a top-mounted viewing screen by an inclined mirror behind the lens. All the artist had to do was put a piece of tracing paper on top of the viewing screen and trace the outline. Thus, the camera became one of the artist's tools.

Photographic Chemistry

Photographic chemistry came rather late in the long history of the development of the camera. Photographic chemistry refers to the use of a light sensitive material to form an emulsion. The first important discovery was made by Johann Heinrich Schulze, a German physicist at the University of Altdorf, near Nuremberg, Germany.

In 1725, Schulze saturated chalk with nitric acid that contained some silver. Exposing this mixture to the sun, Schulze was amazed to discover that the mixture facing the sun turned dark violet, but the portion turned away from the sun remained white. At first, he believed that the darkening was due to the mixture of chalk and nitric acid, but he failed to repeat this experiment. Some time later, he remembered that the mixture had contained silver, as well as chalk and nitric acid. Finally realizing that it was the silver and nitric acid that caused the darkening by light, Schulze prepared ever more concentrated solutions until he was able to form words on the bottles containing the solutions by stenciling out letters and exposing the bottles to direct sunlight. Although Schulze mentioned that it was possible to spread the silver solution on skin, bone, and wood to produce images, he did not do it. At this time, there was no way to make these stencils permanent, and they soon faded away.

The Permanent Image

The next important discovery was made by the Swedish chemist Carl Wilhelm Scheele. He confirmed one of Schulze's discoveries: that the blackening effect of the silver salts was due to light and not to heat. To prove this idea, he spread the white compound on paper and exposed it to the sun for two weeks, during which the paper turned completely black. Scheele then poured ammonia on the powder and discovered that the blackened silver was metallic silver and had become insoluble in ammonia; that is, the ammonia did not dissolve the exposed silver. The ammonia, in other words, acted as a fixer. Scheele did not realize the importance of his discovery—the ability to make a photographic image permanent. Nor did Scheele conceive the idea of photography, an honor reserved for an Englishman, Thomas Wedgewood.

Thomas Wedgewood, the youngest son of Josiah, the famous potter, grew up in a scientific atmosphere. The exact dates of his experiments in photography are not known, although they are presumed to have been around 1800. Wedgewood did not succeed in making the images he exposed through a camera obscura permanent, so none survive today. Although Wedgewood was familiar with Scheele's work, neither Wedgewood nor Scheele realized the importance of the ammonia fixer. Wedgewood was the first, however, to conceive the idea of photography with the use of a portable camera obscura.

The earliest known permanent camera image done from nature was made by a French scientist, Joseph Nicéphore Niépce, at his family's estate near Chalon-sur-Saône in 1826. This culmination of an experi-

View from His Window at Gras, Joseph Nicéphore Niépce, 1826.

Figure 21-2

This image of a courtyard is considered the world's first photographic image. Niepce created it by covering a sheet of pewter with bitumen of Judea, a substance like asphalt that hardened when exposed to light, and exposing it for eight hours in a camera obscura. he dissolved the still soft unexposed parts of the image with lavender oil, leaving a permanent image, which he called a heliograph.

ment begun years earlier ushered in the long history of contributions to the development of photography. Niépce was an inventor who did work with lithography, a process dating from 1796 whereby a drawing made with a grease pencil on limestone can be printed on paper many times over. Originating as a method of reproduction, by 1813 lithography became an art form in its own right. After the drawing is made on the limestone, the stone must be treated with chemicals before it is ready to use for printing.

Niépce's son Isidore made the drawings on the lithographer's stone while Niépce attended to the chemical process. They soon switched to using pewter instead of stone (the material on which the first photograph was made) because limestone was difficult to get locally. After Isidore joined the army, a problem arose because Niépce could not draw. Niépce then began to seek a way to make the action of light etch pictures into the pewter plates.

Heliography

Niépce did not set out to make a photograph. He set out to make a *photo lithograph* to reproduce copies of drawings and paintings. He succeeded in 1822, calling his process heliography (sunwriting). In 1826 Niépce made the first permanent photograph from nature using a camera obscura. This heliograph was made on a pewter plate, and it took eight hours to record the image!

In that same year, Niépce received a letter from a Parisian painter, Louis Jacques Mandé Daguerre, who worked primarily with oils. Daguerre mentioned that he, too, had been working with light images and asked Niépce about his progress. Niépce was at first very cautious in replying to Daguerre, but after Daguerre visited him and the two men corresponded further, they formed a partnership in 1829.

During this time, both Niépce and Daguerre sought a color process. Niépce went so far as to say to his brother Claude, "But I must succeed in fixing the colors." Their partnership, however, did not produce any noticeable improvement in making photography practicable. In 1833, Niépce—the inventor of photography—died.

Daguerre made photography practical. He improved the black and white (monochrome) process so much that he named it the *Daguerreotype* and gave up the search for a color process in the belief that someone would discover a means to capture color once his process became public. In August 1839, the French government honored Daguerre with a life pension and gave to the world, as public property, the daguerreotype process—everywhere, that is, except England, where Daguerre had secretly patented it.

Portrait, subject unknown, J. Sidney Miller, Photographer, c. 1854.

Figure 21-3

Portraiture was the most popular application of the daguerreotype. Most portraits were made with multiple-lens cameras. A full plate (6 1/2 × 8 1/2 inches) could be used to make a series of portraits. This image was a one-sixth plate daguerreotype.

The Daguerreotype

The process of Daguerre involved a sheet of copper plated with silver—the silver surface being well cleaned and highly polished. The silver surface was exposed to iodine vapor in a small box until the surface became golden yellow. The sensitized surface was then placed in a camera obscura, where it remained for five or six minutes. It was then taken from the camera and developed in a vapor derived from mercury. Then the plate was washed and dried, after which it was placed in a case with a sheet of glass over the daguerreotype to protect its surface, which was very easy to rub off the plate.

A well-exposed daguerreotype is possibly the most beautiful form of photography. It possesses brilliance because of the silver surface and shows detail far better than any modern paper print. Of course, there are some serious defects in a daguerreotype. The image can be seen only when it is held in a certain position; otherwise it simply reflects light over its surface because of its mirrorlike quality. Another defect of the daguerreotype was that only one image could be made from each exposure.

Even with these defects, the daguerreotype was the most important photographic process for more than fifteen years, especially in the United States, where many improvements were made. The most important improvement was a shorter exposure time to make the image. At first, the exposure time needed to make a daguerreotype was 5 to 20 minutes—too long to make portraits feasible. By the end of 1840, however, several Americans had made significant improvements so that exposure time was cut to a few seconds. This reduction, of course, made portraits possible, and by 1841 the first chain of portrait galleries was opened by John Plumbe. Among those who taught the art of the daguerreotype was Samuel F. B. Morse, the inventor of the telegraph, who had met Daguerre in Paris while demonstrating his invention.

Morse's students included Edward Anthony, who started the photographic supply house E. Anthony and Company (which later became Ansco and now is known as GAF); Albert S. Southworth, who started the firm of Southworth and Hawes and was the best of the daguerrian artists; and Mathew Brady, who opened his own chain of daguerrian galleries (and, of course, documented the Civil War). Because of his teaching record, Morse became known as the founder of American photography.

The Calotype

People worldwide praised Daguerre and his invention, except one: William Henry Fox Talbot. This English country gentleman saw Daguerre's method as a threat to his own process, the Talbotype—or, as it was known later, the calotype. Talbot began his experiments in 1834 after returning from Italy, where he drew landscapes. His first successful photographic images, made in 1835, were of leaves and lace laid down on sensitized paper and fixed in salt water, which was also Daguerre's first method. (These are negative images on paper, today referred to as *photograms*.) Talbot made little progress in the next three years because his attention was diverted to other matters. It was not until he heard of the impending announcement of Daguerre's method that he sought his own place of honor. His actions from then on appear not to have been those of an English gentleman.

Less than two weeks after the French government had released the news of the daguerreotype, Talbot visited John Frederick William Her-

Figure 21-4

Between 1843 and 1847, painter David Octavious Hill and photographer Robert Adamson made the first extensive use of Talbot's calotype process, producing 450 portraits of the delegates who founded the Free Church of Scotland. The photographs, intended to be used for a composite painting, became more important as photographs.

Hill and Adamson, Calotype print, c. 1845.

schel, a prominent mathematician, astronomer, and chemist who was interested in photography from a chemist's viewpoint. Herschel, a generous man, told Talbot in detail about a chemical he had invented, which he called hyposulphite of soda. This chemical, still in use and known as fixer, makes photographic negatives and prints permanent. Talbot, on the other hand, revealed nothing of his process. He immediately put Herschel's "hypo" to use, and when Talbot wrote to the French government of his method, Daguerre immediately applied it to his own process.

Herschel not only discovered fixer, but he also coined the word *photography*, which comes from the Greek words meaning "light writing." Herschel used the term to differentiate between Talbot's negative paper prints and Daguerre's positive image method that used copper plates.

The calotype process could not compete with the daguerreotype for several reasons. Perhaps the worst stumbling block in its evolution was Talbot himself, who patented the process and its improvements, but who sold them upon receipt of a large amount of money. However, Talbot must receive credit for inventing the photographic process we use today—the negative-positive relationship.

In 1847, eight years after Daguerre and Talbot had made public their discoveries and fourteen years after Joseph Niépce had died, a cousin of the later, Abel Niépce de Saint-Victor, invented a process for sensitizing a glass plate with an emulsion of silver iodide and fresh, whipped

eggwhite (albumen). The mixture, though not very sensitive to light, was capable of rendering fine detail and good tone, which the calotype negative was unable to do. Talbot patented a slight modification of this albumen-on-glass process in 1849, even though this method used a glass negative instead of—as with his calotype—a paper negative.

The Origins of Color Photography

The first color photographs made their appearance within a year after the daguerreotype became public. They were hand-colored black and white daguerreotypes. As yet, no one had discovered a way to make actual color photographs. But the search for a color process continued. Niépce de Saint-Victor, Sir John Herschel, and others found ways to record red, blue, and green colors on silver-chloride–coated materials, but they were unable to make them permanent. In 1851, Levi Hill, a Baptist minister from Westkill, New York, announced that he had perfected a color daguerreotype process. The prospect of a color photographic process on the horizon prompted a drop in the portrait business because everyone wanted to wait until they could get their pictures in color. Six years later Hill published his method, but to everyone's frustration, it turned out to be an accidental combination of elements, which neither Hill, nor anyone else, could repeat.

That light is the source of color had been known since 1666, when Sir Isaac Newton passed a beam of light through a prism, separating the colors that make up the visible spectrum. But a practical solution to photography in color came about slowly. In 1861, British physicist James Clerk Maxwell performed an experiment to prove his theory that red, blue, and green are the primary colors of light and that any color could be recreated through mixing varying proportions of these primaries.

Maxwell hired a photographer to shoot three black and white negatives of a colorful plaid (tartan) ribbon. One was shot through a red filter, another through a blue filter, and the third through a green filter. This produced what we now call separation negatives. These were then contact printed onto film to create three film positives, one for each color. The three film positives were then projected so that the images overlapped onto a screen. Red, blue, and green filters were placed in front of the lens of each projector to match up with the black and white images that had been made through that filter. The result was a crude, but realistic color photograph of the tartan ribbon. The iodized collodion film used for Maxwell's experiment was not sensitive to red light, and scientists were puzzled as to how he got any result. A hundred years later, when Maxwell's experiment was recreated it was found that the dyes in the tartan ribbon fluoresced, and it was because of this fluorescence that he got a red record. Regardless, Maxwell opened the door to further investigations of color photography, and once panchromatic films (black and white films sensitive to all colors of light) were invented, color photography moved forward, utilizing Maxwell's results. Color systems based on the combination of the three primaries to create color are referred to as *additive* systems.

In 1869, two Frenchmen, Louis Ducos du Hauron and Charles Cros, unbeknownst to each other, simultaneously announced a *subtractive* system for creating color images. Their system was based on using cyan, yellow, and magenta, the complimentary, or opposite, colors of the primaries. Cros was a friend of the Impressionist painters and interested in color theory, whereas du Hauron was interested in working out a practical color process. By 1877, after the introduction of panchromatic film, du Hauron perfected the *carbon process*, which led to the *carbro* and *dye transfer* processes, both of which have been extensively used in this century. He also developed color lithography, the method used to print color images on a printing press.

Carbon, carbro, and dye transfer all require separation negatives and are technically complicated processes. Today, only a handful of people make carbon and carbro prints, and dye transfer is slowly dying as newer more practical processes have evolved.

The Wet-Collodion Process

Another important invention was made by an English sculptor, Frederick Scott Archer. Archer learned the calotype process in 1847 and decided to improve it. In March of 1851, he gave the world the "wet collodion" negative. A glass plate had to be cleaned, after which iodized collodion was poured onto the plate, which was then immersed in a silver-nitrate bath and put into the camera while still wet. Development had to be performed before the plate dried, and because of this, it became known as the wet-plate process. Again, Talbot claimed that the wet-plate process was an infringement upon his calotype patent, and he prosecuted anyone who didn't buy a license from him for using it. Finally, in December 1854, the courts found Talbot's claim illegal and released the process.

By 1858, the wet-collodion process was replacing the daguerreotype. One variation, known as the ambrotype. (An ambrotype is an underexposed wet-collodion negative on glass. When the ambrotype is mounted against a black backing, it appears like a positive.) Ambrotypes did not match the tonal range of a daguerreotype. However, because they were quicker to make, they became popular. Like daguerreotypes, ambrotypes could not be duplicated, so copies could not be made.

The tintype was a variant of the ambrotype. Originally called a ferrotype or melainotype, it produced a positive image, usually on a thin sheet of iron (though some were made on leather and other materials). Tintypes were cheaper and easier to make than ambrotypes, and they were unbreakable. However, they lacked the tonal range of an ambrotype. Tintypes were made by the millions up to modern times.

Another popular image in the 1850s, along with the ambrotype, was the *carte de visite*, a photographic visiting card. The fad began in France but soon was found almost everywhere: small photographs, the size of a business card, with a portrait or scene mounted to a cardboard backing. *Cartes de visite* were made from a wet-plate negative, so many prints could be produced. Because they were cheap, their popularity was enormous. (By 1860 ambrotype, tintypes, and *cartes de visite* made daguerreotypes a thing of the past.)

Roll Film

By 1880, the *wet* plate became dry, and thus a picture could be exposed and then developed weeks later. An amateur photographer of this period, George Eastman, became interested in the manufacture of dry plates. In December 1880, the Anthony Company (GAF today) began the sale of the Eastman dry plates. Some people, however, began to dream of a flexible film. On September 4, 1888, Eastman patented a camera that was loaded with a roll of flexible film capable of 100 exposures. The camera sold for $25, and its slogan was "You press the button; we do the rest." It was named the Kodak.

When the 100 pictures were taken, the camera was mailed to the company, where (for $10) the film was removed and processed, prints were made, fresh film was reloaded, and the camera was returned to the sender with the finished prints.

The idea caught on, and in no time "Kodak" was a household name. Photography was now within the reach of everyone.

Advances in Color Photography

Not until the early twentieth century did true color processes become available. The most popular of these was the *autochrome*, invented in

Figure 21-5

Postmortem, tintype, unknown American photographer, c. 1880.

Figure 21-6

This snapshot from a No. 1 Kodak roll camera, photographer unknown, dates from about 1889.

France by Auguste and Louis Lumière, and introduced commercially in 1907. The American photographic pioneers Alfred Stieglitz and Edward Steichen used autochrome as did the photographers for the National Geographic Society, which published images of people from different cultures, forever altering perceptions of what the world was like.

An autochrome is a glass plate coated with tiny grains of potato starch dyed blue-violet, green, and red. The grains were flattened by rollers and dusted with a black powder to fill any cracks. The plates was then coated with a protective layer of varnish. On top of this, a panchromatic emulsion was applied. Because the autochrome plate was made up of tiny grains, the images produced resembled the paintings of post-impressionist painters.

The innovative aspect of the autochrome process was that it was a *reversal process*. Unlike earlier processes that used similar *screen* systems, autochrome was reversed from a negative image to a positive image during development by being reexposed to light. This eliminated intermediate steps and gave a direct positive color image, similar in concept to the color slides and transparencies of today. Dufaycolor and Afgacolor were other screen processes like autochrome, all of which were available for roll film cameras and in use until the early 1930s.

As the advertising and publishing industry grew, photographers relied on the finer resolutions of the carbro and dye transfer processes. They produced separation negatives in large "one-shot" cameras that used mirrors to allow them to expose three black and white color separation negatives in one shot.

The first practical and easy-to-use color film was not produced until 1935. This was *Kodachrome*, which was invented by two musicians turned scientists, Leopold Mannes and Leopold Godowsky, Jr. Based on the 1912 invention of *dye coupling* by Rudolf Fischer, Kodachrome is a reversal film (a positive image transparency film) consisting of three separate emulsions on one support. Each emulsion layer is sensitive to a primary color and uses complementary color dyes to keep the colors segregated. The processing involves complex machinery and cannot be done by hand. Initially a negative image is formed, and then each layer is reversed to a positive image by separate red, blue, and green exposures of light. Subsequently, cyan, yellow, and magenta dyes are formed in place of the primary red, blue, and green, and the silver is bleached away. All modern color films and print processes are descended from this technological breakthrough.

Kodacolor, the first color negative film, was introduced in 1941. It opened the door to the color snapshot, which by the late 1960s became the predominant form of photography. In response to the need for a color transparency film that could be easily processed, Ansco offered

Ansco-Color and Kodak introduced *Ektachrome* color transparency film in 1942.

Color print processes followed the invention of color films. Kodak introduced a positive-to-positive color print process shortly after the introduction of Kodachrome. But contrast problems made this process hard to control, and with the invention of Kodacolor, a film designed specifically for printing, color negative films soon became the primary means for making color prints.

In 1933, a transparency printing process called *Gasparcolor* was invented. Although impractical at the time, it was later refined and reintroduced as *Cibachrome* in 1963 and became extremely popular in the mid 1970s. Cibachrome, now called *Ilfochrome*, became popular with commercial and fine art photographers because of its sharpness, color saturation, and permanence. It was also less expensive than dye transfer, yet provided similar options for retouching and manipulation that other print processes lacked. During the 1970s, other color processes were simplified, and color processing tubes were introduced, making home processing practical for the first time. This led to a boom in the acceptance and use of color photography.

Instant Photography

In 1947, Dr. Edwin Land invented instant photography and introduced the first Polaroid camera, which produced a sepia monochrome print in just 60 seconds. Though its product was initially considered a novelty, Polaroid went on to become an important manufacturer and innovative proponent of photography. In 1962, Polacolor was introduced, providing instant color prints. In 1972, Polaroid again revolutionized photography with its introduction of the SX-70 camera, which brought the magic of watching an image form into broad daylight. The film popped out of the front of the camera and the image formed as you watched it. The SX-70 became instantly popular with snapshooters. In the mid-70s, a well-known New York painter and assemblage artist, Lucas Samaras, began moving the SX-70 emulsion around as it developed; manipulation and artificial applications of color photography in the arts came of age. Shortly thereafter, William Eggleston's more traditional dye transfer color images were shown at the Museum of Modern Art in New York, the museum's first acknowledgment of the importance of color photography.

Polaroid became a major supporter of the photographic arts, providing materials and grants to artists. In the late 1970s, Polaroid introduced

the 20x24- and 40x80-inch Polaroid cameras and provided many artists with an opportunity to use the process in exchange for prints. In 1983, Polaroid introduced instant 35mm color and black and white slide films. Throughout the eighties, John Rueter worked as the technician for the 20x24 cameras and the artist-support program. Through his personal work and exploration, Rueter developed a procedure for transferring Polarcolor emulsions onto other papers, such as watercolor papers. This advance became extremely popular with both artists and the advertising industry.

Directions and Movements in Photography

"Give the people what they want," is an old saying. Without question, people have always wanted portraits: portraits of themselves, portraits of family members and friends, even portraits of people they did not know. Although early portraiture required the sitter to remain still for several seconds, people still flocked to the galleries, which were springing up everywhere.

Portraits done in American before 1855 were generally daguerreotypes. The daguerreotypist, or "artist" as many referred to themselves, generally belonged to one of three groups: the itinerant photographer, the competent small operator, or operators of large studios.

The itinerant photographer was like a peddler going from town to town to peddle wares, in this case, photographic portraits. The aim was not necessarily to deliver the best possible portraits but to make as much money as possible in the shortest time. The portraits these photographers took generally appear primitive, even when compared with other daguerreotypes of the same period. Though some of the daguerreotypes are technically weak, some are quite remarkable as a result of a direct rather than "arty" approach. The itinerant photographers also fulfilled a social need. Because of limited mobility, many who desired a portrait could not get to a gallery or studio. In addition, there simply were not that many practicing professional photographers—and no amateurs.

However, some locales could support a "permanent" photographer, and from many of these small operations some of the most interesting daguerrian art has survived. Because these photographers had personal, social, and business ties with the people they photographed, their work showed pride and higher quality than that of itinerant photographers.

In large population centers, there were many photographers from which to choose. Their galleries, which were frequently showplaces of trends of the time, sometimes ranged to the bizarre.

The owners of big galleries seldom took the photographs themselves. Usually one operator was employed to take the picture, another to

Figure 21-7

Portrait of medical students, photographer unknown, c. 1880s.

develop it, a third to case the image, and a fourth to color it, if necessary. This was standard procedure in the large New York galleries like Brady's or Gurney's and in the Philadelphia firm of Marcus Root. One important exception was the firm of Southwood and Hawes, whose daguerrian portraits are still some of the finest ever done.

Each technical improvement or new process further increased the demand for portraiture because of lowered costs passed on to the customer. By the middle 1860s, the photographic album containing pictures of friends, relatives, or famous people was as common in the home as the family Bible. The only major difference between the family album of then and the family album of today, besides the process employed, was the photographer. Then, the photograph was almost certainly taken by a professional. Today, we each take our own photographs of our friends and relatives.

Photographs of War

The British campaign in the Crimean War of the 1850s was the first war to be extensively photographed. The official photographer, Roger Fenton, outfitted a "photographic van" to serve as a portable darkroom.

Sand Dunes Near Sand Springs, Nevada, T. H. O'Sullivan, 1867.

Figure 21-8

One of the great photographers of the American West, T. H. O'Sullivan, used a photographic wagon as a traveling darkroom to prepare and develop his wet-plate glass negatives while shooting on location.

The process of this time, the wet-plate collodion, required that each negative be developed once it had been exposed. Fenton brought back over three hundred negatives showing battlefields, fortifications, and soldiers. Most of these photographs were taken either before or after a battle because this process did not lend itself to "instantaneous" scenes.

The American Civil War was a more tempting opportunity for the birth of photojournalism. Mathew Brady, whose role in history began when he photographed the famous people of 1850 with the idea of publishing a book, *The Gallery of Illustrious Americans*, felt compelled to document the Civil War. Brady received President Lincoln's consent but no financial backing for that undertaking. However, Brady was a moderately wealthy man and had little reservation about spending his own money, thinking that after the war many people would buy prints of the battles. He assembled a staff of several men and outfitted them with the materials and equipment they needed to make wet-plate photographs. (Two of these men, T. H. O'Sullivan and Alexander Gardner, later became well-known in their own right.) Brady himself rarely left Washington, D.C., so most of the picture taking was done by his assistants.

This enterprise left Mathew Brady practically destitute; people did not want to be reminded of the all-too-recent and horrible war. The negatives were stored in a warehouse and eventually auctioned off. In 1896, Brady died, penniless. Today, however, his negatives are priceless.

The South, too, had its photographers, but for the most part, Southern photographers are lesser known and worked under greater hardships than Brady's men because their supplies had to be smuggled in from the North and from Europe.

Travel Photography

In the mid-1880s, distant lands were being explored and foreign cultures studied. These explorations stirred people's imaginations and created a demand for visual depictions. There were, of course, drawings and engravings, but no other art form could give the reality of photography.

Shortly after Daguerre's process became public, a team under the direction of Frenchman J. P. Girault DePrangey photographed in Egypt. However, widespread distribution of the pictures was not possible until the wet-collodion process was invented. Photographs by Maxine DuCamp, Francis Firth, Charles Negre, Felice A. Beato, and others were soon in demand.

After the Civil War, several government expeditions were sent to the western United States to map and explore the region. A photographer accompanied them to record the details of the areas being explored. Thus, the photographer replaced the artist, the camera replaced the drawing pen, and the photograph replaced the sketch. Civil War photographers T. H. O'Sullivan and Alexander Gardner both went West with these government expeditions as did William Henry Jackson. Other photographers who explored the regions were Carleton Watkins, Eadweard Muybridge, and Andrew J. Russell.

Jackson, perhaps the best known of these men, began to photograph the West with the Hayden survey in 1870, which chiefly followed the Oregon Trail through Wyoming. In 1871, Jackson was probably the first person to photograph the region that became known as Yellowstone National Park. The value of Jackson's photographs is verified by a bill that was introduced in Congress to set Yellowstone aside as a national park.

Time, Motion, and Perception in Early Photographs

Because we now use high speed films with high speed lenses, it seems inconceivable that any exposure should be longer than one second. However, the earlier processes employed a much slower emulsion, which

Stereocard, G. N. Barnard, 1871.

Figure 21-9

Stereophotography, which produced a three-dimensional illusion, was extremely popular during the 19th century. The dramatic 3-D effect required viewing through an apparatus called a stereoscope. This stereocard pictures the aftermath of the Great Chicago Fire.

required exposures that were generally longer than one second. Therefore, people or objects that moved during the exposure time would be blurred, or, if the exposure were long enough, might disappear altogether from the photograph. Daguerreotypes of street scenes often showed no people because they had not remained still long enough to be recorded in the plate.

Stereographic photographs were the most popular and earliest form of photograph to show action as it was taking place. Essentially, a stereograph is composed of two nearly identical views of the same scene taken from two different vantage points, approximately two inches apart. These views are made either by moving the camera laterally or with a double-lens camera. When viewed through a viewer called a stereoscope, the two images blend together to produce a 3-D effect. By the late 1870s, almost no parlor was complete without a stereoscope and a stock of stereo cards.

Sometimes, a fast shutter speed used to photograph a moving object will enable us to see things that are not normally visible to the unaided eye. A camera can, therefore, extend our vision. This fact was demonstrated by Eadweard Muybridge with a series of photographs showing a galloping horse. The photographs proved that the legs of a galloping

Figure 21-11
The Steerage, Alfred Stieglitz, 1907.

Figure 21-10
Animal Locomotion, Plate 187,
Eadweard Muybridge, 1887.

horse were off the ground only when they were bunched under the horse's belly. The results of these and other experiments forced painters to reevaluate their concept of motion.

With the turn of the century approaching, people not only enjoyed looking at photographs of far-away places taken by other people, they were able to take the pictures themselves. George Eastman freed a great many people with his invention. While the turn-of-the-century amateur was busy photographing friends, family, and vacations, some photographers were beginning to explore the aesthetic and social potential of photography.

Early Twentieth Century Photography

One figure who vigorously advanced the cause of photography was Alfred Stieglitz, who was born in Hoboken, New Jersey, in 1864. He spend his student years in Europe and was introduced to photography

Figure 21-12

The Octopus, Alvin Langdon Coburn, 1912.

in 1883. He immediately became obsessed with photography and constantly experimented with it while studying photochemistry at the Berlin Polytechnic. During the nine years he spent in Europe, he traveled, taking pictures wherever he went. By 1889 he was an internationally famous photographer.

Stieglitz returned to New York in 1890 and began publishing *Camera Notes*, a quarterly for the Camera Club of New York. A small group of photographers were drawn to him. These included Clarence White, Gertrude Kasebier, Alvin Langdon Coburn, Edward Steichen, and others—all of them became great and famous photographers in their own right. In 1902, the group broke away from the Camera Club and formed its own group, which Stieglitz named the Photo Secession. One year later, Stieglitz published the first issue of *Camera Work*, a beautifully printed magazine that was devoted to promoting photography as an art form.

The new group met at 291 Fifth Avenue, in a room next to Edward Steichen's, where their photographs were displayed. The room, number 291, became the most famous locale of photography in the century.

The Photo Secessionists agreed on two fundamental principles: exploring new subject matter and concentrating on rendering the subtleties of light. Stieglitz believed a photograph should be straightforward, without manipulation on the paper surface, while others (like Steichen) believed the printing process should be controlled and manipulated. This same argument continues today.

In any event, *Camera Work* not only published the works of certain photographers, it was the means by which many previously unknown artists and writers were introduced to this country. The works of people such as Rodin, Matisee, John Marin, Gertrude Stein, Picasso, Brancusi, and Braque were published toward the end of *Camera Work*. In 1917, after alienating most of his fellow members by drastically reducing the number of photographs he published in *Camera Work*, Stieglitz was forced to close both the magazine and Gallery 291. However, Stieglitz succeeded in the promotion of photography as art. There is probably not a major museum in the world that does not exhibit photography.

The Photograph As a Document

The photograph has an unparalleled ability to document scenes and victims of despair, cruelty, and poverty. In the late 1880s, Jacob Riis, a Danish immigrant living in New York, became the first person to show how photographs could become social documents. Riis had been writing about the conditions of life in the New York slums and began to take pictures to illustrate his articles. Unfortunately, photographic

Figure 21-13

The photographs Hine took as part of a study during the early 1900s documented the need for child labor laws and better working conditions in the United States. Today documentary photographers and photojournalists continue to record social conditions around the world.

Young Millworker, Lewis W. Hine, 1908.

Figure 21-14

Migrant woman and children, Nipomo, California,
Dorothea Lange, 1936.

reproduction was still young, and Riis's pictures appeared in the newspaper as facsimile drawings. However, in 1890, Riis published *How the Other Half Lives*, which contained seventeen photographic reproductions. The book had great impact on people and ultimately caused many housing reforms.

Similar motivations inspired Lewis W. Hine to record the abuses of child labor. In 1900 approximately two million children under the age of sixteen were employed, some under terrible conditions. Hine's photographs helped to pass the first child labor laws.

Social conscience on a governmental level caused President Franklin D. Roosevelt's Assistant Secretary of Agriculture, Rexford G. Tugwell, to appoint Roy Stryker to supervise the photographic recording of farm families during the depression of the 1930s. During the seven year lifespan of the Farm Security Administration (FSA), thousands of negatives were produced, most of them straightforward, strong, and shocking. Stryker recruited a remarkable band of talent for this project, including

Walker Evans, Dorothea Lange, Arthur Rothstein, Ben Shahn, and Russell Lee.

Movements in Modern Photography

The beginning of the twentieth century was a time of great strides in industry, science, politics, and the arts. Art movements, including Surrealism, Fauvism, Dada, and Cubism, began investigating meaning in life and culture while expanding the parameters of art.

In areas of visual design and architecture, no school was more important than the Bauhaus in Berlin. The Hungarian artist Laszlo Moholy-Nagy came to the Bauhaus in 1922. Moholy-Nagy attempted to expand and explore photography, not within the pictorial structure of the 19th century but with a "new vision" compatible with contemporary life. Moholy-Nagy experimented with photomontage, solarization, optical distortions, multiple exposures, and photograms. His hope was to create and expand the visual language of photography.

Another artist working within Dadaist philosophy was Man Ray. The Dada movement stressed that life was full of absurdities, and it was the goal of the artist to create even greater absurdities. Man Ray had little respect for conventional form and technique in photography. He

Sleeping Woman, Man Ray, 1929.

Figure 21-15

An example of the solarization technique.

wrote, "A certain amount of contempt for the material employed to express an idea is indispensable. . . ." Man Ray, like Moholy-Nagy, sought to alter not only the visual image of the photograph, but also the viewers' perception of that image. His photographs were a challenge to the eye and mind.

Photography and the Visual Age

The growth of photography since Word War II has been staggering. It has pervaded all aspects of our culture, especially in the United States. Since the 1960s, courses in photography have been added to the art departments of schools throughout the country. Subsequently, there has been an increase in the public awareness of photography as an art form.

Starting in the late 1940s, photography came of age. Commercially it was booming. *Life* and *Look* magazines popularized the picture story; photojournalism and advertising photography influenced the masses as

Figure 21-16

In the 1950s and 60s, the photo essay was championed by magazines such as *Life* and *Look*. W. Eugene Smith's work was unsurpassed in terms of its beauty and emotional power. This image was part of a photo essay produced for *Life*.

Last Earthly Visit, from *Spanish Village*, W. Eugene Smith, 1951.

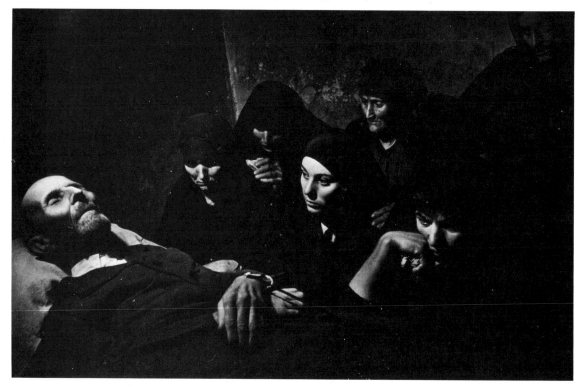

Figure 21-17

Uelsmann maintained a photographic character in his work while producing fantastic multiple images beyond the technical ability of many photographers. Today, the level of technical skill necessary to make images such as Uelsmann's has been simplified by digital imaging and software such as Adobe Photoshop, which makes seamless multiple images much easier to produce.

Figure 21-18

Pricerise, Jim Stone, 1985.

The postmodern movement in the arts questioned the concepts of originality and innovation. For this photograph. Stone "appropriated" a well-known Ansel Adams image and changed the context by adding an electronic bar code and entitling his work to comment on photography, the arts, and the marketplace.

never before. In the late 1960s color snapshots were being made by the billions; the movie industry reached new heights in cinematography; and color television was the norm in the average American home. During the 1970s, fine art photography seemed tied to idealistic notions of higher purposes—personal, social, or aesthetic. Many photographers on the West Coast continued to be dominated by the influence of Edward Weston and Ansel Adams. Among the more traditional photographic artists who had impact during the 1970s on the West Coast were Wynn Bullock, Brett Weston, Jack Welpott, and Judy Dater.

Encouraged by the support and influence of John Szarkowski, the Director of the Photography Department at the Museum of Modern Art in New York, East Cost photographers continued to be known primarily for a documentary approach during the 1970s—often referred

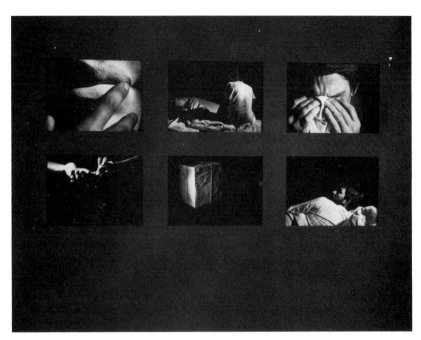

Based on a True Story, Eileen Cowin, 1992.

Figure 21-19

Cowin, who combines still and video images in this piece, is part of the generation of innovative photographers who came of age in the 1980s and widened the traditional boundaries of photography, vastly expanding a medium that has become one of the most active and important areas within contemporary art.

to as *social landscape photography*. Major influences among these slice-of-reality documentarian photographers were Diane Arbus, Lee Friedlander, and Garry Winogrand. The individuals influencing the medium during this period had, for the most part, a strong commitment to the black and white camera image, fine print quality, and a formally finished product.

In response to these influences, other voices sprang up in denial of traditional formal aesthetics. Located primarily in Los Angeles and Chicago, these art-educated photographers embraced conceptualism and mixed-media applications of photography while other artists, who did not identify themselves as photographers, turned to photography as a medium—creating a different vision. Robert Heinecken, Darryl Curran, Robert Fichter, Bea Nettles, Lewis Baltz, and Betty Hahn were among those artists who brought ideas from sculpture, printing, and printmaking to photography. Robert Rauschenberg, Andy Warhol, Ed Ruscha, John Baldessari, and William Wegman were among those who brought photography to the other arts.

By the early 1970s, museums and galleries actively embraced photography. A photo community had evolved by the mid-1970s, which was filled with youthful optimism and energy at the same time; collecting photography became fashionable and prices rose. By the end of the

1970s, color photography had gained acceptance as a fine art and had assumed an important role beyond advertising and family snapshots. Today, the lines dividing the different visual arts are so blurred that they no longer matter. Multi-media approaches, new technology, and pluralism pervade the art world and the photo community has become part of the larger art community.

With breakthroughs in electronic technologies and computer imaging in the 1980s, the differences between painting and photography have turned into common ground. Traditionally, painters have had the freedom to selectively recreate life through the addition or deletion of content. On the other hand, photographers—with few exceptions—were tied to the lens-based camera and selected images directly from life. By the 1990s, however, computer technology had developed that allowed photographers to easily and seamlessly alter existing photographs, offering the control and freedom of painting to selectively recreate or create images drawn from life. This new freedom has opened new creative avenues for photographers and fresh alliances with other art media. This trend seems destined to provide continued change, ensuring the expansion of the applications and influences of photography in all areas of the visual arts.

Bibliography

Aaland, Mikkel, with Rudolph Burger, *Digital Photography*. New York: Random House, 1992.

Abbott, Berenice. *The World of Atget*. New York: Horizon Press, 1964.

Adams, Ansel. *Examples: The Making of Forty Photographs*. Boston: New York Graphic Society, 1983.

———. *The Portfolios of Ansel Adams*. Boston: New York Graphic Society, 1977.

Angel, Heather. *The Book of Close-Up Photography*. London: Ebury Press, 1983.

Arbus, Diane. *Diane Arbus*, An Aperture Monograph. Millerton, NY: Aperture, 1972.

Avedon, Richard. *In the American West: Richard Avedon—Photographs, 1979–1984*. New York: Abrams, 1985.

Avedon, Richard. *Richard Avedon: An Autobiography*, New York: Random House, 1995.

Barratt, Terry. *Criticizing Photographs: An Introduction to Understanding Images*. Mountain View, CA: Mayfield, 1990.

Bravo, Manuel Alvarez. *Manuel Alvarez Bravo*. Boston: David R. Godine, 1979.

Cartier-Bresson, Henri. *The Decisive Moment*. New York: Simon & Schuster, 1952.

Coe, Brian. *Cameras from Daguerrotypes to Instant Pictures*. New York: Crown, 1970.

———. *Colour Photography: The First Hundred Years, 1840–1940*. London: Ash and Grant, 1978.

Coleman, A.D. *Light Readings: A Photography Critic's Writings 1968–1978*. New York: Oxford University Press, 1979.

Crawford, William. *The Keepers of the Light: A History and Working Guide to Early Photographic Processes*. Dobbs Ferry, NY: Morgan & Morgan, 1979.

Davenport, Alma. *The History of Photography: An Overview*. Boston: Focal Press, 1991.

Davis, Phil. *Beyond the Zone System*, 2nd ed., Boston: Focal Press, 1988.

———. *Photography*, 6th ed. Dubuque, IA: Wm. C. Brown, 1990.

Evans, Walker. *Walker Evans: Photographs for the Farm Security Administra-*

tion 1935–1938. Introduction by Jerald C. Maddox. New York: Da Capo Press, 1975.

Frank, Robert. *Les Amèricains.* Alain Bosquet, ed. Paris: Delpire, 1958. U.S. edition, *The Americans.* Introduction by Jack Kerouac. New York: Grove, 1959.

Gernsheim, Helmut, and Alison Gernsheim. *The History of Photography 1685–1914.* New York: McGraw-Hill, 1969.

Goldberg, Vicki. *Photography in Print: Writings from 1816 to the Present.* New York: Simon & Schuster, 1981.

Green, Jonathan. *American Photography: A Critical History.* New York: Harry N. Abrams, 1984.

Grimm, Tom. *The Basic Darkroom Book: A Complete Guide to Processing and Printing Color and Black-and-White Photographs.* New York: New American Library, 1986.

Heinecken, Robert. *Heinecken.* Carmel, CA: The Friends of Photography, 1981.

Hirsch, Robert. *Exploring Color Photography,* 2nd ed. Madison, WI: Brown & Benchmark, 1983.

————. *Photographic Possibilities: The Expressive Use of Ideas, Materials, and Processes.* Boston: Focal Press, 1991.

Horan, James D. *Mathew Brady: Historian with a Camera.* New York: Bonanza, 1960.

Horenstein, Henry. *Color Photography: A Basic Manual.* Boston: Little, Brown, 1995.

————. *The Photographer's Source: A Complete Catalogue.* New York: Simon & Schuster, 1989.

Karsh, Yousuf. *In Search of Greatness.* New York: Knopf, 1962.

Keefe, Laurence E. Jr., and Dennis Inch. *The Life of a Photograph: Archival Processing, Matting, Framing and Storage.* Boston: Focal Press, 1984.

Kertéz, André. *André Kertés: Sixty Years of Photography 1919–1972.* New York: Grossman, 1972.

Lefkowitz, Lester. *Electronic Flash, KW-12.* Kodak Workshop Series. Rochester, NY: Eastman Kodak Co., 1986.

Leibovitz, Annie. *Photographs: Annie Leibovitz, 1970–1990.* New York: HarperCollins, 1992.

Lemagny, Jean-Claude and Rouille, Andre, eds. *A History of Photography: Social and Cultural Perspectives.* New York: Cambridge University Press, 1987.

Lifson, Ben, ed., *Samaras: Photographs, 1969–1986.* Millerton, NY: Aperture, 1988.

Mann, Margery. *Women of Photography: An Historical Survey.* San Francisco: San Francisco Museum of Art, 1975.

Mitchell, William J. *The Reconfigured Eye: Visual Truth in the Post-Photographic Era,* Cambridge, MA: MIT Press, 1992.

Mora, Gilles, ed. *Edward Weston: Forms of Passion.* New York: Abrams, 1995.

Muybridge, Eadweard. *Human and Animal Locomotion: All 781 Plates from the 1887 Animal Locomotion, 3 vols.* New York: Dover, 1979.

Naef, Weston J., and James N. Wood. *Era of Exploration: The Rise of Landscape Photography in the American West, 1860–1885.* New York: The Metropolitan Museum of Art, 1975.

Nettles, Bea. *Breaking the Rules: A Photo Media Cookbook,* 2nd ed. Rochester, NY: Inky Press Productions, Light Impressions Corp., 1987.

Newhall, Beaumont. *The History of Photography from 1839 to the Present Day.* Boston: New York Graphics Society, 1982.

Oakes, John W. *Minimal Aperture Photography Using Pinhole Cameras.* Lanham, MD: University Press of America, 1986.

Reeve, Catherine and Marilyn Sward. *The New Photography: A Guide to New Images, Processes, and Display Techniques for Photographers.* New York: Da Capo, 1987.

Renner, Eric. *Pinhole Photography: Rediscovering a Historic Technique.* Boston: Focal Press, 1995.

Ritchin, Fred. *In Our Own Image: The Coming Revolution in Photography.* New York: Aperture, 1990.

Shaw, Susan, and Monona Rossol. *Overexposure: Health Hazards in Photography,* 2nd ed. New York: Allworth Press, 1991.

Sobieszek, Robert A. *The Art of Persuasion: A History of Advertising Photography.* New York: Abrams, 1988.

Sontag, Susan. *On Photography,* New York: Farrar, Straus and Giroux, 1977.

Stone, Jim, ed. *Darkroom Dynamics: A Guide to Creative Darkroom Techniques.* Stoneham, MA: Focal Press, 1979.

————. *A User's Guide to the View Camera.* New York: HarperCollins, 1987.

Szarkowski, John. *Looking at Photographs.* New York: Museum of Modern Art, 1973.

————. *Photography Until Now.* New York: Museum of Modern Art, 1989.

Vestal, David. *The Art of Black and White Enlarging.* New York: Harper and Row, 1984.

Warren, Bruce. *Photography.* Minneapolis-St. Paul: West, 1993.

Weston, Brett. *Brett Weston: Photographs from Five Decades.* Millerton, NY: Aperture, 1980.

Wilhelm, Henry. *The Permanence and Care of Color Photographs: Traditional and Digital Color Prints, Color Negatives, Slides and Motion Pictures,* Grinnell, IA: Preservation Publishing Co., 1993.

Woods, John Charles. *The Zone System Craftbook,* 2nd ed. Madison, WI: Brown and Benchmark, 1996.

Index

NTC LANGUAGE ARTS BOOKS

Business Communication
Handbook for Business Writing, *Baugh, Fryar, &
 Thomas*
Meetings: Rules & Procedures, *Pohl*

Dictionaries
British/American Language Dictionary, *Moss*
NTC's Classical Dictionary, *Room*
NTC's Dictionary of Changes in Meaning, *Room*
NTC's Dictionary of Debate, *Hanson*
NTC's Dictionary of Literary Terms, *Morner &
 Rausch*
NTC's Dictionary of Theatre and Drama Terms,
 Mobley
NTC's Dictionary of Word Origins, *Room*
NTC's Spell It Right Dictionary, *Downing*
Robin Hyman's Dictionary of Quotations

Essential Skills
Building Real Life English Skills, *Starkey & Penn*
Developing Creative & Critical Thinking, *Boostrom*
English Survival Series, *Maggs*
Essential Life Skills, *Starkey & Penn*
Essentials of English Grammar, *Baugh*
Essentials of Reading and Writing English Series
Grammar for Use, *Hall*
Grammar Step-by-Step, *Pratt*
Guide to Better English Spelling, *Furness*
How to Be a Rapid Reader, *Redway*
How to Improve Your Study Skills, *Coman & Heavers*
How to Write Term Papers and Reports, *Baugh*
NTC Skill Builders
Reading by Doing, *Simmons & Palmer*
303 Dumb Spelling Mistakes, *Downing*
TIME: We the People, *ed. Schinke-Llano*
Vocabulary by Doing, *Beckert*

Genre Literature
Coming of Age, *Emra*
The Detective Story, *Schwartz*
The Short Story & You, *Simmons & Stern*
Sports in Literature, *Emra*
You and Science Fiction, *Hollister*

Journalism
Getting Started in Journalism, *Harkrider*
Journalism Today! *Ferguson & Patten*
Publishing the Literary Magazine, *Klaiman*
UPI Stylebook, *United Press International*

Language, Literature, and Composition
African American Literature, *Worley & Perry*
An Anthology for Young Writers, *Meredith*
The Art of Composition, *Meredith*
Creative Writing, *Mueller & Reynolds*
Handbook for Practical Letter Writing, *Baugh*
How to Write Term Papers and Reports, *Baugh*

In a New Land, *Grossman & Schur*
Literature by Doing, *Tchudi & Yesner*
Lively Writing, *Schrank*
Look, Think & Write, *Leavitt & Sohn*
NTC Shakespeare Series
NTC Vocabulary Builders
Poetry by Doing, *Osborn*
World Literature, *Rosenberg*
Write to the Point! *Morgan*
The Writer's Handbook, *Karls & Szymanski*
Writing by Doing, *Sohn & Enger*
Writing in Action, *Meredith*

Media Communication
Getting Started in Mass Media, *Beckert*
Photography in Focus, *Jacobs & Kokrda*
Television Production Today!, *Bielak*
Understanding Mass Media, *Jawitz*
Understanding the Film, *Bone & Johnson*

Mythology
The Ancient World, *Sawyer & Townsend*
Mythology and You, *Rosenberg & Baker*
Welcome to Ancient Greece, *Millard*
Welcome to Ancient Rome, *Millard*
World Mythology, *Rosenberg*

Speech
Activities for Effective Communication, *LiSacchi*
The Basics of Speech, *Galvin, Cooper, & Gordon*
Contemporary Speech, *HopKins & Whitaker*
Creative Speaking, *Frank*
Dynamics of Speech, *Myers & Herndon*
Getting Started in Oral Interpretation, *Naegelin &
 Krikac*
Getting Started in Public Speaking, *Carlin & Payne*
Listening by Doing, *Galvin*
Literature Alive, *Gamble & Gamble*
Person to Person, *Galvin & Book*
Public Speaking Today, *Carlin & Payne*
Speaking by Doing, *Buys, Sill, & Beck*

Theatre
Acting & Directing, *Grandstaff*
The Book of Cuttings for Acting & Directing,
 Cassady
The Book of Monologues for Aspiring Actors,
 Cassady
The Book of Scenes for Acting Practice, *Cassady*
The Book of Scenes for Aspiring Actors, *Cassady*
The Dynamics of Acting, *Snyder & Drumsta*
Getting Started in Theatre, *Pinnell*
An Introduction to Modern One-Act Plays, *Cassady*
An Introduction to Theatre and Drama, *Cassady &
 Cassady*
Play Production Today, *Beck et al.*
Stagecraft, *Beck*

For a current catalog and information about our complete line of language
arts books, write:
National Textbook Company
a division of *NTC Publishing Group*
4255 West Touhy Avenue
Lincolnwood (Chicago), Illinois 60646–1975 U.S.A.